HEALTH IN A POST-COVID WORLD

Lessons from the Crisis of
Western Liberalism

Sebastian Taylor

First published in Great Britain in 2023 by

Policy Press, an imprint of
Bristol University Press
University of Bristol
1–9 Old Park Hill
Bristol
BS2 8BB
UK
t: +44 (0)117 374 6645
e: bup-info@bristol.ac.uk

Details of international sales and distribution partners are available at
policy.bristoluniversitypress.co.uk

British Library Cataloguing in Publication Data
A catalogue record for this book is available from the British Library

ISBN 978-1-4473-6836-6 hardcover
ISBN 978-1-4473-6837-3 paperback
ISBN 978-1-4473-6838-0 ePub
ISBN 978-1-4473-6839-7 ePdf

Cover design: Robin Hawes
Front cover image: iStock/MicroStockHub
Bristol University Press and Policy Press use environmentally responsible print partners.
Printed and bound in Great Britain by CPI Group (UK) Ltd, Croydon, CR0 4YY

FSC
www.fsc.org
MIX
Paper | Supporting
responsible forestry
FSC® C013604

For Sue, Georgia, Frieda and Mali

Contents

List of figures

Acknowledgements

I would like to thank Jonathan Pattenden, Eric Brunner, Neena Modi, Ted Schrecker, Marie Bontoux, Megan Ellingham and Dave Boydon for their constructive support and suggestions in the development of this work; Goli Tsakalos, Abdurashid Solijonov, Madeline Koch and Caitlin Jarrett for their expertise in advising on and sourcing data; Professors Andy Tatem, Branko Milanovic, Homi Kharas, Brad DeLong, Heidi Larson, Michael Muthukrishna, Lucas Chancel, Chris Lalonde, Leon Feinstein, Miles Corak, Vladimir Gimpelson, John-Paul Rodrigue, John Kirton, Tim Besley, Steven Pinker, Sir Angus Deaton, Peter Goldblatt and Sir Michael Marmot for kindly permitting me to draw on their extensive bodies of work; Drs Camilla Kingdon, Mike McKean and Ian Sinha for their support in communicating the book's ideas across key clinical and healthcare communities. I would like to thank Laura Vickers-Rendall and her colleagues at Policy Press for their professionalism and enthusiasm.

The structure and focus of the book could perhaps most generously be described as unconventional. There are many weaknesses, for which I take whole responsibility. But there are, too, I hope, some points of value in the ongoing discussion about what we mean by human and social development, how we can scrutinise claims of progress in this space, and how health can help in substantiating that debate.

Preface

This book is about health, society and politics. Not so much how socioeconomic and political forces generate health – on which much is already written – but how health illuminates the political and policy choices we make, the values on which we make them, and the kinds of society we get as a result.

Health is arguably the preeminent human good – the condition to which above all others we aspire and on which all our other aspirations depend.[1] In each society – and between countries globally – health reflects back at us in irrefutably objective detail the physical effects of our social and economic principles – the societies they shape embodied, quite literally, for good or ill. My aim, in writing this book, is to present health as a kind of yardstick against which to assess the credibility of the values of the liberal democratic project as they are offered to us today; not to offer glib solutions to wicked problems, but to ask better questions – to use the measure of human health to see where those values are working and, where not, how they might be reimagined.

We are living in turbulent times. A grand convergence of interlinking crises from climate change at the cliff-edge of catastrophic irreversibility and cumulating dysfunction in the global economic system, to tectonic changes in the distribution of geopolitical power and the unravelling of international norms and laws. From splintering party politics and deepening disaffection with democratic process to the performative theatrics of Trump and Brexit and a global landscape of disintegrating state legitimacy,[2] the last decade has witnessed a spiralling failure of faith in the modern liberal institutions and values by which societies have sought to structure themselves over the last 70 years – values of growth and prosperity, of freedom and justice, of democracy and security, and truth.[3]

It is a decade filled with the echoes of the great crash of 2008, reflected back at us through a disorienting mosaic of fractious, antagonistic and increasingly extreme politics (see, for example, Beckett, 2019). But the roots of the crisis go deeper – more than half a century in the making, in the ascendance of a hyper-individualist economic model and the social consequences of economic globalisation, the resurgent power of capital and the slow-motion collapse of societal mechanisms mediating between rich and poor, citizen and state. Accompanied by a sharp and so-far unrestrained rise in economic insecurity and inequality, we have seen an explosive return of populist political agendas – agendas which coopt the tenets of liberal market democracy, twisting them to new and darker purposes. The result is a growing sense of distrust in our systems of governance, in the veracity of the shared values with which for the last seven decades we have coordinated our societies and lives.[4]

In early 2020, the dimensions of that crisis were sharpened by the onset of a global pandemic spreading out of central China and enveloping the world. SARS-CoV-2 (COVID-19) applied new pressure on pre-existing stress fractures in the architecture of the liberal ideal, intensifying both political reliance on – and public scepticism about – the validity of liberal market democracy, driving further apart our interpretation of its values in the way we are governed and the extent to which we consent: values of freedom and security brought into very real conflict as governments imposed levels of public control unseen in modern times; competing versions of democratic process, participation and legitimacy as differing ideological views of health and economic risk sought popular cover under the nomenclature of 'what the people want'; sudden doubts about the sincerity of our governments' commitment to social equality as COVID marked the contours of advantage and disadvantage in radically differing scales of exposure, infection, vulnerability and death; and a renewed assault on science and truth as social media and political pundits adopted, with appalling ease, the tactics of tobacco and fossil fuel energy, through counterfactual obfuscation and the unashamed production of alternative facts.[5]

The approach I take sits somewhat awkwardly between the academic and the popular – possibly satisfying the requirements of neither, but reflecting a belief that the two spheres do not communicate well enough, undermining the power of empirical evidence to inform and support public debate and action. It draws on diverse disciplinary fields – archaeology and literature, economics, history and geography, demography, political science and sociology, philosophy, anthropology, epidemiology, psychology and medicine.[6] Because it is, I think, in the dialogue between 'health' and 'non-health' worlds – subduing our instincts towards disciplinary chauvinism, recognising our own conceptual imperfections, ceding desire for two-dimensional linear certainty in favour of aggregate coherence – that we can achieve a more complete picture of the biological, physical, social, economic and political forces through which societies prosper or decline.

So, to the structure of the book. A short introduction develops the idea of health as a unique measure of society – showing how, over the long course of history, matters of physical well-being, illness and death infuse ideas of civilisation far beyond the strictly biomedical, as our varied cultural, political and technological capabilities have evolved. An introductory chapter then turns to the question of crisis, mapping out a post-war timeline of inflection points in the global landscape and their impact on social, economic and political development, which, I think, lead to the dominant form of liberalism we see around us today and the precarious moment at which it has arrived.

In six following thematic sections, I use evidence from the field of health – of morbidity and mortality, systems of care and social determinants, in countries at all levels of wealth and poverty – to explore, case by case, the values of growth and prosperity, of freedom and justice, of security, democracy and truth, tracing their evolution and asking what health can tell us about the veracity of their contemporary form.

To an extent, each section stands or falls on its own merits – more akin to a series of essays than a single cumulating argument. That said, three consistent themes emerge. First, that there is a critical need to reinvest in the value of collective action – widely corroded by our rapidly superannuating romance with methodological individualism – in the way societies develop, not just for the purposes of equity but because, as we see in multiple dimensions of health, it is simply more efficient. Second, that we need to become much more serious about decentralisation – devolving power to the local level of place and community, and the practices of deliberative dialogue as the essential foundation on which credible governance at national and global levels can be built. And third, that we need radically to revisit our understanding of inequality – not just as the necessary or unavoidable side-effect of economic society, but as a structural malignancy which distorts and degrades the function of all those other values – of growth and freedom, security and democracy, of truth – on which we will need to draw in the process of forging a better post-COVID world.

Notes

[1] In April 2022, an Ipsos MORI global opinion survey found that, around the world, people's number one concern – above money, terrorism, the pandemic, and climate change – was their health and that of their families (see Ipsos Global Advisor, 2022).

[2] From the hubris of Western 'state-building' after the 1990s to the nemesis of state failure in the Middle East, West Asia and North Africa, culminating in the abdication of humanitarian engagement and the allied flight from Afghanistan in 2021–2022; the abandonment of a free Hong Kong reabsorbed with quietly confident brutality under mainland Chinese rule; and a global wave of openly nationalist, kleptocratic and negligently or actively homicidal administrations from Eurasia to Latin America. All of this capped, in the early months of 2022, by Vladimir Putin's murderous invasion of an independent Ukraine, foreshadowing Beijing's predatory gaze over the Taiwan Strait to Taipei.

[3] There is much room for debate about the extent to which the values addressed in this book correspond with a strict reading of historical liberalism. I think they are the ones that most closely map onto a more or less continuous line from the European Enlightenment through movements in 18th and 19th century political philosophy, to the post-war

reformation of a rules-based international order, decolonising challenges to the projection of Western dominance, the proliferation of liberal, market and social democratic models, and the emergence of neoliberalism (see, for example, Zevin, 2022).

[4] I use the term 'we' at various points throughout the book – an attribution which can become irritating without at least some positioning. We is, to some extent inevitably, me or people like me; the *bien-pensants*, the *Gutmenschen*, the smug rump of the baby boomer Old World – internationalist by instinct, centre-left by tradition, small-'l' liberal; full of good intentions but less than effectual and too often actively or unintentionally in enabling cahoots with the institutional, intellectual and economic elites of globalisation.

There are three overlapping perspectives within which I write. First, rooted in a privileged Northern Anglophone tradition, which may place my critique of things 'Western' in a somewhat suspect light; second, from a European standpoint, grounded as I am in my home in the UK – although I hope that the global nature of the evidence presented mitigates this to some degree, as well as direct experience, observation and communication with colleagues in low- and middle-income countries in which I have lived and worked; third, while I have tried to balance reference to mainstream and critical traditions in presenting evidence, the approach I take belongs within a community which challenges the dominant neoliberal interpretation of socioeconomic and developmental discourse.

Over the course of the book, 'we' shifts, becoming more an invocation of people as a global generality – a reference which is problematic given the fractured constituencies I describe as contributing to contemporary liberal crisis. That 'we', though, is the necessary agent of ways forward based on universality and equity.

[5] Each of the book's thematic sections ends by reflecting on the COVID pandemic and the ways in which it has framed and articulated tensions in the contemporary liberal democratic model. Given the kinetic nature of the pandemic, evidence from early phases may support analysis which changes, in some instances significantly, later on. I have tried to clarify the timeframe from onset and phase of transmission in the data and examples presented.

[6] Recognising my inexpertise in many of these fields.

Introduction: health and civilisation

Ideas of health and illness are woven into the roots of what it is to be human. Health links traditional and modern modes of knowledge, embodying in a single conceptual space the long evolutionary continuity of our physical and social selves. Health is perhaps the first and most fruitful of humanity's attempts to extend technological mastery over a frightening and unpredictable Nature. Health endows art with one of its most hard-working metaphorical frameworks, conveyancing frailty of flesh and strength of spirit into grand human narratives of conflict and redemption.

From the earliest societies, health has forged a pathway between intuitive obeisance to the supernatural and a growing sense of the possibility of human agency – mediating our atavistic attachment to ritual with a modernising confidence in scientific method, integrating the magical and the empirical as overlapping modes of inquiry – recognising, in our search for truth, the evidentiary weaknesses of the former and the explanatory limits of the latter.

Between 3000 and 200 BCE, there was an extraordinary flourishing of inquiry into the conditions of illness and codification of cause (Sahlas, 2001). Egyptian papyri of the Old Kingdom reveal an increasingly sophisticated system of medicine manifesting detailed analysis of the major infectious diseases, along with advanced understanding of reproductive and gynaecological disorders and the development of remarkable anatomical and surgical skills. Practical medical concerns, though, merge with questions of deeper social value.

Interest in ophthalmic knowledge, while helpful in addressing common disorders like trachoma, probably speaks to an Egyptian preoccupation with the eye as principal conduit between the worlds of the living and the dead (Andersen, 1997). Intense interest in embryology, from Buddhist and Ayurvedic texts to Aristotle's epigenetics points, doubtless, to the concern for successful procreation, but also to profounder questions raised by fertility – of the ethical origins of life, the nature of the soul, and the critical patriarchal project of codifying male and female reproductive (and thence social) roles (Wellner, 2010).

As civilisations evolve, health forms a bridge between richly imaginative spiritual worlds and the world of bodily necessity – the idea of health and survival as a matter of divine decision gradually supplanted by a nascent sense of humanity's capacity to engineer its own fate. Reliance on magic and ritual in early Old Kingdom texts gives way, over time, to a more methodologically medical model, as successive dynasties gained confidence in the social and

1

bureaucratic systems by which they found they could manipulate the physical environment, assuring a steady supply of food. Interestingly, magical thinking resurfaces as the old empire wanes and its sense of technical power over flood and famine declines (Nunn, 1996).

The Bantu-speaking peoples of precolonial East Africa fashioned a model of health balancing detailed aetiological understanding of everyday diseases – malaria, measles, sleeping sickness – with an elaborate system of spirit causation and developing, between the two, an extensive natural pharmacy of barks, leaves, roots and saps (Feierman and Janzen, 1992). While the Buddhist Pali Canon views *karma* as the major cause of human ills, it nonetheless authorised medicine as one of the four earthly goods monks were permitted to own (Soni, 1976; Haldar, 1992).

Across cultures, health has served as a medium linking systems of religious belief with more material strategies for survival and social organisation. The Mesopotamian Hammurabi Code, around 1750 BCE, was emphatic in regulating medical practice. But it conferred on priests and healers a shared domain of authority as spiritual interpretations of disease merged with a more pragmatic regulation of physical purity, hygiene, food and sexual relations – institutional reliance on divine favour reinsured through the practical management of human behaviour. Ideas of balance – of the spiritual and empirical, the sacramental and secular – weave through images of health in the *I'Ching* of Warring States China and the *Vedas* of pre-Common Era India, incorporating physical and mystical dimensions of human experience in a somatic model which continues to enjoy much interest today (Reddy, 2012; Lu, 2013; Saini, 2016).

Between the establishment of Hippocrates' medical school at Cos in the 5th century BCE and the work of Aelius Galen six centuries later, ideas of 'public health' grew in strength and coherence, emphasising environment, lifestyle and diet as causes of health and illness – physiological and epidemiological evidence competing for explanatory power with more conventional notions of punitive divinity (Berryman, 2012). Athenian city-states appointed and paid for public physicians – a practice later adopted by Byzantium and early medieval European principalities (Porter, 1990). Roman law regulated medics, prohibiting them from suing for payment if their treatments included incantation or exorcism on the grounds that these were probably beyond the realm of credible practice (Carrick, 2001).

Socrates recognises health as the preeminent condition – the *summum bonum* – on which all consequent considerations of life depend. Aristotle's 'good life' describes pretty much item for item the 'social determinants of health' still current in global policy circles today (WHO, 2008). Health and physical decay are central mechanisms of Greek tragedy, its reflections on the virtuous society and the human condition (Cawthorn, 2008; Mitchell-Boyask, 2008; Ormand, 2012).[1]

Ideas of healing, order and salvation are fused in early medieval and renaissance thought and art. Langland's *Piers Plowman* teaches Christ the art of medicine as a way of saving sick souls.[2] Plague is the narrative backdrop to Boccaccio's *Decameron* and Chaucer's *Canterbury Tales*. Healthcare is one of the great social goods in More's *Utopia*. Thomas Browne's *Religio Medici*, published in 1643, brings corporeal body and eternal soul into dazzling proximity through the interior journeys of a growing anatomical and surgical enlightenment (Howell, 2004; Healy, 2011).[3]

Accelerating urbanisation and the growth of transnational trade in the medieval period expanded popular perceptions of disease transmission – most notably, bubonic plague scuttling on and off trading vessels on the backs of rodents and spreading riotously among poor people living in conditions of profoundly unhygienic proximity. Topping the list of conditions, aside from the widely prevalent bloody flux, were leprosy, plague and syphilis, each in its own way mediating change in the public understanding of balance between divine agency and social causation. Patterns of infection and evidence of human-to-human transmission, disease onset linked to social activity and human behaviour, strengthened the sense of temporal effect and the potential power of human agency – health and illness balancing personal responsibility with social causation, moral culpability with natural law (Grigsby, 2003).

Mental health – the murky delineation of sanity and insanity, inclusion and exclusion – shapes tragedy and comedy alike in Shakespeare, signalling Elizabethan anxieties about personhood and state as newly secular concepts of individuality and deviance, social hierarchy and procedural justice displaced more ancient beliefs in witchcraft and possession, blood-line, inheritance and revenge (Bogousslavsky and Dieguez, 2013; Tosh, 2016; Johnson, 2018).[4] Preoccupations with the parameter of reason and madness span the Atlantic – from *Don Quixote* to *Moby Dick* – finally merging in Stevenson's *The Strange Case of Dr Jekyll and Mr Hyde* as the truths of Old World knowledge struggled with the unwritten possibilities of the New.

Images of illness and recovery permeate the European novel through the 18th and 19th centuries creating, in blurred metaphors of the individual and social body, a mechanism through which to resolve conflicts of class, money, marriage and sex as capitalist industrialisation took root (Christ, 1976; Rothfield, 1992; Biasin, 2014). Undifferentiated fevers facilitate the narrative resolution of ill-assorted romantic and economic alliances in Jane Austen and George Eliot, managing processes of psychological crisis among Brontean heroines, and amplifying the space for gender transgression. Dickens uses coma to navigate the genteel resolution of disordered social hierarchy. Smallpox supplies an altogether messier denouement in *Les Liaisons Dangereux* and the unflinchingly unsanitary novels of Zola. Tuberculosis is central to the intense subjectivity of the Romantic poets and the languidly fatal logic of operatic tragedy – the great literary disease of spiritual and social decline in Dumas, Dostoevsky, Turgenev, James and Poe (Vrettos, 1995; Hutcheon and Hutcheon, 1996; Sontag, 2001; Lawlor, 2006; Bailin, 2007; Lawlor and Suzuki, 2012; Hakola and Kivistö, 2014).[5]

Health and illness furnish a language with which to speak about repressive regimes in Latin America in the 1960s and 1970s – narratives of personal triumph and public decay, the pathology of power and the potential for democratic revitalisation, the suspension of physical norms through magical realism providing space to absorb political trauma without descent into madness and despair (Novillo-Corvalán, 2015; Sánchez-Blake and Kanost, 2015).[6] Health as the emblem of necessary balance infuses modern Chinese literature – the reconciliation of physical, familial and social tensions under the ranking imperative of harmony, as important to the Maoist as to the Confucian notion of political order (Ohnuki-Tierney, 1984; Leslie and Young, 1992; Choy, 2016; Lendik et al, 2017). Ideas of pain – physical, spiritual, social, historical – run through contemporary African literature, escaping the blank gaze of colonial disregard and the self-indulgence of neo-colonial guilt, reclaiming Africa from the medicalisations of poverty and underdevelopment, repudiating the idea of the continent as a condition in need of a remedy (Achebe, 1999; Norridge, 2013).

Matters of bodily and psychological dysfunction, public jeopardy and medical prowess, populate the narratives of cinema and television before almost any other theme.[7] The golden age of 1950s Hollywood coincided with a massive expansion in the availability of medical technologies, and commensurate growth of popular faith in public health – the doctor pre-dating both criminal and cowboy as the hero of early film (Harper and Moor, 2005; Glasser and Irvine, 2017). In recent decades, the significance and symbolism of health and illness have proliferated across politics, commerce and media as the state-led emphasis of post-war modernisation gave way to a new liberal economic imagination – of individuals as bounded units of private preference and personal responsibility, their health and illness refashioned as consumption commodities, our appetites almost literally consuming themselves.

Across civilisations, in science and art, health holds up a mirror to social development – a material index of the quality of our communities and societies and an articulate measure by which to assess whether the values we espouse create the kind of society in which we are able individually and collectively to thrive (Kaplan, 1987; Pett, 2018).[8] Health challenges the false oppositions embodied in liberalism – between individual and social, personal and universal – which eat away at the democratic principles of compromise and feed the era of polarisation. Health incorporates multiple value systems engendering a necessary plurality of knowledge, rendering our judgements provisional rather than absolute, creating an interim space in which divergent truths jostle with one another, challenging the validity of reductive political rhetoric – the manufactured confrontations of tradition and modernity; the artificial demarcations of rational and irrational, pure and impure.

Over the course of history, health has served as a bridge between the sacred and the secular, between our spiritual beliefs and our social relations. Health mediates the physiological, the psychological and the psychosocial, mapping inclinations of the body politic on the experiences of the body. Health forges a link between our values and our action – an epistemological framework offering rigorous empirical interrogation while rejecting spurious claims of certainty, embracing instead the properties of complexity and ambiguity and feeding the unending debate which is, itself, the nature and hallmark of the 'good society'.

As we enter a period of unprecedented pressure on the post-war liberal order, emerging from a decade of economic breakdown and the onslaught of COVID-19, health offers a unique medium through which to evaluate the nature of our crisis, and how we propose to move beyond it. In order to plot a course forward, though, we need first, as I will argue in the following section 'Crisis: a timeline', to understand how we got here.

The fall and rise of pandemic society

Health – and its loss – shape human history. Smallpox brought whole civilisations – from the Hittites to the Indigenous tribes of North America – to their knees, killing more people in the 20th century than two world wars combined.[9] Between 1348 and 1447, bubonic plague brought to an untimely end around a third of the population of Europe, reducing workforce and changing the balance of power between peasant labour and landowners, prompting the collapse of feudalism and the birth of the capitalist-industrial economy.

Immunologic vulnerability among the peoples of the precolonial world paved the way for military and administrative occupation, shaping the scope of colonial settlement and laying the foundations for some of the most egregious inequities in global development today (Bewell, 2003).[10] Colonial expansion and the Atlantic slave trade established a transnational exchange of Old and New World pathogens, intensifying the impact of both on hitherto ecologically adaptive populations, profoundly altering the developmental pathway of a whole continent (Taylor, 2012; Ngalamulume, 2017).

Dysentery capped the global aspiration of European naval powers. Typhus likely played a decisive role in the calamitous end to Napoleon's pan-European vision in the frozen wastes of southern Russia (Bray, 1996; Frank et al, 2008; Barro and Ursua, 2009). Emerging in the aftermath of the First World War, Spanish influenza infected half a billion people around the world in a matter of months, reaching remote Pacific islands, penetrating the Arctic Circle, and eventually dispatching between 50 and 100 million innocent souls. It may have changed the outcome of the war as *Blitzkattargh* cut through the German frontlines in the final months of the conflict. The epidemic drove down gross domestic product (GDP) across the world's industrial heartlands, seeding economic depression in Europe and North America and setting up the conditions for the Wall Street crash in 1929 (Brainerd and Siegler, 2002; Honigsbaum, 2013).

Between 1980 and 2020, HIV/AIDS – the great modern plague – killed an estimated 36.3 million people, cutting through working-age adults, mothers and newborns, decimating families, creating whole new generations of orphans and grandparent-parents, reversing growth in sub-Saharan African life expectancy, and reducing the continent's GDP by as much as 17 per cent (Fee and Krieger, 1993).[11] Although tortuously slow to gain real governmental engagement, the global response was, in the end, a watershed. From gay activism in the US to mass civil society lawsuits in Southern Africa challenging commercial ownership of pharmaceutical knowledge; from the establishment of its own, disease-specific global agency (UNAIDS) to the unfurling of unprecedented quantities of international concessionary funding, HIV/AIDS materially altered the struggle for rights-based governance, through the medium of health, leveraging forms of popular inclusion and challenging gender inequity in policy making in ways that had hitherto been little more than idealising aspiration (Buse et al, 2018; Bekker et al, 2019).[12]

We are, it is said, entering a new age of pandemics – their frequency, speed and scale accelerated by compressions of space and time brought about by urbanising globalisation and poorly governed environmental exploitation.[13] New and re-emerging infectious diseases – emboldened by the pace at which we are encroaching on virgin ecosystems, liberating hitherto geographically restrained pathogens – crowd the wings of the global stage waiting for the confluence of circumstances which will sustain another fast-moving, massive outbreak (WHO/Global Preparedness Monitoring Board, 2019).[14]

In late 2002, a new respiratory syndrome, SARS, spread from the markets of Guangdong, via a Hong Kong hotel lift button, to every region of the planet within six months, costing an estimated USD$52 billion in global GDP. Between 2009 and 2010, the H1N1 variant of influenza caused 61 million infections in the United States with 274,000 hospitalisations, killing between 151,700 and 575,400 people around the world in its first year (CDC, 2019). Middle Eastern Respiratory Syndrome (MERS) – a member of the coronavirus family – has been raising its head sporadically since 2012 although for the present, for reasons which are not entirely clear, confined to small-scale localised outbreaks (European Centre for Disease Prevention and Control, 2021).[15] In 2014, Ebola ripped down the trading routes of the West African Mano River Basin, paralysing development in Guinea, Liberia and Sierra Leone before spreading to the Nigerian megacity, Lagos, where it was stopped on the brink of a whole new level of global jeopardy (World Bank/WHO, 2019). Between 2015 and 2016, Zikavirus infected over a million and a half people across the Americas, resulting in thousands of cases of microcephalic birth defect (Boadle et al, 2016).

In the first decades of the 21st century, these proto-pandemics had, so far, been brought under control by a combination of skill and luck. But in 2020, a new coronavirus – SARS-CoV-2 – broke out of central China, moving west into Europe and spreading around the world faster than any comparable global public health emergency of recent years (Figure 0.1) (Chin et al, 2020; Tatem, 2020). By mid-2022, the World Health Organization (WHO) had recorded over half a billion confirmed cases of COVID, with just under 6.9 million reported and 17.2 million estimated deaths. In late 2022, projections of COVID's cumulative impact on global output between 2020 and 2025 rose to USD$28 trillion (WHO, 2022).[16]

COVID-19 may be the first truly global event in human history; a single common assault by Nature on human society, hitting countries in quick succession across the world, activating an unprecedented sequence of contiguous national responses, closing down economies, freezing travel, movement and mobility and placing in head-on collision liberal values – of personal freedom and collective security, democratic decision-making and executive action, economic growth and public health (van Bergeijk, 2021).[17] COVID exploited the unprecedented interconnectedness of our geographical, social, economic, political and cultural globalisation. As we come out of the critical phase, the question is whether we can harness the scale of that global community to mount our best recovery.

Pandemics through history have inspired major change in the structure and function of society. For now, it is unclear whether COVID-19, conforming with the past, will form the gateway to a new paradigm of global social organisation – whether we will learn to use our transnational connectivity to leverage new collective defences, or throw it to the dogs, retreating instead into comforting but self-defeating duck-and-cover insularity; whether we will emerge with a new understanding of the profound incongruity between our economic processes and our planetary capability or simply relapse into business as usual (Horton and Lo, 2015).[18]

Because, as the risk and reality of pandemics grows, our ability to learn and respond appears, if anything, to have stalled. More accurately, we seem to have done well on the 'hardware' of pandemic control: disease surveillance, rapid development of diagnostic testing, preventive vaccines, therapeutics and treatments, but less well on the 'software': the infrastructure of international cooperation; the quality of interface between science and policy; a strategy for strengthening health systems from the grassroots up; and a coherent approach to communication building trust between governments and citizens

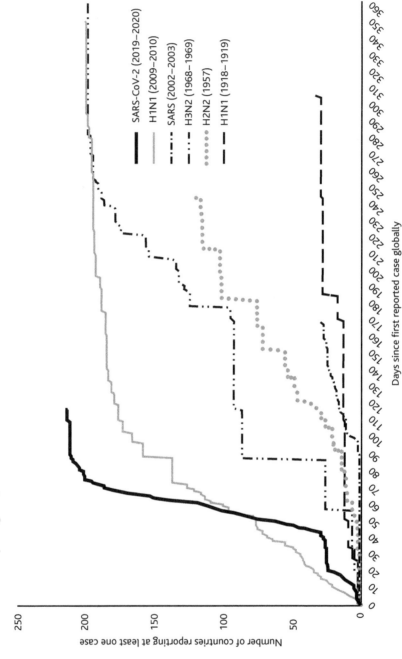

Figure 0.1: Cumulative case reporting rate, COVID-19 and other transnational outbreaks

Number of countries reporting at least one case

Days since first reported case globally

SARS-CoV-2 (2019–2020)
H1N1 (2009–2010)
SARS (2002–2003)
H3N2 (1968–1969)
H2N2 (1957)
H1N1 (1918–1919)

Source: Tatem (2020)

on public health risks and rights. It is as if we are simply unable to retain the repeating insight that the efficacy of our hardware is profoundly dependent on the functionality of the software by which our societies are structured; the value of technical capability shaped by a complex of social and political values within countries and between them.

While COVID has offered us a lesson in humility, we are sadly not known as a species for our ability to be humble. The proper application of that lesson will require truly transformative change across societies – including major change in the distribution of power over political and economic organisation between global, national and local levels. It is not clear that we are ready for this. Another pandemic – one whose case fatality rate is unfortunately unpredictable – may be needed to push us over the edge of that decisional moment. But that that decision is going to have to be taken is now no longer in doubt.

Notes

[1] Some of the greatest of the Greek tragedies may themselves have been inspired by an outbreak of plague in Athens around 430 BCE.

[2] '[A]nd lered hym lechecraft, his lif for to save … and dide hym assaie his surgenrie on hem that sike were.'

[3] On the cusp between Renaissance and Reformation, Donne, Milton and Bacon shared the view of God's 'two books', Scripture and Nature, as inextricably interwoven – the study of one necessitating a study of the other. For all its nanobiological and clinical hyper-specialisation, medicine remains a composite of science and humanity. At the end of the most sophisticated neurological investigations, questions of animating consciousness remain, for the time being, firmly in the domain of the metaphysical.

[4] Hamlet and Ophelia, Othello, Titus Andronicus and the Macbeths are all driven to madness by disruptions of the political order, succession and sex. Lear's breakdown – literally tearing his kingdom apart – speaks to profound political anxiety about the potential collapse of monarchy with the accession of Elizabeth to the throne. Confusions of class, gender and sex structure the stories of *Midsummer Night's Dream*, *As You Like It*, *Twelfth Night* and *The Taming of the Shrew*.

[5] 'Darkling I listen; and, for many a time/I have been half in love with easeful Death/Call'd him soft names in many a mused rhyme/To take into the air my quiet breath.' Tuberculosis was the leading cause of death in Europe and the US in the 19th century, killing as many as one in four. Tuberculosis dispatched Keats' mother and brother before killing him at the age of 25.

[6] See, for example, Gabriel Garcia Marquez's *Love in the Time of Cholera* and *The General in His Labyrinth*.

[7] From *A Matter of Life and Death* to *Angels in America*, by way of *Dr Kildare*, *M.A.S.H.* and *ER*, *Love Story*, *Coma* and *Outbreak*, *Camille*, *Dark Victory*, *Dr Zhivago*, *Carry on Doctor*, *Spellbound*, *One Flew Over the Cuckoo's Nest* and *Awakenings*, *Night of the Living Dead*, *The Satan Bug*, *The Andromeda Strain*, *12 Monkeys*, *An Early Frost*, *Philadelphia*, *Jeffrey*, *28 Days Later*, *I Am Legend*, *Contagion*, *The Happening* and the inexplicably misjudged *World War Z*.

[8] In 1926, Virginia Woolf wrote: 'Consider[ing] how common illness is, how tremendous the spiritual change that it brings, how astonishing, when the lights of health go down, the undiscovered countries that are then disclosed, what wastes and deserts of the soul a slight attack of influenza brings to view ... it becomes strange indeed that illness has not taken its place with love and battle and jealousy among the prime themes of literature' (Woolf, 1926).

[9] Eradicating smallpox, in 1979, is considered to be one of the greatest humanitarian achievements in history.

[10] 'Smallpox, diphtheria, influenza, measles, yellow fever, malaria, mumps, typhoid fever, whooping cough, chicken pox, dengue and scarlet fever, amongst others, often silently preceded and largely made possible the colonisation of the Americas' (Bewell, 2003).

[11] See UNAIDS, 2022.

[12] Although HIV/AIDS has without question shaped the global fight for better governance across health and human development, the results remain uneven – investment and action more focused on the biomedical management of disease than social acceptance of viral status, and heavily dependent on fluctuating political perceptions of economic feasibility and value.

[13] 'There is every likelihood that the next pandemic will come within a decade – arising from a novel influenza strain, another coronavirus, or one of several other dangerous pathogens' (G20 High Level Independent Panel on Financing the Global Commons for Pandemic Preparedness and Response, 2021).

[14] This was written towards the end of 2019, shortly before the onset of COVID-19. Between 1940 and 2004, researchers identified a total of 335 emerging infectious diseases. Meanwhile, the rise of antimicrobial resistance, as infections learn to live with or sidestep our arsenal of antibiotics, threatens the return to a world without effective immune-suppressant cancer therapy, basic surgery or safe hospital care – although for many low- and middle-income countries this would look a lot like business as usual (see, for example, Jones et al, 2008; WHO, 2018).

[15] That said, once within a viably transmissive environment, for example a hospital with a captive population of susceptibles as happened in South Korea in 2015, MERS can move fast and with significant destructive force (see, for example, Gilbert and Green, 2021).

[16] In 2019, World Bank and WHO projections suggested that a new flu pandemic would kill tens of millions and cost 5–6 per cent of global GDP – throwing the world into a prolonged period of economic and social disorder (see Elliot, 2020).

[17] 'The COVID-19 pandemic is the first time in history that closing entire economies has been used as a medical tool, simultaneously and worldwide' (Milanovic, 2020).

[18] 'To the question, "Are we building back better?", the answer is: not yet. The spending announced in 2020 paints a disappointing picture for overall efforts thus far to build forward with green priorities' (O'Callaghan and Murdock, 2021; see also, for example, Roy, 2020).

Crisis: a timeline

Between January and September 2007, starting in the US housing market, the world we thought we knew started to crumble (Edmonds, 2010). Banks – increasingly dependent on mind-boggling algorithmic models – believed they had figured out a way to marketise risk associated with towering Western consumption and debt by blending precarious mortgages with other securities in alchemical investment products so fiendishly complex that, when rising interest rates finally precipitated the rapid spread of defaults and everything started to unravel, no one was able to say where the toxicity lay or how far the contagion would spread.

It was, by many estimates, the worst financial crisis since 1929, ushering in a global recession whose repercussions have expanded and intensified, rippling outwards from financial to economic, economic to social, social to political. In the ensuing decade, as countries struggled to cope and livelihoods suffered, we saw the unwritten and, as it turns out, unenforceable law of human aspiration – that the lives of our children will exceed the limits of ours – dissolve in a fog of turmoil and uncertainty (Barnichon et al, 2018; Cribb and Johnson, 2018; Oxenford, 2018).

Emerging economies were hit by a wave of sharply reversing capital flows. Poor countries were struck by the next wave as demand for primary commodities tumbled and growth contracted. In the most vulnerable countries, 130 million people were pushed back into the poverty world leaders had, a few years earlier, pledged to make history (Griffith-Jones and Ocampo, 2009; World Bank, 2009; Mustapha, 2014; Roderick, 2014; UNESCAP, 2018). Across high-income countries, response to the crisis came in two parts. Between 2009 and 2017, central banks pumped some USD$12 trillion of quantitative easing into the global financial system. On the heels of quantitative easing, however, came a different animal – austerity. In what can only be described as a breath-taking piece of political legerdemain, the crisis was placed firmly at the door of out-of-control government spending, the response to which was to institute some of the most swingeingly punitive cuts to welfare spending in living memory (Ginn, 2013; Lupton et al, 2016).

What was described initially as a 'credit crunch' evolved into a crisis of banking and financial services; from financial calamity into deeper questions of state spending and fiscal management; and from there to a crisis of politics and polarisation – between global and local, cosmopolitan and native, 'us' and 'them'.[1] We arrived, finally, at a crisis of faith in the foundational values which have, over the last half century, been the mainstays of liberal market democracy. Yet, while the travails of recent years are widely ascribed to the crash, they do not start there. To understand the current moment, we need to go further back – to two seminal moments in the post-war period: the OPEC crisis and the fall of the Berlin Wall.

A brief history of the end of the end of history

At 2pm on 6 October 1973 – during the celebration of Yom Kippur – Egypt and Syria launched a joint attack on the Sinai Peninsula and the Golan Heights, occupied by Israel after the Six-Day War. Failure of the military action and a decisive Israeli response prompted Arab states to declare an embargo on oil exports to countries perceived as supporting Tel Aviv. The price of oil quadrupled overnight (Figure 0.2).[2] A second oil shock six years later, following the Iranian revolution, plunged the world into economic recession and political crisis.

Figure 0.2: Import cost of oil (per barrel, in USD$), 1970–2005

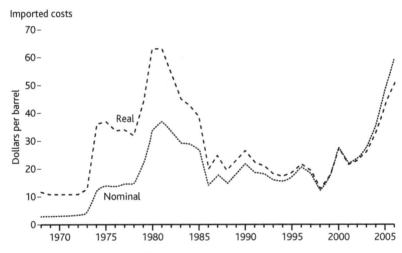

Source: Energy Information Agency (2006)

Crisis, though, brought opportunity. Critics of post-war Keynesianism and state-led reconstruction, quietly building on experimental projects in Latin America, emerged under the banner of 'neoliberalism' to offer an alternative vision of market-led society. Neoliberalism repudiated the Leviathan shadow of the state over social and economic development, viewing government as the problem, not the solution, and collective forms of social organisation as inefficient and repressive. It advocated for a world made up of unique individuals, each rationally bound to the maximisation of their own interests, each rationally self-interested enough to ensure the ultimate welfare of all – and for these individuals to be freed from the chains of an illusory society to engage with one another through the purity of markets undistorted by regulatory control.

Neoliberalism is a curious term – equal parts technical economic reference and shrill ideological bogeyman; overused by those who oppose it and barely acknowledged by those accused of fostering its use (Brand and Sekler, 2009; Cahill et al, 2018).[3] But whether you view the neoliberal turn as a mere flavour of policy or a comprehensive agenda for social reform, there can be little doubt that it has constituted, in its impact worldwide, a profound philosophical reflection on the nature of economic society – depending on your perspective, either radical and emancipatory or empirically impoverished and savage.

In a world of rising unemployment, mounting industrial unrest and escalating social conflict, this new political vision sought to win over voters wearied by fiscal crisis, Cold War contest, and narratives of national decay. It was exceedingly successful – prominently in the electoral victories of Ronald Reagan, Margaret Thatcher and Helmut Kohl, and thereafter in a rapid cascade through countries down the economic development spectrum.[4]

The perfectable society

With the collapse of the Soviet Union after 1990, economic neoliberalism merged with a new brand of American neoconservative democratic evangelism, sharpened by the terrible events of 9/11. These in turn combined with more progressive dividends of the post-Cold War peace – a revived agenda for universal rights, new institutions of international justice, and an agenda for 'human development' embodied in the Millennium Development Goals – to form a vision of the 'perfectable society': a community of nations united under a shared framework of indispensable values – of growth and prosperity, freedom, democracy, security and justice – comprising, together, the destiny, the revealed truth, of human society (Fukuyama, 1992).

Since then, without doubt, the world has changed to an astonishing degree (Pinker, 2018; Rosling, 2018). In 1980, 43 per cent of the world's population lived in extreme poverty; a third of humans were unable to read; one in five children in developing countries did not see their fifth birthday. Children in the rich world had 20 to 30 times the life chances of their poor-world peers. More people lived under autocratic than democratic rule (World Bank, 1980). In 2020, extreme poverty has fallen to 14 per cent; child mortality has fallen from 90 to 43 deaths per 1,000 live births; new HIV infections have reduced by 40 per cent, and people receiving antiretroviral medicines has risen from 800,000 to 13.6 million. Democracies now outnumber dictatorships (UN, 2015; Our World in Data, nd).

These are things worth celebrating. But they are only half of the story (Leatherby, 2017; Smaje, 2018). If conditions of poverty and acute hunger have been mitigated at the very bottom of global society, life continues to be a perennial struggle to find work to make ends meet, to keep the family fed

and stave off hunger, to pay for school and healthcare without being driven
into destitution, to have a meaningful voice in the policy choices shaping
their lives, for perhaps as many as three or four billion of the eight billion
people on the planet. Meanwhile, inequality between nations remains vast,
and inequality within countries is rising (Akinyemi et al, 2015; Hosseinpoor
et al, 2016; Niño-Zarazúa et al, 2017; Alvaredo et al, 2018; Ravallion, 2018).

In the US, all significant income gains between the late 1970s and 2007
accrued to the top 20 per cent of people – much the largest share of this
to the top 1 per cent. The richest 10 per cent own more than 70 per cent
of the country's total wealth (Alvaredo et al, 2018).[5] In the UK, income
inequality – low and steady for three decades after the end of the Second
World War – rose rapidly through the 1980s with the neoliberal turn
(Figure 0.3) (Bourquin et al, 2020).[6]

Figure 0.3: Gini coefficient, UK, 1961–2018

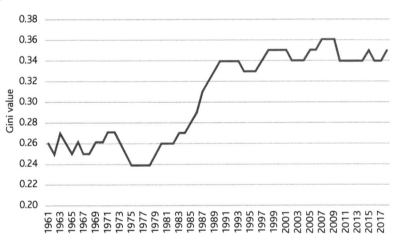

Source: Bourquin et al (2020)

The integration of states in a single global system has without doubt had
considerable benefits in the aggregate. But the local experience of neoliberal
globalisation has been confusing. There is common agreement that it has
created 'winners and losers', but there is less agreement about what this
means in reality – who belongs to which group, and why (Bacchetta and
Jansen, 2011; Gozgor and Ranjan, 2017).

Few people believe that inequality, in and of itself, is a good thing. But
many support the idea that it is a necessary feature – whether temporarily or
permanently – of an economic society which is dynamic and free. There is a
view that inequality tends to move in waves, growing with economic growth
until it reaches a level of social intolerability at which point public opinion and

political influence force a redistributive correction – along a spectrum of possible actions from changes in the tax code to armed revolution (Milanovic, 2016). Under the guiding hand of the neoliberal paradigm, however, I think it is possible that three social mechanisms critical to the peaceful management of inequality – the mediating functions of a traditional middle class, an independent civil society, and meaningful processes of electoral participation – may have become weakened to the point of dysfunction, diminishing our willingness and ability to engage with one another on equitable terms, within and between countries, in defining and delivering a common vision of society.

Class dismissed

The global integration of production and market systems wrought seismic change in the composition and status of workforces around the world. Privatisation and outsourcing saw widespread dilution of workers' rights and protections – epitomised in sweat-shop labour across developing countries, but also in the rich-world meme of the 'gig economy', artlessly rendering exploitative contracts and unliveable wages as freewheeling hipster lifestyle. Offshoring core industrial, manufacturing and service work has hollowed out whole sectors of skilled and semi-skilled workers, leaving a trail of ghost towns across Europe and the American Midwest (Rifkin, 1995; Erixon and Razeen, 2010). Of all globalisation's winners and losers, in the distribution of power between labour and capital, none is more important or instructive than the fate of the old-world middle class.

With its proclivity for entrepreneurial activity, job creation, discretionary spending power and educational status, the middle class has played a key role in curating consensual socioeconomic development over the last 250 years, extending democratic principles and active distributional policies, and guarding against egregious gaps opening up in wealth and power.[7] Under globalisation, a global middle class has expanded significantly. But the centre of its gravity – its power and function – has moved and mutated. Of the next billion entrants into the world's middle class, 88 per cent will live in Asia (Kharas, 2017). As a new middle class has emerged in Shanghai and Kuala Lumpur, the old bourgeois of Europe and America have seen their wealth and status stagnate and decline (Figure 0.4) (Lakner and Milanovic, 2013). The result in rich countries has been a collapse in middle-class identity, along with its unique conciliatory social and political function (Erixon et al, 2010; Cárdenas et al, 2015; Woolf and Schoomaker, 2019).

Research suggests that emerging economy middle classes are less likely to support democratic principles, evincing a preference for strongman politics and showing little interest in redistributive policies (Frank, 2007). Middle-class households in Indonesia, Brazil, Egypt and Thailand reject the idea

Figure 0.4: The 'elephant' curve: relative gain in real per capita income by global income level, 1988–2008

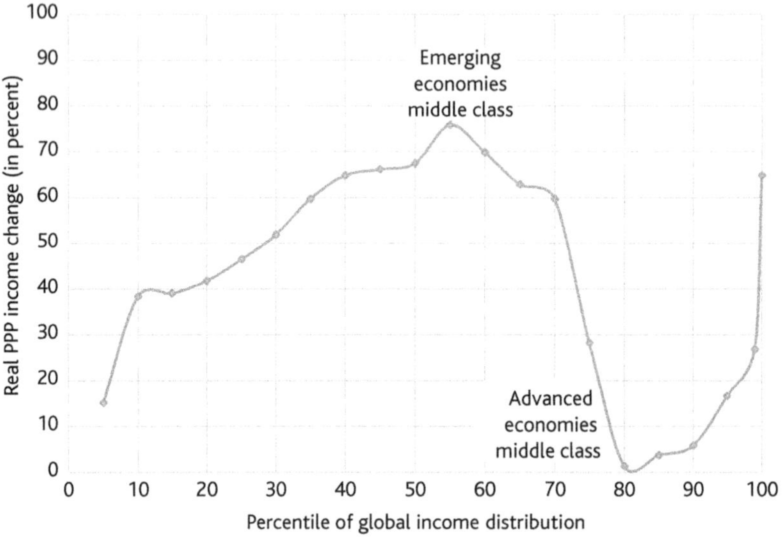

Source: Lakner and Milanovic (2013)

of government and public sector as significant in their success, viewing prosperity as the result of individual merit, work and thrift. This raises a question over exactly how benignly contributory to whole-of-society consensus-building this neophyte global middle class will be (Wolff, 2010; Lobo and Shah, 2015; Klassen, 2016; Rakesh, 2020).

Contracting civil space

Civil society – for long viewed from both left and right as kind of magic bullet for supplying public goods that neither government nor private sector could, would or should – is evolving in ways which, it may be argued, undermine its original form and purpose. Born out of locally self-organising community groups, civil society has proliferated massively. In 1972, 298 nongovernment organisation (NGO) representatives attended the first UN Conference on Human Environment (Salamon et al, 1999; Durant et al, 2004). By 2015, the number of NGOs attending the UN Climate Change Conference was 14,000.

That growth, though, has seen the conversion of loose social groupings into formally constituted legal entities – regional, national and ultimately global organisations, complete with business plans and bottom lines, increasingly driven to expand in competition with one another. As government has withdrawn from provision of public service after public service, NGOs have moved into the widening gap, taking on an increasing proportion of contracts from the state (O'Reilly, 2011). By the late 1990s, two-thirds of NGO business in high- and middle-income countries was devoted to delivering social and welfare services. In countries with the most developed NGO sector, 60–70 per cent of organisational income came from government contracts, with just 15 per cent from public giving.

There is no inherent problem with NGOs taking on management of public sector activities. But in so doing, NGOs have blurred the line between civil society and government, at the expense of their embeddedness in the interests of the populations from which they purportedly arise. This is a subtle process, involving graduations of complicity which can be rationalised or overlooked day to day, but which accumulate in a fundamental repositioning of organisational role, forfeiting the legitimacy of an independent voice representing citizen issues in the face of state and commercial interests (Choudry and Kapoor, 2013; Gideon and Porter, 2016; Alvarez et al, 2017).[8]

Voting with their feet

Through the neoliberal turn, the traditional division of party politics – left and right – dissolved in the goldrush for a fabled 'centre ground'. Spearheaded by the US, UK and Germany, traditional tribal affiliations were supplanted by a new electoral calculus, forged in the social imaginary of a new professional political class (Giddens, 1998). The 'Third Way' aimed to revive the fortunes of centre-left politics by acceding to the immovable truth of market capitalism but subjecting it to some degree of social democratic value. As an electoral strategy, it was strikingly successful. But as a reflection of reality, it failed to engage with profounder problems of structural injustice (Ferragina and Arrigoni, 2016).

The fallacy of centrism is that it overestimates the extent of commonality across electorates, glossing over deep-rooted social and regional inequity, eviscerating real political difference, real contest in the distribution of power (Muntaner and Lynch, 2002; Aronowitz, 2006; Ferragina and Arrigoni, 2016). One notable result has been a flight from democratic engagement, acutely among the young disenchanted by a growing gap between grand political promises and the realities they inhabit (Figure 0.5) (Mahler and Jesuit, 2014; McElwee, 2015; IDEA, 2016).[9]

The resistible rise of the strong man

Over the last half-century, we have witnessed the global proliferation of an economic philosophy of society in which individuals are free to prosper or not in open markets as the role of government is pushed into the margins.

Figure 0.5: Voter turnout, global and regional, 1945–2019

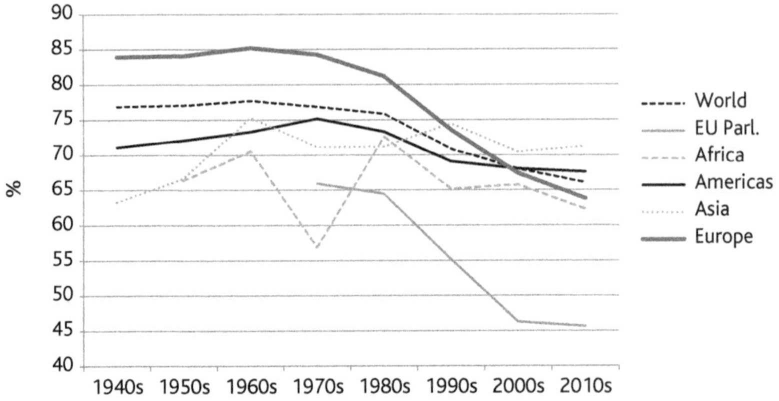

Source: International IDEA (nd)[10]

With the accelerant of the 2007–2008 crash, rising inequality accentuated by a post-crisis decade of recessionary forces, savage welfare retrenchment, stagnating living standards and deteriorating conditions of community cohesion, we have seen mediating social mechanisms which protect and preserve our ability to communicate and disagree with one another dissipate and dissolve. As a result, people have simply started to look for alternative narratives by which to rationalise their experience of society, and alternative leaders to represent that reality.

Between 1990 and 2018, the number of populists in power around the world increased fivefold, bridging left- and right-of-centre politics and manifesting in governments across the democratic–autocratic spectrum (Kyle and Gultchin, 2018).[11] At the core of this surge – cashing in on public feelings of uncertainty, dissatisfaction and fear – lies a common tactic: to destabilise trust in conventional social institutions by undermining our confidence in established modes of information, communication and truth (Algan et al, 2018). Populists coopt the language of the perfectable society and subvert it – challenging what it means to be democratic, what freedom and security truly entail, what constitutes justice. They seize on the necessary uncertainties inherent in science and the scientific method, caricaturing academia, policy and expert knowledge, confronting nuance and pluralist interpretations of social value with the singular assertion of one past and future tradition powered by a nostalgia which is increasingly all that is left to communities exhausted by living in the margins, precariously balanced on the edge of an economic precipice.

They direct our anger at 'elites', disregarding their own wealth and power, dividing society along imaginary lines of a privileged *them* and a dispossessed *us*. Articulating elitism with liberalism and globalism, they extend the division to set native against outsider, driven by the manufactured spectre of uncontrolled immigration and the undeserving migrant. They coopt US-led adventurism and the new polarities of global power, essentialising ethnic and religious identity in order to frame dissent as terror, enabling draconian measures under the powerful new rubric of security.

They deploy constitutional process to challenge constitutional norms. They reject the formal separation of executive and judicial power, claiming direct democracy over representative mechanisms, attacking the role of judges whilst cleaving to legalist challenges and competitive impeachments, extending executive power and compromising oversight. They espouse majoritarian interpretations of public opinion, asserting an absolute mandate for anything above 50 per cent of the vote and absolute loss of mandate for anything less (Palmer, 2017; Brown and Bērziņa-Čerenkova, 2018; Batory and Svensson, 2019; Rachman, 2022).[12] They lay claim to the voice of a silent majority – the voice of the suppressed and oppressed – 'saying it like it is' and offering a space for righteous anger among people who have suffered the depredations of our collective failure to make the perfectable society a reality. They coopt the onslaught of COVID to laughable assertions of national exceptionalism, challenging the collective truths of epidemiology and public health while shielding their eyes from the deaths and the bodies.

On the global stage, they challenge the democratic legitimacy of multilateral institutions from the Geneva Conventions to the Paris Agreement, undermining decades of hard-won concord. They subvert the norms of international relations, manifesting their disdain through extravagantly theatrical extraterritorial executions and horse-trading humans held as collateral for the larger negotiation of business and state affairs.[13] They replace the treaty with the deal, vacating decades of shared value built on collective compromise in favour of temporary arrangements geared to short-term zero-sum gain reversible at the whiff of a better offer and the whim of sharp-suited, cuff-shooting negotiators.

They challenge the language of political discourse, mimicking vernacular forms replete with reference to traditional literature and classical grandiloquence, two-dimensional vocabulary, sensational imagery and bulk use of the superlative. They demonstrate an extreme hostility to traditional media and the filtering capability of formal journalistic outlets, evincing a strong preference for unmediated communication reverting to 'live voice' interactions with their audiences through rallies, banners and posters and the enthusiastic use of social media; the power of live voice – evanescent, deniable, gaslighting its own meanings – epitomising as never before the fragility of truth at the heart of our society (Frankfurt, 2005; Hines, 2017; Brubaker, 2018; Feusatl, 2018; Hunston, nd).

Conclusion

In the last decade, following the global crash, the social, economic and political certainties of the post-war international order have been tested almost to destruction. Faced with catastrophic levels of uncertainty, people seek shelter in hardening positions of insular extremism. Ideas of common interest, shared values – globally, nationally, locally – are giving way to protectionist instincts as families, communities and countries struggle to work out where they stand, to preserve themselves against the maelstrom. As a result, our collective ability to believe in political rhetoric – and the values it embodies – has been all but demolished, leaving in its wake a free-for-all of claim and counter-claim, assertion and accusation, disregarded expertise and the brilliantly obfuscatory invocation of 'fake news'. An emphasis on hyper-individualised consumption turns information into commodity, to be exposed to the market function of choice. Decades of relentlessly hyping the individual as the single meaningful agent in global society – the casual narcissism of the age of the selfie – eventually erodes to the point of breakdown the consensus model of 'truth', the ultimate public good (Haas, 2007).

There has been much liberal soul-searching in the last decade. We thought we were moving beyond the divisiveness of petty national contests; we believed the post-war settlement was solid – that multilateralism was here to stay; that welfare was an indelible feature of domestic policy making, and aid for human development (or at least the relief of egregious suffering) was a bulwark of our international ties to one another. We chose to believe that the privileges of globalisation – of growth, freedom, justice, security, democracy and truth – were commonly shared and equitably esteemed. We were wrong.

In the period ahead as we emerge from the pandemic, we will need to rediscover concrete, shared points of reference – within communities and between countries – by which to review and reconstruct the basic premises of progress through which we aim, collectively, to forge a viable future. The body of this book is devoted to arguing that health offers such a point of reference.

Crisis 2.0

In January 2020, reports started to emerge about a rash of pneumonia-like disease in the city of Wuhan, Hubei Province, central China. Within six months, COVID-19 had circled the planet, reaching into the remotest regions and proliferating, in particular, in the initial instance, among the vulnerable, poor and marginalised in the urban centres of the rich world. One after another, governments introduced 'lockdown' measures, restricting public movement and closing down economic activity – some, more inclined to collective (and authoritarian) action, slickly effective; others more attuned to the libertarian model, stickily recalcitrant. The resulting patterns of global infection – between countries and within them between economic and ethnic groups – have reflected back at us in ineluctable epidemiological detail the pathogenic effects of different systems of value and governance (Figure 0.6).[14]

COVID exposed deep vulnerabilities in the contemporary model of global social and economic development – the long-inevitable confrontation between endless economic growth and necessary environmental stewardship; the disposability of 'global community' and international norms faced with national interest and domestic political pressure; the rhetoric of social justice and the reality of enduring social inequality – exposing the power and the fragility of the liberal world order.[15] While the economies of the rich world look set to recover much lost ground (Ukraine conflict notwithstanding), the full scale of COVID-19, in particular in poorer regions with weaker protective health systems, remains to be seen (World Bank, 2021). COVID brought to a grinding halt most of the processes of social and economic life. In so doing, it revealed the ease with which the absolute assumptions of the modern liberal project – narratives of self-determination and social order – could be unceremoniously stripped away. While we will doubtless recover the material practices of economic life, we will need to work hard to rebuild our confidence in the validity of the social values on which those practices depend (Cooper and Szreter, 2021).

Beyond the loss of life and shattered livelihoods, COVID is a historic moment – a chance to reconsider our ideas of society and to fashion an economic recovery which honours those insights. To reflect on how our model of growth constitutes a source and enabler, as much as victim, of borderless disease; how government, with some honourable exceptions, oscillated between a fear of mounting death and the dread of economic loss, their strategic vacillations often salvaged only by the maturity of popular action – levels of collective compliance extensively underestimated by policy makers steeped in the dubious traditions of behavioural science and methodological individualism (Ham, 2021); how our best technologies were quickly swamped and ultimately dependent for their functioning on simple human decency; how inequality rendered us more exposed and less defended against a virus which is only, ultimately, vanquished by solidarity; how our political leaders fell swiftly back onto the scientific expertise some had spent much time and capital assiduously undermining, shaping the daily narrative of their actions as much to obviate later blame as to lead; how the terrible penalties of lockdown were accompanied by strange new pleasures – of quietude and the momentary rediscovery of a smaller circle of existence – a glimpse of the radical lifestyle changes normally marginalised laughingly by mainstream policy makers and media as wholly implausible.

The scale of COVID's impact, and the fiscal recovery programmes deployed in response, create an epochal opportunity to reframe our social and economic model (UN Environment

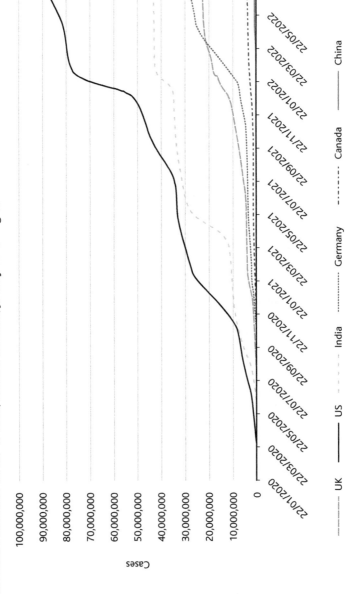

Figure 0.6: Cumulative confirmed COVID-19 cases, selected countries, January 2020–August 2022

Source: Our World in Data (nd)

Programme, 2020). The temptation, among fragmented, frightened, inward-turning governments, will be simply to recreate the tired, inefficient, inequitable and unsustainable but familiar and comforting growth model of the last 40 years, frantically reinflating markets while ruefully justifying a renewal of austerity, as a collective sigh of relief extinguishes the fragile light of shared memory. We will memorialise COVID in the sonorous language of warfare and victory – a heroic battle with hostile Nature – channelling energy towards the fortification of technological remedies and physical walls, instead of looking beyond disease to the human, social and economic causes of vulnerability. This will not bring us the sanctuary we crave. It will feel, for a while, as if it is safe ground. But like the medieval plague city, new-built ramparts will simply camouflage unremediated problems of physical, social and economic decay within.

The true measure of our recovery will be the extent to which COVID revives a common commitment to open global cooperation – sharing the pain and intelligence the pandemic will have bequeathed us and, in the longer term, orienting the global levers of social and economic development – of aid and investment, social protection, tax, credit and debt – to focus on reducing inequality not just among the poorest but across the whole social gradient in ways which honour and build on the local, national and global solidarity we called on during and after COVID.

Notes

[1] Spawning a rather simplistic polarity between 'somewhereists' and 'nowhereists'. In 2016, UK premier Theresa May said: "if you believe you are a citizen of the world, you are a citizen of nowhere". It was a divisive and unhelpful premise picked up in David Goodhart's 2017 work *The Road to Somewhere* (Hurst) (see, for example, Andreouli, 2019).

[2] So serious was the situation that Nixon's administration toyed briefly with the idea of military intervention in the Middle East. In the end it took another 30 years and 9/11 to bring that line of thinking to its messy fruition (see, for example, Peck, 2014).

[3] At the height of its much-bruited policy dominance through the 1980s and 1990s, the term 'neoliberal' largely disappeared from the documentation of economic institutions supposed its greatest cheerleaders. Perhaps, like Keyser Söze's devil, the smartest thing neoliberalism ever did was to persuade the world it didn't exist.

[4] Over the course of following two decades, neoliberal thinking inspired 'structural adjustment programmes' advocating or enforcing deep cuts in public spending and the scale of the state in more than 70 countries (36 of 47 in sub-Saharan Africa). The impact on developing countries continues to be debated today, but there is reasonable evidence that the results hurt millions of the most vulnerable people on earth. In Latin America and sub-Saharan Africa, structural adjustment programmes were associated with slower economic growth, stalled progress in infant mortality and life expectancy, and acceleration of the HIV/AIDS pandemic (see, for example, Lensink, 1996). Between the start of the crisis and 1993, developing country debt burden rose from $785 billion to nearly USD$1.5 trillion.

[5] Between 1987 and 2017, average wealth of the top 1 per cent in the US, Europe, and China rose 3.5 per cent per year compared with 1.9 per cent for average incomes. The top

0.1 per cent increased by 4.4 per cent per year; the top 0.01 per cent by 5.6 per cent. This view of steeply rising inequality in the available data is contested by more recent research on the broad grounds that the redistributive effects of tax and benefits over the periods of measurement are inadequately reflected (particularly in the context of falling US marriage rates among poorer people diluting their share of wealth, and the problem of allocating the 40 per cent of income that does not show up in tax returns) (see, for example, The Economist, 2019: 23–26). The conclusion of this analysis, perhaps unsurprisingly, is that in the absence of firmer evidence redistributive policies should be restrained.

[6] Notably, with the transition from an 18-year Conservative administration to New Labour after 1997, inequality levelled off, but did not fall – suggesting perhaps that a higher level of economic inequality under the centrist model was, in effect, the acceptable new normal (Arias, 2014; Alston, 2018; The Equality Trust, nd).

[7] A confluence of economic interest and political dialogue between rural landowners and urban middle classes in Scandinavia from the mid-17th century may explain, at least in part, the comparatively harmonious model of social development, and extremely positive indices of well-being, we see in that part of the world today.

[8] 'When I give food to the poor, they call me a saint. When I ask why they are poor, they call me a communist' (Dom Helder Camara, 1909–1999). These observations about civil society are not, at all, to discount the upsurge in often spontaneous local, national and transnational civil society movements – from the Arab Spring, Occupy and Black Lives Matter to #MeToo and Extinction Rebellion. But it is to note that these are often the acute manifestation of deeper, long-standing issues rooted in economic, gender, racial, ethnic and environmental injustice, inaction and political inertia, and an expression of frustration in the viability of more traditional modes of engagement between citizen and state (see, for example, Putnam, 2000).

[9] In the US, disengagement from voting is higher among groups who favour higher taxes and government spending on public services, resulting in a self-generating loop of economically conservative voters actively advancing low-tax-and-spend candidates. Meanwhile, concentration of global banking and media ownership has proceeded apace. Between 1995 and 2010, the asset value of the top bank-holding companies in the United States rose from 17 per cent to 64 per cent of GDP; majority control of US media shrank from 50 to five companies (Carroll and Sapinski, 2010; Noam, 2015).

[10] This graph was constructed with the generous provision of tailored data from IDEA's database.

[11] From Hugo Chávez and Nicolás Maduro in Venezuela to Rodrigo Duterte and 'Bongbong' Marcos in the Philippines, Recep Tayyip Erdoğan in Turkey and Viktor Orbán in Hungary, Jair Bolsonaro in Brazil, Narendra Modi in India, Xi Jinping in China and Vladimir Putin in Russia, Donald Trump in the US, Boris Johnson in the UK and Giorgia Meloni in Italy.

[12] A situation associated with increased risk of civil conflict (see Stewart, 2011).

[13] From the execution of Georgi Markov with a poisoned umbrella on the Strand in London in 1978, the Russian state's flamboyant approach to the liquidation of critics has won new fans, attracted perhaps by the theatre of raw power in a purposively lawless world. Alexander Litvinenko killed lingeringly with Polonium 210 and Anna Politkovskaya shot to death in a Moscow lift in 2006, Sergei Magnitsky in a Russian prison in 2009 and Boris Nemtsov in the shadow of the Kremlin in 2015; the attempt on Sergei and Yulia Skripal with military-grade novichok in the cathedral town of Salisbury and on opposition politician Andrei Navalny in August 2020; the dematerialisation of Jamal Khashoggi

inside the Saudi consulate in Istanbul and the killing of Zelimkhan Khangoshvili in Berlin; the drone-strike on General Qasem Soleimani, head of the Iranian Quds Force outside Baghdad airport in early 2020 and the assassination of Mohsen Fakhrizadeh, Iran's top nuclear scientist. Competitive detention has emerged as another model of brutalist diplomacy, from Nazanin Zaghari-Ratcliffe, Aras Amiri, Kylie Moore-Gilbert, Jolie King, Mark Firkin and Anousheh Ashoori in Iran through Paul Whelan and Naama Issachar in Russia, Meng Wanzhou, daughter of Huawei CEO in Canada and Canadians Michael Kovrig and Michael Spavor in China, to the state-sponsored detention of the children of senior Saudi security official, Dr Saad al-Jabri. All spectacular two-fingered salutes to the notion of a global rule of law.

[14] On New Year's Eve 2020, more people in England died of COVID-19 than died as a result of the infection in Australia in the whole of the preceding year (Calvert and Arbuthnott, 2021).

[15] UN Secretary-General, António Guterres, 18 July 2020: "COVID-19 has been likened to an X-ray, revealing fractures in the fragile skeleton of the societies we have built. It is exposing fallacies and falsehoods everywhere … while we are all floating on the same sea, it's clear that some are in superyachts while others are clinging to drifting debris."

.

PART I

Growth

Growth, wealth and health

Growth, we are told, is the principal good and chief preoccupation of the modern world – widely viewed as the most influential economic idea of the 20th century, a condition showing little real sign of diminishing in the early decades of the 21st (Schmelzer, 2016). With remarkable speed and uniformity, an economic notion of development has become installed at the heart of our global values – the core purpose of human society, the primary goal of policy making, and our collective secular religion (McNeill, 2000; Taylor, 2009; Smil, 2019). In 1909, economist and sociologist Thorstein Veblen wrote: '[t]o the modern scientist, the phenomena of growth and change are the ... most consequential facts observable in economic life' (Veblen, 1909).

The idea that growth is the natural condition of human society is curious in at least two respects. First because it is a relatively recent phenomenon. For almost 2,000 years, up to the middle of the 18th century, expansion in global economic output was negligible (Figure 1.1). And second because as a strategy for advancing the human race, economic growth appears to be rapidly running out of road (De Long, 1988; Szreter, 2003; Steffen et al, 2015).

Figure 1.1: Gross domestic product per capita, world, CE1000–2000

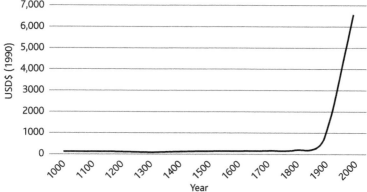

Source: De Long (1998)

This is not to suggest that wealth was somehow absent from the world prior to the Industrial Revolution. Rather that prosperity was created and consumed without being captured through systemic processes of investment and productive development. Long-run average growth in England between 1270 and 1750 appears to flatline at, or close to, zero. But a closer look shows rapid micro-cycles of expansion and contraction between +5 per cent and -5 per cent (Broadberry and Wallis, 2017). Pre-industrial societies were just poorly equipped to preserve and build on these growth spurts – to channel additional productivity to further productive use.

Trade between Europe, Asia, Iberia, Africa and the Americas blossomed between 1350 and 1700.[1] But wealth – concentrated among social and political elites in the midst of gruelling, largely agrarian subsistence – was valued primarily as a matter of consumption and display, designed to manifest the prestige and political power of sultans, popes and princelings, providing collateral and securing lines of credit to pay for military action and territorial conquest (Jardine, 1996).[2] Commercial exchange between East and West, however, revived European access to classical philosophy and mathematics enabling the intellectual flourishing of Renaissance humanities and science. Printing and the commodification of books standardised the transmissibility of accurate information from one part of the world to another.[3] Cartographic and navigational innovations underpinned the expansion of global exploration, trade and conquest accompanied by increasingly sophisticated systems of credit and the quietly seismic invention of double-entry bookkeeping.[4]

A resurgence in physical sciences – shifting from a Ptolemaic to a Copernican view of our place in the universe – expanded the room for manoeuvre between scriptural authority and the practicalities of the business world, not least by gradually removing compound interest from the schedule of mortal sins.[5] The process of secularisation, capped by the Treaty of Westphalia in 1648, formalised the legal idea of nation-states within an international order of sovereign governments presiding over defined juridical territories – creating the space for new institutional frameworks, refined by Enlightenment epistemology, through which wealth would finally be put to the services of growth through the Industrial Revolution over the following 250 years.

Dismal perhaps, but scientific?

As each generation became richer than the last, amateur interest in the dynamics of production and consumption became formalised under the title of 'economics'.[6] From Smith and Malthus, Ricardo, Marx and Mill, Pareto and Schumpeter, Keynes and Galbraith, Hayek, Friedman, Harrod and Domar to Myrdal and Ostrom, Arrow and Becker, Prebish, Frank and Wallerstein, Bergmann, Kahneman, Stiglitz and Krugman, Banerjee and Duflo – a pantheon of intellects,[7] running the ideological gamut, has created a rainbow of theoretical schools, all wrestling with the intersecting behaviours of capital, labour and technology, institutions and incentives, in an effort to understand their fundamental properties and the deep continuities by which they shape social production, productivity, change and growth (Zhao, 2019). In this they have been both ingeniously inventive and almost comedically incapable of consensus.

The growth of economics demonstrates two trajectories strikingly at odds with one another. On one hand, with the speed and execution of a model army, economics has come, in a very short space of time, to dominate all other academic disciplines, ascending to a kind of imperial status in the dog-eat-dog hierarchy of policy making and media reportage. But in precisely the same process, it has become detached from the reality of our lives, evolving from a composite of grounded historical, sociological, anthropological and psychological analyses – the observations of Adam Smith's philosopher-speculator – to a suite of disembodied quantitative methods embedded in, and shrouded by, stupefyingly complex mathematical modelling, struggling to connect vast macroeconomic assumptions of system function with the endless microeconomic intricacies of human behaviour and in the process, too often, encouraging the transubstantiation of perfectly decent working hypotheses into unhelpfully dogmatic truths (Schumpeter, 1952; Fine, 2000).

At the heart of economics is a problematic tendency to essentialise humans and their society – *economies* conceptualised as definitively closed or definitively open systems, based on archetypes of capital and savings, population growth and technological innovation; *markets* as perfectly competitive, populated by households and firms rendered in mathematical formulations taking scant account of actual behaviour or historical context;[8] and the relentless conceptualisation of *individuals* as rational agents responsive to crudely drawn incentives, working in splendid isolation towards a utility framed in zero-sum terms of more and less (Jorgenson, 1991; Kocherlakota and Yi, 1996; Amirkhalkhali and Dar, 2019).

Economic models are a necessary and often elegant way of attempting to capture, clarify and comprehend immensely complex systems of production and consumption predicated on myriad factors conditioned by the monstrous variability of human decision-making and behaviour (Rubinstein, 2012). It is perfectly reasonable, for the purposes of efficiency, to proceed on the basis of some assumptions about rationality and predictability in the way people behave. But these models have proved poor (at least prospectively) in explaining determinants and processes of growth across the development spectrum – particularly the nebulous properties of power which shape the rules governing the accumulation of wealth, within and between countries (King, 2016).[9]

Exogenous growth theory advanced by Robert Solow and Trevor Swan in 1956 predicted that poor countries would gradually converge with the rich world – an effect we have yet, in any full sense, to see.[10] In 1961, Paul Rosenstein-Rodan generated GDP growth projections for 66 countries up to 1975. Of these, six turned out to be accurate (17 were high; 43 low). Hollis Chenery and Adam Strout predicted gross national product (GNP) growth rates for 45 countries between 1962 and 1975. They got 11 right. In the mid-1970s, based on the average growth rate of developing countries between 1960 and 1975, it was estimated that it would take the People's Republic of China 2,900 years to close the gap in absolute per capita income with the average of Organisation for Economic Co-operation and Development (OECD) countries – almost six times slower than the predicted rate for Lesotho (Morawetz, 1977). Cross-country growth studies, proliferating through the 1990s, were notable mainly for their consistent failure to achieve stable, coherent results (Kenny and Williams, 2001).[11] Few economists prior to 2008 foresaw the greatest financial crash to hit the world for eight decades (King and Kay, 2020).

In the aftermath of the crash, economics seems to have become riven between a metaphysical crisis of faith in the accepted truths of macroeconomic lore, and an almost evangelical revival of confidence in the capacity of microeconomics, through randomised control trials, to illuminate individual incentivisation as key to questions of social organisation (Meldrum, 2000; Ravallion, 2018). While it would be naïve to deny the critical importance of economics to social policy formation, it is probably just as unwise, as John Maynard Keynes observed, to invest economics with the imprimatur of science or the quasi-religious authority it seems now to enjoy in shaping political and strategic decisions which impact real lives (Carroll and Summers, 1991; Wheelan, 2010; Sedlacek, 2011).

The idea of growth as primarily economic in nature is, in any case, a much more recent phenomenon, spreading rapidly in the second half of the 20th century shaped in part by growing Cold War competition, and facilitated by the development of GDP as a new measure of national economic health (Figure 1.2) (Foley et al, 2019).[12]

GDP is probably the most familiar economic measure in public perception and the most influential acronym in modern policy making.[13] Principally a measure of production, it has become widely misapplied as a proxy for societal welfare and prosperity in a much broader sense – legitimising the idea that a growing GDP is the precondition of other social goods. This is problematic. The assertion of GDP growth as the preeminent policy goal in the present – on

Figure 1.2: Frequency of references to 'economic growth' in US, UK and Chinese language, 1900–2020

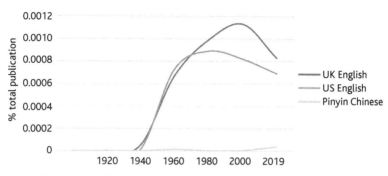

Source: Google Ngram (2021)

which future societal investment depends – displaces attention to welfare obligations in the present which are, in theory, unconditional according to widely accepted principles of rights, inclusion and justice, rendering them as if contingent on increases in national wealth which may be achieved in the interim, it might be inferred, by other less benevolent means.[14]

GDP is also a poor metric. It excludes high-value non-market activities – from crime to housework and social care – which offer distinct social value and risk but are hard to quantify and measure. It offers no insight into the distribution of wealth within a society. It omits national wealth in the form of infrastructure, land, forest, minerals and human capital, nor does it account for externalities in relation to these in the form of pollution, environmental deterioration and depletion of non-renewable natural resources, or the potential collapse in mental health consequent on the social estrangements and economic stresses of life under globalisation – resulting in a pricing of economic activities which is incrementally wildly inaccurate. GDP is perfectly good for counting items of industrial and manufacturing production but is progressively less able to encapsulate a society's productive value as maturing economies become more heavily dependent on the protean processes of knowledge and technology.[15] While it would be specious simply to dismiss GDP without considering workable alternatives, its original virtue as the least-bad metric by which to assess countries individually and rank them globally is increasingly threadbare as a defence of its continuing power over our collective social vision and the extent to which it exerts a gravitational force on policy (see, for example, Costanza et al, 2014).

A notion of economic growth, replete with academic credentials, measurement methods and mathematical models, has only really entered into our public discourse in the last 70 years, making its meteoric trajectory into the normative centre of our social and developmental values all the more striking – and worthy of careful scrutiny. In 1956, Peter Wiles wrote: 'the prime end of economic man is material plenty, he wants to have as much of everything as possible. In order that this state of affairs should be achieved, the economy must grow' (Wiles, 1956). Yet, as Aristotle notes, 'wealth is evidently not the good we are seeking ... it is merely useful for the sake of something else'.

We should ask, then, whether growth has become too powerful in the imagination of our best purposes. Is it possible that we focus on achieving growth without adequately reflecting on the objectives to which we put it (see, for example, Sen, 1999)? Notwithstanding worthy efforts to wrest a broader imagination of what we mean by society, welfare and development from the sweaty grasp of economic orthodoxy over the last 40 years, growth remains the foundational article of our common global faith, apotheosised in a kind of developmental tautology as both the means and end of social progress – perpetual and universal, rather than dynamic and contingent.

Growth and health

There is every reason to believe that, in human society, the conditions of health and wealth are closely linked. The rich today, generally speaking, live longer than the poor. Rich countries have better life expectancy than poor ones.[16] On the face of it, a rational inference is that the accumulation of wealth should be one of the most powerful strategies a society can adopt if it wants to secure for its population a better class of health and an extended span of time on earth. If this is true – and if we value a long and healthy life above all other goods – then economic growth is rightly the central concern of our societies and governments. If it is not, then we need to reassess the formidable grip growth exercises on our imagination.

Until roughly 300 years ago, life for the majority was characterised by chronic malnutrition, fragile immunity, stunted growth and early death. Life was, as Hobbes put it, 'nasty, brutish and short'. For two millennia, up to 1750, calorific intake remained low and flat, adult stature was frozen at around 160–170cm, and average life expectancy hovered between 30 and 40 years (Haldane, 2018). After 1750, starting with the Industrial Revolution in Britain, growth in wealth and incomes accelerated, adult bodyweight increased by 50 per cent, male height rose by 5–10cm, infant mortality fell by 40 per cent and lifespan doubled (Pritchett and Summers, 1993; Fogel, 1994; Eggoh et al, 2015).[17] In the early 20th century, alongside growth in real incomes, industrialised countries saw a dramatic fall in mortality, raising life expectancy by three decades. Between 1950 and 1980, developing countries experienced similar gains to the average span of life.

Over the last 50 years, a rich body of research has mapped the interaction between growth, wealth and health. There is widespread agreement that correlation exists but much less agreement as to which way it runs causally, how or why the one produces the other, and – critically – to what degree of effect (Bloom et al, 2018). This is more than an academic debate. It motivates the social policies our governments espouse and the kinds of welfare society in which we will find ourselves in years to come (Barro, 1996; Jamison et al, 1998; Wang et al, 1999; Gallup and Sachs, 2000; Arora, 2001; Mayer, 2001; Meer et al, 2003; Bloom et al, 2004; Frenk, 2004; Cutler et al, 2006). If increasing wealth is the engine of better population health, a sensible government will invest in economic growth on the reasonable basis that health will, eventually, take care of itself. If, on the other hand, health is a prerequisite for growth, that same government may be expected to invest in the health of its population – up to the point at which better health translates into greater economic productivity.

In the first case, society spends little on health. In the second, society spends only as much as will guarantee a viable workforce and mitigate additional costs on the economy. In both cases, if health is viewed primarily in its relation to growth and wealth – as an instrumental investment rather than a social goal in its own right – action on health will be narrowly conceived and limited in scope. These are, of course, characterisations. Few government policies are so starkly drawn. But the tendency to view health as subsidiary or secondary to growth is very real, with very real consequences for the way social development is conducted. When push comes to shove, as it does in political life – when the choice is between health and wealth – health too often ends up taking the bus.

In 1975, demographer and sociologist Sam Preston decided to test the relationship between life expectancy and per capita GDP across developed and developing countries. The result – the 'Preston Curve' – has become a standard point of reference in discussions of the wealth–health nexus (Figure 1.3) (Preston, 1975).

While the curve continues to provoke academic debate to this day, one interpretation – that income growth is instrumental in improving longevity – has come to dominate vernacular readings of the graph most frequently cited in policy making circuits (Bloom and Canning, 2007).[18] It is an incomplete reading – an eloquent example of the plasticity of empirical evidence, moulded through sedimentary processes of confirmation bias, subjugating the data to our entrenched faith in growth as the animating force of the human universe.

The shape of the curve is capable of two readings – on one hand, that increasing income is the manifest key to greater life expectancy; on the other, that income has little, in any necessary sense, to do with it at all. Reading horizontally, left to right, countries appear to experience very significant

Figure 1.3: The Millennium Preston Curve, 2000

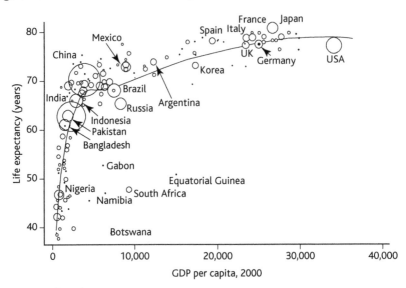

Source: Baker (2008)

gains in life expectancy for very small increments in per capita GDP, with the wealthiest countries (beyond the transition from a predominance of deaths in youth to mortality clustered in late-age) living longest (D'Acci, 2011; Dickinson, 2011; Coyle, 2017; Jorgenson, 2018; Lange et al, 2018). A vertical reading, though, suggests more or less the opposite – that countries at roughly equivalent (low) levels of GDP can experience dramatically different amounts of life expectancy (Davis, 1956). In 2000, China and Nigeria enjoyed similar per capita incomes, yet Chinese people lived on average two decades longer than their Nigerian contemporaries. At a little over USD$2,000 as the curve elbows and flattens, further gains to life expectancy irrespective of additional prosperity shrink almost to nothing.[19] At the time of the graph, Mexicans lived only a marginally shorter life than their American cousins, but at one quarter of the national income (Friedman, 2006).

Disentangling the direction of influence between wealth and health is a challenge. Increasing national income can translate into better living conditions, nutrition, healthcare and education. Improving health can translate into stronger economic performance and greater overall wealth. There is nothing inherently wrong with the idea that growing income is good for people's health. In poor countries, small increments in the stock of resources *can* make a radical difference in basic conditions of survival and living. Increasing wealth in rich countries *may* support investment in costly technological innovations as ageing populations manifest increasingly complex chronic conditions. But there is nothing automatic in these effects. Waves of globalisation from 1870 to 2015 show lengthy periods in which economic growth and human development are almost entirely uncorrelated.[20] The suggestion that increasing GDP is the *necessary* precursor to improving social welfare and development is spurious. The relation between wealth and health is mediated by public choices – benefit determined as much by political will as by monetary value (Deaton, 2013; Lange and Vollmer, 2017).[21]

The Preston Curve has been re-estimated many times since the original. The shape of the distribution remains the same over time, as the whole sample moves up and right. A dip at the 'shoulder' of the curve, appearing during the 1990s, reflects sharp deteriorations in adult life expectancy associated with the HIV/AIDS crisis in sub-Saharan Africa and crash implementation of economic reform as the Russian Federation emerged from the USSR. Both examples demonstrate the impact of systemic shocks on population health in countries where the protective effect of government and institutions of governance is chronically weak or suddenly removed.[22]

A seminal study in 1982 sought to understand why some poor countries enjoyed levels of life expectancy beyond what would, according to the income hypothesis, have been expected.[23] Results had little to do with growth and everything to do with the quality of governance people enjoy – effective bureaucracies able to innovate and adapt within often severe resource constraints; administrative systems responsive to population needs even in the context of natural disasters and economic disruption; and political commitment to a wider concept of human development and to the provision of universal basic services in infrastructure, healthcare, education and gender equality (Balabanova et al, 2013). In 1980, WHO observed: 'Perhaps nothing has arisen ... of more significance than the explicit recognition that health development is a reflection of conscious political, social, and economic policy and planning ... [that] development itself is more than the mere growth of national product' (WHO, 1980).[24]

It is estimated that in poorer countries improving basic household and community conditions by reducing indoor air pollution, encouraging safer sex, improving domestic hygiene, expanding breastfeeding and enhancing nutrition, and extending uptake of oral rehydration and vaccination – simple, low-cost effects of government action and social behaviour change – could enhance life expectancy by 14 per cent, an increase which would require an uplift in per capita income of some 3,200 per cent (Georgiadis et al, 2010).[25] Preston himself argued that access to social development and health technology was likely responsible for a significant part of the increase in lifespans, with income accounting for just 10–25 per cent (Garcia et al, 2016; Lutz and Kebede, 2018).

There is no question that growth and health are powerfully linked – but not in the crude calculus of tradable values which has characterised development strategy over the last half-century. By articulating growth and health as variables in a fixed relationship we lock ourselves into a hierarchical framework enforcing preference for one over the other in prioritisations which are either unrealistic or inefficient or both. That economic growth contributes to human welfare is not in dispute – when it is directed towards productive social uses, used efficiently, and distributed equitably across the population. But evidence shows that if growth is pursued as its own priority without attention to the equitable expansion of basic living standards, it can entrench vicious cycles of poor performance and underdevelopment (Haines and Heath, 2000; Ranis et al, 2000; Mustafa et al, 2017). As economies grow, the marginal utility of further GDP falls, meaning that simply cleaving to growth as the paramount policy imperative without periodically re-estimating its importance relative to other human and social objectives is increasingly nonsensical (Rosendo Silva et al, 2018; Cole, 2019).

Notes

[1] As well as the extensive naval expeditions mandated by the Chinese imperial court and led by Admiral Zheng He in the early 15th century.

[2] Renaissance art manifests an intense interest in rare and luxury goods – spices and dyes, woven fabrics, silks and brocades, gems, tapestries, porcelain, palatial and garden architecture, rare books and maps – a tendency recognisable in the dynamics of contemporary global wealth (Jardine, 1996).

[3] In 1516, in Cologne, Albrecht Durer was able to buy two books containing contemporaneous accounts of the existential struggle between Martin Luther and the Holy See for the price of a pair of shoes (Jardine, 1996).

[4] An accounting method essential to the 20th-century development of National Accounts and GDP.

[5] Roman law banned compound interest as the worst kind of usury; Einstein reportedly called it the most powerful force in the universe; former Bank of England Chief Andy Haldane calls it 'magic' (Haldane, 2018).

[6] The emergence of economics as a discrete field is often dated, more or less, to Adam Smith's *Wealth of Nations* in 1776, though earlier writings reflect increasingly sophisticated interest in economic concepts from Thomas Aquinas and Ibn Khaldun to William Petty and Antoine Lavoisier.

[7] Albeit with a depressingly predictable gender profile.

8   In 2013, reflecting on the greatest financial crash for 80 years, former US Federal Reserve Chairman Alan Greenspan manifested an almost touching bewilderment that the foundational credo of his professional life – that bankers would operate purely to maximise the interest of their shareholders – had not turned out to be the case (see Tett, 2013).

9   Attempts to incorporate environmental cost into long-run macroeconomic modelling – for example William Nordhaus' 2018 Nobel Prize-winning dynamic integrated climate-economy (DICE) – tend to attract praise and blame in equal measure predicated as they are on the choice of discounting rate applied to the value of future risk – a rate which epitomises assumption-driven guesswork.

10 This, of course, oversimplifies fiendishly complex calculations and underestimates the fruitfulness of learning from failed hypotheses. But failure has real consequences too. While commodity prices collapsed in the 1970s and 1980s, the World Bank continued to forecast rising prices on primary commodity markets, such that in the end projected revenue was 4–5 times actual price, leading poor primary producer countries to take on unmanageably high levels of debt (see Deaton, 2010).

11 See, for example, Morikawa (2019).

12 'It is only by outgrowing the enemy that we can keep on winning [the Cold War]' (Wiles, 1956).

13 GDP was originally proposed by economist Simon Kuznets in 1934, although with substantial reservations. It was adopted as the principal metric of national economic progress in the post-war planning meetings at Bretton Woods in 1944. 'GDP is a key metric because it is widely held to be synonymous with citizens' welfare' (Oishi and Kesebir, 2015.

14 The 'fiscal event' fronted by UK Chancellor Kwasi Kwarteng announced on 23 September 2022, following the 'bold' shift in narrative from distribution to growth under newly arrived premier Liz Truss is a good example of this problem.

15 Technology – progressively the preeminent driver of growth as economies mature – is particularly challenging to quantify and predict. Technological change is described by US economist Moses Abramovitz as 'the measure of our ignorance'.

16 People in Monaco (89.5 years) can expect to live almost 40 years longer than people in Chad (49.8 years).

17 Between 1870 and 1976, average working hours fell sharply, from 3,200 to 1,800 a year. With improved systems of sanitation, nascent systems of social protection and improving nutrition, along with new capabilities in public health and medical care, improvement in living standards accelerated beyond anything experienced in human history – each generation 50 per cent better off than the one before. Growth in household resources, at least in industrialising countries, became the norm handed down from parents to children.

18 'If policymakers want to prolong people's lives, economic growth appears to be the predominant medicine' (Jetter et al, 2019: 1387–1403).

19 Among rich countries, once you are above, say, USD$20,000 in per capita income, further GDP growth on its own buys you little additional life. Above USD$30,000 per capita the relationship between wealth and health is flat; and above USD$40,000, the relationship appears to turn negative. Income may lead to health in poor countries, but causation seems to reverse in the rich world. Indeed, as high-income countries get richer, the relationship between income and longevity may eventually evolve into an inverse-U as

older populations create what is described, perhaps rather ungenerously, as a deadweight effect on the economy (see, for example, Biciunaite, 2014).

[20] See, for example, Prados de la Escosura (2019); see also Chen (2016).

[21] There is a striking parallel between health and growth and growth and happiness. At any given moment, rich people tend to be happier than poor ones. Richer societies, living beyond the precarious insecurities of subsistence are, on average, happier than their poorer counterparts. But over time, as countries grow, happiness does not follow. At low levels of wealth even small differences in per capita GDP are associated with large changes in subjective well-being, but as countries get wealthier the slope of the relationship falls to close to zero (Czapinski, 2013). In the UK between 1973 and 2000, GDP rose 70 per cent while psychological well-being remained unmoved. In the US between 1955 and 2005, people reporting themselves 'very happy' hovered at around a third of the population, unaffected by steady increase in per capita wealth.

This may be because people adapt quickly to rising standards of living, or due to the mood-dampening effect of inequality as neighbours and colleagues appear to get richer faster. Either way, as economies grow, the value of growth itself as the source of subjective as well as objective well-being is increasingly doubtful. Some policy makers have become energised by the idea of happiness as an explicit goal of social policy. But how far do we want our governments to expend scarce resources attempting to engender in us, through bureaucratic processes, feelings which are deeply subjective, constitutionally complex, and at the best of times ephemeral. There is a distinct risk, particularly in an era of rising populism, of policy being shaped along similarly short-run, capricious or superficial lines. Health is, by contrast, one of the most robust correlates of happiness in countries the world over (Mauss et al, 2011). See also Easterlin, 1974; Inglehart, 1996; Subramanian et al, 2005; Clark et al, 2008; Veenhoven, 2008; Diener et al, 2010; Knight and Gunatilaka, 2011; Sabatini, 2014; Tapper, 2022.

[22] Life expectancy in Botswana fell from 65 in 1990 to 49 in 2000, returning to 66 in 2011; in Zimbabwe, life expectancy was 60 in 1990, 43 in 2000 and 54 in 2011. In South Africa, life expectancy fell from 63 in 1990 to 57 in 2000, partially recovering to 58 in 2011 – during a period in which GDP per capita grew seven-fold.

[23] Sponsored by UNICEF, the *Good Health at Low Cost* study reviewed factors associated with longevity in China, Cuba, Costa Rica, Sri Lanka and the Indian state of Kerala. The study was re-run in 2013, this time including Bangladesh, Kyrgyzstan, Thailand, Ethiopia and Tamil Nadu (Balabanova et al, 2013).

[24] '[D]espite massive economic growth and technological progress following World War II, the same basic complex of infectious, parasitic, and respiratory diseases, compounded by nutritional deficiencies, still accounts for most of the world's deaths. ... There is now a clear shift towards the measurement of social development and changes in well-being by non-monetary indicators and away from excessive reliance on such indicators as per capita gross national product' (WHO, 1980).

[25] In comparative modelling of 300 Indian districts, increasing female literacy from 22 per cent to 75 per cent reduced under-five mortality from 156 to 110 per 1,000 live births, while a 50 per cent reduction in poverty incidence reduced child deaths from 156 to 153 (Murthi et al, 1995, cited in Sen, 1999).

Health, development, capital and trade

By the end of the 1980s, confidence in economic growth as the engine of development – a mechanical process through which developing countries would gradually approximate their rich world counterparts[1] – was in crisis (Singer, 1989; Ghislandi et al, 2019). Developing economies, laden with unmanageable levels of debt, were struggling under an aggressive regime of fiscal retrenchment. GDP growth had stalled. Food production in Africa was in decline and social development in the least developed countries had come to a standstill (Nandi and Shahidullah, 1998; Easterly, 2001).

In 1990, the UN adopted a new framework of metrics, the Human Development Index (HDI), fusing measures of health and education with per capita GDP to create a more nuanced way of estimating country progress (UNDP, 1990). A decade later, 189 countries signed the Millennium Declaration and launched the Millennium Development Goals (MDG), aiming to rid the world of extreme poverty, hunger, ill health, illiteracy and gender inequality, to strengthen environmental protection and build a union of nations.[2] The Declaration proclaimed with customary UN grandiloquence an era of 'freedom … equality … solidarity … and tolerance', expanding the development narrative beyond economic growth (Vandemoortele, 2011).[3] On paper, it was transformational. In practice, it was a rather thinner broth.

Goals are excellent as a means of galvanising large groups of people with heterodox views and interests – for example governments – to concentrate on areas of common interest (or at least common enterprise in gaming the data) (Sachs, 2012). They are, in the parlance of management consultancy, SMART.[4] But they are not a particularly effective way of stimulating lasting locally led change in deep-rooted historical, political and institutional arrangements shaping quality of life in the world's multiplicity of countries and cultures.

The MDGs were in many ways a stunning humanitarian accomplishment. Global health improved dramatically. Between 1990 and 2015, maternal mortality fell by over 40 per cent; under-five mortality by 53 per cent. High and rising trends of HIV, tuberculosis and malaria infection were successfully confronted and forced into some degree of retreat – global malaria mortality fell by 58 per cent, new HIV infections by 40 per cent between 2000 and

2013. But if they represent a triumph of collective (albeit Westernised) action, they embody too a failure of concept – indentured to an unreconstructed economic vision of progress.

At the heart of the goals was the problem of poverty (MDG1) – poverty construed in terms of income, reduction in income poverty as the key to progress, with technical fixes in health and education as complementary strategies supporting the accumulation of humans rendered as capital for the purposes of increasing productive capability in countries where other forms of capital were thin on the ground (Baldacci et al, 2004; Sachs, 2005; UN Millennium Project, 2005; Chang and Ying, 2006; Ogundari and Awokuse, 2018).[5]

The MDG approach to health can be viewed, similarly, as the commodification of survival rather than the creation of deeper capabilities in human flourishing – framed in disembodied units of morbidity and mortality and effected through changes which were, without question, remarkable in scale but disappointing in depth, superimposed through the technical circumvention of disease and death rather than a profounder transformation in the societal arrangements which create health and shape life chances in the first place (van Bergeijk and van der Hoeve, 2019). Progress was secured through narrowly defined technical interventions delivered within standardised templates heavily conditioned by the top-down influence of specialised global agencies and donors (Kabeer, 2015; WHO, 2015).[6]

Advances in selected health indicators relied on a massive escalation of external financial support. International aid for health rose fivefold between 2000 and 2015, but the pattern of spending – the money for vertical disease control programmes towering over comparatively negligible investment in the building blocks of sustainable health systems such as trained personnel, basic infrastructure and administrative capacity (Figure 2.1) – looks more like an attempt to purchase outcomes than genuine commitment to sponsoring processes of structural change.[7] Instead of staking out new ground for health as an intrinsic article of the developmental contract, the goals instrumentalised health, cleaving to an older orthodoxy of its subsidiary role in the larger process of economic advancement. Domestic spending on health in developing countries was lower in 2014 than it was in 2000.

In the guileless lexicon of global averages, the MDGs may be construed as an historic triumph over the dehumanising forces of deprivation, disease and death. Country by country, though, performance was distinctly more erratic. While this level of heterogeneity makes the search for success factors a matter of debate, the association between economic growth and the MDGs is ambiguous at best. Progress on goals was stronger in resource-poor, low-growth African countries than in their resource-rich, high-growth neighbours. Annual GDP growth among low- and middle-income countries rose strongly in the 1990s prior to the MDG launch

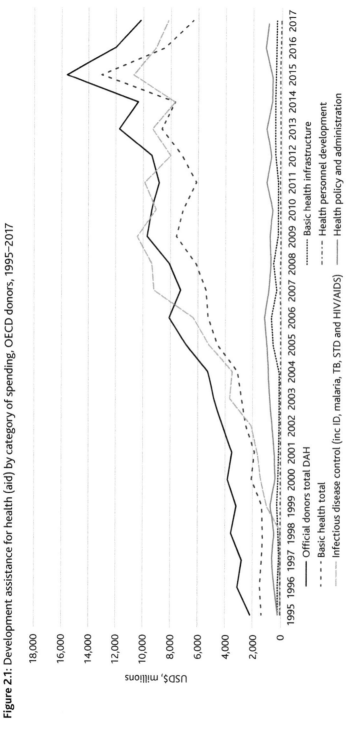

Figure 2.1: Development assistance for health (aid) by category of spending, OECD donors, 1995–2017

USD$, millions

18,000
16,000
14,000
12,000
10,000
8,000
6,000
4,000
2,000
0

1995 1996 1997 1998 1999 2000 2001 2002 2003 2004 2005 2006 2007 2008 2009 2010 2011 2012 2013 2014 2015 2016 2017

—— Official donors total DAH

– – – Basic health total

······· Infectious disease control (inc ID, malaria, TB, STD and HIV/AIDS)

········ Basic health infrastructure

–·–·– Health personnel development

—— Health policy and administration

Source: OECD Creditor Reporting System (nd)

(albeit from a lower level), but declined overall between the early 2000s and 2015 as indicators of health and education moved sharply upward.[8] In 2013, public surveys across sub-Saharan Africa found that rates of 'lived poverty' had barely changed over the course of a decade of MDG implementation – neatly articulating the awkward dissonance between statistical development and the grittier reality of lives on the ground. Average incomes across sub-Saharan Africa in 2013 were just 7.7 per cent higher than in 1974 (Arndt et al, 2016).[9]

The disconnect between MDG progress and economic growth does not imply unimportance in the dimension of growth.[10] But it does point to the intuition that growth serves human development when it is mediated through the prism of good governance. Not governance in the form of shrill denunciations of corrupt practice popularly aimed by Western voices at poor country governments, blithely overlooking our own deeply sophisticated systems of financial misdirection which are so often the necessary counterpart to this miscreance, but in the form of quietly determined political willingness and administrative ability, in countries at all levels of economic development, to tackle entrenched inequalities, translate national wealth into local welfare systems, and ensure that a reasonable share of rising GDP manifests concretely in the day-to-day lives of low-income households (Nissanke and Ndulo, 2017; Niaz Asadullah and Savoia, 2018).[11]

In their eagerness for outcomes, epitomised by the health goals, the MDGs underpowered attention to process – systemic change in the quality of governance across political systems (Fukuda-Parr, 2017).[12] Yet it is precisely that species of change – radically reorienting approaches to the domestic governance of growth, distribution and welfare, supported by radically reimagined global governance of economic and human development, the creation of public goods and the probity of financial flows – that will determine both the sustainability of the MDGs' achievements and the achievability of the Sustainable Development Goals (SDG) (Melamed et al, 2010; Asongu, 2014; World Bank, 2016).

Sustainable what?

Launched on 25 September 2015, the SDGs – now 17 in number – took over and expanded the MDG agenda, extending the timeline to 2030. The SDGs preserve a focus on poverty and hunger, education, health, gender, water and sanitation, but add energy, employment, industrialisation, growth, urbanisation, production and consumption, equality, climate action, environmental stewardship, peace and global partnership – all entailed under the imperatives of social equity and environmental sustainability.[13] It's a tall order.

The transformational credentials of the SDGs are in their universal application – this time obligating *all* countries, not just the developing ones, in a compact of collective action newly woke to the distributional requirements of global development within a tightening noose of finite planetary resources. The SDGs seek to fuse the imperatives of economic growth, human development and environmental preservation in a single coterminous enterprise, aligning the interests and needs of rich, emerging and poor developing countries.

While there is much discussion of virtuous synergy between goals and sectors and countries, the SDGs articulate with equal clarity the possibility of existential confrontation between rich and poor worlds, over objectives which are simply incommensurable: between growth to maintain rich-world lifestyles and growth to change the poor world's poverty profile; between economic expansion and environmental conservation; between ecological conservation and agroindustrial economics; between rural communities and rapid urban growth; between the technological opportunities and costs of dirty and clean energy – all orbiting the ill-defined and untested twelfth goal, 'responsible production and consumption', the privilege of economic modernity that the wealthy world seeks to protect and the poor world seeks to acquire (Obersteiner et al, 2016).[14] A heat map of challenges and priorities for sub-Saharan African and OECD countries illustrates this (Figure 2.2) (Pradhan et al, 2017; Sachs et al, 2017).

It is possible that (as in Figure 2.2 overleaf) a disconnect between poor and rich world priorities – unmet basic human development needs (dark grey, left) facing off against politically unpalatable environmental measures (dark grey, right) – will necessitate a grubbier transactional approach to the SDGs, as rich countries exchange continuing financial support for poor countries' abandoning dreams of a conventional industrialising route to development.

It sometimes seems that the semantic pivot of the global goals, from 'millennium' to 'sustainable', rather glosses over what is in reality a much profounder shift from *fin-de-siècle* self-assurance in the Western development model to a somewhat queasier recognition of our collective vulnerability, and the inevitability of a new global order of responsibility. Whether you view the SDGs as admirably optimistic or disturbingly sophomoric,[15] they articulate a future in which progress will depend on complex trade-offs within and between countries – trade-offs between economic advancement and public well-being which are hard for ministries to agree domestically, for politicians to sell publicly, and for countries to agree globally (Osborn et al, 2015).

Figure 2.2: SDGs (numbers 1–17) progress, priority and 'overspill', sub-Saharan countries (left) and OECD countries (right), 2017

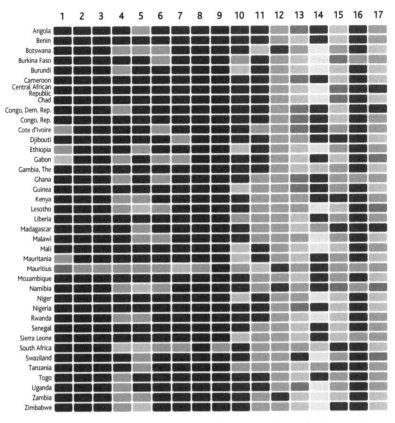

1. No poverty 2. Zero hunger 3. Good health and well-being 4 . Quality education
5. Gender equality 6. Clean water and sanitation 7. Affordable and clean energy
8. Decent work and economic growth 9. Industry, innovation and infrastructure
10. Reduced inequalities 11. Sustainable cities and communities
12. Responsible consumption and production 13. Climate action 14. Life below water
15. Life on land 16. Peace, justice and strong institutions 17. Partnerships for the goals

Source: Sachs et al (2017)

Take food. The way we produce and consume food is critical to species survival, to world hunger, to health, and to the achievement of the SDGs. The global food system, currently worth over USD$8 trillion a year, is of great consequence to international trade and the prospects for global growth, not to mention the life chances of hundreds of millions of farmers and urban labourers. Food availability is a matter of national security. Cheap food is enormously popular and hence of profound political significance. A marginal shift in relative market price can tip communities into food

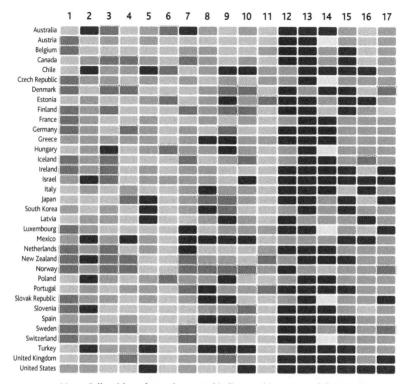

Note: Cells with perforated surround indicate achievement of the SDG target; lighter and darker grey cells indicate closer to and further from targets respectively.
Source: 2017_sdg_index_and_dashboards_report.pdf

insecurity and eventually famine; removal of staple subsidies can bring down governments, while political refusal to nanny away our attachment to delicious but, as it turns out, deadly fats and sugars is, we hear, the hallmark of democratic liberality.

Food is life. But with globalising production and consumption, it is also a powerful driver of illness and death. Rapid expansion and liberalisation of global food trade over the last 40 years has seen a dramatic increase in the consumption of highly processed foods associated with escalating incidence of food-related disease and death (Magnusson, 2019).[16] In 2019, around 70 per cent of avoidable deaths worldwide were the result of noncommunicable diseases (NCDs) – rising and potentially catastrophic epidemics of obesity, diabetes, heart and respiratory disease, cancer and mental illness (see, for example, Magnusson, 2019). Four-fifths of these deaths occurred in low- and middle-income countries – 40 per cent of them associated with nutrition

(Beaglehole and Yach, 2003; Nugent and Feigl, 2007; Venkat Narayan et al, 2010; WHO, 2011, 2013; Alleyne et al, 2013; Di Cesare et al, 2013; Walls et al, 2019).

Between 2000 and 2016, global undernutrition fell from 14.7 per cent to 11 per cent. But 'overnutrition' doubled, rising to 600 million people or 13 per cent of the world's adult population. Most low- and middle-income countries are now affected by the 'double burden of malnutrition' – parallel processes of unresolved household hunger and rising household overweight and obesity. There can be few more persuasive examples of human development having somewhere gone quite badly wrong (Popkin et al, 2020). In the early 2010s, the global cost of obesity was estimated in the region of USD$2 trillion (McKinsey, 2014).

Balancing national and international interests in food – sitting at the intersection of global goals for poverty, hunger, health, growth, climate and conservation of land and sea – entails delicate arbitration (Nilsson et al, 2016).[17] As things stand though there is no new forum through which that arbitration will be managed.[18] Instead, competing or conflicting SDG interpretations will fall under the existing architecture of global governance – an architecture which tends to default in favour of the economic over the social, of trade and growth over health (Price et al, 1999; Labonté and Sanger, 2006; Thomas and Gostin, 2013; O'Laughlin, 2016; Gopinathan et al, 2019).[19]

The confrontation of growth, trade and health

Global trade is administered through a relatively robust legal system overseen by the World Trade Organization (WTO). To become a member of the WTO countries must submit to around two dozen separate binding agreements, subjecting themselves to a dispute resolution mechanism capable of enforcing decisions through hard economic sanctions.[20] Global health, by contrast, is governed through a largely voluntary patchwork of non-binding treaties and soft law managed under the auspices of WHO (Gostin and Taylor, 2008; Gostin and Sridhar, 2014). With 7,000 staff in 150 country offices, six regional centres and a gleaming Geneva HQ, WHO is an organisational behemoth with a USD$5.7 billion budget in 2020–2021. WTO is comparatively diminutive – a staff of 450, one Swiss office and a 2018 budget of USD$203 million. WHO is technically authoritative but politically subservient to its members' endless reinterpretation of health, science and value. WTO is constituted rather more ethereally as a court – in its own language, a 'forum', a 'set of rules' – a disembodied space elevated above the political fray by the framework of legally enforceable powers entailed to it by its members in the process of joining.[21]

Trade asserts a sweeping jurisdictional authority over almost all sectors of society. Health, by contrast, struggles, with an oddly wistful combination of angrily frustrated timidity, to exert force much beyond the synthetic boundaries of its biomedical silo (Taylor, 2015; Marks-Sultan et al, 2016; Gostin et al, 2017).[22] When interests in growth and health clash – for example over the international trade in food – disputes are arbitrated by WTO (Blouin et al, 2009; Labonté et al, 2011; Kaldor, 2018; Labonté, 2020).[23] A government proposing to regulate food trade for the purposes of health can be challenged to demonstrate that there is no other intervention capable of achieving the same outcome but with less disruption to economic activity.[24]

The problem is that, while this is a perfectly viable evidentiary requirement for the purposes of the legal process on which trade depends, it is profoundly at odds with the scientific method on which health is founded (see, for example, Kaye, 1992). Demonstrating with absolute certainty a causal epidemiological link between consumption and disease is tough.[25] Attempting to prove the unequivocal public health superiority of a particular regulatory intervention in the complex chain of factors from global food production, through national nutrition policy, to local marketing practices – all mediated through the appallingly complex prisms of social and behavioural science, biological and genetic predisposition, and health outcomes therefrom – is a virtual impossibility.[26]

In order to obstruct attempts to regulate trade to protect or promote health, opposing interests need do little more than exploit the obligation of science not just to acknowledge, but to relentlessly pursue the intrinsic uncertainties and ambiguities in its own evidentiary method. Challenges to food trade regulation are now the largest category of arbitration managed by WTO. An estimated 74 per cent of challenges to food-related controls over the last 20 years were mounted by wealthier against poorer countries. Few challenges proceed to full dispute resolution. Where parties are unequally able to furnish legal expertise and absorb costs of litigation, the effect of a challenge may be to force the weaker party to move to informal resolution or to defer in favour of voluntary models of intervention, placing the burden of protective change on consumers and leaving commercial interests unmolested. When the Thai government proposed a traffic-light system to label snack foods, high-income countries challenged on the grounds that it was unnecessarily restrictive. No formal arbitration was made, but the Thai government abandoned the policy (Toebes, 2015; Thow et al, 2018; Friel and Jamieson, 2019).[27]

Countries are, of course, entitled to defend themselves and their people's health through the domestic use of tariffs and taxes to control imports and moderate demand. But liberal (or neoliberal) trade norms discourage such regulatory controls (Kniess, 2018). The formal system is, in any case, dwarfed by endlessly opaque and fluid networks of informal influence, often between profoundly unequally empowered countries. Comparing the authority of official global treaty law with the vast hinterland of unofficial manipulation and inducement populating the margins of every diplomatic conference and international summit is a bit like using electric telegraphy to police Facebook. Moreover the global system, however imperfect, is itself weakening, undercut by a welter of bilateral and regional trade agreements and the more recent recurring rash of protectionist theatricals. In the absence of a global point of reference, norms and rules governing trade could become more fragmented and competitive in the economic space, and less likely to prioritise compromise in the space for health (Mitchell and Voon, 2011).[28]

Health is a human right; but trade is a fundamental freedom – the inviolable liberty of individuals and nations to engage with one another in economic transaction. Which trumps which is increasingly moot. But in the rough-and-tumble of realpolitik, trade has a tendency to win (Ruckert et al, 2022).[29] Disregarding for a moment the perennial problems of black and grey markets, freedom to trade is largely deliverable within a society's existing legal and administrative systems. The right to health, by contrast, is only ever partially within our gift – balanced awkwardly at the confluence of research and policy, medical skill and the vicissitudes of a powerful and capricious Nature. The right to health is a promise based on a wish; the freedom to trade is a matter of actionable law.

Trade is widely prized as the engine of global growth – its benefits immediate, tangible and appetising to politicians and their policy teams. Health is still, too often, viewed as a cost on economies, as a non-productive sector, a luxury good – a black hole consuming endless amounts of capital whilst generating returns which are of limited value to policy, popular or electoral purposes, hard to differentiate economically, diffused across whole populations, and dissolving in a longer-run future than is sufficiently meaningful to the conventional political life-cycle (Saltman et al, 2007; Frenk, 2010; Mackintosh and Tibandebage, 2016).[30]

As a commitment to collective enterprise the SDGs constitute a positive advance in human development. But as a set of concrete global aims they have the potential to become the world's largest scoreboard for political pusillanimity and statistical subterfuge (see, for example, Alston, 2020). The voluntary nature of the goals and the extent to which states may cherry-pick targets strongly suggest that progress will be partial at best.

The goals will do us a profound disservice if we allow them to stand as the idealisation of our best intentions, determinedly disregarding our actual behaviours – as individuals, communities and countries; to paint a picture of integration and synergy without properly delineating the inevitable sacrifice they necessarily entail. Perhaps we should approach the SDGs not as a roadmap to be marked out by public disappointment and political dissembling en route to unachievable utopia, but as a conceptual framework, a heuristic device, through which we can shape a more robust, transparent and evidence-based debate within and between countries about the true scale of compromise needed to make better, fairer and more survivable progress – what we wish to achieve and what we are willing to forego to get there.[31]

The value of economic growth is not in doubt. What is in doubt, is the notion that growth alone – unrestrained, poorly governed – is the solution. What health shows is that the broad social benefit of growth – its real value – lies in the way it is used, the quality of the systems of governance by which, within and between countries, we determine through fair process the best uses of our common wealth. The question of governance has never been more critical. The nature of the world to come – the susceptibility of our bodies to ageing and complex chronic disease and the inability of the environment to tolerate much more wastefulness – is already forcing upon us the realisation that things cannot go on as they are, that we now have monumental decisions to make about a change of course, both in our model of health and our idea of growth.

Notes

[1] Typified by Walt Rostow's 'five stages of economic take-off' (Rostow, 1959).

[2] MDG1: reducing poverty and hunger; MDG2: increasing primary education; MDG3: strengthening gender equality and empowerment of women; MDG4: reducing child mortality; MDG5: reducing maternal health; MDG6: halting and reversing HIV/AIDS, malaria, and other diseases; MDG7: improving environmental sustainability; and MDG8: reaffirming the global partnership for development.

[3] www.un.org/en/ga/search/view_doc.asp?symbol=A/RES/55/2

[4] 'Specific, Measurable, Achievable, Realistic, Timebound' – a triumph of the acronymer's art, forcing messy reality, like sausage meat, into fat shiny units of delusionally self-confident development managerialism.

[5] In 1993, the World Bank's annual World Development Report, *Investing in Health*, dramatically annexed policy terrain hitherto occupied by WHO with its concept of health as intrinsic to human rights and development. The World Development Report '93 urged investment in health as a contribution to stronger growth. Some argued at the time that this economic framing justified a 'costly retreat from rights-based approaches to health and education', among them Professor Agnes Binagwaho, former Rwandan

Minister of Health (in Jamison et al, 2013). In 2018, the World Bank launched a new global development metric – the 'Human Capital Index'. Differentiated from human development, it was designed to measure states' commitment to health and education as inputs to productive labour and GDP growth, and to serve as a guide for global capital investment (see Stein, 2018; Botev et al, 2021; see also Elson, 2005).

[6] Over eight years, between 1994 and 2002, six global agencies were established, focusing on vertical programmes in HIV/AIDS, tuberculosis, malaria, vaccines and immunisation, and nutrition: UNAIDS (founded in 1994); Roll Back Malaria (1998); Stop TB (2000); the Global Alliance for Vaccines and Immunisation (GAVI, 2000); the Global Fund for AIDS TB & Malaria (GFATM, 2002); and the Global Alliance for Improved Nutrition (GAIN, 2002). Between 2000 and 2010, the proportion of aid allocated to HIV/AIDS, tuberculosis and malaria rose to 60 per cent of all global health aid.

[7] During the 2014–2015 Ebola outbreak in West Africa, we heard repeatedly that the epidemic had collapsed health systems in Guinea, Sierra Leone and Liberia. But the reverse is true. Ebola perfused the region through gaping institutional holes where a functioning, socially embedded system of health and care should have been. In 2015, in Sierra Leone, between 15 per cent and 25 per cent of children presenting at government hospitals across the country died. In 2020, regional and district hospitals still lacked reliable access to electrical energy and clean water. Supplies of basic medicines from paracetamol to ampicillin were intermittent. Roughly half of the nurses working in these facilities were not receiving a salary [personal observation, Sierra Leone, 2016–2022] (see, for example, WHO/UNICEF, 2022).

[8] World Bank. GDP growth (annual per cent) – Low- and middle income countries (https://data.worldbank.org/country/XO); an MDG evaluation in 2009 was unable to detect correlation between reductions in household poverty and improvement in the goals for health and education (see Bourguignon et al, 2010).

[9] See, for example, McArthur and Rasmussen (2018).

[10] Average GDP growth across developing regions was stronger in the 2000s than it had been in the doldrum years of the 1980s and early 1990s. The problem was not growth, but the conversion of growth into equitable welfare. Ethiopia enjoyed GDP growth rates around 10 per cent per annum in the first decade of the 21st century, but achieved a per capita income of just USD$567 in 2014, remaining firmly in the bottom tier of the Human Development Index, 173rd out of 185 in the same year.

[11] The term 'governance' has been rather degraded in recent decades – coopted during the ill-fated 1980s by, among others, the World Bank to delimit the developmental role of government, opening up space for markets. Governance remains, notwithstanding, an important concept in development, growth and health (see, for example, Lange and Vollmer, 2017).

[12] Between 2005 and 2018, the quality of governance among poor African countries, as measured by the World Bank's Country Policy and Institutional Assessment (CPIA) index, averaged 3.2 (out of 6) – remaining low and stagnant throughout the period with a marginal decline to 3.1 between 2015 and 2018. Between 1996 and 2018, the quality of 'government effectiveness' in 51 low and lower-middle income countries in Africa and Asia declined from -0.76 to -0.9 (World Bank, World Development Indicators, 2019).

[13] The MDGs assessed progress at aggregate country level with lesser attention to the distribution of benefit within populations. The SDGs include explicit objectives to improve

equity though whether distributional outcomes will rely on a rights- or market-based model remains to be seen (see, for example, Frey, 2017). Only two of the seven targets on inequality (SDG10) are given concrete indicators.

[14] 'Regrettably, Goal 12 is particularly vague and thus difficult to operationalise' (Loewe and Rippin, 2015). In 1992, in the run-up to the Earth Summit in Rio de Janeiro, President Bush declared: "The American way of life is not up for negotiation. Period." Much has changed since then, but how much countries' commitments to environmental sustainability now outweigh domestic interest in maximising growth remains to be seen in the post-COVID era. Quantitative analysis suggests that it will be physically impossible to achieve both the SDG targets for economic growth and the goals for CO_2 emission and resource consumption. Something's got to give (see Schiermeier, 2019; Spaiser et al, 2019).

[15] The SDGs have been described as 'fairy tales, dressed in the bureaucratese of intergovernmental narcissism, adorned with the robes of multilateral paralysis, and poisoned by the acid of nation-state failure' (see Horton, 2015).

[16] FAO, IFAD, UNICEF, WFP and WHO, 2018. Establishing causal relations between global and regional trade agreements and health outcomes is challenging. However, there is relatively robust evidence that implementation of trade agreements and associated policies is correlated with higher cardiovascular disease incidence and higher Body Mass Index (BMI) (see, for example, Barlow et al, 2017). The economic cost of unhealthy work forces and escalating healthcare is projected to hit USD\$47 trillion by 2030.

[17] See, for example, WHO's *Global action plan for the prevention and control of noncommunicable diseases 2013–2020*.

[18] See, for example, the removal of explicit references to 'diet' in the weakened second draft of the COP27 agreement text (Draft Decisions 1/CP.27 and 1/CMA.4).

[19] The popular idea that emphasis on economic value reflects consciously inhumane policy making is neither easily verifiable nor particularly helpful. There are likely as many proponents of the benefits of trade in WHO as there are defenders of health in WTO. Lions don't eat antelope because they demean the species or find them especially tasty. They eat them because it is in their nature to do so.

[20] For example, Samoa had to rescind a ban on the appealingly named 'fatty turkey tail' as condition of entry into WTO; 84 per cent of Samoan adults are overweight or obese.

[21] A similar state of affairs applies in the comparatively weak statutory powers of the Centers for Disease Control (CDC), vis-à-vis other federal agencies more closely associated with trade, in the US (see, for example, Hearne, 2022).

[22] The International Health Regulations (IHR), arguably WHO's most powerful regulatory instrument, are primarily designed to act on infectious diseases capable of causing mass epidemic and pandemic outbreaks thus compromising the viability of international trade. Notifiable IHR diseases are: smallpox, polio, human influenza, SARS, cholera, pneumonic plague, yellow fever, Ebola, Lassa, Marburg, West Nile fever, dengue fever, Rift Valley fever and meningococcal disease. Public health emergencies of international concern (PHEIC) have been invoked under the IHR seven times: for H1N1, polio, Ebola (twice), Zika, COVID-19 and monkeypox. But they make no explicit mention of HIV/AIDS, TB or malaria, or noncommunicable disease (see, for example, Taylor, 2018).

[23] Mainly through the Committee on Technical Barriers to Trade. WHO has no comparable adjudicative power.

[24] Agreement on Technical Barriers to Trade (TBT) Art. 2.ii, www.wto.org/english/doc s_e/legal_e/17-tbt_e.htm (see also, for example, WTO/WHO, 2002).

[25] Thousands of peer-reviewed journal papers mapping the association between tobacco and cancer were produced after 1950 before action was taken to limit the global trade in cigarettes.

[26] Particularly so where the precautionary principle is subordinated to existing international agreements as it is in WTO Sanitary and Phytosanitary (SPS) regulations.

[27] See, for example, Labonté et al (2019).

[28] Margaret Chan, former WHO Director-General: 'International trade has many consequences for health, both positive and negative. One particularly disturbing trend is the use of foreign investment agreements to handcuff governments and restrict their policy space. ... In my view, something is fundamentally wrong in this world when a corporation can challenge government policies introduced to protect the public from a product that kills' (speech at World Health Assembly, 2014). Tobacco is a unique commodity – the only legal product that kills up to half of its users. Disease associated with tobacco causes around six million deaths a year, killing more people than HIV/AIDS, malaria and tuberculosis combined. On current trend, 100 million tobacco-related deaths in the 20th century will rise to 1 billion in the 21st. In Africa, the number of adult smokers is expected to increase from 77 million in 2013 to 572 million in 2100 (Kniess, 2018).

[29] Notwithstanding much warm rhetoric about the intrinsic value of health, the WTO, International Monetary Fund (IMF) and World Bank, G7, G20 and Brazil, Russia, India, China and South Africa (BRICS) share an institutional commitment to the idea of health as primarily a consequence of growth and growth therefore as the policy priority (see, for example, Labonté and Sanger, 2006; Gopinathan et al, 2019; McBride et al, 2019).

[30] 'We pledge to do more to help you to make the case for fiscal policies, and to demonstrate that health expenditure is an investment, not a cost' (World Heart Federation, UN High Level Meeting on Universal Health Coverage, 23 September 2019). See also, for example, Stein and Sridhar (2019) and Chang and Ying (2006).

[31] The conduct of human development, according to Amartya Sen, rests on our ability – globally, national, locally – to engage in open, inclusive debate about priorities and preferences to arrive at more genuine consensus. The credibility of the development debate depends not just on the transparency of the forum, but also on a common language of values and standard of evidence reconciling scientific and legal concepts of proof. But having the right voices in the debate, the right people in the room, is a basic requirement. Between 1997 and 2016, the TBT heard 82 challenges to regulatory controls on food trade for nutritional health. Technical representation on behalf of health, whether as a matter of science or of rights, was conspicuously absent (see, for example, Barlow et al, 2019).

3

'They go on because they have begun'

The decades after the Second World War – the liminal space between violent transnational chaos and the establishment of new global order – were rich in opportunities to shape future society (Middleton, 2000; Skidelsky, 2009). Between national processes of reconstruction and the international reconfiguration of rule-bearing institutions, new models of growth and health emerged, powered on one hand by industrialising production and mass consumption, and on the other by national health systems operationalised through proliferating systems of epidemiological surveillance, fuelled by a miraculous expansion in curative capabilities and a newly minted biomedical vision of the individual and the body.[1]

Conceptually conjoined, these models settled into a deep popular sedimentary conviction, and commensurate political promise, that increase was the natural human condition, whether measured in dollars or life-years – an endless vista of life and wealth mediated by mass commercialisation and underpinned by technological innovation (Blasco-Fontecilla, 2014).[2] That conviction has come under increasing strain in recent decades, both in the increasingly evident limitations of the biomedical model for public health and the increasingly urgent environmental limits to our appetite for growth.

The limits to growth

The trajectory of health system development in almost all low- and middle-income countries in the post-war period broadly followed the contours of the developed world's biomedical model – allocating the lion's share of resources to managing individual and disease, with often little more than residual attention to the social and economic factors which generate illness as societies develop and grow (Miranda et al, 2008; Samb et al, 2010; Yusuf et al, 2015; Asante et al, 2016; Gmeinder et al, 2017; Xu et al, 2018; Wendimagegn and Bezuidenhout, 2019).[3] There is no question that curative care is a powerful expression of social progress and a vital dimension of human health. But it is inefficient and costly. Economic growth and technological development have equipped the biomedical model with increasingly sophisticated – and expensive – technological and pharmaceutical capabilities ill-adapted to preventively dealing with escalating global epidemics of chronic disease creeping quietly through the arteries of modernising societies.

Health systems in high-income countries – super-specialising, hyper-individualised – are already reaching the fiscal limits of politically palatable public fundability; beyond which limits lie the inevitability of rationing and the riskier option of discharging a growing proportion of health services into the private sector (Ferguson, 1999). Global health spending doubled between 2000 and 2013 to USD\$7.35 trillion, most growth driven by technology costs and rising demand (see, for example, WHO, 2017). In 2021–2022, OECD countries spent an average of around 9.5 per cent of GDP on healthcare – the US spending a heftily inefficient 17 per cent (OECD, nd). In 2020–2021 alone, US expenditure on prescription medicines was USD\$348 billion – the upper end of total estimated annual costs of achieving universal health coverage across all countries by 2030 (see NHE, nd). Any even remotely genuine attempt at universal healthcare incorporating access both to basic public health and more advanced NCD treatments would drive many low- and middle-income countries into a form of health bankruptcy within months (Jakovljevic and Getzen, 2016; Papanicolas et al, 2018).

Developing countries struggle to afford a 'basic package of health services' set out in the Lancet Commission on Investing in Health in 2013. In 2016 half of all lower-middle income countries could not afford this package; in the poorest countries, none could. Without a fundamental change in the direction of global health and care, the consequence will be new axes of inequity, between individuals within countries and between countries internationally, as rich-world capacity to manage chronic diseases pulls further away from the pack, and as private providers – already the major source of healthcare in most developing countries – step into an expanding field of care left vacant by government, confining future access to state-of-the-art medicine to those with the ability to pay.[4]

The problem of a biomedical model promising endless future health improvement mirrors the problem of endless political assurances about advancing material wealth. The environmental limits to economic growth have been known for decades.[5] Change is now inevitable – the only uncertainty being how long we propose to continue the game of chicken between our economic aspirations and the world's ability to accommodate them (Meadows et al, 1972; Nordhaus and Tobin, 1972; Hirsch, 1976; Ekins, 1993; Meadows et al, 2005; Eisenmenger et al, 2020).[6] Arguments in favour of technological, ecomodernist and 'green growth' solutions are appealing but would be more credible if underpinned by detail regarding how they will work in practice and, crucially, how their benefits will be made equitably available around the world.[7] Between 1990 and 2017, the annual global 'material footprint' accelerated from 43 to 92 billion metric tons; it is projected to grow to 190 billion metric tons by 2060, outpacing both population growth and economic output. The material footprint of high-income countries is 13 times that of low-income ones (UN, 2019; see also Parrique et al, 2019).

At a global level, the immense disparity in economic development between high-income and other countries suggests that a meaningful correction towards equitable sustainability must require significant growth restraint on the part of the rich world accompanied by larger, more stable resource transfers to countries struggling with basic human development (Figure 3.1). In this context, rhetoric about 'shared prosperity' and 'levelling up' looks either bewilderingly cynical or unfathomably stupid.

A global development trajectory which is genuinely sustainable depends on the deliberate choice of more modest growth aspirations in high-income settings combined with better systems of domestic revenue in the low- and middle-income worlds – systems which require much improvement in national and local governance, but also in a global system too often dominated by rich-country interests: from better access to global markets; independent legal and technical support for engagement in rule-setting forums; strengthening remuneration lower down global value chains; sharpening rules on transnational business formation, tax and investment; and enhancing technical support for producer countries to negotiate commercial contracts in particular in natural resource extraction.

Visceral resistance to lowering growth is palpable across all country groups of economic development, if perhaps most stridently among the rich (IMF, 2019; OECD, 2019). But it is based on lopsided judgement. For a start, the rate of GDP increase in OECD countries has been steadily declining over the last 60 years, quietly undermining the urgency of the growth discourse (Figure 3.2).[8]

Analysis suggests that slowing growth in the rich world is achievable without losses to human development (Barroso et al, 2016). The challenge of a low-growth future may be less a matter of material deprivation, and more to do with the political difficulties of rebalancing deep-rooted socioeconomic norms of property and ownership, consumption and choice (Malmaeusa and Alfredsson, 2017).[9] Public attitudes to slowing growth may be more flexible than policy makers assume. When life-and-death variables are added to growth models, the marginal value of further consumption falls more or less to zero (Jones, 2016).

Lower-growth economies, appropriately structured, could see significant improvement in physical and psychosocial health with reduced pollution improving air and water quality, localising production chains improving diet, modified regimes of labour and employment lowering levels of stress-related physical and mental illness, and decelerating ecological encroachment

Figure 3.1: Per capita gross domestic product, low-, lower-middle-, middle- and high-income countries, 1960–2021

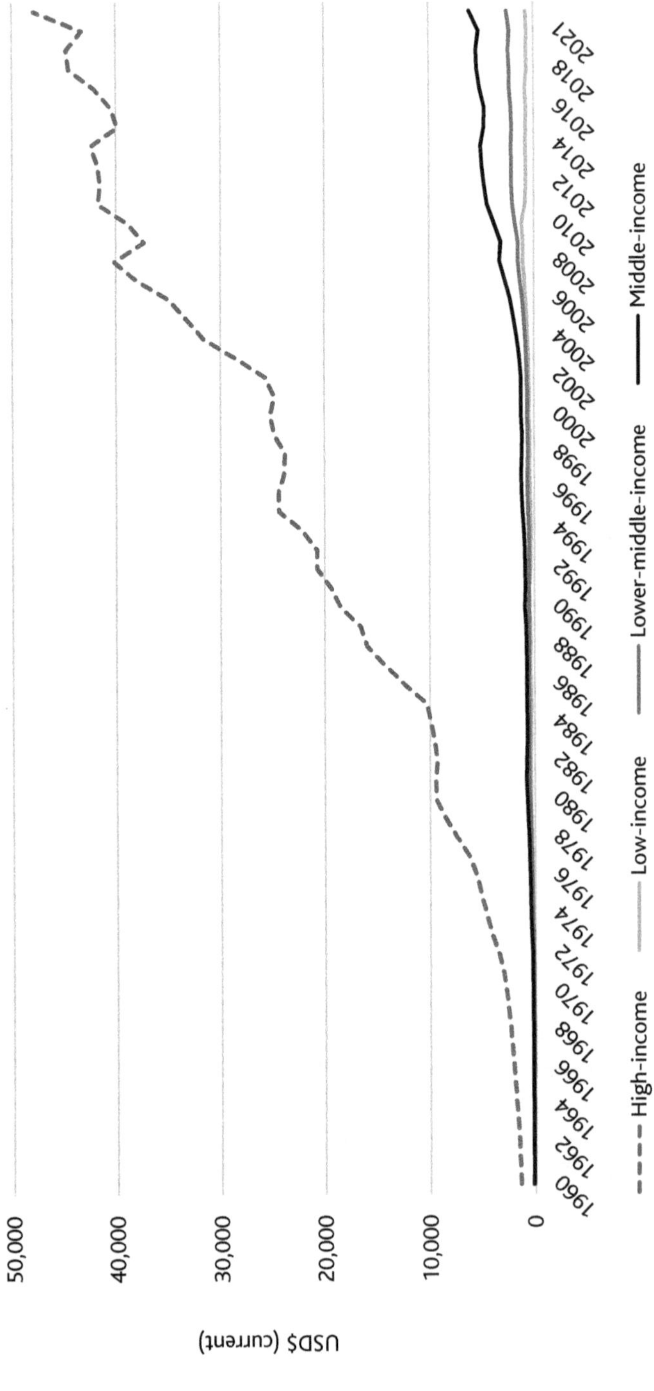

Source: World Bank data GDP per capita (current US$) data (worldbank.org)

Figure 3.2: Per capita GDP, % growth rate, OECD countries, 1961–2021

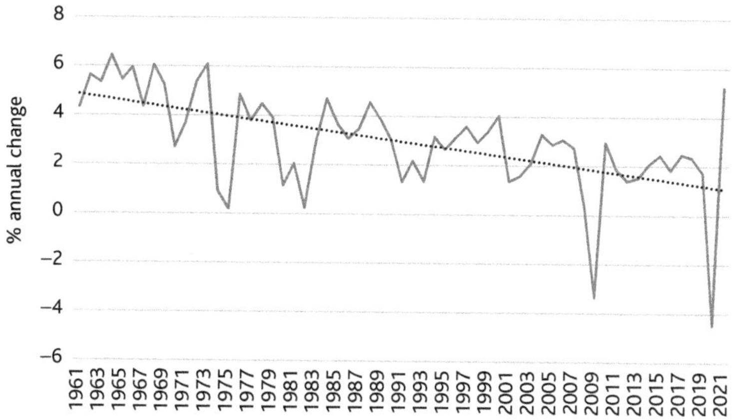

Source: World Bank

mitigating exposure to new zoonotic pathogens. Slower rich-world growth – shifting the emphasis from quantitative expansion to more efficient and equitable resource use and distribution within and between countries – may be more feasible than we are led to believe (Daly, 2008; Borowy and Schmelzer, 2017; Jackson, 2019).[10]

Japan's three-decade stagnation has had remarkably little adverse impact on population health and health inequality.[11] Between 1980 and 2016, age-adjusted all-cause mortality in Japan was the lowest among a group of high-income countries, continuing a steady downward trend after the onset of growth stagnation in 1992, and appearing to avoid the mortality reversal – the 'deaths of despair' – witnessed in the US and UK during the decade of austerity and opioids after the 2008 global crash. What appeared at first to be sustained economic misfortune may in fact turn out to be a rather more positive illustration of what can happen in a country when it reaches the limits of its ability to enrich and consume (see, for example, Chiavacci and Hommerich, 2017; Tanaka et al, 2017; Curry et al, 2018; Krugman, 2020).

Conclusion

The answer to the intersecting crises of healthcare and growth is surely not to repudiate the miracles of biomedicine. Nor is it, though, as many governments appear to prefer, to continue embroidering a biomedical business-as-usual model with hopelessly subaltern health prevention, promotion or social determinants sub-strategies and initiatives, shackled to an unreconstructed and increasingly pathogenic economic orthodoxy. The response must be to exploit the coming reconfiguration of our growth paradigm to forge a new model in which better health and better growth coalesce in a single strategic proposition – a model which could be adopted commonly across countries, adapted for level of development and resource availability, as a set of standards by which to shape progressive economic health.

A model which channels social investment towards low-cost, high-impact policies and interventions which incentivise healthier lifestyles but, recognising that lifestyle is shaped by material circumstances, expedite behaviour change among individuals through systematic reduction in underlying socioeconomic inequality between groups;[12] which concentrates public policy attention and allocates resources more efficiently around key life-course transitions – from non-negotiable protection for sexual and reproductive rights to meaningful parental and family support; from high-quality antenatal care, maternal welfare, breastfeeding and universal vaccination to harnessing the network of opportunities for early child development; from securing educational progression, particularly for girls, to active mental health, through schools and workplaces, intensively addressing the plasticity, promise and perils of adolescence; from a more informed dialogue on public health, risk screening and preventive interventions, capitalising on the public good possibilities of telemedicine and big data, to a somewhat less irrational approach to the personal value and public potential of older age (Luyten et al, 2015; Wang et al, 2016; Allen et al, 2017a; Arredondo et al, 2018; Marmot and Bell, 2019; Hensher et al, 2020).

A model which enforces basic labour rights, building labour productivity not just through the sometimes brutalist effect of technological and managerial reorganisation, but through serious commitment to constructive long-range engagement between workers and their firms; which designs social protection systems to foster inclusion rather than simply perpetuating a kind of tolerated marginality among those deemed as manageably poor; which invests in the physical and technological infrastructures of community cohesion, decentralising resource use and accountability to the local level and defending rather than coopting the scrutiny of an independent civil society; which applies rigorous precautionary science to the regulation of market activity whether for health or environmental protection, incentivising long-term, 'patient' capital, financing more modest but stable profit over 'hot' capital's rapacious hunger for the rapid return.

A model which, returning to Professor Veblen, engages with growth as an evolutionary rather than a static property, as a tool rather than a faith – whose utility changes over time as the centre of our economic gravity transitions from the obsessive conceptualisation of wealth as individual value to a more coherent vision of wealth as common good.

Post-COVID growth – new wine or old bottles?

The immediate impact of COVID-19 on the global economy was little short of cataclysmic. Economic output contracted by 4.3 per cent in 2020 – around USD\$3.6 trillion of goods and services lost. Global trade shrank by 20 per cent. The pandemic systematically disrupted all of the daily human, social and logistic processes of production, manufacturing, commerce and consumption. Advanced economies leveraged hitherto unthinkable amounts of liquidity, placing whole economic sectors in an induced coma to insulate them from harm. Low-income countries were exposed to heavy recessionary effects of lockdown and the inflationary consequences of rich-country stimulus. Eighteen months into the pandemic, rich and poor worlds faced very different post-COVID prospects for recovery (Figure 3.3). How much that dampens incentives to invest in a new growth paradigm remains to be seen – wealthier countries seeking to regain continuity in the economic functions they spent so much to preserve; poorer ones disinclined or unable to afford the uncertainties of a new economic pathway (Gostin, 2021; Kwame Morgan et al, 2021).[13]

Faced with scarring in the global supply chain and entrenched inflationary pressures, governments in rich, emerging and poor countries alike will be tempted to rebuild their balance sheets on risk-averse reversion to popular and conventional pre-pandemic modes of growth – of fossil-fuelled energy and maximising GDP.[14] In mid-2021, recovery strategies were already bending towards the old magical thinking – that marginally moderating CO_2 production and pollution can justify a continuation of the conventional production and consumption growth model, exhausting natural resources, crippling climatic and planetary systems, and defraying risk on an incurious acceptance of technological advance as the future gamble absolving political decision-makers from unpopular action in the present.[15]

At the same time, governments and corporate counterparts pump up the 'net-zero' narrative, whose cosmetic calculus reduces the need for *actual* decarbonisation in highly carbon-reliant economies by invoking 'nature-based solutions' and technological fixes as yet unproven at scale; framing the problem as 'carbon footprint', shifting environmental responsibility onto consumers and away from major economic and industrial actors (Meckling and Allan, 2020; Le Billon et al, 2021; Taherzadeh, 2021). In late 2021, the proportion of recovery investments extending finance to green options was tellingly small.[16]

Meanwhile, widening disparity and increasing fractiousness between countries and regions – exacerbated by the Ukraine conflict – undermine calls for greater global cooperation, throwing us back into a more transactional model of national interests, compromising collective action on environmental commitments, weakening cooperative communication on emerging disease and deadening, more broadly, the energy behind a

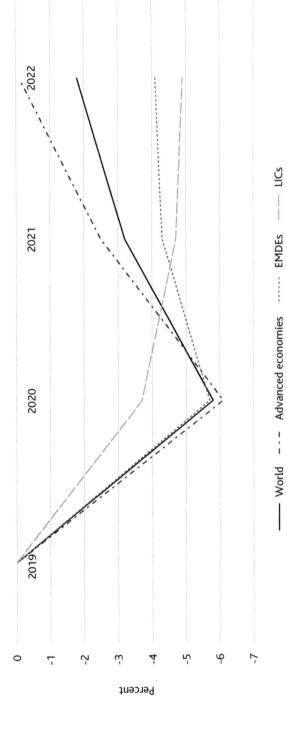

Figure 3.3: Projected deviation from pre-pandemic output, by country economic category, 2019–2022

Notes: EMDE: Emerging Market and Developing Economies; LIC: Low-income Countries.

Source: World Bank (2021)

new vision of positive global governance. Such a vision, though, is more needed than ever. If COVID showed us the horror of an abrupt end to our daily patterns of growth-fuelled consumption, it points to the need for much stronger collectively agreed control over the modes of resource exploitation through which that growth is produced (Bernstein et al, 2022).

It is estimated that a new disease emerges somewhere around the world every four months. Around three-quarters of emerging infectious diseases are zoonotic in origin, the result of pathogens jumping the increasingly permeable boundary between the animal and human worlds (McDermott and Grace, 2012; Salata et al, 2019). Change in land use – accelerating exploitation of new terrain for the purposes of human settlement, crop cultivation and commercial activity – is believed to be the leading cause of zoonosis. Humans have cleared almost half of the world's forests in the last 10,000 years – a process of deforestation accelerating rapidly in the last five or six decades – intensifying the interface between human and nature, increasing the frequency of rural–urban interaction through trade in foods and wildlife commodities, and increasing the scale and mechanisation of livestock and poultry production feeding the growing global appetite, as household wealth rises, for animal proteins (McMichael, 1993; Saker et al, 2004; Allen et al, 2017b; Wu et al, 2017; Napolitano Ferreira et al, 2021).

The problem of economic growth is that it is operationalised primarily as a matter of sovereign national strategy – while its externalities are increasingly global and its implementation remains defiantly local. Multilateral governance over resource exploitation is managed largely through weakly voluntary norms and compacts; local governance – in real communities where the animal spirits of growth and the forces of zoonosis collide – veers wildly between the negligible and the complicit, lacking genuine engagement with the people whose livelihoods are most directly affected (Loh et al, 2015; Gostin and Katz, 2016; Weiss and Wilkinson, 2018; Hargrove et al, 2019; Lee and Piper, 2020).[17] The lesson of COVID for global growth is that we need a great transformation in the architecture by which global growth is governed – to mend the long-standing disconnect between a macro-level of multilateral policy and the myriad micro-worlds of economic livelihood (Manstetten et al, 2021).

The key to transformational change is, perhaps paradoxically, the nation-state itself (Polanyi, 1944). National governments must use their uniquely mandated authority to divest themselves of power, ceding decision-making both upwards and downwards. Governments will have to accept that growth can no longer be viewed as the exclusive domain of individual national strategy, relinquishing to the global level a much greater degree of binding control over the acceptable parameters of the growth they wish to pursue (Buchholz and Sandler, 2021; Khan and Munira, 2021). And they will need to extend far more convincingly to the local level the devolved power, distributive investment and legal protection necessary for such strategies to be meaningfully interpreted, adapted and enacted. In this transformational process, the state leverages its vital status within the international system to mediate the transnational regulation of local practice and the local tolerance of global norms.

It is a vision of transformation which may seem, at the very least, wishful – not to say absurdly unlikely.[18] But the shock of COVID and the 'fat tail' threat of a future zoonotic disaster – a single pathogenic jump but this time equipped with greater capacity for mutation, transmission and lethality – gives the woolliness of the vision a sharper edge (see, for example, Taleb, 2007). Virus – capable of leaping from bat or bushmeat to human, colonising the world within months and forcing its vital economic rhythms to a wholesale grinding halt – demands a closer coherence between local reality and global response. It draws together in a single continuous piece the management imperatives of the global and local, the macro- and the microscopic. It links the index case of a new disease with every other member of the human race, each point of zoonotic origin with every other geographical point on the planet. It necessitates a grand convergence of global agreement and hyper-localised implementation, unhindered by the assertion of sovereign space, demanding an inviolable openness of borders unseen in modern history.

The virus – our experience of COVID, its convergence with climate crisis, and their collective roots in a dangerous and poorly governed model of growth – finally tests to destruction the Westphalian concept of state autonomy and the imagination of a defined domain of 'domestic' affairs, suggesting that sacrificing the freedoms of a national growth model are amply repaid by the greater freedom from global collapse.

Notes

[1] Although concepts of biomedicine date to the development of the germ theory of disease, the biomedical era really opens with the discovery of antibiotics after 1940 and the 'molecularisation' of health science, with the proliferation of experimental empiricism and the ascendance of the randomised control trial (see, for example, Quirke and Gaudilliere, 2008).

[2] See also Smil (2019).

[3] Major improvements in infectious disease control and perinatal mortality in low- and middle-income countries were largely funded through post-war aid, public–private partnerships and global philanthropy (Jamison et al, 2013). Domestic health spending across developing countries was – and is – much more heavily concentrated on facility-based curative services. Around 70 per cent goes to in-patient hospital services, with 8 per cent on prevention. Among OECD countries, 79.9 per cent of health spending goes to curative services and medical goods with 2.8 per cent to disease prevention. In the UK, an estimated 5.29 per cent of the National Health Service budget in England was spent on prevention in 2014/2015; public health spending in the US was 2.65 per cent in 2014 (see, for example, Davies et al, 2016).

[4] A state of affairs with the potential to become ugly quickly (see, for example, Frankel, 2003).

[5] Although the 'limits to growth' remains disputed by some economists and demographers who favour confidence in technological solutions, as well as policy makers fearing a public backlash against the loss of material wealth.

[6] See, for example, Pascual et al (2022) and also Victor (2010).

[7] Technological solutions can incur a 'rebound effect' resulting in increased rather than decreasing resource consumption. At the start of the 20th century, steam engines in the UK were 36 times more efficient than those of 1760, but a 2,000-fold growth in steam-power use resulted in hugely increased coal consumption (see also, for example, Robertson and Mousavian, 2022).

[8] Average per capita growth rates in Western Europe continuously decreased from around 5 per cent annually in the 1950s to around 1 per cent (or 1.6 per cent for OECD average) in the 2000s. Growth in China, the US and the European Union was projected to fall between 2015 and 2021, from 2.9 per cent to 1.6 per cent, 2.1 per cent to 1.3 per cent, and 6.9 per cent to 6 per cent, respectively. In 2021, global growth was projected to continue softening to 3.2 per cent in 2023 (World Bank, 2022a). These projections looked somewhat rosy subsequently in the face of the COVID pandemic, which saw world government and private sector debt rise by an additional USD$15 trillion to 365 per cent of global GDP, followed by significant growth-dampening effects associated with the Ukraine invasion including disruptions in global supply chains, sharp energy price hikes, inflationary and stagflationary signals, and rising interest rates.

[9] See, for example, Saito (2020).

[10] See, for example, Brunner (2020).

[11] Although suicide in specific social groups and employment sectors has increased.

[12] Poorer people in developed and developing countries are more likely to drink alcohol, use tobacco and consume insufficient fruit and vegetables. In low-income countries recommended daily consumption of fruit and vegetables represents almost 52 per cent of household income, compared with 2 per cent in rich countries. It is estimated that the poorest households in England would have to spend over 70 per cent of their income to follow national healthy eating guidelines (see, for example, Stringhini et al, 2010; Petrovic et al, 2018).

[13] Just before the onset of COVID, in 2019, almost half of poorer economies were already assessed to be in or at high risk of sovereign debt distress (IMF, 2022). Projections for post-COVID global recovery have been several times adjusted downwards as a result of the impact of the Ukraine conflict on energy, food, stability, inflation and interest rates (see, for example, World Bank, 2022b).

[14] See for example the extraordinarily underpowered 'fiscal event' announced by the UK's Liz Truss and Kwasi Kwarteng on 23 September 2022.

[15] Or, as Greta Thunberg puts it, 'blah, blah, blah' (September 2021).

[16] Around 1 per cent of the USD$11–12 trillion stimulus during the 2007–2008 financial crash was allocated the 'green economy'; following the crisis, emissions of CO_2 soared (see, for exampe, Cifuentes-Faura, 2021). According to the International Energy Agency (IEA), global emissions of CO_2 rose by 5 per cent on pre-pandemic levels in 2021,

increasing by an estimated 1.5 billion tonnes (Global carbon dioxide emissions are set for their second-biggest increase in history – News – IEA).

17 The post–war international system was hobbled from the outset by a governance structure controlled by its members, who were and remain reluctant to surrender control, to subject themselves collectively under a truly global authority characterised by legally binding, enforceable provisions. The shift, between Kyoto (1997) and Paris (2015), from binding targets to 'nationally determined contributions' is a good example of governments' dislike of committing to suprastate enforcement. At the other end of the spectrum, while it is important not to romaticise the 'local' as if inherently more virtuous, informed or wise, it is important, too, to recognise the failure of global and national systems of governance to optimise the real potential of localities by understanding and mitigating the complex local power structures which can sustain exclusion of certain groups and communities from decision-making processes.

18 An important reservation in this respect is the potential loss of legitimising national democratic decision-making. This is a reasonable concern, but enhanced localisation may actually invigorate democratic participation, while a growing volume of popular interest – acutely in solutions to climate crisis – seeks speed and uniformity of action which exceeds what conventional democratic politics appear able to supply.

PART II

Freedom

4

The nature of freedom

There can be few more celebrated principles in contemporary political life than freedom – and few more bitterly weaponised.[1] Our ability to choose and shape a preferred pathway through life is arguably the most powerful social and political value of the last 250 years.[2] According to economist Amartya Sen, freedom is foundational to human development – instrumental to the functioning of participatory politics and to the engines of economic growth, but intrinsic, too, to the essence of what the 'good society' represents. In the early 21st century, an ethics of freedom has come to underpin our most basic conception of how we should be governed, and how we envisage our everyday lives (Rose, 1999).

Yet freedom is inherently paradoxical. It is, as Hannah Arendt says, the unsquareable circle of conscience and consciousness, the collision between a causal universe and our irrepressible sense of will – humanity suspended somewhere between angel and beast (Arendt, 1961). Freedom is an endlessly contested construct, an aspiration incapable of completion but requiring constant effort and attention in balancing the societal values of the individual and the collective, the particular and the universal (Gallie, 1955). The language of freedom exercises great moral and symbolic weight yet the word is, in and of itself, curiously void – given sense only by the objects and objectives to which it is attached. Freedom from what or whom? Freedom to do what, for what purpose? Isaiah Berlin notes over 200 working definitions of the word – its forms and representations inevitably selective and ideological, capable of legitimising everything from extreme libertarianism to totalitarian control (Berlin, 1969). The history of freedom is, if nothing else, a struggle for meaning.

In the course of two and a half centuries, a proliferation of philosophical and sociological theories – of Kant, Rousseau, Hegel, Marx and Foucault, Hobbes, Locke, Hulme, Mill and Hayek, Montesquieu, Tocqueville, Berlin, Arendt and Sen – have created a densely woven, complex and contradictory field of ideas blending raw conjecture, metaphysical intuition and empirical observation about the possibilities of freedom – as MacGilvray puts it, from the legal privileges distinguishing freeman from slave in the forums of ancient Athens and Rome – suffused with moral order yet deeply inequitable – to the apotheosis of individual autonomy in the modern marketplace – supremely egalitarian but drained of connective moral content (Locke, 1689; Montesquieu, 1748; Mill, 1860; Streissler, 1969; Taylor, 1984; Allison, 1990; Prakash, 1996; Franco, 1999; Krause, 2005; Oksala, 2005; Macdonald and Hoffman, 2010; MacGilvray, 2011).[3]

In more recent decades, however, the richness of the idea of freedom has been narrowed and honed, diluted and bowdlerised, accelerating through the relentless cycle of modern political and media packaging – from human condition to economic paradigm; from complex construction of collective governance to the cruder proposition of individual entitlement; the precondition rather than medium of social engagement; debased from the rallying cry of great social movements to the shrill political punchline for every purveyor of cut-price populist snake-oil selling simplistic visions of progress in an increasingly complex world (see, for example, Korich, 2017).

Development as freedom – political versus economic

The currency of modern freedom was forged in the political crucible of Enlightenment science as new laws of physical causation weakened the foundations of divine authority and the tenure of increasingly sclerotic monarchies grown over-reliant on celestial endorsement. From the American and French revolutions through the Spring of Nations to the wave of postcolonial independence and the fall of the Berlin Wall, the modern idea of freedom took practical shape in the revolutionary emancipation of peoples and nations from the iniquity of oppressively unjust governance (Arendt, 1966–1967). In Isaiah Berlin's formulation, this 'negative freedom' placed emphasis on protecting people from the arbitrary imposition of state power.

The complementary idea of 'positive freedom' – a hazier notion of personal realisation which, progressively rationalised as common human condition, risks leading paradoxically to the subordination of the individual, ultimately, under an authoritarian collective – fared less well, tarnished by association with the 20th-century rise of fascist and totalitarian ideologies. Confronted by the horror of the concentration camp and the gulag, negative freedom came to be viewed as, if not better, then certainly the safer option – embodying deliverance from the spectre of over-reaching government, and of government as in some fundamental sense antagonistic to the notion of liberty (Berlin, 2002; Crowder, 2004; Tiedermann, 2006).

The idea of freedom as restraint of arbitrary power fed on and nurtured new discourses of citizen and human rights emerging as a natural counterpart to the overthrow of obsolete regimes.[4] Rights, construed as unconditional and legally binding, offered a pragmatic solution to the capriciousness of absolute power and the inefficient economics of traditional hierarchy. The articulation of human rights constitutes an epochal advance in socioeconomic and political justice. But rights also, in their nature, directed attention to the legal person – to the core protections of body, property and conscience, focusing on the instance of abuse and specific corrective action and – perhaps – diminishing attention to the structural, systemic drivers of wider injustice, the deeper pathologies of power.[5] Over time, the concept of freedom operationalised through an architecture of rights came to be viewed as individual in nature – rooted in the foundational moral value of human autonomy and the sovereignty of person (Howard-Hassmann, 1995; Rose, 1998; McCorquodale, 2003; Mackenzie, 2008; Villa, 2008; Rudanko, 2012).[6]

The interlocking of freedom and rights cultivated a concept of society composed of discretely interacting individuals, meshing neatly with the emerging neoclassical notion of a rationally self-interested *homo economicus* operating through open markets (Hurst, 1956; Campus, 1987; Udehn, 2001; Urbina and Ruiz-Villaverde, 2019). Through the 19th and early 20th centuries, as the market steadily replaced more traditional institutions as the principal mechanism for social organisation and the distribution of value, freedom in civil and political terms became increasingly tightly yoked to liberalism in the economic sphere. Over time, the ideas of freedom *in* the market and freedom *of* the market have fused, eventually rendering an imagination of the market as the embodiment of freedom itself.

The modern model of freedom, then, gradually draws together three core features – repudiation of government as inherently suspect; celebration of the individual as the supreme expression of society; and the reimagination of society as, primarily, individuals interacting through markets. It was a freedom which offered protection from political interference in legal economic activity, where such interference could be construed as man-made and hence unjust; but one which was much less interested in the consequences of economic function in terms of wealth and poverty, viewed as natural conditions and hence unproblematic. It was a model which offered political protection of economic freedom, but not the economic protection on which political freedom relies (Hertel and Minkler, 2007; Steiner et al, 2008).[7]

Ideas of freedom permeate the aftermath of the Second World War, forming the basis of the Atlantic Charter, giving shape to the post-war international order, the foundation of the UN and the Universal Declaration of Human Rights (UDHR).[8] Rapidly advancing industrial technologies and momentum for agrarian reform in a newly defined world of 'developed' and 'developing' nations – all jostling for position within the polarising spheres of Cold War ideology – brought capital and labour, citizen and state into complex new relations; the creation of welfare institutions in the industrialised world and new systems of development cooperation between

Figure 4.1: Communication between President Roosevelt and Prime Minister Churchill towards agreement of the Atlantic Charter, 12 August 1941

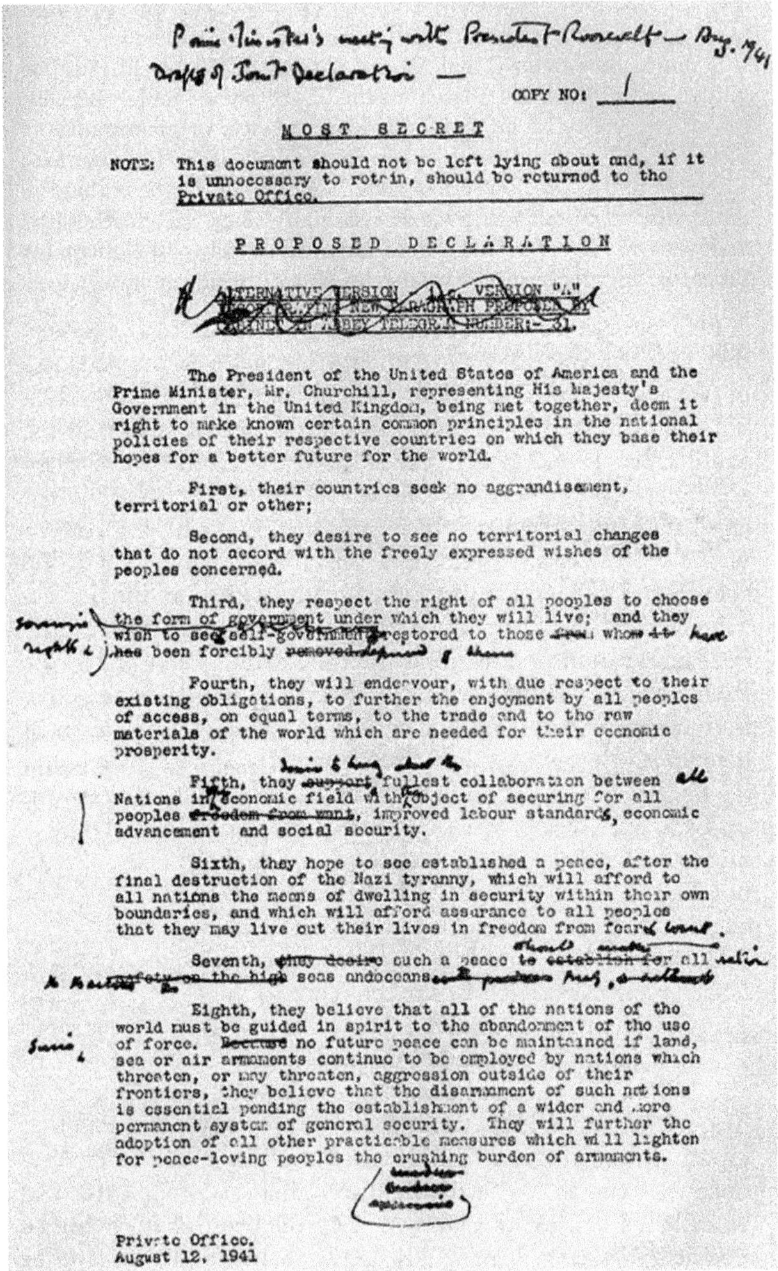

Prime Minister's meeting with President Roosevelt — Aug. 1941
Drafts of Joint Declaration —

COPY NO: 1

MOST SECRET

NOTE: This document should not be left lying about and, if it is unnecessary to retain, should be returned to the Private Office.

PROPOSED DECLARATION

ALTERNATIVE VERSION (i.e. VERSION "A") INCORPORATING NEW PARAGRAPH PROPOSED BY [illegible] TELEGRAM NUMBER:- 31.

The President of the United States of America and the Prime Minister, Mr. Churchill, representing His Majesty's Government in the United Kingdom, being met together, deem it right to make known certain common principles in the national policies of their respective countries on which they base their hopes for a better future for the world.

First, their countries seek no aggrandisement, territorial or other;

Second, they desire to see no territorial changes that do not accord with the freely expressed wishes of the peoples concerned.

Third, they respect the right of all peoples to choose the form of government under which they will live; and they wish to see self-government restored to those from whom it has been forcibly removed.

Fourth, they will endeavour, with due respect to their existing obligations, to further the enjoyment by all peoples of access, on equal terms, to the trade and to the raw materials of the world which are needed for their economic prosperity.

Fifth, they support fullest collaboration between Nations in economic field with object of securing for all peoples freedom from want, improved labour standards, economic advancement and social security.

Sixth, they hope to see established a peace, after the final destruction of the Nazi tyranny, which will afford to all nations the means of dwelling in security within their own boundaries, and which will afford assurance to all peoples that they may live out their lives in freedom from fear.

Seventh, they desire such a peace to establish for all safety on the high seas and oceans.

Eighth, they believe that all of the nations of the world must be guided in spirit to the abandonment of the use of force. Because no future peace can be maintained if land, sea or air armaments continue to be employed by nations which threaten, or may threaten, aggression outside of their frontiers, they believe that the disarmament of such nations is essential pending the establishment of a wider and more permanent system of general security. They will further the adoption of all other practicable measures which will lighten for peace-loving peoples the crushing burden of armaments.

Private Office.
August 12, 1941

Source: Pictorial Press Ltd/Alamy Stock Photo

rich and poor countries engendering new possibilities in the balance of political freedom and economic progress.

But realpolitik outpaced rhetoric and the separation of political and economic ideas of liberty remained firm (Malinowski, 1947; Gibbons, 1953; Paterson, 1973). In US–UK negotiations on the wording of the Atlantic Charter, Churchill removed 'freedom from want' in Roosevelt's draft, eliminating the alleviation of poverty as a direct objective of the new global order (Figure 4.1). Harry Truman's 1949 'Four Point Plan' speech, setting out the terms of a new 'free world', offered American technology and capital to developing countries in exchange for opposition to the oppressions of the Soviet bloc – the mitigation of poverty again constituted as the consequence of political reform rather than an aim in itself.[9]

Between 1966 and 1976, in a rare case of East–West consensus, UN member states agreed to repackage the Universal Declaration in two covenants, one devoted to 'civil and political' the other to 'economic, social and cultural' rights.[10] In effect, both sides of an increasingly bitter Cold War found themselves in tacit agreement that while human freedom based on civil and political rights was defined and enforceable, freedom predicated on a universal standard of economic, social and cultural livelihood constituted a commitment too far (Hunt, 1993; Ioana, 2014). In the new regime of universal rights, freedom from political oppression was viewed as legally actionable and economically viable. Freedom from poverty was not.[11]

Global economic and fiscal crises of the late 1970s, and the ascendance of neoliberal ideas in global economic and political policy-setting in the following decade, sharpened the emphasis on economic individualism, the repudiation of government and the premise of freedom in and through the market. By the end of the 1980s, though, a 'lost decade' of stagnating development indices, acutely among poor countries, brought about a critical reappraisal of radical liberalisation, recognising – perhaps a little late – that populations mired in the multiple unfreedoms of poverty, illiteracy and disease would struggle in practice to avail themselves of economic opportunity however freely available in principle.

After 1990, in response, the international community signed up to a series of global commitments – the MDGs and later SDGs – aimed at mitigating poverty viewed as more than simply economic, to enhance wider social functions in education, health, gender and inclusion as, in themselves, instrumental to a fuller concept of human freedom (Sen, 1987, 1999).[12] There is no doubt that the concept of 'development as freedom' helped moderate the preceding decade's fierce ideological concentration on market-led progress. But Sen's vision is an adaptation of the liberal market concept rather than a more radical reworking. There was, in the construction of the global goals, a tacit acceptance of poverty as a condition relevant only to the particular social group – the afflicted – rather than an expression of the social hierarchy as a whole, thus invoking managerial solutions visited on 'the poor' as if a separate species, rather than through profounder whole-of-society change.[13]

The idea of freedom we have inherited is at best incomplete and at worst toxic. It emphasises the individual at the expense of the collective. It offers the notional freedom of political rights without accounting for the economic circumstances people need to be meaningfully free. It diminishes the value of government as arbiter of social equity – endowing wholly imperfect market mechanisms with the awesome responsibility of determining freedom's distribution (Neumann, 1953; Friedman, 1962; Becker, 1981; Bauman, 2000; Brown and Baker, 2012; Krause, 2015). This is not to suggest that collective action is intrinsically superior to individual motivation, nor that government tends to be the best judge of social value. Neither is remotely necessarily true. Simply that an artificially narrow interpretation of freedom – in any ideological direction – is likely to produce poor outcomes.

Complexity and nuance have been stripped out of the contemporary dominant notion of freedom – lionising autonomy, fostering hyper-individualised identity and increasingly hermetic and antagonistic group affiliations. We are left with a version of freedom which is universal but cut-throat; which sets us at odds with one another in societies whose principal function is to facilitate individual preference and singular flourishing; a version which disregards – or even celebrates – inequality which, rising around the world, renders the experience of freedom increasingly exclusive and politicians' pronouncements about freedom increasingly hard to stomach.[14]

Whilst a relationship between health and freedom is intuitive – a deep sense of the interaction between liberty of mind and body and physical and mental well-being – the relationship is by no means automatic or unilinear. Health is generally understood to be a special good, underpinning the fulfilment of more or less all notions of what human freedom entails (Sen, 2010; De Jong et al, 2019). If, then, a prevailing version of freedom fails to substantiate our health – or undermines the social and economic conditions on which good health depends – that freedom fails a basic test of its own validity.

In the three chapters that follow, I use examples from the world of vaccines and immunisation, the management of noncommunicable 'lifestyle' diseases, and the structure and function of health systems to illustrate how a predominantly negative model of freedom – privileging individual autonomy over collective action, political rights over economic protections, and market allocation over distributive governance – undermines conditions of social reciprocity and cohesion essential both to the practical improvement of population health and the wider social and economic freedoms that health makes possible.[15]

Notes

[1] Literally as well as figuratively. After a brief flirtation with the improbable 'Operation Infinite Justice', the US War on Terror following 9/11 was named 'Operation Enduring Freedom' and then 'Freedom's Sentinel' after 2013 – a freedom mission which has, to no observable benefit, eventuated hundreds of thousands of unnecessary and violent deaths. In September 2020, the ill-conceived 'US Commission on Unalienable Rights' convened by former US Secretary of State and career mediocrity Mike Pompeo warned: '[I]n today's interconnected world, the defense of freedom at home may require the United States to come to the aid of friends of freedom abroad in repelling the aggression of freedom's enemies.' Final Report of the Commission, www.state.gov/commission-on-unalienable-rights (see Gourevitch and Robin, 2020). According to Fox & Friends (2019), 'If you hate capitalism, you hate freedom' (3 December).

[2] According to Arthur Schlesinger, '[t]he conception of the free society ... is the crowning glory of Western civilisation' (Schlesinger, 1949; see also Foner, 1998).

[3] 'Freedom' has been deployed to justify an array of moral propositions, from the brutalisations of colonial occupation to the struggles against slavery; from the totalising violence of two world wars to the Western assertion of moral high ground in the ensuing Cold War world; from the liquidation of imperial holdings in Africa and Asia to the suite of ill-fated regime change projects authored mainly by the US in the Middle East, Latin America and West Asia over the last five decades.

[4] From the Declaration of the Rights of Man and the Citizen in France in 1789, through the Universal Bill of Rights in 1791, to the Universal Declaration of Human Rights under the newly formed United Nations in 1948.

[5] The individuation of rights can result in competitive claim and counter-claim – for example between a wealthier neighbour's right to a healthy environment and the slum-dweller's right to a home – undermining social solidarity. The resources needed to pursue rights claims can disadvantage poorer, marginalised people and communities, privileging those with higher status, leading to 'queue jumping' and increasing inequality.

[6] See, for example, Charvet and Kaczynska-Nay (2008), Fox and Mason Meier (2009), Elsayed-Ali (2019), Kapcynski (2019) and Da Silva (2020).

[7] Two of the best examples of liberation in the modern era illustrate the problem of political versus economic freedom. During the emancipation of Russian serfs in 1861, around half of the agricultural land in European Russia was transferred from gentry to peasant ownership. The selection of land and the price of transfer, however, remained under the control of the landowners, resulting in a mass of nominally free serfs economically trapped by high-interest loans and marginally productive soil. The ending of slavery in the US saw cohorts of Americanised Africans liberated from servitude into a political economy of racial segregation and crippling indebtedness, with profound long-run consequences for racial inequality and social fragmentation in the US today. As Martin Luther King noted in 1963: "Five score years ago, a great American ... signed the Emancipation Proclamation. But 100 years later, we must face the tragic fact that the Negro is still not free" (see, for example, Stanley, 1998; Figes, 2002; Desmond, 2019).

[8] FDR's State of the Union 'Four Freedoms' speech delivered on 6 January 1941 – "freedom of speech, freedom of worship, freedom from want and freedom from fear" – shaped the development of the Charter.

[9] "Democracy alone can supply the vitalizing force to stir the peoples of the world into triumphant action, not only against their human oppressors, but also against their ancient

enemies – hunger, misery, and despair" (President Truman's inaugural speech, 1949; see Millis Simons, 1950; Rockefeller, 1951).

[10] Notwithstanding the conventional view of Western and Soviet preferences as respectively for human rights and social development, as well as the still-ongoing experimentation with economic liberalisation and political control in China after 1978. See www.ohchr. org/en/professionalinterest/pages/ccpr.aspx

[11] 'Those in favour of drafting two separate covenants argued that civil and political rights were enforceable or justiciable, or of an "absolute" character, while economic, social and cultural rights were not, or might not be; that the former were immediately applicable, while the latter were to be progressively implemented; and that, generally speaking, the former were rights of the individual "against" the State, that is, against unlawful and unjust action of the State while the latter were rights which the State would have to take positive action to promote' (*Annotations on the text of the draft International Covenants on Human Rights*, 1 July 1995, UN Doc. A/2929, para 10). 'The issue that needs to be confronted ... is that these [ESC] rights present genuinely different and, in many respects, far more difficult challenges than do civil and political rights ... [I]t is a much more complex undertaking to ascertain what constitutes an adequate standard of living, or whether a state fully respects and implements its population's right to education or right to work. Vexing questions of content, criteria, and measurement lie at the heart of the debate over "justiciability" yet are seldom raised or addressed with any degree of precision' (Stewart, 2004: 253–310; see also Kalantry et al, 2010).

[12] A view best set out in Sen's *Development as Freedom* (1999).

[13] Sen's freedom is founded on the potential of communities to engender common purpose fuelling collective action. Yet his philosophy of freedom remains subject to the greater belief in people's natural heterogeneity, in the liberation of individuals to pursue the 'life they have reason to value'. It is a vision of freedom which, paradoxically, leads back to a society in which autonomy overrides the collective action on which developmental progress depends. See, for example, Gasper, D. (2020) 'Amartya Sen, social theorizing and contemporary India', International Institute of Social Studies, Working Paper No. 658; Graf, G. and Schweiger, G. (2014) 'Poverty and freedom', *Human Affairs*, Volume 24, Issue 2; Chandler, D. (2013) 'Where Is the Human in Human-Centred Approaches to Development? A Critique of Amartya Sen's "Development as Freedom"', *The Biopolitics of Development*, 16, 67–86.

[14] "'You're free' they keep telling us. But freedom is always coming in the hereafter ... and the hereafter is a hustle." Jesse Williams, BET Awards, June 2016.

[15] Negative freedom mirrors the biomedical model – focusing on the emancipation of the body from the impositions of disease but without the complementary emphasis on a more muscular public health promoting positive well-being analogous to positive freedom (see, for example, Hyland, 1988; Azétsop and Rennie, 2010; Azétsop, 2016).

The vaccine society

After clean water, vaccines are widely considered to be the greatest contribution to human health. Ever. Nothing in history has killed more people than the arsenal of infectious diseases – from familiar ancient enemies to newly emerging pathogens – against which vaccines provide a widening umbrella of protection (Streefland, 2001; Lee, 2020; Nnaji et al, 2021). No other public health intervention provides comparable societal benefit for the same per capita cost (Jit et al, 2015; Doherty et al, 2016).

In the last two decades, vaccines are estimated to have prevented 2.7 million cases of measles annually, 2 million cases of neonatal tetanus, 1 million cases of pertussis, 600,000 cases of paralytic poliomyelitis and 300,000 cases of diphtheria, averting 2–3 million deaths worldwide each year (Remy et al, 2015; Kennedy, 2019).[1] Between December 2020 and December 2021, COVID vaccinations are estimated to have averted between 14.4 and 19.8 million deaths (Watson et al, 2022).

National immunisation programmes in the United States since 1980 have seen a decline of greater than 92 per cent in cases and 99 per cent in deaths from diphtheria, mumps, pertussis and tetanus – entirely eliminating endemic polio, rubella and measles (until recent resurgence of the latter) – preventing 33,000 deaths and 14 million cases of disease in each birth cohort, saving USD$10 billion in direct costs and $33 billion in disability and lost economic productivity (Roush et al, 2007).[2]

In the early 1960s, roughly a third of African children died before their fifth birthday – most killed by infectious diseases like smallpox and measles. Vaccine coverage in developing countries was abysmal, widely in single figures. In the decades following the launch in 1974 of the Expanded Programme on Immunisation aggregate rates of national coverage for a basic schedule of routine vaccines rose steeply to between 80 per cent and 90 per cent, and vaccine-preventable mortality plummeted (Figure 5.1) (Greenwood, 2014).[3]

Between 2000 and 2016, measles-related deaths fell by 84 per cent, averting 20.4 million avoidable deaths. Smallpox has been eradicated – the first instance in human history of a natural pathogen removed from the ecosystem.[4] Between 1988 and 2013, the rate of death among newborns as a result of preventable tetanus fell 94 per cent from 787,000 to 49,000 a year. The Global Polio Eradication Initiative has reduced the incidence of paralytic poliomyelitis from 350,000 cases a year at its launch in 1988 to 102

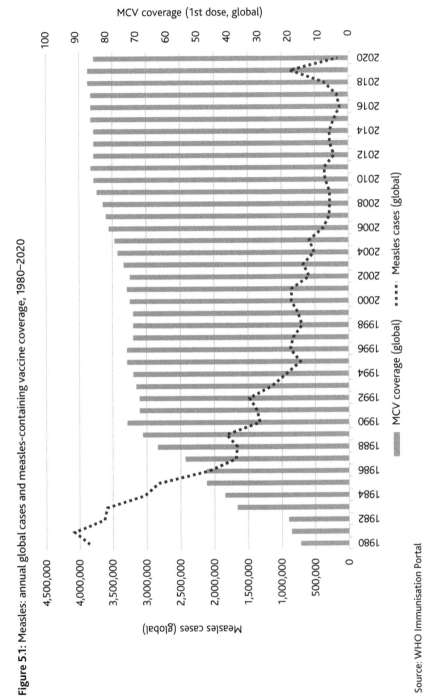

Figure 5.1: Measles: annual global cases and measles-containing vaccine coverage, 1980–2020

Source: WHO Immunisation Portal

cases worldwide in 2020.[5] The impact of COVID-19 demonstrates with brutal clarity the importance of immunisation – the single credible pathway to global recovery of the physical, social, psychological and economic freedoms taken from us by the pandemic in every country and community on the planet (Ecclestone-Turner and Upton, 2021).

Vaccination brings ideas of health and freedom into unique focus (Mooney, 2020; Colgrove and Samuel, 2022). To work effectively – to engender herd immunity – vaccination requires mass public compliance.[6] This is problematic from the perspective of liberty as autonomy. Collective freedom from the risk of disease depends on the enforced or elective adoption of individual unfreedom (Allen and Allen, 1986; Gostin et al, 2020). The entire vaccine edifice relies on the willingness of individuals to forego a measure of choice or, rather, to recognise individual freedom as reliant on cooperative action – the individual efficacy of our technologies determined by the collective force of our social cohesion. Vaccination collapses the conventional distinction between individual and communal risk-benefit creating a category of utility intelligible only through the concept of reciprocity. The practice of vaccination embodies the social contract – one in which cooperation is not just morally but functionally superior (Korna et al, 2020). If that contract starts to fail, so too does the viability of the vaccine society.

Over the last 200 years, the pace of evolution in immunological science has been remarkable.[7] But rapidly expanding schedules of routine vaccination, multiplying combinations of multi-antigen shots and fractional doses, new generations of live and killed vaccine, advanced adjuvants and novel molecular and genetic technologies – rooted in a practice whose origin story among the cows and cowherds of Edward Jenner's Gloucestershire feeds on deep human apprehensions about the proper balance of science and nature – have put public understanding and acceptance under increasing pressure (Figure 5.2).[8] Radical acceleration of discovery and production processes – driven in particular by Ebolavirus in West Africa and COVID in the last half-decade – have sharpened concerns about due diligence and vaccine safety (see, for example, Dudley et al, 2020). In fairness, balancing risk and benefit, vaccination is one of the safest public health interventions on record. Chance of serious harm is almost always vanishingly small. But it is not non-existent. And it is perhaps fair to say that the global vaccine community has been guilty of a kind of science-culture complacency, relying on the self-evidence of objective benefit without adequately acknowledging less positive or more challenging interpretations arising in diverse social and cultural contexts. Partly as a result, but partly also as an effect of changing social relations at a

Figure 5.2: Gillray's 'The Cow-Pock', 1802

Source: Library of Congress, Prints and Photographs Division, Cartoon Prints, British

larger scale, the golden era of vaccine confidence, flanked by the discovery of polio vaccines and the eradication of smallpox, has given way in the last two decades to an era of growing vaccine scepticism.

In 2020, progress in the global uptake of vaccination had stalled and, in some instances, started to reverse (see, for example, Paules et al, 2019; Hoffman, 2020; Johnson, 2022). In 2020, one in five children worldwide was not fully vaccinated, with 1.5 million deaths annually from preventable disease. Global vaccine uptake has stagnated over the last decade at around 86 per cent. Measles, once all but eliminated from the US and Europe, is once again rearing its ugly head. The number of reported cases in Europe in 2018 was triple that in 2017 which was 15 times that in 2016. In the first half of 2019, 364,808 measles cases were recorded in 182 countries – the highest number since 2006.

Certainly, a significant part of the problem is the persistent, and in some cases abject failure of governments, predominantly but by no means exclusively in low- and middle-income countries, to invest adequate resources in ensuring universal access to this extraordinarily cost-efficient life-saving public health measure.[9] But along with supply-side obstacles is a growing trend of public uncertainty, anxiety and, at the extreme, hostility, leading to vaccine refusal on the demand-side – a behavioural condition called 'vaccine hesitancy' – under which a small but sometimes growing minority of individuals, households and communities begin to question the premise of vaccination and, in a proportion of cases, simply vote with their feet and walk away (Gowda and Dempsey, 2013; Williamson and Glaab, 2018; Tull, 2019; Kennedy, 2020).[10] The question is why?

The roots of refusal

Vaccine scepticism, hesitancy and refusal are discernible in countries at all levels of wealth. Vaccine hesitancy manifests in rich and poor families, bridging political polarities of left and right, liberal and conservative.[11] The causes of hesitancy are manifold and interact in complex ways – from technical fears about adverse reaction and misgivings over vaccine efficacy, concerns about vaccine composition and ingredients and the strict necessity of immunisation among ostensibly disease-free communities, to anger at the bureaucratic imposition of social norms on individual choice, and resentment at government failure to bring other development goods to impoverished communities struggling with chronic poverty.

Mass vaccination programmes, dependent on near-universal coverage and high levels of public compliance, represent one of the few occasions when marginalised communities are able to capture the attention of the national and global policy making community. Vaccine refusal in northern Nigeria – frequently interpreted as the action of largely illiterate communities inflamed by rumour and misinformation – was in reality the effect of those communities rationally attempting to exchange vaccine compliance for modest improvement in local development investment, and larger historical struggles between state and federal levels of the Nigerian political economy.[12]

The dominant policy response to vaccine refusal falls into two categories – enforcement or enlightenment. Enforcing vaccination, based on the ethical and legal judgement that individual freedom cannot imperil the freedom of others, is attempted by a minority of countries, and is weakly implemented – presumably reflecting both a deep uncertainty about the appropriate balance of power between state and individual in the matter of health, and the unappealing optic of health workers physically imposing vaccination on overpowered families and children.

Attempts to enforce smallpox vaccination in Britain and America in the 19th century met with legal challenge, anti-vaccination societies and public rioting (Earl, 2005). Militarisation of smallpox eradication in the 1970s left deep scars in the same impoverished areas of northern India and Nigeria where resistance to polio vaccination emerged decades later. Deployment of security services to support polio campaigns in Pakistan in the last ten years, whilst providing essential protection to vulnerable vaccinators, has done little to improve relations between the government in Islamabad and marginalised Pashtun communities at the epicentre of continuing viral transmission (Silverman and May, 2001; Walkinshaw, 2011; Flanigan, 2014;

Patryn and Zagaja, 2016; Grzybowski et al, 2017; Pierik, 2018; Giubilini and Savulescu, 2019; Buttenheim et al, 2020).

Perhaps reflecting these problems, enlightenment – mainly in the form of 'information, education and communication' (IEC) programmes – is by quite some distance the most popular approach to addressing vaccine hesitancy (Figure 5.3) (Jarrett et al, 2015).

The essential premise of enlightenment is that hesitant and resistant individuals, households and communities are somehow imprisoned within a circuitry of false knowledge, victims of bad information, ignorance or irrationality – whether the over-privileged rejection of Western science and state authority among rich-country communities luxuriating in the absence of the very diseases vaccines prevent, or the much-vaunted, if poorly evidenced, susceptibility to misinformation of people in low-income communities whose poverty and illiteracy (sometimes encoding the insinuation of a deeper religious or cultural obscurantism) renders them peculiarly prone to 'myth and misperception'.

The idea that vaccine hesitancy is based fundamentally on people's inability to understand the science grossly oversimplifies a history of resistance which is founded in rather more lucid economic, political and cultural interests, anxieties and instincts. An association between vaccines and sexually transmitted infection, manifesting through popular rumours in India and Nigeria in the mid-2000s that oral polio vaccine (OPV) was infected with HIV, harks back to 19th-century epidemiological studies in the US and UK showing a correlation between early smallpox inoculations and syphilis – probably the result of poor hygiene in early vaccine and variolation practices. The association was likely amplified by widely debunked claims in Edward Hooper's *The River* (1999) that OPV production using central African monkey kidneys in the late 1950s facilitated the zooanosis of simian immunodeficiency virus into the human population as HIV.

Rumours of OPV re-engineered to sterilise poor Muslim populations reported in India reflected concrete experiences of political oppression and religious conflict amplified by memories of forced sterilisation in the 1970s delivered in many cases by the same health workers subsequently offering unexplained vaccines, for free. Opposition to pertussis vaccine in wealthy countries in the mid-1970s fed on research reporting plausible, but ultimately unfounded, risk of neurological damage. Ironically, one of the most tenacious vaccine controversies – that of an association between the Measles-Mumps-Rubella (MMR) vaccine and autism – has no particular historical basis, raised simply by one subsequently debarred doctor's unethical, dishonest and incompetent research, published in *The Lancet* in 1998.

In the end, enforcement and enlightenment arrive at uncomfortably similar illiberal positions. Enforcement is problematic for reasons which are self-evident. Enlightenment – drawing on the idea of refusal as a form of

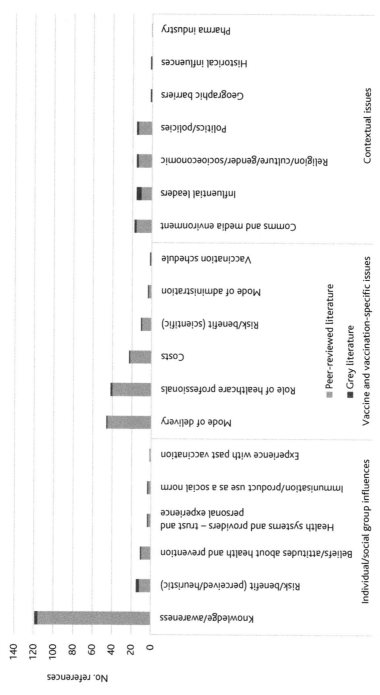

Figure 5.3: Approaches to vaccine hesitancy, a global review

Source: Jarrett et al (2015)

unfreedom created by ignorance or delusion – depends on a relatively firm demarcation of right and wrong knowledge, and the necessary correction of those labouring under the latter, such that the heterodoxy of resistance can be converted through a process of education into voluntary submission to the collective truth of vaccines, drifting awkwardly towards the totalitarian notion of liberating people from false consciousness and forcing them, for their own good, to be free.[13]

More importantly, both enforcement and enlightenment suffer from the additional difficulty that neither, in its own terms, appears to be compellingly effective (Hobson-West, 2003; Lewin et al, 2014; Nyhan et al, 2014; Dube et al, 2015; Gellin, 2020; Jacobson et al, 2020). This may be to do with the fact that opposition to vaccination often has little to do with vaccines themselves.[14] Without doubt, hesitancy is articulated through material concerns about the nature, efficacy, safety or necessity of vaccines (Figueiredo et al, 2020) – and sustaining public support for vaccines will require a much more sophisticated engagement with discourses of anti-vaccination than the relentless simplistic projection of pro-vaccine education, consigning opposition to a failure of intellect (see, for example, Tafuri et al, 2011).

But it is becoming increasingly clear that these concerns are frequently the immediate expression of deeper seams of anxiety about the legitimacy of the institutions – national and international, public and private – which promote vaccination as biological imperative and social norm (Benin et al, 2006; Navin, 2016; Kraaijeveld, 2020). Growing vaccine resistance around the world maps onto a widening crisis of trust in contemporary systems of social, economic, political, cultural and environmental governance – a crisis fuelled by escalating economic inequality, increasing concentration of the influence of capital, the progressive withdrawal of the state from the provision of public goods, and the outsourcing of responsibility for welfare to individuals and households struggling in an increasingly complex risk society (Brownlie and Howson, 2006; Lee et al, 2016; Taylor et al, 2017; Iriart, 2017; Baumgaertner et al, 2018; Dew and Donovan, 2020; McCoy, 2020).[15]

Viral diseases are uncannily adept at seeking out and exploiting conditions of social inequality. From country to country, COVID assiduously mapped social faultlines – those most oppressed by the unfreedoms of economic poverty and low social status most exposed to disease and least able to afford the forfeiture of freedoms necessary for lockdown (Blundell et al, 2020; Bowleg, 2020). In a reverse fashion, vaccines offer a powerful opportunity to confront disease, now and in the future. But it is an opportunity predicated on high levels of social cohesion, based on equitable socioeconomic conditions, in order to achieve maximum technical efficacy.

The future of vaccines, and the freedom they provide, depend ultimately on our willingness to work together to a common agenda. Degradation in collective vaccine faith risks a catastrophic collapse in one of humanity's greatest technological achievements. But collective willingness in the technological space depends on public perception in the social space – of basic fairness and shared responsibility, a perception which is weakened by the relentless dynamics of competitive individualism. Rebuilding and reinforcing social equity requires purposive government leadership and a model of governance founded in a different vision of freedom (Varoufakis, 2020) – a freedom which is relational rather than individual, in which autonomy is negotiated rather than absolute, which acknowledges the interdependence of our sovereign choices, and which places reciprocity at the heart of what it means to be free.[16]

Notes

[1] In the decade to 2020, vaccines and immunisation averted around 23.3 million deaths worldwide.

[2] Between 1947 and 2007, the value of immunisation in the UK is estimated to have been GBP£6.6 billion a year. www.abpi.org.uk/new-medicines/vaccines/economic-and-social-impact-of-vaccines/

[3] Although this masks significant inequality between countries depending on health sector function, level of economic development and exposure to conflict and instability. Among the poorest countries in 2018, 7 per cent of children were fully immunised. Within countries, immunisation varies widely – between male and female, urban and rural, regions demarcated according to economic or political significance, and mainstream and marginalised population groups. In Nigeria, immunisation for diphtheria, pertussis and tetanus ranges from 79.6 per cent in the wealthiest quintile to 7.4 per cent in the poorest and in Pakistan from 88 per cent to 29.9 per cent (see, for example, Hosseinpoor et al, 2016).

[4] Eradication of smallpox is estimated to have prevented 150–200 million deaths between 1980 and 2013.

[5] Excluding cases of circulating vaccine-derived polio virus (cVDPV).

[6] Population coverage required to reach herd immunity varies by disease and antigen but rises to as high as 93–95 per cent for highly infectious conditions like measles.

[7] Vaccines for plague and cholera (1895 and 1897); tuberculosis (1890–1950); diphtheria (1913); tetanus toxoid (1923); yellow fever (1935); pertussis (1948); polio (1950–1961); measles, mumps and rubella (1963–1969); hepatitis B (1975) and A (1995); haemophilus influenza type-B (Hib, 1985); rotavirus (1998–2006); pneumococcal conjugate vaccine (PCV) and human papilloma virus vaccine (HPV) (2006); Ebolavirus (2016). Some 321 candidate vaccines for COVID-19 were in development in October 2020, with 42 in clinical trials. By November, two vaccines (Pfizer-BioNtech and Moderna) were registered at 95 per cent efficacy in phase III trials, with an 'Oxford-AstraZeneca' vaccine at a slightly confused aggregate 70 per cent efficacy in hand, as well as Russian (Sputnik V) and Chinese (Sinopharm) candidates adopted without complete transparency in their

national jurisdictions. The principles of vaccination are now being turned to NCDs from cancer and diabetes to hypertension and Alzheimer's, as well as therapies for allergy, autoimmune disease and addiction.

8   Although the idea of complementarity between disease and cure has been part of medical thinking from the application of dog hair to bites in Jin Dynasty China, through the ingestion of snake venom by 10th-century Buddhist monks to inure themselves to attack, and the variolation of smallpox pustules in disease-free subjects as a prophylactic measure during epidemics. It is perhaps ironic that an intuition which led to one of the world's greatest medical discoveries also feeds homeopathy, a strong candidate for its most worthless.

9   A situation exacerbated by the extent to which COVID-19 has drawn on scarce health sector capacity.

10 In 2019, WHO named vaccine hesitancy one of the top ten threats to global health.

11 Vaccine refusal in the United States unites middle-class families losing faith in the value of inclusive society and African American communities distrustful of government viewed as presiding over their systematic exclusion (see, for example, Reich, 2016; McCoy, 2017).

12 Personal observation based on discussion with local public health administrators, community leaders and local households in northern Nigerian states, as well as more formal research between 2001 and 2013.

13 The false knowledge idea of vaccine refusal is further flawed in that it tends to take the reasons people give for refusal – however outlandish – as a genuine reflection of what they believe, rather than the tactical use of popular narratives consciously deployed to advance more strategic aims, for example leveraging compliance with vaccination against diseases they do not experience as risk for other benefits they have reason to value (see, for example, Larson et al, 2018).

14 'When it comes to vaccination programmes, the debate is rarely about the disease itself but about the relationship between the individual and the state' (Olterman, 2020).

15 As well as proliferating use of dense social media networks to promote distrust in formal scientific, institutional and governmental sources of information, supportive of populist and conspiratorial agendas (see, for example, Bonner, 2022; see also Roth et al, 2011; Tacke et al, 2020).

16 'To think of humans as freedom-loving you must be ready to view nearly all of history as a mistake' (Gray, 2013).

6

The freedom to fail

For most of human history up to this point, life and death have been shaped chiefly by infectious disease – smallpox, tuberculosis, plague, leprosy, syphilis, cholera, typhus, measles, malaria – along with the perils of childbirth and the traumas of violent injury. In the last century, though – as socioeconomic development, medical technology and disease control initiatives radically reduced the scale of pathogenic illness, improved perinatal survival and mitigated accidental risk – NCDs (primarily cancers, cardiovascular and chronic respiratory disease, diabetes and – shamefully late – mental illness) have emerged as a new frontline in global health. NCDs are responsible today for 73 per cent of mortality worldwide with the highest rates of death in low- and middle-income developing countries.

Mounting effective strategies to tackle NCDs will be critical, in coming decades, to our chances of maintaining socioeconomic progress in countries at all levels of development – which makes what can only be described as a singular listlessness in the international response all the more intriguing. Worldwide, 1.1 billion people have hypertension, 425 million adults have diabetes, about 40 per cent of adults are overweight or obese and almost 800,000 people die annually from suicide. Yet global leadership on NCDs has been slow to emerge – decentralised to selective national policy making, and reliant on voluntary engagement from increasingly powerful multinational corporate actors. 'In 2014 NCDs constituted half of the entire global burden of disease but received less than 2 per cent of all international health aid (US$492 million out of US$36 billion). In contrast, HIV represented 4 per cent of the global burden of disease but received 29 per cent of global funds' (Nelson Allen, 2017).[1]

Aetiologically rooted in the ways we live, NCDs are commonly described as 'diseases of lifestyle' – associated most immediately with the food we eat, our levels of physical exercise, the recreational substances we consume, and the stressors we absorb. If infectious diseases are conceptualised as an external assault on human society by a pathogenic nature – a battle in which the protective intervention of the state is not only warranted but required – NCDs can be viewed by contrast as internal to the individual, emerging from within our bodily selves – the physical manifestation of the choices we make and the preferences we pursue, amplified by a combination of genetic and biological propensities. For the state to intervene in a similarly protective way in the causes of NCDs would look worryingly like intervention between the individual and their sovereign right to choose how to live. In a world dominated by the discourses of market democracy, small government and individual freedom, such intervention is heavily discouraged.

The idea that individual lifestyle is at the root of the NCDs we experience leads to the belief that our diseases are caused by the consumption choices we make and the behaviours we freely adopt. In reality, though, behaviour and choice are quite distinct mechanisms – behaviour a sub-set of choice, and choice itself heavily circumscribed by the material conditions in which individuals, households and communities live. It is intellectually dishonest to attempt to separate out the notional freedom of individual behaviour from the limits to choice imposed on people by the social, psychobiological, economic, cultural and political constraints through which they navigate their daily lives (Taylor, 2015).

In the last 30 years, a rich literature of research on the 'social determinants of health' – the social, economic, political, cultural and environmental conditions in which we are born, grow, live, work and age – has shown, with considerable empirical consistency, the influence society has on our health and life chances.[2] We know that, for condition after condition from heart disease to suicide, where you are in the social hierarchy shapes your risk of disease and death – profoundly challenging the notion of freedom as essentially individual (Figure 6.1) (Shaw et al, 2016). The systematic association of socioeconomic status and NCD risk profoundly challenges the notion of freedom as essentially individual.

Figure 6.1: Prevalence of hypertension by economic category and metropolitan classification, United States, 2013

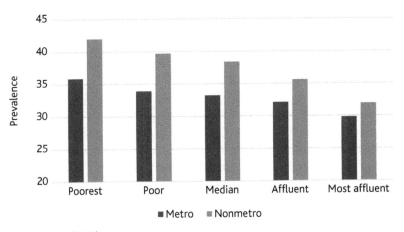

Source: Shaw et al (2016)

Acknowledging the influence of social determinants, NCD policy in countries around the world is replete with the language of 'multisector … multi-level … multifactorial' approaches. But the end result – in money and action – remains weighted towards investment in programmes which focus on individual responsibility and lifestyle management. National action plans dutifully map out colourfully tiered targets from individual to societal level. But in the conversion of easy idealisations into politically charged reality, the policy maker's concentration drifts back downstream to personal behaviour and choice, leaving behind in a mist of distal intentions the more radical reform of social structures and market regulation which – while substantially more effective in reducing NCD threat – invoke a level of government intervention distinctly problematic for the modern model of freedom (Schrecker and Taler, 2017).[3]

Increasing involvement of multinational corporate actors in setting the agenda for NCD action tends, too, to concentrate on an individualised model of disease prevention and, unsurprisingly, on a voluntary model of corporate responsibility (Clark, 2014). Corporations are able to draw on considerable commercial and public relations muscle to shape and then invoke the idea of a popular demand for freedom of choice. They dominate the informational market with materials and messages supportive of their preferred approach, over time establishing a dubious claim to 'win-win' symbiosis with governments who are fiscally unable or politically unwilling to undertake a more balanced programme of individual choice and regulatory control (Anderson et al, 2009).

From the 1970s, powerful commercial interests, in particular those representing food and tobacco, expanded strategic funding to epidemiological studies bolstering their arguments in favour of individualised prevention, especially where it dovetailed with the promotion of their products (Clark, 2019). Increasingly, the demarcation between commercial and governmental thinking has blurred in a 'Third Way' compromise of public–private partnerships (PPPs) financing research and science-policy communication as public sector budgets have dwindled. In the early 2020s, industry continues to wield enormous influence over national policy, through sophisticated and well-financed formal and informal channels around the commodification of food and the scope for regulatory control (see, for example, Lencucha and Thow, 2019; Tangcharoensathien et al, 2019). Governments outsource their statutory role to a seemingly endless stream of governance compacts and exercises in corporate social responsibility, constituting commercial actors as part of the solution rather than origin of the problem. Opaque, well-funded lobbying, informal political patronage and shell NGOs complete the ecosystem of discursive construction, promoting the protection of individual freedom to consume from the evils of state intervention (Wiist, 2010; Gilmore et al, 2011; Bartlett and

Garde, 2015; Fooks et al, 2017; Seitz and Martens, 2017; Bartlett, 2018; Steele et al, 2020).

A consensus of government and private sector ends up promoting behaviour change as key to the empowerment of individuals and their freedom to choose, disregarding the scant evidence that these behavioural intervention methods have any significant impact, in so doing deflecting attention from the need for systemic reform and a more collective societal level of action (Arnott et al, 2014; Brown et al, 2014; Pearce et al, 2014; Alageel et al, 2017; Cradock et al, 2017; Murray et al, 2017; Oosterveen et al, 2017; Holman et al, 2018; Byrne, 2019; Champion et al, 2019; McCrabb et al, 2019; Varkevisser et al, 2019; Adom et al, 2020).[4] The global rise of obesity is illustrative (Sell and Williams, 2020).[5]

Feeding freedom

One in nine people in the world today – 820 million – are hungry, one in eight of these approaching starvation. At the same time, one in three adults, or a little under a third of the world's population, is overweight or obese, projected to rise to one in two by 2030 (InterAcademy Partnership, 2018). It is a picture of the world which could most charitably be described as dysfunctional.[6] Countries at all stages of economic development are seeing the emergence of a double burden of under- and over-nutrition. In 2000, WHO declared obesity a global pandemic. Yet national and international policy responses are fragmented. Progress towards nutrition targets is slow, if moving at all (Traverso-Yepez and Hunter, 2016; Global Nutrition Report, 2020).

Policy responses to the problem of obesity rely heavily on the idea of individual responsibility, supported by a looped feedback of corporate messaging and public opinion linking diet with personal preference and obesity with moral failure (Crawford, 2006; Varman and Vikas, 2007). Voluntary change in food industry practice is favoured by national governments, WHO and the food industry (Kaldor, 2018). Mandatory state intervention in the supply side is assiduously avoided or steeped in institutional ambivalence for fear of appearing unduly to encroach upon the twin principles of market freedom and lifestyle choice (Boddington, 2010; Brownell et al, 2010; Lund et al, 2011).[7] Yet the scope of freedom in food people truly possess is extremely limited – hamstrung between an inner world of neural pathways hijacked by sophisticated environmental cues shaping appetite and addiction, and an outer world of rising inequality, growing market power and intransparent agreements in the global trading systems through which food is produced and supplied.

Few sensible people consider individuals capable in any meaningful sense of perfect sovereignty or autonomy (Ayer, 1972; Gostin and Wiley, 2008).

Environmental conditions override psychological regulatory systems, diminishing the reality of personal freedom (Vandevijvere and Kraak, 2019). The informational conditions necessary for unqualified moral responsibility are sufficiently extreme – acutely so under the combined pressures of material poverty and psychosocial stress – that we simply cannot be confident that what people actually do is a reliable measure of what they choose (Kass, 2001; Childress et al, 2002; Gostin and Gostin, 2009; Conly, 2013; Levy, 2018). Obesity is intimately responsive to socioeconomic status – clustering among the poor in high-income countries, rising initially among the wealthy in low-income and emerging economies, but travelling down the economic distribution as those countries develop, seeming to seek out deprivation as its natural milieu (Templin et al, 2019). Confronted by these dynamics, consigning obesity to personal responsibility is at best naïve and at worst cynical. A rhetoric of personal freedom means little when hedged in by the unfreedoms of psychosocial and economic powerlessness intensifying in the world around us (Standing, 2011; Owens and Cribb, 2013; McGill et al, 2015).

Over the last four decades, concentration of power in a globalising food system has created a web of unfreedoms constricting the ability of individuals, families and communities to secure adequate healthy food on their own terms – from a commercial model switching out complex carbohydrates, micronutrients and dietary fibre for quicker, more convenient energy-dense products loaded with the sensory compensation of fats, sugars and salt; aggressive marketing of highly processed cheap foods feeding an obesogenic cycle of desirability, affordability, ill-health and social stigma; unbalanced domestic agricultural policies favouring income-earning export-oriented monocrops, increasing market volatility and distorting local food availability; to mounting levels of transnational equity converting smallholder farming into agro-industrial investment, raising levels of debt and default among poor rural communities, feeding the swell of rural out-migration into spreading urban slums or sprawling suburban neighbourhoods bereft of space to exercise, characterised by income poverty, 'food desertification'[8] and the gravitational drift of households towards energy-rich, nutrient-poor low-cost obesogenic diets (Modi and Cheru, 2013).[9]

The example of obesity – and the nature of the global response – points to a policy discourse immersed in the ideology of individual freedom and personal choice, in the teeth of overwhelming evidence that such freedom and choice are dwarfed by wider social and economic forces. The systematic patterning of NCDs – biology shaped by environment, environment shaped by concentric circles of increasingly distal determination far beyond the influence of local will – suggests that emphasising personal responsibility and individual choice is an inadequate response to this intensifying global health challenge (Eikemo et al, 2016; Marmot and Bell, 2019).

This does not suppose unimportance in the realm of personal responsibility – simply that behaviour is frequently outgunned by the social, economic and political forces that generate the freedoms and unfreedoms under which people operate. It supposes, rather, that liberating people while failing to supply the conditions through which they can manage their liberty is an ineffective, inefficient and ultimately rather cruel idea of freedom.

Notes

[1] See Nugent (2019).

[2] As well as the 'commercial determinants of health' increasingly rooted in globalising systems of production and trade (de Lacy-Vawdon et al, 2022).

[3] Over the last 40 years, for example, while UK governments have increasingly acknowledged the role of social conditions in driving health and inequality, policy has continued to concentrate on individual behaviour and the 'empowerment' of choice (Kriznik et al, 2018; see, for example, Popay et al, 2010).

[4] Evidence for the efficacy of behaviour change interventions is weak, where it is assessed at all. Across diverse lifestyle fields from diet and weight loss, through alcohol reduction and smoking cessation, to physical exercise and transport use, results are frequently small, negligible or non-existent; where positive, they tend to be poorly sustained over time. The powerful influence of socioeconomic context suggests that an excessive emphasis on individual behaviour and choice will be least effective among poor communities in wealthy countries and in large urban and rural populations in the low- and middle-income world (Toomey et al, 2020; see, for example, Chater and Loewenstein, 2022).

[5] I focus on food in this section. But psychobiological addictions relating to alcohol and drugs use illustrate similar patterns of constraint on the notion of freedom in terms of consumption choice, with severe impacts on population health.

[6] 'It is unacceptable that, in a world that produces enough food to feed its entire population, more than 1.5 billion people cannot afford a diet that meets the required levels of essential nutrients and over 3 billion people cannot even afford the cheapest healthy diet' (FAO et al, 2020).

[7] Framed in the tediously effective discourse of the 'nanny state'. In 1941, Bronislaw Malinowksi observed: 'Medical science can demonstrate that certain forms of diet are indispensable, while other dishes are harmful. The decision whether you prefer to gorge yourself with fried capons soused in Burgundy and steer towards stomach ulcers and arthritis, or on medical advice keep to a reasonable diet, remains with the individual.' Eighty years later, little has changed: '[W]hile it is clear that consumption of artificial trans fats poses a significant risk to human health, it is not clear how societies should respond to this risk. ... Although [bans] may have a positive impact on human health, they open the door to excessive government control. ... To protect human freedom and other values, policies that significantly restrict food choices ... should be adopted only when they are supported by substantial scientific evidence and when policies that impose fewer

restrictions on freedom, such educational campaigns and product labelling, are likely to be ineffective' (Coggon, 2018; see also Resnik, 2010).

[8] A primarily urban process in which commercial outlets offering healthy, affordable food are gradually displaced within a neighbourhood by outlets offering cheap, unhealthy fast foods (Bellian, 2019).

[9] Global food prices fell by 75 per cent in real terms between 1974 and 2005. This trend, however, does not protect against relative price spikes. Globalisation of the food production system has accelerated industrialisation of agricultural production in low- and middle-income countries, increasing monocropping, reducing the physical and economic space for family farms and diversified local production, exacerbating biodiversity loss, expanding smallholder reliance on modified seeds, intensifying use of pesticides and fertilisers, shifting production from cereals and legumes to dairy and meat to feed the dietary preferences of modernising society and encouraging greater resource-intensive use of new arable land released through poorly regulated exploitation of virgin territory (see Kaur, 2020). In 2022, disruptions to global supply chains and inflating production costs caused sharp upward movement in prices of vital basic foods in countries across the economic development spectrum.

7

The dead hand of care

The emergence of modern healthcare – drugs, technologies and treatments – offers us today a freedom from illness and death unimaginable just a century ago. Healthcare is perhaps the most concrete expression of the point where individual need meets societal response. How we are – or are not – able to access critical care will become, at one time or another, an existential question for most of us. Once we are past the point of prevention through action on the broader determinants of disease, the healthcare system is, in some form in every country on earth, the thin blue line standing between individuals and a world of pain and loss.

Over the 20th century, almost all industrialised countries pursued a collective, population risk-pooling approach to the development and provision of healthcare, from Bismarck's model of social insurance to the National Health Service (NHS) of Beveridge and Bevan.[1] With escalating levels of technological sophistication, ageing populations, increasing demand and spiralling cost, however, most of these countries have started seeking alternative models to reduce the fiscal burden on the national budget (Schieber and Poullier, 1989; Busse et al, 2017).

Emerging out of colonial health services, many low- and middle-income countries entered independence with weak and underdeveloped systems of healthcare. In the ensuing decades, low levels of domestic investment, limited local resources, structural adjustment and aid dependence have constrained public sector leadership and the formation of public health systems, rationalising instead the necessity – and putative efficiency – of privately contracted medical services in countries roiled by high levels of mortality, disease and debt.[2]

Over the last 40 years, it has become evident that neither the rich- nor the poor-world experience of healthcare, confronted with expanding need and escalating technological possibility, is practically or ethically sustainable. As a result, the notion of 'reform' has become a permanent feature of health sector policy making, and a battleground in the ideology of freedom – whether to liberate care, as a private good, into the hands of market provision and consumer choice, or to unify care, as a public good, statutorily accessible to all. While most governments attempt to thread the needle, espousing both objectives in some degree of combination, the direction of reform has drawn heavily on the negative model of freedom – repudiating the state as intrusive, inefficient or inept, advocating the liberation of healthcare as a market commodity and the emancipation of individuals to choose the care they consume (Dougherty, 1992; West-Oram, 2013; EXPH, 2015; Gaynor et al, 2016; Almgren, 2018).

During the 1980s, accelerating after 1990, health systems across the developed and many parts of the developing worlds have seen an extensive drive to move away from the idea of direct government-led healthcare – the dead hand of the state – towards an increasingly powerful role for non-state commercial interests: from corporate investment in hospitals, clinics, private insurance and private–public partnerships, to corporate philanthropy and the financialisation of healthcare provision encouraged in low- and middle-income countries through a patchwork of often conflicting and incoherent experimentation with outsourcing, user fees and 'results-based financing' (Mackintosh and Koivusalo, 2005; O'Laughlin, 2016; Wu and Mao, 2017; IFC Global Private Health Conference, 2019; Marten, 2019).

Empowering individuals to understand and engage with the care they receive is a vital principle of health system development in countries at all levels of economic capability. Harnessing the role of private sector actors in healthcare delivery is an inevitability which can only sensibly be approached as a virtue, in particular in low-income country contexts (Musgrove, 1996; Wadge et al, 2017). But the systematic marginalisation of government in healthcare – the fragmentation of care among a constellation of often poorly regulated providers, and the gradual repositioning of care as a commodity whose availability is predicated on people's economic means – is a doubtful strategy whether in terms of efficiency or equity.

Shrinking the role of government in healthcare in order to free people from oppressively monopolistic state behaviour is partly based on the imputed superiority of market dynamics – generating innovation and competition, enhancing efficiency and leading to better outcomes. But looking at the available evidence, this argument is hard to sustain. Private-for-profit hospitals in the US and Canada incur higher costs and increased risk of death compared with equivalent not-for-profit facilities (Devereaux et al, 2004; Herrera et al, 2014). Outsourcing and privatisation of NHS services in the UK after 2012 has been linked (albeit not necessarily causally) with a sharp resurgence in treatable mortality (Goodair and Reeves, 2022). In Italy's widely privatised health system, public spending is associated with significantly lower mortality while private expenditure shows no comparable effect (Cecilia Quercioli et al, 2013).[3] In sub-Saharan Africa, public sector spending maps onto better health outcomes, including for neonatal, infant and under-five mortality (Oxfam, 2009; Novignon et al, 2012; Novignon and Lawanson, 2017).

State-led healthcare in China between 1949 and 1979 saw infant mortality fall from 200 to 34 per 1,000 live births, while life expectancy almost doubled. Premier Deng Xiaoping's market-oriented reforms after 1980 produced such sharply rising inequality, in particular between rural and urban communities, that substantial elements of the system were subsequently returned to government management (Tang et al, 2008).[4] Out-contracting health service delivery, whilst popular with global health financiers, appears overall to do no better than government-led provision, with performance depending heavily, in any case, on the organisational type and operational ethos of the sub-contracting agencies (Lagarde and Palmer, 2009; Odendaal et al, 2018; Petrou et al, 2018).[5]

Part of the problem is that the evidence, while voluminous, is as often inconclusive. Within a vast research literature both warmly supportive and fiercely critical of healthcare marketisation, findings seem largely dependent on how studies are structured and what values are analysed (Coarasa et al, 2017). Private providers tend to do well in terms of timeliness, patient dignity and convenience, but worse in terms of equity, accessibility and efficiency, partly the result of perverse incentives to over-test and over-treat the wealthy while underserving the poor. Public providers tend to do worse in terms of equipment, drugs supply and staff but better in terms of equity. Overall, findings are plentiful but ambiguous. The result is obfuscation. In the absence of consensus, reform processes shifting care from state responsibility to commercial opportunity have been shaped ideologically rather than empirically – grounded in a narrow idea of the interaction between freedom and liberalisation (Hanson et al, 2008; Montagu et al, 2011; Basu et al, 2012; Torchia et al, 2015; Turcotte-Tremblay et al, 2016).

Of over 100 PPPs in global health in the last two decades, many concentrate on vertical disease control with heavy emphasis on technological solutions. PPPs are widely praised for injecting new life into a moribund global policy environment coming out of the 1990s, innovating technical, financial and administrative approaches. But at the same time PPPs have balkanised healthcare into internally competing disease priorities, delivering services through a plethora of state and non-state agencies, including both private organisations and NGOs, bypassing government, undermining national planning and administration, and squeezing the space for community participation in priority-setting and evaluation of impact (Storeng et al, 2019).

The question of public and private in healthcare is rarely, if ever, constituted as zero-sum, but rather as one of a variety of shades of composition – especially so in developing countries where private provision dominates. But what we *mean* by 'private sector', particularly in low- and middle-income countries, is often poorly defined – ranging from super-specialised hi-tech urban tertiary centres, through international and local NGOs, to variously qualified medical practitioners, unlicensed pharmacists and drug shop owners, traditional healers, herbalists and shamans. In fact, if unaccredited providers are stripped out of analysis, the scale of private provision in low- and middle-income countries falls dramatically (Oxfam, 2009; Mackintosh et al, 2016). This is important not least because private sector performance appears to be strongly influenced by the structure and performance of the public sector, suggesting that whatever the benefits of private care services, they are determined by the strength of the sector as a whole (Morgan and Waters, 2016).

Healthcare is, moreover, strikingly prone to market failure (Barber et al, 2019).[6] Profit motives disincentivise extension of services to those less able to pay, and increase the incentives to over-provide to those who can (Tibandebage and Mackintosh, 2005).[7] Healthcare markets underinvest in diseases prevalent in poor countries and among poor communities, undervaluing externalities generated by good health including the public benefit of infectious disease control and the economic value of a healthy workforce. The net effect – combining a structurally weak public health infrastructure with a poorly defined and regulated private sector – is a fragmentary patchwork of care which government struggles to control and households struggle to understand (Light, 2003; De Costa and Diwan, 2007).

In the end, the question revolves around what we believe about the nature of healthcare and the care system – what they are and what they are for.[8] If care is viewed primarily as a private good – an assemblage of intellectual property, technological capability and pharmaceutical commodities – the system can be construed simply as a marketplace of technical transactions, capable of astonishing curative feats but with high levels of inequality (Mahnkopf, 2008). But healthcare, and perhaps more specifically the *system* through which care is delivered, is more akin to public good than a transactional space through which diagnosis is provided and treatment consumed (Karsten, 1995).

Health is sufficiently foundational to our ability to live fulfilled and flourishing lives – the determinants of health so deeply embedded in the social, economic, political and cultural arrangements by which we organise society – that the equitable promotion, protection and advancement of health through a system of care takes on a special practical and moral character in the relationship between individual and society. The care system is a flesh-and-blood manifestation of the social contract, a microcosm mirroring the society in which it sits, reflecting the heights to which we can rise and the degree to which we fall short (Kawachi and Berkman, 2000; Armstrong, 2001; Chuang et al, 2013).

Healthcare systems, even where fragile and underdeveloped, are an expression of belonging – the promise of support when lightning strikes. Health systems map out the body of the nation in arterial networks of clinical infrastructure and social inclusion – hospitals and health centres, clinics and community centres; doctors, nurses and midwives; a dense network spreading outwards from the central level of policy, standards and guidelines through a myriad of planners, managers and administrators; academics, researchers, teachers and students; surgeons, super-specialists and family physicians; lab technicians, pharmacists, paramedics and porters; public health practitioners, biomedical clinicians, epidemiologists, public sector workers and private entrepreneurs; psychiatrists and psychologists, physiotherapists and nutritionists; primary care workers and community volunteers.[9]

The healthcare system is not simply an effect, but an engine of social development. It is a physical and institutional space in which progressive forces challenge the regressions of obscurantism and hierarchy – advancing education over gender, professionalism over class, technical expertise over social status, public duty over private privilege; a space in which individual biology, medical technology and public priority are mediated through the architecture of scientific objectivity, in which the universality of individual need coalesces in a common sense of solidarity; a space which forges dialogue – between clinic and community, patient and provider, healer and health worker; between physical frailty and the power of knowledge; between tradition and modernity. Healthcare systems, in each country, represent a space in which different ideas and ideologies – of the nature of people, society and state – can engage in constructive contest founded in the safety of shared value (Janzen, 1978).

The care system cannot, on its own, create health. But the existence of a system, in and of itself, creates a sense of security which makes the vagaries of fate and illness manageable. Public belief in statutory entitlement – the guarantee of care – engenders a security which liberates individuals, households and communities from risk which, in past generations, foreclosed much social participation and economic enterprise. An inclusive health system fosters the cohesion and trust on which the wider freedoms of a thriving society depend (Gilson, 2003; Whetten et al, 2006; Gille et al, 2015; Heymann et al, 2015; Blair et al, 2017; Wenham et al, 2019). If meeting individuals' health needs is instrumental to their normal social functioning; if normal social function is intrinsic to individuals' freedom to live life and flourish; and if equality of opportunity to live and flourish applies to all individuals in society – then a genuinely equitable healthcare system is essential to a complete condition of freedom (see, for example, Culyer, 2014).

More equitable care will not emerge naturally out of fragmented systems and intensive individualisation of consumption behaviour. It requires muscular arbitration and stewardship – the 'progressive hegemony' that only states are mandated to provide (Srivastan and Shatrugna, 2012; Flavin et al, 2014; Gilson et al, 2017).[10] From the vantage point of health, freedom requires more, not less, government – and not the pusillanimous, once-removed oversight of 'light-touch' governance, artlessly off-loading responsibility onto underfunded localities, arm's-length bodies and sub-contracted service providers, creeping gingerly back in from the political wings only when things go egregiously right or unambiguously wrong. It requires vigorous articulate government creatively present at the centre of the national system, radiating outwards in nodes of care to the periphery, manifesting the positive potential of government not as a displacement of local delivery but as the empowerment of that diversity within a framework of accountability in which universal, equitable access is an absolute commitment rather than aspirational promise.

Conclusion

Freedom is an axiom of the good life and a vital dimension of social progress.[11] But 'liberty for its own sake is an empty vessel'.[12] Freedom functions as a medium rather than an outcome – as a vehicle for debate rather than an absolute assertion.[13] Unfortunately, we have arrived in contemporary political and media discourse at a version of freedom which is both increasingly strident and incomplete – dogmatically negative in tone, fixated on the sovereign individual liberated from the clutches of intrusive government into the endless economic opportunity of society as market (MacCallum, 1967).

A freedom which teaches autonomy as its best expression eventually corrodes the collective action and social cohesion which underpin the power of our greatest technological capabilities. Vaccines demonstrate how individual freedoms interanimate with one another through decision-making processes in which cooperation is both functional and ethical. This freedom is relational and reciprocal, not individual and absolute (Brown, 1995; Bittner, 2019). It is populous, contingent, negotiated, fluid – a medium of engagement through we continuously seek equilibrium of interests.

A freedom which invokes individual choice and personal responsibility as key to health and chronic disease – assiduously disregarding the influence of global markets shaping preference and limiting alternatives – liberates people to prosper or to fail according to factors substantially outside their control. It is a freedom which offers the political right to choose health without supplying the economic means through which that choice is made practicable; a freedom which, calibrated against individual wealth and social status, is progressively less available the poorer you are.

A freedom which aims to liberate the collective basis of medical and social care from the control of government in favour of markets risks sacrificing coherence and equity in favour of ideological purity. Healthcare is more than a set of services and transactions. It is a reflection of our social relations – fragmented and self-seeking, or progressive and inclusive. If access to healthcare is a measure of basic fairness and if maintenance of equitable access requires active governance, then this form of freedom requires more, not less, government.

We are, without doubt, living in an era of unparalleled human freedom (Welzel, 2013). We are freer now as a species than at any other time in our history. But it is an incomplete freedom.[14] And at the heart of that incompleteness, nourished by the corrosive force of excess individualism, is the problem of inequality. While we may be free in the aggregate – possessed of global wealth and technological capability unprecedented in human history – our freedom is by no means equitably distributed, within countries or between them.[15]

The individualist model of freedom is generally viewed as indifferent to inequality – or actively receptive to it, as freely interacting individuals prosper or not according to putatively natural capability and merit (Charvet, 1981; Schmidtz and Pavel, 2018). Equality, in this view, is antagonistic to freedom, framed as a kind of enforced sameness among differentially deserving people. But this is a one-sided interpretation – the liberation of individuals for better or worse within social systems over which they exercise only limited control; a freedom which is, as Tennyson puts it, 'red in tooth and claw'. Viewed from the perspective of health, it may be that we have things the wrong way around. Perhaps it is not that freedom comes at the necessary and inevitable cost of social inequality, but that social inequality is itself the last great barrier to human freedom.

A freedom-loving people

Without effective vaccine or treatment, initial national responses to COVID-19 during 2020 relied almost entirely on voluntary or enforced restrictions on social and economic activity. One of the commonest approaches was the imposition of 'lockdown' – the compulsory cessation of work, activity and interaction in public spaces between and among citizens. As a strategy for managing a public health emergency, there are few more complete examples in peacetime of an organised assault on freedom by the state.[16]

Degree of lockdown, speed of imposition from declaration of pandemic, and level of enforceability varied substantially between countries – between a swift, intensive and widely effective model in countries including China, Taiwan, Singapore, South Korea, Vietnam and Rwanda, and a hesitant, fragmented and ambiguously authorised model in, among others, the UK, US, India and Brazil (Allcott et al, 2020; Independent Panel for Pandemic Preparedness & Response, 2021). Policy ambivalence was based in part on the fear of economic loss, and of economic growth and public health as in some basic sense opposed to one another rather than complementary. But it drew also on a deeper notion of freedom – the conviction that people would cleave to their inviolable right to choose a preferred level of exposure to disease, compromising their collective willingness to comply with restrictions.[17]

In the UK, expectations of weak compliance based partly on the dubious notion of 'behavioural fatigue', ultimately disavowed by academics but widely deployed by policy leaders and politicians, resulted in delays in locking down. Over nine days between 14 and 23 March 2020, as restrictions on social activity were mooted, the number of UK cases rose from 200,000 to 1.5 million. There was an institutional belief that the public would not accept heavy control measures. On 12 March, UK Chief Medical Officer Chris Whitty said: "[a]n important part of the science on this is actually the behavioural science, and what that shows is ... that people start off with the best of intentions, but enthusiasm at a certain point starts to flag". Modelling compliance with measures like household isolation assumed a low and unstable rate of adherence: 'These interventions assume compliance of 50 per cent or more over long periods of time. This may be unachievable in the UK population and uptake is likely to vary across groups' (UK Scientific Advisory Group for Emergencies, 2020).

As it turned out, compliance in the UK was extensive. 'Mobility dropped to 15 per cent of the norm during the first weekend after lockdown was enforced' (Jeffrey et al, 2020). In other words, public willingness to subordinate individual freedom for collective good – was extremely high at the outset, although rates declined over following months as incoherent easing, rule changes and localised lockdown were brought in. Astonishingly, the UK's government made a more or less identical error in late September 2020 as a new wave of cases rose. In fact, the onset of COVID-19 stimulated a remarkable display of flexibility in our idea of freedom – public attitudes shifting swiftly from concern about resource scarcity and civil liberties to a sense of shared responsibility and collective purpose (Dayrit and Mendoza, 2020; Pascoe and Stripling, 2020). In the end, political credence in negative freedom shaped a pandemic policy which was, to put it bluntly, fatal. In the UK, delayed lockdown was linked to 20,000 avoidable deaths – a high price for ideological purity (Mahase, 2020; UK/ House of Parliament, 2021). In the first wave of the COVID pandemic, societies able to draw on deeper resources of collectivism appeared to see lower rates of infection than those which clung to the immutable individuality of freedom (Figure 7.1) (Oliu-Barton et al, 2021).

If COVID teaches us anything, it is that the value we attach to freedom is modifiable according to a finely calibrated balance between individual and collective good.[18] Attachment to an absolute form – individualism liberated from the paternalist state – has resulted in hundreds of thousands of personal tragedies. That sense of a balance thrives in conditions of social cohesion, which are reliant on perceptions of social equity. In the end, the freedom required to confront a global pandemic in future will rely on public conviction that the society in which they are asked to participate is to an adequate degree fair.

Figure 7.1: Country collectivism and log of COVID-19 case trajectory

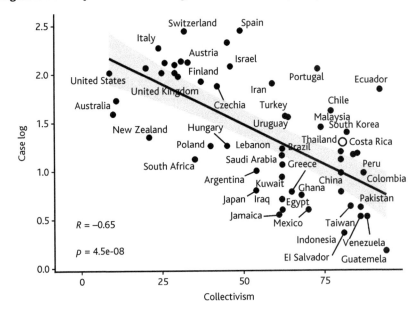

Source: Muthukrishna (2020)

Notes

[1]   Public spending accounted for 71 per cent of health provision across OECD countries in 2017. The principal high-income outlier is the private insurer/provider system adopted by the US, with higher levels of avoidable mortality and lower levels of quality of care (Partanem, 2017; OECD, 2021: data available at: www.oecd.org/health/Public-fund ing-of-health-care-Brief-2020.pdf; www.healthsystemtracker.org/chart-collection/qual ity-u-s-healthcare-system-compare-countries/#item-start

[2]   In low-income countries in 2017, 51 per cent of health spending was 'out of pocket', paid by individuals and households to service providers at the time of use (World Bank data). Unlike higher-income developing countries, the trend in out-of-pocket payments in poorer countries is rising. In Nigeria, India and Pakistan, countries which collectively account for a large proportion of global under-five mortality, the proportion of out-of-pocket healthcare spending in 2018 was 77 per cent, 62 per cent and 60 per cent, respectively (WHO data). See, for example, https://data.worldbank.org/indicator/SH.XPD.OOPC.CH.ZS; www.who.int/data/gho/data/themes/topics/health-financing

[3]   In 2020, weaknesses in public health capacity rendered northern Italian states acutely vulnerable to the early and uncontrolled spread of COVID-19.

[4]   So politically damaging was the impact on inequality that in 2008 the Chinese government announced that the idea that 'the medical and health care system should be market-oriented depending on market forces to meet the medical care needs of the people ... is a wrong concept in the socialist market economy' (*The Economist*, 2008).

[5]   'Public financing is more efficient, protects against medical impoverishment and is the only real option for countries hoping to provide a sustainable healthcare system' (Jamison et al, 2016 see also Sudhir and Ravallion, 1993).

[6]   In 1971, Julian Tudor Hart framed an inverse law of healthcare: 'The availability of good medical care tends to vary inversely with the need for it in the population served. This ... operates more completely where medical care is most exposed to market forces, and less so where such exposure is reduced' (Nambiar and Mander, 2017).

[7]   In the US, improper Medicare fee-for-service payments are estimated to result in losses of USD$12–23 billion per year, or 7–14 per cent of the programme's total cost.

[8]   In the interests of transparency, while I think the arguments for a coherent approach to hybrid private and public healthcare provision are the most likely way forward, I am opposed to the idea of healthcare as profit-bearing. The spectacle of parents watching a child suffer or die for want of money to pay for treatment, still far too frequent a reality, is the hallmark of civilisational failure.

[9]   Notwithstanding massive global variance in capability from the hi-tech tertiary hospitals in New Delhi to Basic Health Units in South Sudan, the underlying premise – a space devoted to physical assistance and service – is universal.

[10] In global opinion surveys, 92 per cent of people in low- and middle-income countries view government as principally responsible for healthcare. Pew Research Center Global Attitudes Survey, Spring 2015. Available at: https://worldpublicopinion.org/

[11] The imposition of a New Security Law by the Chinese government in Hong Kong in early 2020 was a masterclass in the resurgent use of raw power – a widely televised illustration of the fragility of freedom.

[12] 'To me the question whether liberty is a good or a bad thing appears as irrational as the question whether fire is a good or a bad thing? It is both good and bad according to time, place and circumstance' (Stephen, 1874; see also Samek, 1981).

[13] Maintaining and expanding the space for public engagement in policy debates is time-consuming and beset by challenges in countries at all levels of wealth and poverty. If, though, we accept a version of development and freedom delivered to us by an increasingly professionalised political class, without much more aggressive participation and scrutiny, we are poorly placed to complain when the results are underwhelming.

[14] Reflected in the title of Barak Obama's 2020 memoir, *A Promised Land*, published by Penguin.

[15] Momentary events – the manifest injustice of the Grenfell Tower fire in London; the killing of George Floyd in America; the impact of COVID among poor and minority ethnic communities around the world – illuminate, every once in a while, the deep, systematic racial, ethnic, gendered and economic inequalities woven into our daily lives. We are shocked when the mechanics of organised inequality become momentarily visible. We protest, investigate and inquire, eventually wondering whether the original offence was more than a tragic exception, an outlier, a 'bad apple' – gaslit by the bureaucratic turgidity of our process. Tutored to cleave to negative freedom, we end up salami-slicing change

in the minute mitigation of individual abuse rather than asserting the broader principle of inalienable protections; to focus on the individual and the anger, rather than on the structure which supports deeper unfairnesses day after day.

[16] "We have never before seen restrictions as severe, extensive and prolonged as those experienced for most of 2020" (Justice Samuel Alito, National Lawyers Convention Keynote Speech, 13 November 2020).

[17] Boris Johnson: "[O]ur country is a freedom-loving country … it is very difficult to ask the British population, uniformly, to obey guidelines in the way that is necessary" (see Matharu, 2020).

[18] Prime Minister Johnson's forlornly sub-Churchillian formulation (22 September, 2020), "[N]ever in our history has our collective destiny and our collective health depended so completely on our individual behaviour", inverts the reality that, through the pandemic, our individual health depended fundamentally on our collective behaviour.

PART III

Justice

8

The poverty of justice

If justice is the rock on which political civilisations are founded, its currency in public discourse seems oddly volatile (Greenberg and Cohen, 1982). Vernacular interest in justice throughout modern Europe peaks in the first half of the 19th century as revolutionary democratisation, economic industrialisation and evolutionary science engendered new concepts of biological individualism and social causation, merging natural and moral orders with more material questions of capital and labour, productivity and wealth.[1] But its salience wanes over the following century – perhaps under the pressure of early globalisation, as soaring inequality through the *Belle Époque* and the Gilded Age gives way to economic nationalism and the onset of two world wars (Figure 8.1).

Figure 8.1: Frequency of published references to 'justice', English language, 1800–2019

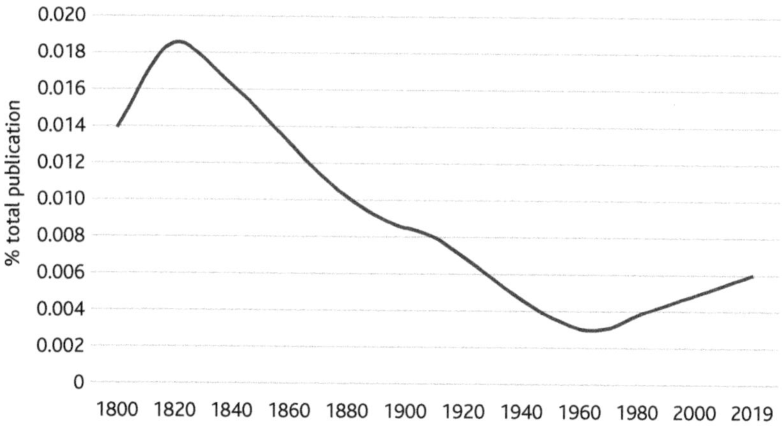

Source: Google Ngram (2021)[2]

That trajectory, particularly in ideas of 'social justice', starts to reverse between 1900 and 1950 – likely fuelled by revolutions in Russia and China and the 'great levelling' of wealth and welfare in industrialised countries following the Second World War; rising faster from the 1960s, as struggles for colonial liberation and escalating opposition to racial injustice in the US combined with feminist, gay and Indigenous rights movements – all in the larger context of socialist and market economic ideologies competing, in cold conflict, for the offer of a better way (Figure 8.2).

Figure 8.2: Frequency of published references to 'social justice', English language, 1800–2019

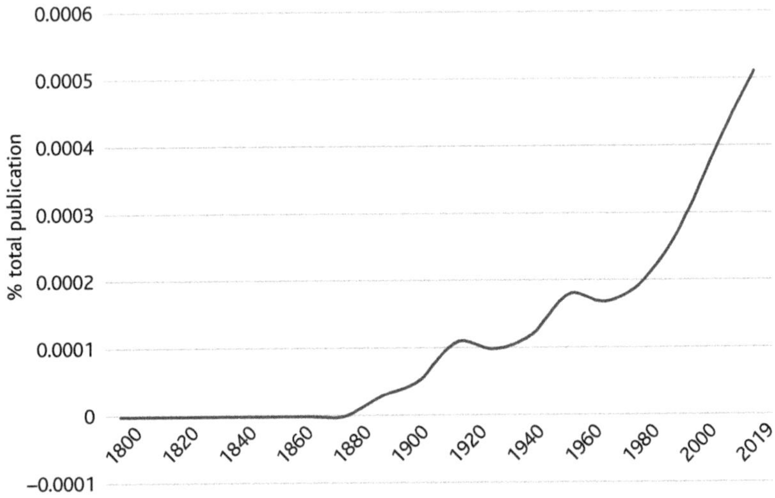

Source: Google Ngram (2021)

The question of 'global justice' emerges more recently, rising sharply in the last 20 years, driven by growing concern for issues whose transnational nature is increasingly hard for states to sidestep, including a new wave of economic globalisation, resource exploitation and trade and the persistent challenges of poverty – all progressively overshadowed by the question of human survival as climate crisis and environmental damage provoke ever fiercer wars of words over science, truth, political liability and the fair distribution of responsibility (Figure 8.3) (Della Porta et al, 2007; Guo et al, 2019).

We know injustice when we see it (Figure 8.4) (Nagel, 2005). Yet our ability to define and agree what it requires, let alone to convert that into reality, seems trapped in a state of permanently incomplete philosophical gestation – rich in concept and contest but poor in concrete practice. Confronted with images of human suffering, we invoke the urgency of humanitarian assistance – little of which, one may argue, does any lasting good. Presented with the manifest divisions of global advantage and disadvantage, we evolve baroque languages of trade, development and diplomacy through which to convert appalling realities into manageable units of often entirely inadequate action (Buchanan et al, 2009).

Social justice, it seems, is always one step removed – either framed prospectively, through the meticulous arrangement of ethical axioms by which to organise the good society, assiduously disregarding thereafter the extent to which we fail them; or offered retroactively, through bureaucratic

Figure 8.3: Frequency of published references to 'global justice', English language, 1800–2019

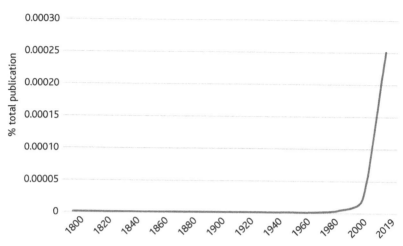

Source: Google Ngram (2021)

Figure 8.4: Mumbai City seen from the slums

Source: Pixabay/ameeq/3 images[3]

processes of remediation for the wrong of injustices already incurred. Between the prospects of a brighter future and compensation for a blighted past we seem to live, in the present, in a world from which justice is persistently, tantalisingly absent. If the arc of the moral universe bends towards justice, we are entitled, eventually, to ask how long it proposes to take – and to ask whether we are doing as much as we can to push it along?[4]

Justice and its limits

Over the last century we have witnessed the rise of rights, inclusion and tolerance enshrined in national legislation, multilateral treaty and global compact.[5] Yet progress towards a greater justice remains limited. The nominal universalisation of women's suffrage has not, to date, produced anything remotely approaching gender equality, whether in public office or private life – from pay, welfare and childcare to reproductive control. In 2015, a woman's earnings were on average 24 per cent lower than a man's 'whilst women around the world do almost two and a half times as much unpaid care and domestic work' (UN Women, 2019).[6] In 2019, one in four seats in national legislatures around the world was occupied by a woman (Shannon et al, 2019) – and the tragedy is, that reads like an achievement.[7]

An estimated one in seven humans living on the planet today has some form of disability – yet communities of disability continue to experience extraordinary levels of exclusion from education, employment, welfare, healthcare, transport and housing (Munsaka and Charnley, 2013; Brown, 2019).[8] Meanwhile, familiar chauvinisms – towards the migrant, the immigrant and the refugee – are busy cloaking themselves in newly sanitised animosities; in clumsily manufactured 'culture wars' designed to drive divisive electoral strategy; and in the resurgence of a vicious moral panic among patriarchies enfeebled in the face of gender transcendence and sexual plurality (Seguino, 2016; van der Vossen and Brennan, 2018; Wang, 2018). Discrimination continues to trace the well-worn contours of class, caste and race (UNDESA, 2020b). Indigenous groups and First Nations, progressively stripped of natural patrimony, cluster at the bottom of index after index (Hernández et al, 2017; Coffey et al, 2019).[9]

Openness in global trade has expanded steadily since 1970, cross-country wealth indices have risen, and extreme poverty has fallen dramatically.[10] Yet deprivation remains deeply entrenched, and inequality is climbing to levels which are little short of catastrophic (Figure 8.5).[11] 'The reality', according to the UN's rapporteur on extreme poverty, 'is that billions face few opportunities, countless indignities, unnecessary hunger and preventable death ... too poor to enjoy basic human rights' (UN, 2020).

Democracy spreads, but dissatisfaction in the last quarter century has risen from 47.9 per cent to 57.5 per cent – disillusion with the failure of equitable opportunity corroding faith in collective enterprise (Foa et al, 2020; Freedom House, 2020). Artificial intelligence promises undreamt-of freedoms in efficiency and leisure while at the same time amplifying machine-learnt bias, accelerating informalisation of just-in-time employment and the casualisation of an increasingly precarious global labour force, weakening decades of progress against coercive and exploitative forms of work (Moore, 2014; Korinek and Stiglitz, 2017; Criado Perez, 2019; De Stefano, 2019;

Figure 8.5: Share of national income accruing to top 1 per cent versus bottom 50 per cent, US, 1980–2016

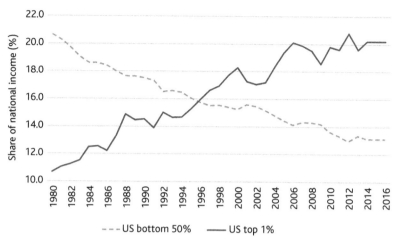

Source: Alvaredo et al (2018)

Vandergeest and Marschke, 2020). While humanity scales ever greater heights of technological mastery, populations around the world watch with growing bewilderment the paralysis of political will to confront imminent environmental disaster, the hammer blows of which are already falling hardest on those least able to protect themselves (Sachs, 2017).[12]

To assert the persistence of injustice is not to discount the waves of social movement, gathering new pace and energy in the last decade or so in impressively creative intersecting strategies of virtual and real-world activism. But it is to challenge the tendency towards a kind of triumphal 'presentism' – the insistence that we should celebrate today because it is so plainly better than yesterday. It is to ask whether we have come as far as the stories we tell ourselves suggest. And it is to point to a woeful institutional complacency in civil and political discourse which calls endlessly and earnestly for justice in the midst of densely woven, minutely orchestrated unfairnesses reproducing themselves with apparently consummate efficiency around the world every day.

There is a kind of cognitive dissonance, today, between the escalating volume of political and philosophical traffic around the question of justice and a world in which justice seems still a distant aspiration – invoked more in proportion to its absence than its realisation, wielded more often by those interested in defining and delimiting its claims than by the people from whose suffering those claims arise. To borrow Pogge's metaphor, we seem more often to be looking for ways to reorganise the game of poker humanity is playing – a game in which some players keep winning and others losing – rather than asking whether we should reject poker altogether and seek another form of recreation. The problem is that human society is not a game that we join on our own terms. We are born into it, on terms set long ago, playing out in intensifying waves of generational advantage and disadvantage. And unlike most games, if we challenge the rules, society reserves the right to exercise violent coercion to secure our continued participation.

Justice, poverty and opportunity

In the history of contemporary political philosophy, two voices – those of John Rawls and Amartya Sen – have come to exert a powerful influence on the idea of justice in social policy. Rawls imagines a just society founded on agreement between hypothetical citizens who, unable to know where they will find themselves in a prospective world, are assumed to arrive at the most disinterested and thus fairest arrangement for all (Rawls, 1971).[13] As a thought experiment, it conjures institutions which are elegant and attractive. But it relies on a form of transcendent human impartiality that is at best implausible, and an idealisation of cooperative agency rarely seen.[14] Sen takes a more pragmatic approach, accepting society as non–ideal and seeking not a world of perfect fairness but one which is simply 'a little less unjust' – a society founded in processes of public deliberation by which citizens agree the fundamental human 'capabilities' required for a worthwhile existence, committing to the provision of essential public goods and services as universal entitlement (Sen, 2009; Venkatapuram, 2011; Meshelski, 2019).

For both Rawls and Sen, human freedom is the end point of justice – and the rational individual is the primary agent of that freedom (Harsanyi, 1980; Samek, 1981).[15] Both prioritise two fundamental objectives in the quest for social justice – that, on one hand, social progress must prioritise reduction in disadvantage among the most impoverished and, on the other, that improving fair opportunity must be the primary mechanism of that progress. Both allow that, where these objectives can be claimed as met, whatever inequality remains is acceptable (Cohen, 2008).[16] Under the circumstances, it is not hard to see how poverty reduction and the creation of opportunity have become central tenets of policy which claims to seek a more equitable human and global development.

Equality of opportunity is preferred as the feasible alternative to equality of outcome which, we are told, given people's natural differences is not only undeliverable but would be problematic to the notion of individual freedom, allowing for an excessively intrusive state.[17] But a reliance on opportunity accepts too readily the surface assumptions of formal institutional process – the idea that simply enhancing the space of notional choice available to all will be enough to overcome the material, social and cultural forces which appear, from one society to another, systematically to help some advance and hold others back.

Opportunity understates the profound power of social status and hierarchy shaping domination and subordination, inclusion and exclusion; the myriad intersecting identities which mould advantage and disadvantage – of nationality, gender, class, ethnicity, race and tribe, all embedded ultimately in the fiendish intricacies of kinship and family, their heterogeneous logic of value and distribution regulated by unparalleled quantities of violence and love (Lucas, 1972; Feinberg, 1974; Reis, 1984; Matsuda, 1986; Nussbaum and Glover, 1995; Sandel, 1998; Okin, 2005; Choules, 2007; Gledhill, 2012). The opportunity model of justice is one which consents too easily to a natural quantum of inequality without adequately challenging the sinuous political forces through which that inequality is unfairly created and sustained.[18]

Justice as a lesser inequality

In the absence of an effective paradigm for social justice, attention has turned to the more practical question of inequality as an economic phenomenon (Shepelak and Alwin, 1986; Young, 1990; Raphael, 2001; Alfani, 2020; Gugushvili et al, 2020; Balasubramanian et al, 2021).[19] This model too, though, struggles to find its moral feet. In the contemporary liberal vision of individualist society, wealth and income are viewed as derived from talent and effort – roundly protected under a fierce commitment to the sanctity of property. As such, difference in people's means is widely understood not just to be naturally occurring, but the expression of a well-functioning society of free individuals.

Normative economic policy recoils from the avoidable imposition of artificial limits on private affluence, or the enforcement of statutory restriction on how much richer the rich can be than the poor. As a result, inequality has become interpreted as, essentially, a problem of those at the bottom of society rather than of society as a whole – on economic inequality as a matter of poverty and on the poor as a kind of residual social category, the unfortunate side-effect of growth whose upsetting presence can be resolved, or even made statistically to disappear, through targeted technical intervention (Kaplinsky, 2005; Moellendorf, 2009; Mosse, 2010; Wesley and Peterson, 2017).[20]

Poverty reduction strategies, broadly speaking, have converged on the objective of expanding opportunity among the poor for social and economic advancement – through redistributive fiscal measures, better and fairer provision of basic developmental goods like healthcare and education, directly subsidised livelihood goods and, in some cases, straight cash transfers (de Barros et al, 2009; Kanbur and Spence, 2010; Milanovic, 2015; UNDESA,

2015; Xu, 2016).[21] It is a paradigm which offers hope that inequality, constituted as basic want, can be remedied without unduly disturbing other, wealthier sections of society; and one which imagines society itself as an open space within which individuals from whichever level can move up (or down) according to merit and fair chance. This seems reasonable so long as advancement is mainly determined by effort or accident undistorted by the resources people inherit or the social and political hierarchies into which they are differently born (Piketty, 2020a). But the 'poverty-opportunity' paradigm fails to acknowledge the extent to which already-existing social inequality, itself, undermines the mobility necessary for the marginalised to break out of their disadvantage. Evidence suggests that the greater a country's level of inequality, the lower its intergenerational mobility – systemic inequality, in effect, locking poorer people into poverty from one generation to the next (Figure 8.6).

Figure 8.6: The 'Great Gatsby' Curve: correlation of economic inequality and intergenerational immobility

Source: Miles Corak (2012)

Over the last 40 years, in high-income and developing countries, social mobility has decelerated and, in many cases, stalled entirely (Commission on Social Mobility, 2018; Major and Machin, 2018; Grigoryev and Pavlyushina, 2019; Präg and Gugushvili, 2020).[22] To continue to invoke mobility as the engine of justice is disingenuous in the absence of greater attention to the deep social factors determining opportunity's outcomes. Social mobility requires the kind of meritocracy rarely realised – or realised in ways which worsen the problem it seeks to resolve.[23]

The poverty-opportunity paradigm overlooks, or studiously ignores, the extent to which individual merit is overwhelmed by the power of social position – the unearned attributes of family, history, inheritance, cultural capital and social status shaping, for example, the extent to which the effects of innate intelligence and education are subordinated to underlying privilege (Figure 8.7) (Feinstein, 2003; Bourguignon et al, 2009; Funjika and Gisselquist, 2020).[24]

Using the World Bank's threshold of USD$1.90 a day, extreme poverty globally fell from 1.9 billion people in 1990 to 736 million in 2015 – from a third of the world's population to one in ten (Development Initiatives, 2019). This is, on the face of it, an extraordinary achievement. But declarations of 'mission accomplished' are premature. For a start, progress was measured against dubious baselines (Jolliffe and Beer Prydz, 2021).[25] And a large part of the reported reduction is attributable to a small set of emerging economies, like India and China. Using an updated USD$2.50 poverty line, and excluding China, headcount poverty worldwide barely changed between 1990 and 2010 (Fischer, 2018; Munoz Boudet et al, 2021).

More importantly, during the same period, far from diminishing, the problem of inequality has evolved in complex and intensifying forms.[26] On one measure, global inequality – assessed as simple difference from richest to poorest individuals – has fallen since 1990. This, though, is partly the artefact of shifting economic power as emerging economy middle classes (mainly in Asia) have raised the world's median income. Meanwhile, the GDP wealth gap between developed and developing countries remains vast. And the difference between the very poor (mainly in Africa and South Asia) and the very wealthy has grown (Goda, 2016).[27] Over the last 20 years, 'the absolute gain in mean daily income of the world's poorest 5 per cent was 7 cents per person, while for the richest 1 per cent it is conservatively estimated at $70' (Ravallion, 2017).

Inequality in high- and middle-income countries has risen significantly over the last four decades. In the US, the CEO-to-worker pay ratio rose from 20:1 in 1970 to 303:1 in 2010. China's Gini coefficient has risen by 15 points since 1990, although levelling off after 2008. Following economic liberalisation in 1991, the share of national income accruing to the wealthiest 10 per cent in India rose from 34 per cent in 1990 to 57 per cent in 2018 (Förster, 2012; Assouad et al, 2018).[28] Inequality in developing countries rose through the 1980s and 1990s, in many cases to dangerously high levels, splintering thereafter in multiple trajectories, demonstrating simultaneously that inequality is not an inevitable feature of economic development – that it can be effectively addressed through well-designed policy – and that genuine

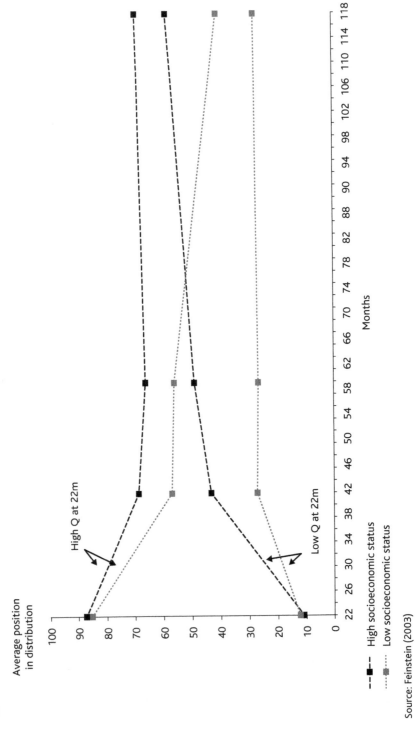

Figure 8.7: Socioeconomic status and cognitive development (Q) in children, 22 months to ten years (1970 cohort), UK

Source: Feinstein (2003)

commitment to confront inequality is still very far from a universally shared political objective (Klasen, 2016; Venkatasubramanian, 2017).

The case against economic inequality should by now be open and shut. It distorts social institutions governing property rights and justice, weakening investment and productivity; it undermines growth and poverty reduction. It tears at social cohesion, and it makes people unhappy (Glaeser et al, 2003; Easterly, 2007; Oishi et al, 2011; van Deurzen et al, 2014; Freistein and Mahlert, 2016; Galbraith, 2016; Bandyopadhyay, 2017; Vandemoortele, 2019).[29] What causes inequality to rise or fall remains a matter of historical debate (Piketty, 2013; Milanovic, 2016; van Bavel, 2016; Scheidel, 2017; Alfani, 2019; De Zwart, 2019; van Bavel and Scheffer, 2021).[30] But it has also become clear that inequality is neither a natural nor necessary feature of human economy nor an inevitable phase of the development process. It is, rather, a political choice – one with which too many countries and governments appear much too comfortable (Cornia and Martorano, 2012; Salomon, 2013).

A supply-side justice

In the end, the poverty/opportunity vision of justice is a rather thin one. It is a justice which remains tied to the orthodox truths of contemporary liberalism and the inviolability of the individual (Alkire, 2002; Detels et al, 2015); which rests on the status quo, abjuring abuses of power but struggling to challenge or change the iniquity of power itself.[31] It is a justice which aims to moderate despair at the bottom of the economic distribution, but not to challenge the nature of hierarchy distorting the shape of society as a whole;[32] which aims to open up access to opportunity, but to reject responsibility for the persistent, structural disparities in life outcome that follow, pushing these back onto the shoulders of the poor and the choices they are assumed freely to make once opportunity has been supplied; one which is defined and shaped at the discretion of the powers that be, through existing systems of governance with limited incentives towards more extensive – and disruptive – forms of equality; and one which is framed, globally, through the calculus of humanitarian dispensation rather than an enforceable community of states interacting through agreed norms and laws.

The result is, ultimately, a 'supply-side' vision of justice, limited to what prevailing power will tolerate, rather than what populations are entitled to demand. Yet a vision of justice confined to the mitigation of gruelling material want at the bottom of the economic distribution is simply insufficient to the task of forming a more genuinely equitable society. A vision of justice fashioned through the notions of individual opportunity and social mobility will continue to fail in addressing and changing embedded systems of identity, hierarchy and power through which the patterning of advantage and disadvantage is sustained, with blinding predictability, from one part of the world to another, one generation to the next.

Notes

1   'Those who study the physical sciences, and bring them to bear upon the health of Man, tell us that if the noxious particles that rise from vitiated air were palpable to the sight, we should see them lowering in a dense black cloud above such haunts and rolling slowly on to corrupt the better portions of a town. ... Then should we stand appalled to know that where we generate disease to strike our children down and entail itself on unborn generations, there also we breed, by the same certain process, infancy that knows no innocence, youth without modesty or shame, maturity that is mature in nothing but in suffering and guilt, blasted old age that is a scandal on the form we bear' (Dickens, *Dombey & Son,* 1848).

2   I recognise that Ngram is an imperfect way of representing global discourse, covering texts in English, French, German, Italian, Spanish, Hebrew, Russian and simplified Chinese but omitting multiple other European and non-Western languages. But it offers a shorthand way to trace trends in language and public interest – without asserting anything definitive in the resulting profile. See, for example, Koplenig (2017) and Zhang (2017).

3   https://pixabay.com/photos/mumbai-slums-poverty-poor-ghetto-5250402/

4   This, reputedly Barack Obama's favourite quotation from Dr King is, in fact, the adaptation of a more equivocal reflection by Theodore Parker in 1853: 'I do not pretend to understand the moral universe. The arc is a long one. My eye reaches but little ways. I cannot calculate the curve and complete the figure by experience of sight. I can divine it by conscience. And from what I see, I am sure it bends towards justice.

5   www.un.org/ruleoflaw/thematic-areas/human-rights/equality-and-non-discrimination/

6   An estimated 70 per cent of frontline workers bearing the brunt of COVID-19 were women, while women made up less than a quarter of pandemic response decision-making roles.

7   The lowest proportion in South Asia and the Middle East (17–18 per cent) and highest in Nordic countries (43 per cent). In 2017, one third of countries offered no legal protection against sexual violence in the home (see, for example, Hirschmann, 2008; UN Women, 2015; Tavares and Wodon, 2018; Khandaker and Narayanaswamy, 2020).

8   The rights, needs and capabilities of people with disability are reported to be being systematically excluded from national planning processes following COP commitments on climate change (McGill Centre for Human Rights and Legal Pluralism et al, 2022).

9   Indigenous peoples, compared with non-Indigenous peers, experience higher rates of heart disease and HIV/AIDS, higher infant and maternal mortality, and lower life expectancy (Curtiss and Choo, 2020).

10   https://data.worldbank.org/indicator/NE.TRD.GNFS.ZS; Legatum Institute (2019).

11   In 1968, income among Black Americans was 60 per cent of Whites, a ratio unchanged in 2008. In 2016, the median net worth of White Americans was USD$171,000, and of Black Americans, USD$17,600 (see, for example, McIntosh et al, 2020; see also Bloome, 2014; *The Economist,* 2020).

12   See, for example, Chelstowski (2012), Stoner and Melathopoulos (2015) and Lopez (2022).

[13] Society designed by individuals operating from behind a 'veil of ignorance' with regard to the status they may expect in the resulting society and thus, in theory, self-protectively inclined to support more equitable distributive norms.

[14] Rawls notes: 'for the most part, I examine the principles of justice that would regulate a well-ordered society. Everyone is presumed to act justly and to do his part in upholding just institutions' (Rawls, 1971).

[15] '[F]reedom of thought and liberty of conscience; political liberties ... freedom of association, as well as the rights and liberties specified by the liberty and integrity of the person; and finally, rights and liberties covered by the rule of law' (Rawls, 1971). 'The success of a society is to be evaluated ... primarily by the substantive freedoms that the members of that society enjoy' (Sen, 1999: 18).

[16] Rawls' 'difference principle' (or 'maximin') permits divergence from strict equality so long as the inequalities in question make the least advantaged in society materially better off than they would otherwise be. This though is vague, creating a broad latitude for the interpretation of acceptable inequality, including significant increase in the wealth of higher-income groups as long as that increase can be construed as the best way to benefit the poor in the long run – a principle which could, in theory, be invoked to defend 'trickle-down' theory. Sen prioritises improving equitable access among the poor to key human development resources like healthcare and education, expanding their opportunity to pursue, as successfully as they can, their personal life goals.

[17] 'Equality of opportunity is ... set up as the mild-mannered alternative to the craziness of equality of outcome' (Philips, 2004: 2).

[18] Emphasis on self-interest also undervalues the idea of sacrifice in how individuals and communities determine a just distribution in complex social relations. Rawlsian justice stops at the water's edge – viable within societies but substantively inoperable between them, insofar as it is only within the nation-state, he believes, that individuals can be viewed as having any kind of moral, statutory – or enforceable – relation to one another. Although in later work he recognises some duty between states (see for example Rawls, 1999), he continues to view difference in wealth and other conditions between countries, assuming basic levels of proper governance, to be morally unproblematic. Others like Sen, Thomas Pogge and Martha Nussbaum take a more cosmopolitan view, arguing that being human is enough to constitute a formal obligation between people universally, notwithstanding that the global architecture necessary for enforcing such obligation is very largely non-existent and prey to the political whims and interests of individual member states (Pogge, 1989). At a global level, their justice, it seems, remains at best optional and at worst illusory – subject to the realpolitik of conventional international relations and reliant, in the absence of a more radical shift towards enforceable global governance, on the capriciousness of humanitarian largesse (Eyal et al, 2013).

[19] Income inequality has been described by Barack Obama as 'the defining challenge of our times' and by Pope Francis as 'the root of social evil'; by the IMF's Christine Lagarde as a major challenge to democratic stability, and by IMF chief Kristalina Georgieva as the harbinger of global calamity (see Christiansen and Jensen, 2019; Qureshi, 2020; UNDESA, 2020a).

[20] According to UNDESA (2020), '[p]overty eradication has been retained as the highest strategic priority of the post-2015 development agenda ... an indispensable requirement of sustainable development and a matter of basic justice and human rights. While high and growing income inequality is fuelling polarised political debates around the globe, a

consensus has emerged that all should enjoy equal access to opportunity.' OECD (2019: 18) argues that '[r]educing absolute, rather than relative, inequalities could be construed as a more realistic policy objective'. In early 2021, President Xi Jinping announced that China had completely eradicated extreme economic poverty – an historic achievement but one using a poverty line of USD$1 a day, aggressive and potentially unsustainable interventions, and occurring against a backdrop of strongly rising inequality.

[21] Although frequently in forms which are flagrantly inadequate to the task of creating meaningful change. Take one example from either end of the global wealth spectrum – the nugatory, but hotly debated GBP£20-per-week uplift in basic income support for poor families in the UK announced as part of the government's COVID-mitigating measures, subsequently removed shortly before the onset of the 'cost of living crisis'; and the allocation of USD$5–8 per capita for an outsourced Basic Package of Health Services in Afghanistan, widely acknowledged to be far below the true minimum cost of provision (see, for example, UNDESA, 2020a; Mir Ahad Saeed et al, 2022; see also Kanbur and Wagstaff, 2014; Kanbur and Vines, 2000; UNESCO, 2014; OECD, 2019).

[22] Although with large regional variation. One in ten adults born in the 1980s in Africa had a higher level of education than their parents, compared with eight in ten in parts of the East Asia and Pacific region (see, for example, Narayan et al, 2018; Sen, 2019).

[23] The idea of meritocracy being originally based on a dystopian satire of education progressively captured by those with status and resources, creating a new kind of elite professional political class. The protagonist of that story concludes: 'No longer is it so necessary to debase standards by attempting to extend a higher civilisation to the children of the lower classes' (Young, 1958; see also Young, 2001).

[24] In a social experiment in India, high- and low-caste children were found to perform equally well on cognitive tests while their caste status was unknown. When asked to reveal their caste, lower-status children performed significantly worse, perhaps reflecting an internalised understanding of the unequal rules of the wider social game in which they were being asked to operate (see Hoff and Pandey, 2004; Platt and Zuccotti, 2021).

[25] Using a threshold aggregating multiple national poverty lines, 'social poverty' has fallen since 1990, but at a much slower pace than absolute poverty.

[26] Inequality rising in China, Russia, India and Indonesia but falling in Thailand, Malaysia and Cambodia; falling inequality across the countries of Latin America, but from a comparatively high level; and a spread of effects in sub-Saharan Africa between falling inequality in Guinea, Mauritania, Niger, Mali, Burkina Faso and rising inequality in Ghana, Mozambique, Kenya, Zambia and South Africa (see Simson, 2018).

[27] See Milanovic (2018) and Piketty (2020).

[28] See, for example, Yang (2002), Li et al (2013) and Jain-Chandra et al (2018).

[29] Richard Wilkinson and Kate Pickett led work on the pervasive effect of inequality on social relations and quality of societal systems (see, for example, Wilkinson and Pickett, 2009).

[30] Social inequality is generally dated from the establishment of sedentary agricultural societies and growth of complex social, administrative and industrial hierarchies. The economic historian Simon Kuznets concluded that inequality follows a predictable trajectory, rising in the early stages of economic development, and falling as political economies mature (Kuznets, 1955) – a theory challenged by resurgent inequality in high-income countries in the last four decades. More recent historical research suggests that periods of rising

economic inequality are punctuated by 'levelling' associated with exogenous shocks such as epidemic disease and war or endogenous processes of social reorganisation. The scale of levelling, however, depends on the quality of prevailing political institutions such that some cataclysmic events are actually followed by increase in inequality. What happens in the aftermath of the COVID pandemic will be an object lesson in this respect.

[31] Rawlsian justice relies ultimately on conventional forms of juridical law and the agencies through which this is enforced. Sen's justice is manifested through the assured provision of capabilities underpinned by fair access to public goods and services – of water and sanitation, nutrition, healthcare, education, labour and employment markets. Yet the extent of provision and degree of entitlement to those goods and services remains substantively defined by the ideological preference and fiscal judgement of the government of the day.

[32] As Guo et al (2019: 522) note: '[G]overnment, as the primary agent of justice, has the responsibility to distribute *basic* social goods to ensure that *basic* rights are met and satisfied ... [to] maintain a *basic* social order to protect citizens' security, provide primary materials for citizens' *basic* survival' [my italics]. But how basic is 'basic'? And who decides?

9

Just health, just care

Unlike wealth, which is mainly instrumental in facilitating other life goals, health represents both instrumental and intrinsic value – the necessary condition of 'normal functioning' and the substance and quality of life itself (Frankena, 1976; Nussbaum, 1999; Rid, 2008; Sen, 2017). As such, health enjoys a special status in the question of social justice.

It is widely agreed that egregious inequality in people's health and lifespan is unattractive, undesirable and even morally offensive.[1] But the idea of an enforceable level of equality in what is widely viewed as a quintessentially fateful human property is equally generally regarded as both practically implausible and unacceptably intrusive in the space of individual freedom (Venkatapuram, 2019). Between the fundamental affront of avoidably unequal lives and the impossibility of strictly equal existence, political philosophy and public policy have struggled – and continue to struggle – with the specific terms of a health justice (Arneson, 1989; Anand et al, 2004; Boylan, 2004; van Raalte et al, 2018).

Rawls rejects health, viewing it as a natural good – a matter of individual luck randomly distributed and thus provoking no question of fairness in distribution.[2] Sen and colleagues recognise health as a key dimension of social justice, but with notable differences in the extent to which society can be held responsible – ranging from supporting the opportunity to be healthy through adequate provision of the basics of human development, but without any guarantee of a healthy life outcome, to an Aristotelian list of social conditions on which health depends, but with diminishing clarity, as the list lengthens, about which public institutions, if any, can be reasonably held accountable for their provision (Daniels, 1985; Sachs, 2010; Sen, 2010; Nussbaum, 2011; Daniels, 2012; Kelleher, 2013).[3]

Loaded with overwhelming ambiguity, the idea of health as justice has become enmired in a kind of ethical no-man's land. At the heart of the problem is an intense uncertainty about physical causation and moral responsibility – uncertainty about how far health is the reflection of individual characteristics or societal arrangements; about how much health and lifespan reflect lifestyle choices or brute luck, and how much they are the net effect of the many intersecting ways society shapes our lives; about how far therefore society, through the state, should take responsibility for difference in citizens' health; about how much of this difference can be defined as inequitable (and by extension unjust), and how much simply the natural variation in people's life chance (O'Neill, 2002; Prah Ruger, 2004; von dem Knesebeck et al, 2016; Fritz and Cox, 2019).

Empirical uncertainty – reinforced by an armoury of linguistic obfuscation – aids governments and policy makers, unwilling or unable to shoulder the mountainous implications for societal reform of a social model of health, to frame health as primarily a matter of biomedical care, and the core offer of health justice (like the problem of economic poverty) on the more manageable task, within and between countries, of improving care services, most urgently among the very poor and sick (CNDSS, 2008; Kriznik et al, 2018; Plamondon et al, 2020).[4]

Justice as healthcare

Healthcare is, evidently, critical for physical and mental well-being.[5] Advancing medical technology and public health have seeded extraordinary improvements in global health in the last century. Miraculous advances are revolutionising technological capabilities – in rapid diagnostic testing, high-resolution imaging and artificial intelligence, robotic surgery, organ replacement and bio-mechanical communication, immunology and immunosuppression, and the exponential growth in genome science and gene editing, building hitherto unimagined capacity for personalised screening, cell-based therapies and regenerative medicine. Immunisation continues to be a global game-changer – development of Ebola and COVID vaccines moving from bench science to mass application in a timespan unthinkable ten years ago. Unprecedented financial and technological commitments under the MDGs and now SDGs have enabled mass expansion of public health programmes, healthcare services and access to therapeutic drugs, radically changing the global landscape for diarrhoeal diseases and respiratory infection, tuberculosis, malaria and HIV/AIDS (Barreto, 2017; Holst, 2020).

Progress has been, in many respects, impressive. In 1950, global life expectancy was 49 years. In 2015, it had risen to 70.5, an increase of 44 per cent – much of it concentrated in poorer developing regions (Goesling and Baker, 2008).[6] Between 1990 and 2015, maternal mortality globally fell by nearly 44 per cent from 385 to 216 deaths per 100,000, the lifetime risk of maternal death declining from around 1 in 73 to 1 in 180 (WHO et al, 2015). Between 1990 and 2019, mortality among children dying before age five fell 59 per cent, from 93 to 38 per 1,000 live births (Figure 9.1; WHO, nd). These are no mean achievements. They reflect historic advances and point to the potential for further future gains. But to what extent do they constitute justice?

Figure 9.1: Proportion of children born alive dying before age five, by global region, 1950–2019

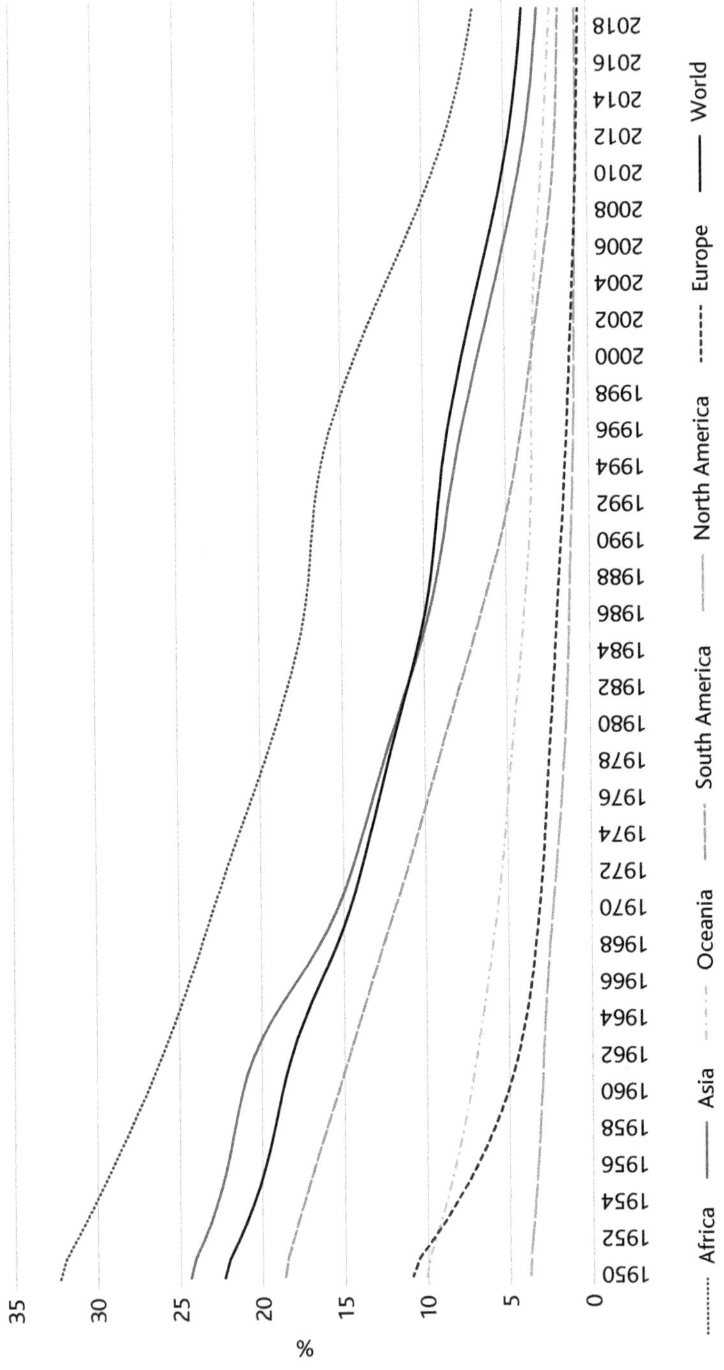

Source: Our World in Data (nd)

.... Africa   —— Asia   ········· Oceania   ——— South America   ——— North America   ------ Europe   —— World

From a bird's-eye perspective, global health appears to be on course for a grand convergence in life chances, drawing to a universal vanishing point health inequality in countries rich and poor. But it is a vision which, like the poverty reduction paradigm, draws on the same dubious interpretation of inequality as basic lack at the bottom of the development distribution (Jamison et al, 2013; Boyle et al, 2015).[7] From the 'worm's-eye view', things are less rosy.

The geographical and social distribution of health remains deeply inequitable (Casas-Zamora and Ibrahim, 2004; Prah Ruger and Kim, 2006; Norheim and Asada, 2009; Benfer, 2015; Yourkavitch et al, 2018; Shawky, 2020; Netter Epstein, 2021). Around 80 per cent of deaths among children under five years of age are now clustered in two regions – sub-Saharan Africa and South/Central Asia. African children are 14 times more likely to die before their fifth birthday than in any other part of the world. In 2015, one in 500 children in Iceland might be expected to die before age five, compared with one in 10 in Angola (Unicef, nd). Developing countries now account for 99 per cent of maternal deaths globally – around two-thirds of these in sub-Saharan Africa. A mother in Sweden has a 1 in 10,000 chance of dying in childbirth. In Chad it is 1 in 16.[8]

In 2018, a resident of Hong Kong could expect on average 32 more years of life than a citizen of Lesotho.[9] There is a two-decade gap in average life expectancy between the highest- and lowest-ranking countries on the HDI, and while global inequality in human development fell between 2000 and 2015, inequality within countries, particularly poorer ones, grew (Nino-Zarazua and Jorda, 2017; Barker, 2020; Permanyer and Smits, 2020).[10] Between 1990 and 2017, relative global inequality in the burden of disease registered an improvement of just 2 per cent (Steinbeis et al, 2019).[11] However impressive in the aggregate, progress is not the same as justice – and should not be accepted as a substitute.

Relying on healthcare as the principal vehicle for health justice is problematic for a number of reasons. For a start, it is a strategy unsupported by the historical record. Major improvements in population health in today's wealthy countries significantly pre-date the wide availability of new medical technologies (Figure 9.2). Those improvements, while amplified by expanding health science and care, as well as the professional socialisation of key public health cadres like nurses and midwives – were driven by change in the distribution of underlying 'determinants' which shape population health – the social, political, sanitary, nutritional, educational and labour conditions of rapidly urbanising communities in the industrialising world (McKeown et al, 1975; Szreter, 1992, 2004). Indeed, it was rapid improvement in mortality in the first wave of now-developed nations, accelerating after around 1860, that drove global progress in the early 20th century, sharply widening inequality in health and welfare between rich and poor regions and inspiring a new agenda for development following the Second World War (Cutler et al, 2006).[12]

Figure 9.2: Global child mortality per 1,000 live births, 1800–2017

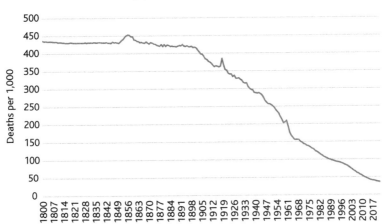

Source: Gapminder (nd)

That agenda – an integrated uplift in the social conditions comprising human development – is today enshrined in the SDGs. Halfway to the deadline, however, progress is variable and the premise of an holistic approach to the determinants of health appears beleaguered (see, for example, UN, 2020; Goalkeepers Report, 2022; UNDP, 2022). Between 2014 and 2019, global food insecurity rose; access to clean water continued to improve, but progress on safe sanitation remained slow;[13] 'slum' populations continued to rise as a proportion of urban residence; labour conditions worsened, in particular for informal sector and younger workers (Schmidt-Traub, 2015; Bhutta et al, 2020; Sachs et al, 2020).[14]

Achieving the full range of SDG targets – many of them determinants of human health – is projected to cost USD$5–7 trillion a year to 2030, costs which may seem feasible in the hyperbolic breathlessness of the multilateral conference but are deeply challenging for resource-poor countries impacted by COVID, shifting international access to aid and credit, and the gathering effects of climate change (Kumar et al, 2016; Vorisek and Shu, 2020). Achieving health through the targets under SDG3,[15] by contrast, is estimated to cost in the region of USD$274–371 billion a year (see, for example, Jamison et al, 2017; Stenberg et al, 2017). Perhaps unsurprisingly, action on global health remains concentrated on action in healthcare, and in particular on realising the SDG commitment to 'Universal Health Coverage' (UHC).

The roots of justice

UHC is a vital commitment in its own right. But as a mechanism for justice, it is confronted by some awkward realities. As healthcare develops, it gets more expensive.[16] As economic societies mature, their population health demands become more chronic, complex and costly. Spending capacity in the health sector today ranges from USD$5,252 per person in high-income countries to USD$40 in low-income ones.[17] For every dollar spent on healthcare in poor countries in 2016, wealthy countries spent USD$130 – a ratio projected to remain at similar levels in 2050 (GBD, 2019). The chances of poor countries and regions 'levelling up' to the scale of healthcare available in the wealthy world, in the foreseeable future, are somewhere between slim and none. In 2017, half of the world's population lacked access to essential health services. In low-income countries, 12 per cent to 27 per cent of people had access to the tracer services by which UHC is measured (WHO, 2019).

Under the circumstances, UHC is confined to a duty on states to ensure equitable access to a minimum level of essential care services. The choice of language – 'coverage' rather than 'care' – is notable, imposing a duty on governments to officiate over provision of care, for example through insurance mechanisms, without necessarily being accountable for the quality or efficacy of the resulting care delivered (Sanders et al, 2019; Rajan et al, 2020). UHC does not secure for people a full range of healthcare services – only those that are defined as 'essential'.[18] What is viewed as essential today in the US or France may be viewed as wholly unrealistic in lower-income countries for decades to come. What is selected as essential by wealthier, more powerful groups in a society may have little relation to the needs or preferences of poorer communities (Chalkidou et al, 2016).

Healthcare has an unfortunate, but quite possibly inherent, tendency to channel and intensify social inequality (Cookson et al, 2021).[19] Provision favours politically networked, wealthier, urban populations – people's ability to negotiate access and maximise benefit of care services shaped by their differential resources of knowledge, status and power. From Ghana and Bangladesh to China and America, social inequalities of geography, gender, race and ethnicity, age, legal status, wealth and education define people's ability to access most major forms of healthcare – from antenatal, maternal, outpatient and secondary referral services, through immunisation and early child development, to treatment for chronic conditions, mental health and access to social insurance (Grintsova et al, 2014; Hosseinpoor et al, 2016; Restrepo-Méndez et al, 2016; Li et al, 2018; Moscelli et al, 2018; Pulok et al, 2018; Abekah-Nkrimah, 2019; Mulyanto et al, 2019; Satinsky et al, 2019; Barasa et al, 2021; Kifle et al, 2021).

Between 2005 and 2015, across low- and lower-middle-income countries, three-quarters of people in the wealthiest quintile had access to essential maternal and child services, compared with 17 per cent in the poorest communities (WHO and International Bank for Reconstruction and Development/World Bank, 2017). In Ethiopia, 90 per cent of mothers in Addis Ababa deliver at a health facility, compared with a little over one in 10 in the geographically remote – and politically troublesome – Afar region. In Nigeria, child vaccination ranges from around 80 per cent in the wealthiest areas to less than 10 per cent in the poorest – from 76 per cent in the southern Anambra State to 5 per cent in northern Sokoto (National Population Commission and ICF, 2019).

Early child development services – critical for long-run life chances in education, employment, family and the onward generational cycle of poverty and disadvantage – are systematically better in wealthier than poorer countries, and within countries among richer urban than poorer rural families. '[C]hildren in the poorest quintile or in rural areas are being left behind and consistently scoring worse on all four indicators of ECD [early child development] than peers in the richest quintile or urban areas. In many sub-Saharan countries, more than half of young children were exposed to stunting or extreme poverty, indicators that have robust associations with poorer status on school learning, labour market productivity and health' (Lu et al, 2020: 9).

Healthcare is a good example of supply-side justice – what is deemed essential, the scale and orientation of investment, the degree of commitment to equality all substantively determined by the provider of last resort, the state or, globally, by the international community. The extent of this justice is shaped by what prevailing authorities determine to be ideologically digestible, socially necessary, economically efficient or fiscally manageable. Take, for example, immunisation. At the start of the 1980s, spurred by the Expanded Programme on Immunisation, rates of childhood vaccination rose dramatically. Once reaching around 80 per cent, however, progress slows to a plateau (Figure 9.3). Between 2000 and 2015, worldwide vaccine coverage rose from 72 per cent to 85 per cent. Between 2015 and 2018, the rate of increase generated little more than an additional 1 per cent.[20]

Reaching every community, every household and every eligible child is one of the great global challenges of immunisation – a challenge in all societies, but acute in countries struggling with limited resources, with populations fragmented by region or ethnicity, fractured by conflict and territorial

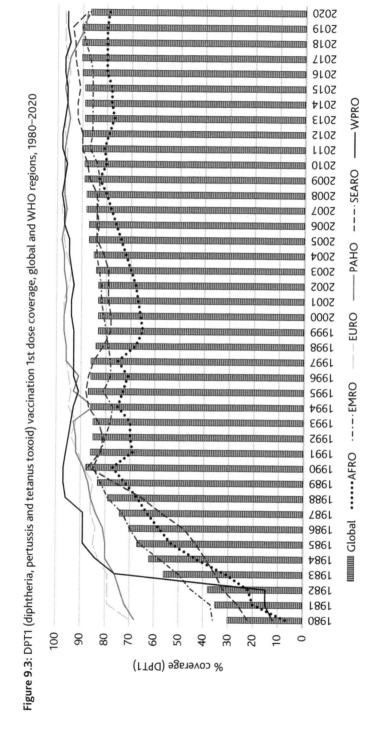

Figure 9.3: DPT1 (diphtheria, pertussis and tetanus toxoid) vaccination 1st dose coverage, global and WHO regions, 1980–2020

Source: WHO Immunisation Database

insecurity, or simply confronted with the logistical difficulties of reaching remote communities isolated by topography. It is also, though, a measure of commitment to justice. The slackening pace of progress certainly reflects increasing difficulty of accessing and engaging with progressively harder-to-reach residual populations. But the extent of the loss of pace at around the point of achieving herd immunity points to the satisfaction of a utilitarian requirement and a marked reduction in the urgency of a more ethical goal. The incremental costs of reaching the one in five missed children – especially in epidemiologically unthreatening, economically unpromising or politically unfriendly areas – appear to outweigh the intrinsic value of justice manifested through a relentless commitment to universal immunisation. Once use-value has been achieved, the equity-imperative appears to fall away.

Strengthening the quality, availability and accessibility of healthcare to all parts of the population in countries across the world – the universalisation of healthcare – is a vital task, and the hallmark of civilised development. But it is the beginning, not the end, of justice. Reduction in absolute health inequalities around the world over the last few decades points to the success we have had in remediating basic human need among the poor. But persistent relative disparities suggest a continuing failure to address the deeper drivers of inequality inscribed in the architectural design of society as a whole (Reidpath and Allotey, 2007). Massive investment in maternal and child health has brought down avoidable mortality in the early years, extending global life expectancy dramatically. But the gap in life chances between society's privileged and poor remains entrenched; and the difference in adult and older-age longevity between developed and developing regions is widening (Liou et al, 2020).

The promise of universal care is progress but inadequate in and of itself in the search for equitable global and national health, a process for which, according to Amartya Sen, much more radical social and economic transformation is required. UHC is justice on a budget – 'the affordable dream', enticing on its own terms yet from the perspective of justice inadequate (Sen, 2015). Successful implementation of UHC would constitute a momentous humanitarian achievement. But it could also be framed as prodigious failure in the face of larger moral questions.

This problem is likely to escalate as societies' technological capacities expand. Advancing health science eventually, necessarily, exceeds the ability of even the wealthiest governments to finance from the public purse. Unwilling, under the liberal market model, to impose limits on privately funded demand, governments preside over the gradual emergence of two-tier systems, encompassing a 'basic' package of statutorily universal care and an upper level of elective treatments affordable only by the socially, economically and politically privileged minority – already the broad reality in most low- and middle-income countries (Lehoux et al, 2018; Abrishami and Repping, 2019; Malbon et al, 2019; Salamanca-Buentello and Daar, 2021).[21] While we reject inequality in healthcare associated with poverty at the bottom of society, we cannot bring ourselves – yet – to repudiate inequality in healthcare associated with wealth at the top. Diverging access to increasingly powerful health-enhancing and life-extending technologies, in the absence of greater regulatory intervention, may lead over time to new forms of existential inequality as an emerging bio-elite quietly detaches itself from the physiologically residual majority.

Concentrating on healthcare sustains a biomedical model of health, medicalising inequality as natural or inevitable physiological difference – enabling policy makers to claim marginal adjustments within the healthcare domain as justice delivered without the trouble of tackling deeper social inequity with commensurately greater risk of ideological, hierarchical or electoral instability (Lynch, 2017).[22] But a focus on technical solutions largely confined within the health sector will not, ultimately, address the dynamics of inequality in health because the causes of health inequity are tied to fairness in the distribution of power across society and between social groups rather than to biological variance and amenability to technological intervention between individuals (Petter Ottersen et al, 2014; Vega and Sribney, 2017).

Notes

[1] Political interest in health inequality has proliferated over the last 30 years. Since the early 1990s, initiatives on health inequality have been launched by the European Union, the UK, the US, New Zealand and Canada; the World Bank, the Pan-American Health Office, EQUINET, the Global Health Equity Initiative, the International Society for Health Equity, and the WHO Commission on Social Determinants of Health.

[2] Rawls takes good health as a given for the individuals in his well-ordered society.

[3] For Sen, states are responsible for providing citizens with the opportunity to be healthy, but not for their health outcomes. Yet, as he notes, '[g]iven what can be achieved through intelligent and humane intervention, it is amazing how inactive and smug most societies are about the prevalence of the unshared burden of disability' (Sen, 2009: 261). Martha Nussbaum outlines the constituent capabilities of human health including: life; bodily health; bodily integrity; senses, imagination and thought; emotions; practical reason; affiliation; other species; play; and control over one's environment (Nussbaum, 2000). But capabilities, like rights, allow for progressive realisation through public process and prioritisation, dependent on the economic means of the supplier state, and thus entertaining potentially large inequalities over an interim of undefined length.

[4] Where Europe favours the language of 'inequality', America prefers the term 'disparity' – a choice which may reflect different ideas of where injustice originates – social class in the Old World, race in the New (Reed and Chowkwanyun, 2012). 'Inequality' is used to describe any difference in health between individuals or groups without reference

to fairness – for example, the sex difference in average life expectancy between men and women. 'Inequity' describes differences which are viewed as unfair – which are 'unnecessary, avoidable or remediable' (Graham, 2009; Braveman et al, 2018). This definition, though, remains open to quite wide political and policy interpretation. In the 1980s, the UK government replaced 'health inequality' with 'health variation', directing attention to quantity of divergence and away from cause (see, for example, Khan, 2015).

[5] Martin Luther King believed that 'of all the forms of inequality, injustice in health care is the most shocking and inhumane'. According to Dr Julian Tudor-Hart, putting the welfare of the sick ahead of all other consideration is probably the most civilised thing we can do. Thomas Pogge views health as a matter of global justice but recognises the contradictory role of global institutions in simultaneously asserting and undermining the rights of the poor.

[6] Overcoming reversals in the 1980s and early 1990s associated with HIV/AIDS in sub-Saharan Africa and post-Soviet economic shock therapy in the emerging Russian Federation. Between 1960 and 2018, life expectancy at birth in high-income countries increased 17.7 per cent, from 68.5 to 80.7 years; by 51 per cent in middle-income countries, from 47.6 to 71.9 years; and by 60 per cent in low-income countries, from 39.7 to 63.5 years.

[7] At the 2013 World Health Assembly, World Bank Group President Jim Yong Kim said: "We can bend the arc of history to ensure that everyone in the world has access to affordable, quality health services in a generation." Global convergence, however, is confined to a specific group of care services, for mothers and newborns, and in the control of major childhood infectious diseases. It omits the growing global burden of noncommunicable diseases and injury, and the much wider landscape of social determinants.

[8] The lifetime risk of maternal mortality in high-income countries is 1 in 3,300. In low-income countries, it is 1 in 41 (World Health Statistics, 2018).

[9] In Hong Kong, 82.3 years and, in Lesotho, 50.5 years. In 1950, the difference in life expectancy at birth between India and Sweden was 35.5 years.

[10] While global food production exceeds 100 per cent of the world's total dietary need, one in six children in low- and middle-income countries is underweight, poorer families suffering proportionally more, and almost half of all under-five child deaths are associated with underlying malnutrition (see, for example, Barros et al, 2018).

[11] In 2017, people in low disease-burden countries lost less than 20 per cent of healthy lifetime to illness while those in high disease-burden countries lost over 70 per cent.

[12] UHC High Level Meeting in New York in September 2019. Heads of state and government and representatives of states and governments 'reaffirm that health is a precondition for and an outcome and indicator of the social, economic and environmental dimensions of sustainable development and the implementation of the 2030 Agenda for Sustainable Development, and strongly recommit to achieve universal health coverage by 2030' (Political Declaration of the High-level Meeting on Universal Health Coverage 'Universal health coverage: moving together to build a healthier world', p 1).

[13] Possibly related to fact that clean drinking water is highly amenable to market commodification while sanitation requires extensive, generally state-led, infrastructural investment.

[14] Conditions which may well deteriorate further in a post-COVID world with intensifying informalisation and new weaknesses in legal labour protection.

[15] The goal dedicated to 'good health and well-being'.

[16] Global spending on healthcare rose to USD$7.8 trillion in 2017, or about 10 per cent of world GDP, up from USD$3.5 trillion in 1995.

[17] From USD$10,036 per person in Switzerland to USD$436 in China and USD$19 in the Democratic Republic of Congo.

[18] SDG 3.8: to 'achieve universal health coverage, including financial risk protection, access to quality essential health care services, and access to safe, effective, quality, and affordable essential medicines and vaccines for all'. Attainment of the target is measured by 'average coverage of essential services including reproductive, maternal, newborn and child health (RMNCH), infectious diseases, non-communicable diseases and service capacity and access, among the general and the most disadvantaged population by 2030'.

[19] The 'inverse care law', formulated by Dr Julian Tudor-Hart in 1971. There is an 'inverse equity law' too – that new healthcare interventions tend to be taken up more quickly and effectively by higher status groups (see Victora et al, 2000).

[20] High-level political forum on sustainable development, convened under the auspices of the Economic and Social Council Progress towards the Sustainable Development Goals: Report of the Secretary-General. 2020 session 25 July 2019–22 July 2020.

[21] See, for example, 'Justice and Access to Health Care' (2008) (substantive revision October 2017). Justice and Access to Health Care (Stanford Encyclopedia of Philosophy).

[22] 'Construing socially- and politically-created health inequities as problems of technocratic or medical management depoliticises social and political ills', Lancet-University of Oslo Commission on Global Governance for Health, 2014.

10

A kingdom of ends

All lives are existentially arbitrary. First by the chance of geography into which you are born and the wealth or poverty of the family you inherit – the ineffable coincidence of you being born you; then by the biological and genetic make-up predisposing you to long life or an early grave, and the lifestyle preferences, choices and accidents that will corral you along that path. Yet in each of these concentric spheres, the ostensible randomness of individual luck and choice masks the deeper systemic effect of political choices and societal arrangements – within countries and between them – shaping the material conditions and level of empowerment into which you are born and through which you grow, learn, earn, age and die.

Between 2015 and 2018, infant death in the United States was 2.3 times higher among Black Americans than White, and three times higher in poorer, rural communities. Risk of maternal mortality was 2.4 times higher for Black than for White American women – 120 per cent higher for mothers in the most-deprived areas (Singh et al, 2017; Singh, 2021). Inequality in life expectancy between rich and poor quintiles in the US has grown in the last three decades from five to 12 years for men, and 14 for women, an effect strongly correlated with race and ethnicity (NAS, 2015; Dwyer-Lindgren et al, 2017).[1]

In the last decade, Washington, DC, Baltimore and Glasgow have seen a 20-year gap in male life expectancy between wealthy and poor neighbourhoods (Marmot, 2015; Matheson et al, 2020). Travelling from midtown Manhattan to the South Bronx in New York City, life expectancy declines by ten years – six months foregone for every minute on the subway (Berwick, 2020). Across Europe, increases in life expectancy have concentrated among the socially and economically better-off; in the UK, longevity in the most deprived areas has stalled and started to fall, widening the gap in life expectancy – a phenomenon not seen since the late 19th century (Leon, 2011; Bennett et al, 2018; Mackenbach, 2019; Marmot, 2020).

Across the world, people with lower social status live shorter, less healthy lives. Poor families experience higher levels of infant and child mortality than their rich neighbours (WHO, 2008; Suzuki et al, 2012). Although inequality in child mortality fell during the MDGs period, in 2015 the rate of child death in poor households was still 12.2 times higher than in wealthier families. Countries with the fastest rates of aggregate child survival improvement also saw inequality along socioeconomic and cultural lines widen (Cha and Jin, 2020).

In China, maternal mortality ranges from 3.4 deaths per 100,000 live births in well-heeled Nanhu District in the eastern seaboard province of Zhejiang, to 830 in ignorable Zanda County on the western edge of Tibet (Li et al, 2017; *The Lancet*, 2020; Crimmins, 2021). In India in 2015–2016, under-five mortality ranged from 7 per 1,000 live births in Kerala to 74 in Uttar Pradesh – maternal, perinatal and child mortality all systematically higher among scheduled castes, tribes and other 'backward' classes (International Institute for Population Sciences and ICF, 2017). In the late 2000s, life expectancy was between 11 and 14 years lower for Australian Aboriginal than non-Aboriginal peoples (Shepherd et al, 2012). Canadian First Nations account for around 4 per cent of the population, but 12.5 per cent of new HIV infections; incidence of diabetes is three to five times higher than in non-Indigenous communities (Greenwood et al, 2018). The rate of suicide, acutely among the young, rises in eerily steady increments (right to left along Figure 10.1), as their sense of control over history and community deteriorates and 'cultural continuity' is lost (Chandler and Lalonde, 1998; Das-Munshi and Thornicroft, 2018).

Figure 10.1: Youth suicide among First Nations by number of factors of cultural continuity

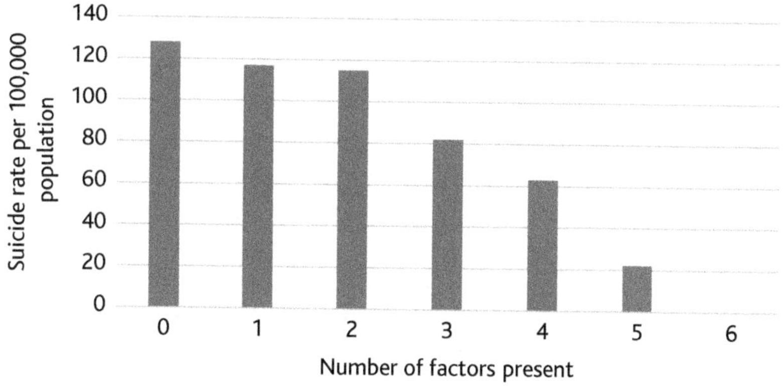

Source: Chandler and Lalonde (1998)[2]

These are not simply failures of opportunity. They are the wholly predictable effects of inequitable opportunity compounded by the unfair distribution, across different social groups, of the capability to convert opportunity into outcome over the whole life course. Equality of opportunity is an insufficient formula for justice. Health is not a matter of moments – 'opportunity' and 'outcome' artificially segmented as separable moments instead of continuous, overlapping cycles of circumstance, choice, luck and effect through which, over time, our lives are determined; the equalisation of people's life chances at some imaginary societal starting line, shaped thereafter by a combination of personal choice and biological fate mitigated by medical care. Health is the expression over time of our biological and social selves – the net of our interactions with one another in a social ecology which is, above all, relational (see, for example, Lundberg, 2020).

Rather than focusing, disproportionately and disingenuously, on individual opportunity, we can better gauge the quality of our social justice by the outcomes we enjoy.[3] A greater focus on outcomes builds a more honest approach to justice – acknowledging that systematic difference between groups arbitrarily defined by identity and social status is indefensible in the just society, recognising such outcomes as the embodiment of multiple, intersecting conditions, or 'determinants' – all of them together, not each on its own, constituting a fundamental failure of fairness for which society itself bears substantive accountability (Marchand et al, 1998; Krieger, 2001; Whitehead and Dahlgren, 2006; Graham, 2009; Olshansky et al, 2012; Singh and Siahpush, 2014; Elgar et al, 2015; McCartney et al, 2019; Sartawi, 2020; Bergen et al, 2021).

The 'social determinants of health' framework (Figure 10.2) offers us a map showing how health inequality is fashioned by the societal conditions in which we live – a heuristic through which we can reverse the order of opportunity and outcome, tracking backwards from right to left – from physical outcome through immediate genetic, biological and behavioural causes, to the material circumstances which modify these, moving further back through the levels of education, employment and income that shape those circumstances, and finally to the forms of governance, politics and policies that set the foundational terms of a society's inequality.[4]

Social determinants research demonstrates – in clinical outcome after clinical outcome, social factor after social factor – a deeply nuanced pattern of advantage and disadvantage lying behind the unequal physical lives we enjoy; a 'social gradient' – the stepwise interaction between people's socioeconomic circumstances and their health (Figure 10.3).

The shape of the gradient illustrates the subtle power of health inequality – presenting not as a simple cliff-drop between general well-being and a disadvantaged minority but rather as a smooth differentiation down the hierarchy – the position of each intimately linked to the positions of others (Powers and Faden, 2006; Marmot, 2017).[5] The ubiquity of the social gradient across countries at all levels of economic development, and the tenacity of the slope as economies mature – modifying in pitch but rarely disappearing – suggests deeper continuities than simple lack of income or medical care in the way inequality is produced (Allen et al, 2017). The implications of the gradient are profound – that health inequality involves everyone in society; that unequal health is rooted in systems of power

Figure 10.2: The social determinants of health conceptual framework

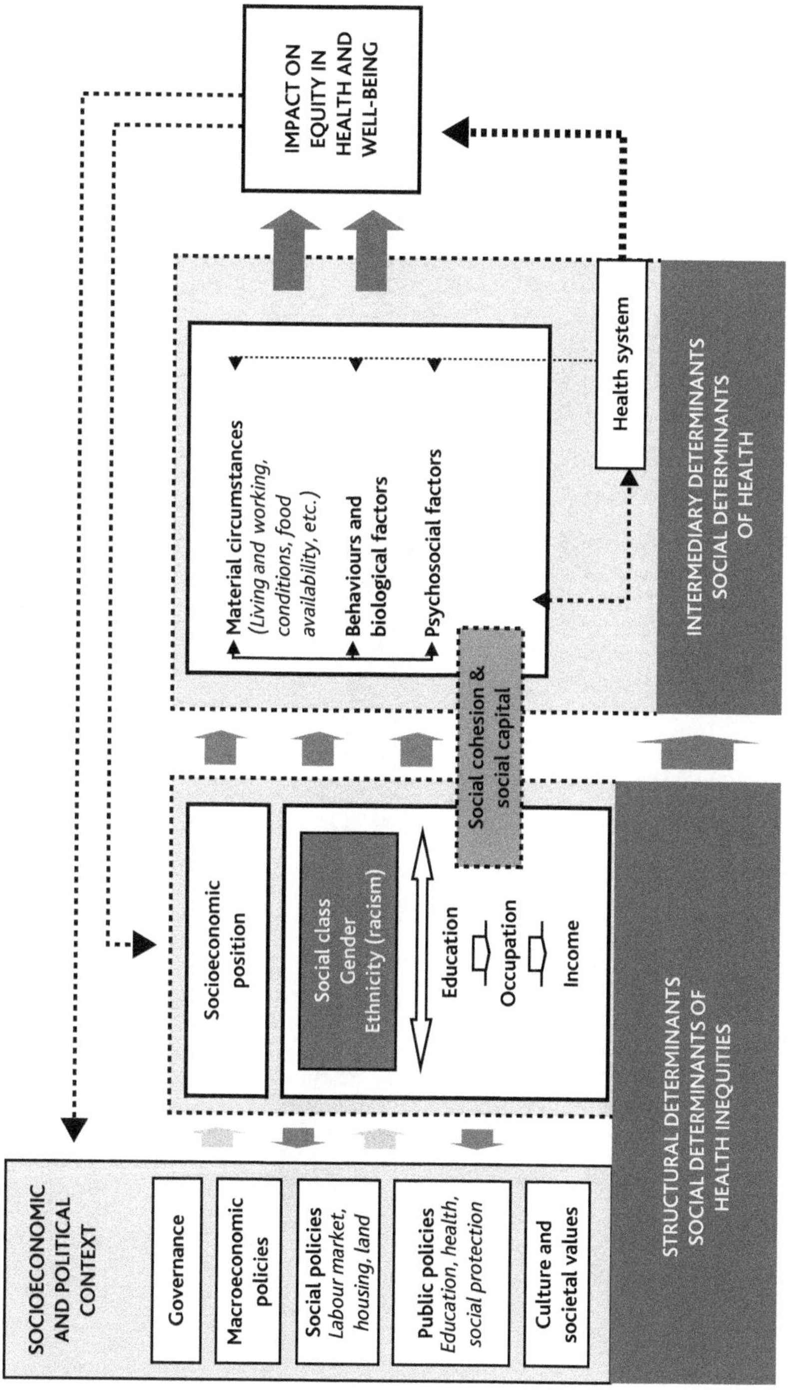

Source: WHO (2010)

Figure 10.3: Female life expectancy/disability-free life expectancy, UK, by neighbourhood deprivation, 1999–2003 and 2009–2013

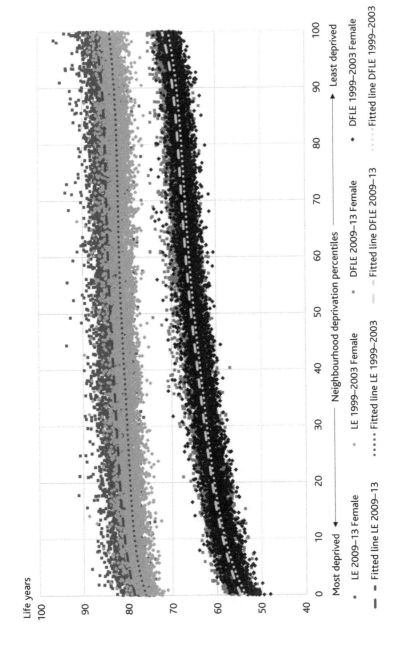

Source: Institute of Health Equity[6]

and discrimination; and that meaningful action thus implies an agenda for reform which is necessarily radical, whose reach extends far beyond the biomedical model.

Around the world, though, action on the social determinants remains muted – policy making caught between the idealisations of health activism and the rigours of academic research which, cleaving to provable evidence of 'downstream' correlations between health, biology and social position leave deeper but empirically murkier 'upstream' effects less robustly scrutinised (Embrett and Randall, 2014; Lucyk and McLaren, 2017; Baker et al, 2018). It is a combination of effects which enables governments unsure about the moral or practical imperatives of inequality to muddy the water, contesting causation or at least sowing uncertainty, and thus moderating often to marginal levels the action deemed necessary for meaningful justice (von Andreas et al, 1998; Clougherty et al, 2010; Lynch, 2020; Nutbeam and Lloyd, 2021).

Reductive approaches to inequality focus on technical fixes within siloed sectors – the mindless insistence on 'quick wins' and an abiding faith in magic bullets; the emphasis on individual manifestations of social status – of gender, race, class or caste – as if independent characteristics which interact discretely with wealth, education, housing, employment and so on; on mitigating specific dimensions of social disadvantage – being poor, being female, being a minority – as if these were hermetic linear effects rather than cumulating facets of the same groups of disadvantage over and over again (Brown et al, 2016; Hernández et al, 2017; Sundari Ravindran, 2017).[7]

Because the determinants of health do not operate in isolated streams. They intersect and interact, reinforcing and amplifying one another. Multiple material disadvantages cluster in the same communities and groups of identity. It is not gender *or* race *or* class that determines socioeconomic status; it is the intersectionality of gender *and* race *and* class acting cumulatively to create systemically entrenched dispossession. Poor households are not simply, or mainly, economically poor. Their disadvantage is plural and overlapping – composed of asset poverty and chronic livelihood insecurity; punishingly poor geographical, residential and housing options; educational marginalisation, oppressive labour and employment relations, inadequate income and marginal space for skills growth – all integrated in a single, continuous organic lived whole, transmitting from generation to generation; and all founded in the single, super-determinant – inequality of power, of voice (Blacksher, 2012; Hicken et al, 2017; Eikemo and Øversveen, 2019).[8]

Viewed through the lens of the social determinants of health, social justice entails a fundamental reconsideration of power – not a marginal shift in the economic status of those at the bottom, nor provisional extension of nominally better opportunity in one or another intermediating determinant. It is an acknowledgement that different life outcomes are neither simply natural force nor technical misadventure, but the embodiment of unequal power, among and between social groups, over the form and function of society itself – the degree to which people believe themselves capable of commanding the social resources necessary to achieve a life which is, and feels, secure; the degree to which people are – and believe themselves – able to participate meaningfully in the decision-making through which such resources are allocated; their sense of agency, not just in accessing better benefits within the status quo society, but of agency in setting – and contesting – the rules by which that society is structured (Gkiouleka et al, 2018; Bond and Singh, 2020; Nedel and Bastos, 2020). It is the recognition that justice entails a change not in the distributive calculus of who gets what but in the formative process of who gets to have an audible voice in deciding – justice defined not by its techniques of supply but by its force of demand (Deveaux, 2018).

Health, knowledge, power

Power is rarely handed over spontaneously by the powerful. Meanwhile, the status quo of supply-side justice has delivered outcomes which are, to date, disappointing. If greater justice depends on a more urgent demand, it will require considerably more organised public engagement and action (Stroebe et al, 2019; O'Neill, 2001).[9] And herein lies a problem.

People generally estimate social position by comparison with immediate reference groups – family members, friends, neighbours – people much like themselves. There is, as a result, a popular tendency to believe that the societies in which we live are more equal than they really are (Hauser and Norton, 2017; Huber, 2017; Knell and Stix, 2017; Gimpelson and Treisman, 2018; Kenworthy and McCall, 2018; Macchia et al, 2019).[10] Moreover, our sense of what is unjust is cautiously calibrated. We view individual disadvantage as acceptable if it occurs in a society we believe broadly equitable, assigning inequality to personal responsibility rather than systemic unfairness (Ku and Salmon, 2013).[11] In the end, the more we believe that the world we see around us represents the distributional norm, however inequitable in reality, the less we will feel justified in pressing for structural change and the more we will be inclined to endorse political and policy agendas which push individual action rather than more radical transformation.[12]

Our expectations of justice are shaped over time, too, by the experiences we bring to the judgement. In resource-poor developing countries, support for improving the simple availability of basic services like healthcare significantly outweighs interest in the fairness with which they are distributed, while in more highly developed countries, where people enjoy comparative socioeconomic security, interest in the equity of public services is stronger. It may be that equality is viewed as a luxury affordable only in countries above a certain level of wealth or, conversely, that justice is viewed as incrementally implausible as we descend the distribution of resources until, in very poor and excluded communities, it is viewed with a combination of humour and despair.

Poor communities – on the rare occasion they are actually asked – show subtle understanding of the social, economic and political factors affecting their unequal life chances. But they are frequently reluctant to acknowledge inequality – possibly to avoid the psychosocial costs of the stigma that comes with it; perhaps as a means of asserting agency in the face of the persistent inferiorisation, cleaving instead to ideas of individual behaviour and personal responsibility as principal causal factors – those most heavily impacted often least able, or willing, to countenance structural explanations for the disadvantages in health they suffer (Popay et al, 2003; Macintyre et al, 2005, 2006; Davidson et al, 2008; Putland et al, 2011; Lundell et al, 2013; Garthwaite and Bambra, 2017; Smith et al, 2017; Smith and Anderson, 2018). Long-run, day-to-day deprivation may undermine people's belief in the possibility of a fairer deal (King et al, 2013). Generations of structural inequality, whether among African Americans in the United States or scheduled castes and tribes in India – perpetuated through systematic discrimination, residential segregation and economic and political marginalisation – in the end normalise the experience of an unequal lot (Fehr and Fischbacher, 2000; Fehr and Schmidt, 2006; Graham, 2008; Trump, 2020; Aldama et al, 2021; Gillispie-Bell, 2021).[13]

Under the terms of liberal socioeconomic discourse, inequality has been successfully positioned in the public psyche as a necessary side-effect of economic function – the key to competitive efficiency, a precondition for progress, and a mechanism through which elite inspiration trickles down in blessings to the lesser mass (Dorling, 2015). Inequality has been established as the appropriate price of recognising individual ability and talent, promoting dynamic economy and protecting property rights (Kluegel and Smith, 1986; Ornstein, 2017).[14] The construction of inequality as the natural human and thus necessary social condition itself feeds parasitically on a deeply held human need to believe that the world is an ordered, stable and hence just place (Feinberg and Willer, 2011; Ahrens, 2019).[15] As inequality deepens, confronting this narrative – challenging the manifestations of injustice and the social system from which it grows – comes with increasingly punishing costs, costs which fall hardest on the most dispossessed, sometimes turning the system's most disadvantaged into its strongest advocates (Kay and Friesen, 2011; Payne, 2017; Jost et al, 2018; Goudarzi et al, 2020).[16]

Conclusion

Justice is not satisfied by the provisional promise of a lesser poverty. Nor will it be realised through the isolated artifice of 'opportunity', endlessly, vomitously parroted by political pundits. Justice, rather, grows out of equitable involvement, by all social groups, in setting collective goals, shaping strategy and monitoring progress – through systems of governance which are meaningfully, genuinely decentralised, with real political, economic, social and fiscal decision-making power devolved to the multiple localities where inequality clusters.

Real social justice, in this sense, grows out of the local – out of the empowered engagement of communities, built into the statutory framework of the state, based on genuine decentralisation and devolution. Not the cynical Potemkin form of 'community development' and local 'resilience' – shifting responsibility for welfare onto people in their own neighbourhoods, while withdrawing the state from wider systems of critical public service; directing communities to adapt internally, drawing cannibalistically inward on dwindling assets, rather than seeking change in the broader structures of power and privilege within which localities of advantage and disadvantage are situated (Popay et al, 2020).

Justice, in this framing, is founded on a much more muscular interventionist approach which confronts and reverses the divergent universes of wealth and poverty; encouraging us to live more closely with one another regardless of identity or means – to experience one another's worlds through active policies of socially mixed housing, education, transport and neighbourhood development; through much more equitable approaches to the infrastructure of physical and virtual interaction; policies consciously designed to break down the segregations of place, colour, religion, wealth which underpin unequal lives (see, for example, Chetty et al, 2022); in communities networked, one with another, between municipalities, across regions.[17]

The just society is one which continuously – intentionally – challenges itself, subjecting its values and the evidence of their impact to unremitting, transparent interrogation; seeking to stimulate rather than manage or stifle public challenge. The society which, by contrast, tolerates inequality and undermines or actively suppresses the evolution of public capacity to debate its policies through informed critical appraisal, cannot claim, regardless of its level of wealth or growth in the aggregate, to be just.

A plague on all our houses

COVID-19 created a landmark moment of clarity about what it means to be a truly globalised species – confronted at all points on the planet by the shared experience of a common enemy, and by the commonality of its consequences across economies, societies and countries. After COVID, we will never – or not for a very long time – look at one another in the same way again. We will never have been so close to one another, nor more distant. The infection has exposed the intensity of our interdependence, and the degree to which contemporary political discourse struggles with the full significance of that fact.

Cataclysmic events – pandemic, war, revolution and financial crash – have historically been accompanied by a levelling effect, with substantial reductions in social and economic inequality. COVID-19 appears – so far – to be going the other route, sustaining and intensifying pre-existing social injustice.[18] We are not 'all in this together' (see, for example, Goldin, 2021). In the UK, age-standardised COVID mortality was 55.1 per 100,000 population in the most and 25.3 in the least deprived English boroughs (with poor areas of London reporting rates upwards of 140, and some affluent postcodes reporting a mortality of zero) (Davenport et al, 2020).[19] The US saw extremely high mortality among Black Americans – making up 33 per cent of the population of Chicago but over 50 per cent of COVID cases and nearly 75 per cent of deaths (with similar disparities reported in Louisiana and Michigan, in Milwaukee and New York) (Krouse, 2020). In Rio, incidence of disease was higher in wealthier neighbourhoods in the first months of the outbreak, but mortality was higher among the deprived as COVID gravitated towards marginal communities (Cifuentes et al, 2021; Silva and Ribeiro-Alves, 2021). Across countries and regions, COVID mortality was associated with level of income inequality (Elgar et al, 2020).

Poorer countries in Africa and Asia appeared, in the initial waves of infection, to evade the scale of impact felt in the wealthy world, the disease engendering a curious form of global compensation for historic injustice. Over time, though, more complete data suggest that age-specific infection fatality rates were twice as high in poorer societies compared with the high-income world (Levin et al, 2022). In any case, by mid-2021 – with vaccine roll-outs moving at pace in high-income countries and a third wave of increasingly infectious variants spreading in a growing body of lower-income countries – the putative advantages of poverty appeared to wane. The true scale of death in the developing world, among swathes of community unregistered in any formal system of governance, may never be fully counted – a posthumous headcount excluded through the great global injustice of unenumerated lives.

Within countries, COVID has illuminated the scale and tenacity of social inequality – continuing, systemic failures of social justice articulated through the familiar set of health determinants. The pandemic amplified intergenerational inequity, killing disproportionately in older age groups while impacting economically most heavily on the young. It struck hard in Black and minority ethnic communities, interleaving vulnerabilities of economic poverty, poor housing, poor health and the additive exposure of low-income frontline jobs (Ewing and Hendy, 2020).[20] Pandemic control measures magnified inequalities of gender and race – hitting hardest the sectors most occupied by working women worldwide, resulting in reduction or complete loss of income, disproportionately intensifying the global precariousness of domestic and migrant workers.[21] In high-income countries, the ability to 'work from home' was concentrated in higher-income households, falling among households with lower education, less skilled employment, and workers in the public sector and social care. In low- and middle-income countries, fewer than one in ten urban jobs could be carried on remotely, lockdown hitting informal sector labour particularly hard (Gottlieb et al, 2021). Social and economic distancing measures pushed the poorest, subsistent households and communities to the edge of survival. The pandemic weakened formal sector employment while the demands of informal sector work weakened pandemic controls (Barnett-Howell et al, 2021).

Between countries, COVID has shattered the rhetoric of global justice. Wealthy countries in Europe and North America led the investment and science that produced multiple viable vaccines in record time, but went on to secure stocks significantly in advance of their predicted needs,[22] leaving many low- and middle-income countries struggling to access anything approaching the stocks they needed and reliant on the WHO-led COVAX global vaccination initiative (Ekström et al, 2021).[23] By the end of November 2020, wealthy countries had pre-ordered or secured options on nine billion doses. COVAX, meanwhile, had secured enough for around 250 million people – far below what low- and middle-income countries needed (*Nature*, 2020). In January 2021, in excess of 39 million doses of vaccine had been given in 49 higher-income countries, with 25 doses delivered in one poor country. By June 2021, around 2.7 billion doses had been administered globally, around eight out of ten in high and upper middle-income countries. Around 1.5 per cent of total vaccine stocks had been delivered across the entire African continent (WHO/AFRO, 2021). Offers by wealthy countries to release 'surplus' stock once their own populations had been fully covered manifested a perfectly proper attention to their domestic obligations, but also a perfect reflection of the provisional approach to global justice which would be comic were it not so morally shameful and epidemiologically incompetent.[24] At the 2021 World Health Assembly, WHO Director-General Dr Tedros Adhanom Ghebreyesus said: "The world is on the brink of a catastrophic moral failure and the price of this failure will be paid with lives and livelihoods in the world's poorest countries."[25] By September 2021, five billion vaccines had been administered worldwide – almost 75 per cent in just 10 countries. Africa, meanwhile, had coverage of 2 per cent.[26]

In an attempt to establish more equitable access, a group of countries with leadership from Eswatini, India, Kenya and South Africa, tabled a proposal at the UN to waive aspects of the Agreement on Trade-Related Aspects of Intellectual Property Rights, allowing low- and middle-income countries to start producing their own stocks using Big Pharma knowledge made openly available as a global public good. High-income countries, including the US, Canada, Norway, the UK and members of the EU, rejected the proposal, ostensibly on two counts: first, that they could not countenance weakening international property law, regardless of the unparalleled global crisis; second, that poorer countries were incapable safely of reproducing the complex vaccine technologies spearheaded by the wealthy world (Engebretsen et al, 2021).[27] The rationalisations of resistant rich countries betray an overriding commitment to knowledge as private property, and a determination to maintain the vast and inefficient inequality in technological capability and production capacity between developed and developing regions based on dubious, and self-reinforcing, premises of poor country absorptive constraints.[28]

But this is just the start of the new wave of global inequity on which COVID shines a harsh light. Even assuming access to adequate vaccine stocks, chronic weaknesses in healthcare systems in many low- and middle-income countries, and massive inequalities in access to basic services including routine immunisation, will impose huge and unequal barriers on mass vaccination delivery, with the lowest performance among the poorest, most marginalised regions and communities. Technical preparations for vaccine distribution are well in advance of the social engagement processes on which vaccine confidence and uptake rely. In Spring 2021, initial assessments of national vaccine preparedness showed that 85 per cent of countries had a national COVID immunisation plan and almost three-quarters had established vaccine safety systems. Only 30 per cent, meanwhile, had developed processes to train the army of locally trusted vaccinators they would need; and one in four had put in place a strategy for social mobilisation and public engagement to encourage people to get vaccinated. Given the extent of vaccine hesitancy emerging in the early phases of global roll-out, associated with distrust of government in communities accustomed to marginalisation, such strategies are going to be vital in ensuring that rising supply is able to connect with adequate demand (Sachs et al, 2022).[29] If global inequality undermines local vaccine access, and local inequality undermines vaccine acceptance, confronting inequality – simultaneously within countries and between them as necessary dimensions of a coherent concept of justice – must lie at the heart of the prospects for success of post-pandemic recovery.

Notes

[1] Between 1980 and 2010, life expectancy at age 50 in the US increased strongly for the richest 20 per cent; flatlined for the middle 60 per cent of Americans; and for the poorest fifth of the population, fell from around 83 to 78.3 years. Race, poverty and geography were particularly strongly associated with inequality in mortality and morbidity from cardiovascular disease, cancer, diabetes, chronic obstructive pulmonary disease, HIV/AIDS, homicide, psychological distress, hypertension, smoking, obesity, and access to quality healthcare (Dwyer-Lindgren et al, 2017).

[2] When all six facets of cultural continuity are present (right hand), rate of suicide is negligible; when all six are lost, the rate is appallingly high – over ten times the global average. Factors of cultural continuity affecting youth suicide include: 'achieved a measure of self-government; litigated for Aboriginal title to traditional lands; accomplished a measure of local control over health, education and policing services; & had created community facilities for the preservation of culture. First Nations youth suicide rates are estimated to be between 5 and 20 times higher than that of the general non-Native population' (Chandler and Lalonde, 1998).

3   To combine the highest possible average level of healthy longevity with the least amount of dispersion around that mean – a formula suggested by Bill Foege, architect of the strategy through which smallpox was eradicated, during a Commission on Social Determinants of Health meeting in Vancouver in 2007.

4   The social determinants of health framework reflects factors as if within a single notional society but recognising the growing influence of transnational and global policy influence.

5   The 'social gradient' is a field of analysis, arguably one of the most important in the understanding of society and health, spearheaded by the work of Professor Sir Michael Marmot, originally based on the Whitehall Studies he led.

6   Data obtained from Office for National Statistics, which is licensed under the Open Government Licence v3.0.

7   For example, politicising debate over the relative contributions of race and wealth in explaining Black/White health differentials in the US, ultimately weakening policy action on both (see, for example, Davis, 2020).

8   'The angry, despairing victims of inequity, and their supporters, marching in the streets of the US despair in part because they and their parents and their grandparents and generations before have been waiting far too long. They find no moral law in evidence, no social contract bilaterally intact. They do not believe in promises of change, because for too long people remain hungry and homeless, with the doors of justice so long closed' (see Berwick, 2020: 226).

9   'Justice has to be realised, even wrested from, imperfectly just states through forms of collective action' (Chandhoke, 2013: 312).

10 Using a variety of large, cross-national surveys, research shows that people consistently perceive a more equitable level of Gini coefficient than is the case in reality (Gimpelson and Treisman, 2018; see also Sen, 2017).

11 When presented in research with the problem of obesity in a highly unequal society, respondents tend to focus on the structural effects of social system, and to support interventions which target inequality. Confronted by the same problem in a society described as relatively fair, people favour measures based on personal responsibility.

12 As part of the scientific secretariat to the Commission on Social Determinants of Health, I remember being perplexed by the absence of mass public rioting by people confronted with the objective evidence of egregious, unnecessary inequality in life's most precious resource (see, for example, Edsall, 2015; Samuels, 2015; Nangwaya and Truscello, 2017).

13 In behavioural economics games, participants appear to favour fairness within the group over individual advancement. Where participants are able to exercise reciprocal control over one another's resources, their preference for fairness rises. Where each player has perceived autonomy, their tolerance for inequality grows. Where power is experienced as collective and shared, people seek to achieve fair outcomes; where it is felt individually, inequality becomes more acceptable. One way or another, our understanding of inequality is deeply linked to our sense of power – or powerlessness – over the social conditions in which we find ourselves (see Luttig, 2013).

14 In Indonesia, almost 50 per cent of survey respondents believed that the poor were so due to 'internal' reasons such as laziness, and that rich people gained their wealth

through hard work (see, for example, World Bank, 2015). Belief in high social mobility and fairness of the economic system in the US reconciles people to large income gaps and a relatively conservative approach to redistribution in public policy (see Davidai, 2018).

[15] People who espouse the 'equal world' worldview experience lower levels of depression and anxiety (see, for example, Lima And Morais, 2015; Hecht et al, 2022).

[16] In the US, low-income groups and African Americans were more likely to believe that economic inequality is legitimate and necessary and were more averse to criticising government; poor Latinos were more likely than wealthier peers to trust government; low-income households were more tolerant of large pay disparities and believed them necessary to foster motivation and effort; poor African Americans in the South were more likely to subscribe to meritocratic ideologies than more affluent African Americans from the North (see, for example, Jost et al, 2003).

[17] Education is key. Where it is deployed parsimoniously as the basis of human capital and labour productivity, its results are predictably narrow and instrumentalised. Education should instead be designed to 'equip individuals with the skills necessary to participate in the social life of their community and to change the nature of the social order as needed' (see Counts, 1978).

[18] *The Economist* Finance and Economics (2021) 'The pandemic has widened the wealth gap. Should central banks be blamed?', *The Economist*, 10 July: In India, in June 2021, Mercedes recorded the highest ever sales of its super-luxury SUV as people choked for want of oxygen outside hospitals swamped by volleys of patients they could no longer treat (see, for example, Subbarao, 2021).

[19] See also Johnson et al (2020).

[20] Women constitute 70 per cent of those employed in health and social work. In the US, people of colour make up 60 per cent of warehouse and delivery workers and 74 per cent of cleaning services workers (see, for example, Paremoer et al, 2021).

[21] In Latin America, women were 44 per cent more likely to lose their jobs than their male counterparts at the onset of COVID-19 (see Heinemann and Beegle, 2021).

[22] Between 150 per cent and 500 per cent of estimated requirement.

[23] At the end of 2020, all of Moderna and 96 per cent of Pfizer/BioNTech vaccine had been acquired by high-income countries. A large proportion of Oxford/AstraZeneca vaccine was expected to be taken up by large middle-income countries like China and India (see, for example, Goodman, 2020; Oxfam, 2020).

[24] Moderna, which received around USD$2.5 billion from the US government, aimed to pitch its vaccine at USD$32–37 a shot (though costing in the end closer to USD$15–18 in the US and EU respectively); Pfizer turned down public finance, spending around USD$2 billion of its own money, but in partnership with BioNTech who received a little under half a billion euro from the German government and the EU, aiming to recoup around USD$13 billion initially at an estimated cost of USD$15–20 a shot; Oxford/AstraZeneca committed to produce and distribute vaccine at cost in perpetuity for low- and middle-income countries (around USD$3–4 a shot). Johnson & Johnson promised to make their single-dose vaccine available at cost during the pandemic at USD$10 a shot. Much of the contractual language in which pharmaceutical companies' pledges to provide at cost limited that commitment to the 'duration of the pandemic' and stipulated the right of the providers to define when the pandemic was over.

25 WHO Director-General's opening remarks at the 148th session of the Executive Board. Geneva: World Health Organization, 18 January 2021. Available at: www.who.int/direc tor-general/speeches/detail/who-director-general-s-opening-remarks-at-148th-session-of-the-executive-board.

26 WHO Director-General's opening remarks at G20 Health Ministers Meeting – 5 September 2021. Rome, Italy, 5 September 2021. Available at: www.who.int/director-general/speeches/detail/who-director-general-s-opening-remarks-at-g20-health-minist ers-meeting---5-september-2021

27 "Now is the time to reject protectionism, the narrow nationalism, and the disinformation that can divide us, and can hinder the response to this common threat. After all, COVID-19 affects every nation. Because we are all human" (subsequently sacked UK Secretary of State for Health, Matt Hancock, at G7, 26 January 2021).

28 In May 2021, the US reversed its opposition to IPR (intellectual property rights) waiver, with more positive noises from the EU and WTO. But by early June WTO talks had once again foundered, with the EU, UK and Switzerland among high-income countries continuing to block progress on movement to a text. In January 2022, the stand-off on the Agreement on Trade-Related Aspects of Intellectual Property Rights was still unresolved, India's request for a ministerial meeting to take forward the proposal for IPR sharing blocked by the EU as 'premature'. In February, evidence emerged of resistance among vaccine-producing pharmaceutical companies to the WHO's programme to build a vaccine production 'hub' on the African continent. By June 2022, member states at the WTO had failed, again, to reach consensus on a vaccines waiver (see, for example, Davies, 2022).

29 According to Vitor Gaspar, director of the IMF's fiscal affairs department, '[p]re-existing inequalities have amplified the adverse impact of the pandemic. And, in turn, COVID-19 has aggravated inequalities. A vicious cycle of inequality could morph into a social and political seismic crack. Unequal speeds of recovery through vaccination, in concert with potentially rising global interest rates associated with large fiscal stimulus, could hit middle- and low-income countries with losses to growth and high debt. See Miller and Curran (2021); Strauss and Wheatley (2021); Noonan and Smith (2021). See, for example, Bibby et al (2020); also World Bank (2021).

PART IV

Security

11

War and peace

The pursuit of security is probably our earliest human instinct – rationalising a willingness as individuals, households, communities and ultimately societies to consent to the concentration of political power in exchange for protection from a world of peril.[1] Security forms the founding contract between citizen and state – constituted for much of the last 250 years primarily as a matter of national defence, legitimising a suite of military, judicial and policing policies deemed necessary to guard against the aggression of other countries and to underwrite the stability of social order at home (Hoppe, 2003; Šulović, 2010).[2]

In the 20th and 21st centuries, 'security' peaks twice in public discourse – in the 1950s, in the interstices between the end of the Second World War and the birth of the Cold War; then again, following the early 2000s and the epoch-shaping aftershocks of 9/11 (Kvartalnov, 2021). Over time, however, the defining character and form of this most fundamental value – what security means, what it entails and, crucially, how it is delivered – has broadened and deepened, becoming in the process both more encompassing and benign and more elusive and sinister.

Confronted by a variety of revolutionary movements across 19th-century Europe, the classical outward-facing notion of military security evolved an inward, domestic counterpart focusing on maintaining social stability by containing public dissatisfaction and, in an associated manner, mitigating extreme forms of popular deprivation.[3] In America, Roosevelt's 'New Deal' and the 1935 Social Security Act – placing novel emphasis on security in the form of jobs, financial and market participation – pre-dated the National Security Act, National Security Council and the formal establishment of a Central Intelligence Agency.[4]

This tension in our idea of security – between national defence and social welfare – is epitomised in a growing compulsion, led by some high-income administrations, to declare 'war' on all manner of ills – criminal and civil, domestic and international.[5] Seeking to build the 'Great Society', Lyndon Johnson launched wars simultaneously on both poverty and crime.[6] Sadly, if predictably, programmes aimed at improving opportunity among economically marginalised, largely African American communities overlapped awkwardly with interventions in enhanced law enforcement focusing on criminal delinquency perceived to originate in precisely the same neighbourhoods. Sweeping cuts to US welfare spending, accelerating through the neoliberal turn of the early 1980s and accompanied by rising investment in domestic enforcement capacity resulted, over time, in one of the most awe-inspiring – or horrifying – paramilitarised police services in modern history, imposing an external order on communities starved of the resources necessary to build the internal cohesion on which willingness to comply is based (Hinton, 2017).[7]

Security: from national to human

On the international stage, the concept of security had started to widen from the early 1970s – from post-war focus on military and intelligence matters to problems of food scarcity and malnutrition, population growth, humanitarian disaster and mass migration, access to energy, environmental degradation and the emerging world of informatics and cybercrime (McInnes and Rushton, 2013; Zwierlein, 2018). Around 1990, with the end of the Cold War and the revelation of a world, beyond bipolar détente, still immersed in poverty and political instability, a new paradigm of security began to form – a vision of international stability organised around the rights-based imperative of protecting the human, the individual person, as much as, or even in preference to, the nation and the state (Commission on Human Security, 2003).

In 1994, the moral urgency of that vision was given concrete form in the Rwandan genocide and the resounding failure of the international community to intervene – both covered in excruciating detail by globalising mass media. Out of the ashes, the UN launched a new paradigm – 'human security' – refocusing the value of security away from defence of the nation and towards protection of the person, away from the militarised value of enforceable strength and towards the social imperative of individual socioeconomic well-being manifested in adequate access to food and healthcare alongside protection from personal, community, political and environmental threats (UNDP, 1994; Haq, 1995). It was in principle a seismic shift, reframing the balance of power between national sovereignty and the universal sovereignty of the rights-bearing individual. And within a few years, the premise of human security – sharper-featured sister to the 'human development' agenda – would be interwoven with the eight great global commitments to millennial development (Kiwan, 2019).[8]

In its origins, human security was clearly, at least in part, a benign attempt to give human development teeth. But beset by absent or hazy definition, its agenda has been subject to widely varying interpretation[9] – a latitude which, critics argue, has resulted in cooption to some highly questionable policy positions (Christie, 2010). By emphasising the responsibility of states to supply their citizens with a basic modicum of survivable socioeconomic development, at the same time asserting the continuity of that security as the inalienable property of all people regardless of location, human security placed in jeopardy the inviolable sovereignty of any government failing to fulfil its developmental mandate.[10]

By shifting security's centre of gravity from the nation-state to the universal person, human security breached the Westphalian principle of non-interference, paradoxically rendering countries with persistently poor performance on indices of individual rights and human development liable to the indignity of legitimate international and ultimately military intervention. Under human security, poverty itself – construed as a threat to stability within countries and between them – becomes a justifying *casus belli* (see, for example, Commission on Human Security, 2003). In a world shaped by a growing maze of interlinking transborder risks, human security merged the state's responsibility to protect its citizens with the international community's right to insist.

Over time, the blueprint for a new more muscular internationalism has gravitated towards the multilateral legitimation of an older national security discourse – developmentally weak states constituted as an existential threat to world order and, through damage to global economic systems, to the material interests of advanced industrial countries, gingerly joined by emerging economies, often through increased participation in multilateral peacekeeping missions, seeking comparable cover for the satisfaction of their own transnational needs (Chandler and Hynek, 2010). Underdevelopment in the form of poverty, marginalisation, vulnerability and inequality becomes, itself, a threat, implicitly presented by the poor world to the non-poor (Duffield, 2001). Security – ultimately enacted through forcible intervention – becomes a legitimate development strategy.[11]

The terrible events of the morning of 11 September 2001 accelerated the conflation of underdevelopment, insecurity and the legitimacy of force projection, as a traumatised America was jolted out of its global unipolar status by the startling reality of an asymmetric world. The subsequent declaration of a 'War on Terror' – never quite clarifying whether the fight was against our own or our enemy's fears – brought us a step closer to the dystopian 'forever war', collapsing the formal notion of the internal and external state, reconstituting insecurity as a pervasive condition, everywhere at all times, justifying the extension of the security state domestically and the possibility of regime change internationally. The War on Terror seeded global confusion – massively strengthening the legitimacy of state control whilst withdrawing the imprimatur of state inviolability; revitalising the discredited 'clash of civilisations', empowering an increasingly militarised frontline between the imaginary forces of darkness and light – the resistance of tradition to the blandishments of modernity – drawn in improbably sharp Manichean lines yet populated by combatant and non-combatant, militant and civilian, merged in a single indistinguishable mass of suspect humanity.[12]

In the following 20 years, a 'development-security nexus' has created a blurry policy space in which divergent concepts vie for dominance – whether global security is better achieved through investment in human development, or development achieved through the enforcement of social order; whether national security comes more readily through the internal resilience of cohesive societies, or through the top-down capability of states to enforce protective measures against attack from within or without; whether security grows out of our social ability to behave cooperatively, or our institutional – and ultimately militarised – capacity to police conformity; whether global security reflects the cooperative architecture of states engaging on equal terms through a system of common purpose and shared rules, or the legitimation of transnational intervention and the enforcement of controls by some on others, largely dominated by countries with the loudest policy voices and the most economically to lose (Gebresenbet, 2014).

Global health security

From the Venetian *quarantina* of the mid-15th century, through the International Sanitary Conferences in 1850s Paris, to the Health Office of the League of Nations in 1923 and the establishment of WHO in 1948, the emerging architecture of global health has coalesced, almost exclusively, around the problem of fast-moving, epidemic infectious diseases and the threat they pose to the security of national and transnational economic activity.[13]

Over time, growing evidence of zoonotic risk – from HIV and rabies, through Creutzfeldt-Jacob Disease and Bovine Spongiform Encephalopathy, to anthrax, avian and swine flu and SARS – inspired increasing investment in an integrated concept of 'One Health Security', drawing together military, security and intelligence communities with those of social development, agriculture, commerce, veterinary and environmental science. Fears of biochemical or nuclear contamination incurred accidentally or otherwise, in the new world of terror rising in the aftermath of the First Gulf War, completed the field of transnational health risks feeding the increasing attention of global policy-setting institutions over the last four decades (Figure 11.1).

But the pattern of attention – sharp peaks of interest and equally steep troughs – speaks to a short-run, reactive cycle of panic and neglect, concentrated on securitising high-income country populations from the

Figure 11.1: Emerging global health governance – G7/8 communications; no. references to health, 1975–2021

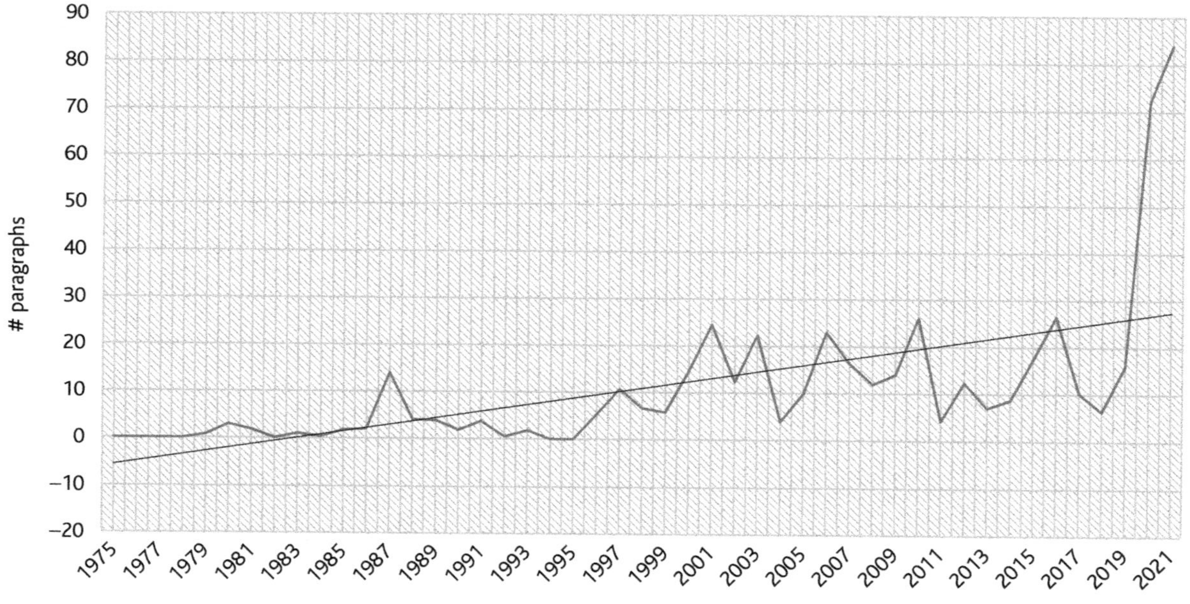

paragraphs

Source: Kirton and Koch (2021)[15]

incidence of risk, protecting people from periodic exterior attack rather the steadier process of building a global resilience from within (Kirton and Mannell, 2005; Schäferhoff et al, 2019).[14] This notion of health security remains firmly anchored in a classical concept of national security and the practices of securitisation – on health characterised primarily as an external threat to the body politic, legitimising a hard security response in the form of monitoring and containment (Stoeva, 2020); a pattern which prioritises control of effect over mitigation of cause; on threat arising in the poorly governed hinterlands of human-ecological interaction, associated with rapid urban expansion and impoverished populations – the condition of underdevelopment itself constituted, once again, as a source of insecurity (Ruger, 2005; Castillo-Salgado, 2010; Rushton, 2011; Gronvall et al, 2014);[16] a security which seeks to protect the political economy of globalisation from the human propensity to disease, rather than to protect human health from the effects of global economic practice (McInnes and Lee, 2006; Davies, 2009).[17]

Securitising AIDS

Emerging in central sub-Saharan Africa in the early decades of the 20th century, AIDS probably originated in the zoonosis of bush meat diets, spreading across borders and through populations within the central region largely undocumented for a good five or six decades before being picked up in a rash of rare lung infections and aggressive cancers among young gay men in Los Angeles, San Francisco and New York in the early 1980s. The origins of HIV are cloaked in the obscurity of Africa's exclusion from history – given name and clinical identity only once arriving in the biomedical heartlands of the wealthy world (De Cock et al, 2012; Faria et al, 2014; Pepin, 2021).[18] The securitisation – and desecuritisation – of AIDS is a case study in the way the dominant practice of global health security has evolved.

The first decade of its enumerated existence was characterised by an extraordinary display of political diffidence rooted in uncertainty about the degree of risk HIV presented, and to whom. Perceived to confine itself to poor African countries and, in higher-income nations, to socioeconomically and culturally marginal groups, public health efforts to raise the alarm were met with governmental ambivalence, confused communication, and quickly proliferating social stigma (Merson, 2006). Gradually, though – initially through the services of the intelligence-gathering community – awareness of HIV as a potential threat to Western security interests began to emerge. In 1987, the Central Intelligence Agency named HIV as one of a group of infectious diseases constituting a threat to domestic security, a position reinforced in 1992 by the US Institute of Medicine,[19] boosted by Laurie Garrett's seminal report *The Coming Plague* in 1994, and in 1996 by Bill Clinton's Presidential Decision Directive on Infectious Diseases and US Security. Four years later, the first US National Intelligence Council report on health linked HIV/AIDS with American national security flowing from falling life expectancy in other parts of the world, and the consequent potential for social instability and conflict (National Intelligence Council/US Government, 2000; Luo, 2002).

By 2000, HIV/AIDS had thrown rising life expectancy across highly-affected African countries into catastrophic reverse (Figure 11.2). Seven countries in sub-Saharan Africa were estimated to have infection rates above 20 per cent of the adult population – some above 30 per cent. Projections – probably in hindsight somewhat exaggerated – suggested that as many as one in four adults in sub-Saharan Africa would die of HIV/AIDS, crippling military and police forces, bureaucratic and administrative functions, degrading productive activities in agricultural production, depleting household income, escalating food insecurity and destroying the social fabric of everyday relationships.[20] Between January and July 2000, 19 years after the first cases were detected in the US, the UN Security Council made history by citing HIV as a risk to global stability, particularly in conflict-affected countries and peacekeeping settings (De Waal, 2010).[21] Confronted by the prospect of widespread social disruption and political collapse, the global community dramatically ramped up its response. HIV was given its own MDG. Management of the epidemic was wrested from the WHO and invested in a new multilateral agency, UNAIDS. New funding mechanisms – the Global Fund for TB, AIDS and Malaria (GFATM) and the President's Emergency Plan for AIDS Relief (PEPFAR) – were launched. Between 2000 and 2005, after a decade of inattention, global action on HIV/AIDS took off (Figure 11.3).[22]

That there has been, in the end, a remarkable humanitarian response to HIV/AIDS is not in doubt. But the form and trajectory of spending point to motives which remain instrumentally linked to the preservation of high-income countries' interests rather more than to the sustainable welfare of people and countries most heavily impacted. First is the large proportion of rising HIV funding allocated to high- and upper-middle-income countries. This may well relate to greater ability to finance and deliver treatment and hence larger cost. But the modest and relatively flat rate of expenditure in low-income countries speaks to a limited concern for wider, longer-lasting welfare that a deeper funding relationship might entail. Second is the proportion of funding allocated to 'care and treatment' compared with the much smaller amount dedicated to 'prevention' (Figure 11.4).

Again, while this may relate to the widening availability, from the mid-1990s, of effective medicinal and therapeutic options, the small and diminishing

Figure 11.2: Life expectancy, world, sub-Saharan Africa and selected African countries, 1960–2020

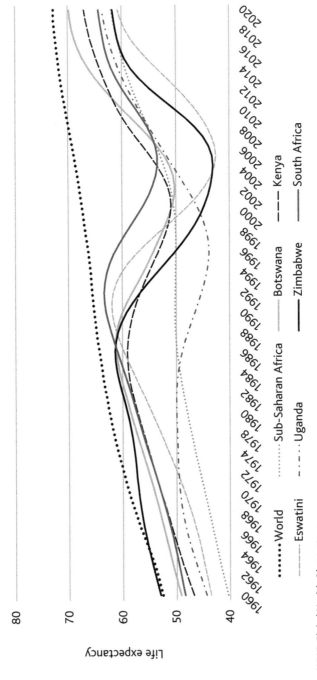

Source: WHO Global Health Observatory

Figure 11.3: Development assistance for health – HIV allocation by source, 1990–2021

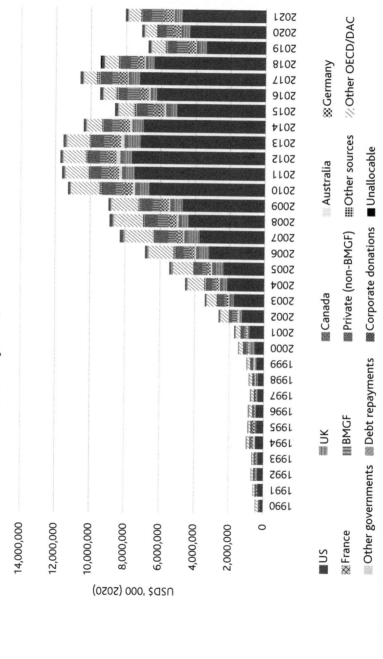

Source: Dieleman et al (2018)

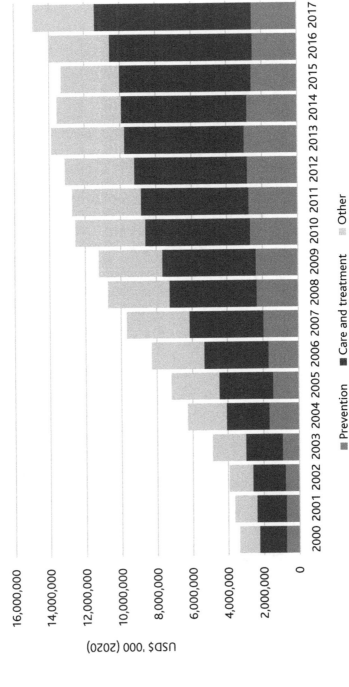

Figure 11.4: Development assistance for health – HIV allocation by function, 2000–2017

USD$ '000 (2020)

■ Prevention   ■ Care and treatment   ▓ Other

Source: Dieleman et al (2018), with updated data generously provided by the Institute for Health Metrics and Evaluation

focus on disease prevention points to a preference for biomedical intervention to control the pathogen over an inclination to fund the development of social resilience to the broader risks and consequences of infection.

And this leads to the third observation. Global funding for, and prioritisation of, HIV/AIDS appears to reach an inflection point between 2010 and 2015. Once under pharmaceutical control, alarm about potentially uncontrolled and fatal HIV/AIDS transmission has started to wane. Once converted through effective treatment from a deadly infection to a chronic condition, and as poor countries take on an increasing proportion of disease control cost, the incentives for continuing engagement among high-income donor countries start to diminish – not because the disease is done with, but because its perceived threat to the national and international interests of a particular group of comparatively powerful economies has been mitigated (UNAIDS, 2022).[23] Investment continues in advancing science – for example the ongoing search for a vaccine – but drains away from support to the development programmes which enhance communities' ability to prevent and manage infection through local, social means (Dieleman et al, 2018; Verrecchia et al, 2019).[24]

North and South

What 'security' is allowed to mean – and how it is enacted – are processes of social, political and technological evolution: from raw national interest to collective global good, from protection through military capability to defence of human welfare; from the brute matter of enforceable control to the more complex challenge of social resilience. How far we have come along this evolutionary trajectory is an open question – a question which is particularly tested under the acute conditions of pandemic disease outbreak.

Global health security mandates a selectivity in our approach to health and human welfare – which kinds of disease we view as threatening to security, and which we view as unfortunate but inconsequential, defines the circumstances in which we are prepared to mount a global response, and desecuritises those with which we continue to live in an uneasy peace (Feldbaum et al, 2006; Newby et al, 2021).[25] Whether we view health security as primarily the protection of domestic and international economic functions, of orderly society, or of human life, significantly shapes the kind of strategy we pursue.

When we choose to identify a disease as a risk to global security, and for how long we maintain that stance, is influenced by our technological ability to exercise effective control over the causal agent – such that energy and attention are focused more on infectious diseases with definable pathogens to attack than on chronic conditions resulting from complex biological processes shaped by individual behaviour and social status. Once a pathogen can be placed under the control of biomedical intervention, it can – as we see with HIV/AIDS – be removed from the health security agenda with whatever continuing ill effect on humans relegated to the 'normal' range of management processes within society. What remains unclear across these fundamental questions is: who defines the terms of a global health security threat, to what extent is there multilateral consensus on these processes and, where there is not, whose voices are decisive (WHO, 2007; Davies, 2019; Kuznetsova, 2020)?

These are questions around which the global policy making community continue to revolve in tense and distrustful groupings. The commonest concern is that global health security is promoted mainly by high-income countries as a means of sanitising a rather selfish instinct – to protect themselves, their peoples and their economic way of life from the risk of massive disruption perceived to be primarily the problem of underdevelopment intermingling environmental exploitation, poverty-driven zoonosis and fragile health systems. Global health security remains a field of struggle between cooperation by all for all, and cooption of the majority to the interests of the few; a framework in which we make each other safe, or we make ourselves safe from each other (de Bengy Puyvallée and Kittelsen, 2019).

Lack of consensus among UN member states on the meaning of 'global health security' feeds fears of hidden agendas and a growing impasse in processes of multilateral coordination and cooperation around global health.[26] Russia, China and France manifested significant behind-the-scenes resistance to the UN Security Council's 2000 resolution on HIV/AIDS on the grounds that health was a problematic matter for arbitration under the rubric of security.[27] The anarchic global response to COVID has revealed the frailty of the liberal order's rhetoric about global health security and collaborative international intent (Patrick, 2020; Gostin, 2021; Malik et al, 2021; Sachs et al, 2022). In the event, the absence of definitional consensus, married to a narrow, reactive model of action, made the collective reversion to a savage protectionist insularity and moralising parochial unilateralism disturbingly easy (Stein, 2003; Heymann and Rodier, 2004).

After Ebola, calls proliferated for a worldwide, militarisable, supranational authority capable of responding decisively to outbreaks of infectious disease. As COVID came under some degree of vaccine-enabled management, the global policy community quickly turned its attention to the establishment of a new global architecture to defend us better next time (Blinken and Becerra, 2021; Nikogosian and Kickbusch, 2021; Wenham et al, 2021).[28] Around the popular idea of a pandemic treaty, a veritable cascade of new institutional ventures contributory to this architecture is forming. But it is an architecture with a particular flavour – profoundly weighted in favour of Northern scientific and managerial oversight; focused on the extension of surveillance implicitly anchored in rich-world capabilities and on the ability (or right) of high-income countries to extend direct access in poorer regions, to acquire and analyse evidence of pathogenic emergence, underpinning public-private collaborations in the research and development of biomedical technologies in response (Levich, 2015).[29]

These institutional formations look very much like an attempt to fortify a global system of surveillance dominated by Northern interests and strengths and – implicitly or explicitly – targeting poorly governed peripheries of social and economic underdevelopment, projecting light into the opaque spaces of rural–urban interaction where global health risk is perceived to cluster; to acquire data about people at risk – to secure access to the interior world of viruses and variants in the bodies of the infected, rather more than to help them create the conditions under which structural risk of infection is itself reduced; to build a kind of epidemiological panopticon[30] – operationalised under the technological superiority of the wealthy world – its gaze directed outward into the obscurities of poverty and inequality, the victim and vector of global health risk that we are not yet ready to properly address.[31]

Notes

[1] The language of 'security' originates in the classical Roman world ('se-curia', without care) as a subordinate condition of the greater concept of 'pax' (peace) – evolving over time from the formation of mutually exclusive territories after the Westphalian settlement of Europe's religious wars through the high-alert détente of the Cold War world to the architecture, after 1990, of multiple domestic and international state interests interacting through an escalating narrative competition over legitimacy, authority and power in a world of disintegrating normative cohesion (see, for example, Bobbitt, 2002; Zwierlein and Graaf, 2013).

[2] Woodrow Wilson believed that security was the necessary foundation of democratic government – a position rendered marginally less convincing by the fact that administrative democracies were responsible for a substantial portion of the estimated 170 million violent deaths during the 20th century.

[3] From Bismarck's prototype welfare state in 1880s Germany, through the UK's Liberal welfare reforms between 1906 and 1914, to Beveridge, Roosevelt and Truman.

[4] The International Labour Organization's 1944 Philadelphia Conference presaged inclusion of social security as a human right in the UN's UDHR of 1948.

[5] Wars on drugs and terror being two notable examples – the first linking criminal and social drugs use and dysfunction in the US with increasingly militarised international cooperation, in particular in Central and South America, the consequences of which are still discernible today in the entrenched logics of state and non-state violence plaguing the region; the second an ineffectual and ultimately counterproductive attempt to impose the hard enforcement of traditional national security on deeply held religious, cultural

and ideological values among individuals, groups and nations espousing often violently anti-Western doctrine.

6   The 'War on Poverty' was announced in Lyndon Johnson's State of the Union speech on 8 January 1964. In the following year, Johnson proclaimed 1965 "[t]he year when this country began a thorough, intelligent and effective war against crime". In March 1966, he concluded: "The war on crime will be waged by our children and our children's children. But the difficulty and complexity of the problem cannot be permitted to lead us to despair. They must lead us rather to bring greater efforts, greater ingenuity and greater determination to do battle" (in Hinton, 2015).

7   The Office of Economic Opportunity was established in 1964 and decommissioned by Ronald Reagan in 1981. The 'War on Crime', meanwhile, enjoyed rising levels of investment, accompanied by escalating rates of extrajudicial killing and mass incarceration, with around 3 per cent of America's population – an indefensibly large proportion of them African American – under some form of penal restraint in the late 2010s (Shrider et al, 2020).

8   Human security – including job security, income security, health security, environmental security and security from crime – cuts across multiple sectors incorporated in the MDGs and SDGs (see, for example, Seidelmann, 2010).

9   'Like other fundamental concepts, human security is more easily identified through its absence than its presence. And most people instinctively understand what security means' (UNDP, 1994: 3).

10   The adoption of the 'human security' paradigm coincided with the tentative emergence of a 'Responsibility to Protect' (R2P) doctrine, following the Rwandan genocide. R2P was and remains a controversial idea, promoted by some countries primarily in the old rich world but repudiated by others. R2P creates a somewhat murky space in international norms incorporating both a state's obligation to protect its citizens with the right – and duty – of other countries to intervene where that initial obligation fails.

11   The post-9/11 interventions in Iraq and Afghanistan are a good example of this – merging objectives of military action, regime change, public security and socioeconomic development such that the failure of human development and rights is itself offered as a justification for war, and war is presented as a necessary route to development and rights (Sovacool and Halfon, 2007).

12   On the 20th anniversary of 9/11, President Biden declared the War on Terror over; the end of 'forever wars'. It is not clear, though, that this entails a withdrawal from the projects of global security – instead perhaps a shift of emphasis from catastrophically misjudged attempts at 'boots on the ground' to more remote technology-enabled management (for example through keyhole surveillance, air power and deployment of autonomous security capabilities) and cooption of local indigenous leaders and forces where needed – a return to the 1970s model of inter-state security placing rights and freedoms in new jeopardy.

13   The European *lazaretti*, originally designed to manage leprosy, were repurposed to control the spread of bubonic plague carried on trading vessels; the Paris conferences focused on epidemic cholera; the Pan-American Sanitary Bureau (PASB), the League of Nations and the Office International d'Hygiene focused substantively on plague, leprosy, cholera, typhus and yellow fever; the original 1969 IHR covered three diseases – plague, cholera and yellow fever; following renegotiation between 2005 and 2007, the revised IHR allow for classification of any transnational health threat as a 'public health emergency of international concern' (PHEIC) – but the list of notifiable diseases remains concentrated

on a subset of fast-moving, highly-transmissible infectious diseases capable of disrupting trade and economic activity between countries and across borders. In 2001, the World Health Assembly (Resolution 54/14) authorised epidemic alert and response, within and between states, as a strategy for global health security. Between 2005 and 2007, WHO member states reformulated the IHR to 'minimize vulnerability to acute public health events that endanger the collective health of populations living across geographic regions and international boundaries' (WHO, 2007).

[14] US health security financing rose from USD$0.1 million in 2013 to USD$133.1 million in 2020.

[15] The graph tracks the volume of documentary output devoted to health in each year's G7/8. While the trend of attention is broadly upwards, it is characterised by peaks and troughs – a pattern of reactive engagement around emergent issues threatening 'home' interests, from the Chair's statement on HIV/AIDS in 1987 stimulated by evidence of escalating global transmission, through the doldrum years of the early 1990s, resurgent interest in the linkage between health and economic growth articulated by the Commission on Macroeconomics and Health in 2001 rising again with the shock of SARS in 2003 and the subsequent renegotiation of the IHR between 2005 and 2007, a lull in engagement after the 2008–2009 global crash, reversed in 2015 by the rapid onset of West African Ebola and topped, in 2020–2021, by the towering shock of COVID-19.

[16] The Global Health Security Agenda – a collaboration of over 70 state and non-state actors established in 2014, focuses on infectious disease risks 'whether natural, deliberate or accidental', The Global Health Security Agenda 2024 Framework (ghsagenda.org); the Global Health Security Initiative, including Canada, France, Germany, Italy, Japan, Mexico, the UK, the US and the European Commission, with WHO as observer, focused initially on biological, chemical or radio-nuclear terrorism, with pandemic influenza added subsequently, Global Health Security Initiative – Global Health Security Initiative (ghsi.ca). In 2019, G20 Ministers of Health agreed to focus on health threats caused by: acute infectious diseases, biological or chemical agents, environmental or nuclear factors and other emergencies which 'pose a significant risk not only to public health but also to national and global security and stability as well as sustainable and inclusive growth'. Okayama Declaration of the G20 Health Ministers, Okayama, Japan, October 20, 2019; http://www.g20.utoronto.ca/2019/2019-g20-health.html. The UK's first National Security Strategy, published in 2008, focuses on bioterror and infectious disease, particularly pandemic influenza – partly explaining its unpreparedness for coronavirus a decade later (see HM Government, 2008).

[17] See for example the World Bank's ill-fated attempt to incorporate pandemic risk within the global financial system. The Pandemic Emergency Facility (the 'Ebola Bond') aimed to attract private capital to finance pandemic responses around the world, by selling a bond into the market. Simplified to its basics, the bond stipulated that if, over a defined period (say, three years) a pandemic outbreak did not occur, investors got their money back with interest (around 12 per cent). If a pandemic did occur, their money was forfeit. Hindsight is a wonderful thing – but the flaws in this model might, in the design phase, have been seen from space. The key, of course, is defining when a pandemic occurs, and who gets to control that definition (a situation equally crucial during COVID, in determining contractually when pharmaceutical companies providing new vaccines could shift from a concessionary to a profit-making model). The Pandemic Emergency Facility proposed to use mortality thresholds – releasing 30 per cent of the fund at 250 confirmed deaths in two or more countries; 60 per cent at 750 deaths; and the final tranche at 2,500 deaths. Two problems are immediately apparent. First, interested parties might well attempt to

influence the interpretation of mortality data to mitigate the likelihood of a pay-out (a relatively easy task in the context of many chronically weak national health information systems). Second that, in the nature of fast-moving infectious diseases, pay-out *following* confirmed deaths is likely to be too late. In 2019 the World Bank put the Pandemic Emergency Facility on ice (see, for example, Grépin, 2015; Brim and Wenham, 2019; Erikson, 2019; *Financial Times*, 2020; Commission on a Global Health Risk Framework for the Future, 13 January 2016).

[18] A history of HIV's early transmission within and then beyond the African region was reconstructed through genetic mapping using archival blood samples whose preservation was as often as not simply a matter of luck (see, for example, Gilbert et al, 2007).

[19] A judgment disregarded by George Bush Sr.

[20] International Crisis Group (2001). In 1998, one in seven civil servants in the South African government were thought to be HIV positive (see *New York Times*, 1998). In Angola and the Democratic Republic of Congo, estimates of HIV prevalence in police and army services were as high as 60 per cent (see, for example, Hsu, 2001).

[21] 'AIDS is not just a humanitarian crisis. It is a security crisis – because it threatens not just individual citizens, but the very institutions that define and defend the character of a society.' US Vice-President Al Gore, chairing UN Security Council meeting, 10 January 2000. UN Security Council Resolution 1308 (2000) on the Responsibility of the Security Council in the Maintenance of International Peace and Security: HIV/AIDS and International Peace-keeping Operations.

[22] Dieleman et al (2018). In 2002, the Alberta G8 committed to eradicate the disease, and at Gleneagles in 2005 announced unprecedented commitments of additional finance (Global Burden of Disease Health Financing Collaborator Network, 2020).

[23] 'The idea that global health security only refers to prevention and protection against diseases that might kill people in rich countries is neither moral, sustainable nor practical. Will we allow COVID-19 to become, like we did with HIV, TB and malaria, another lingering "residual pandemic" we care much less about because it only kills the poor? Or will we take COVID-19 as the catalyst to rethink what we mean by global health security?' Peter Sands, Executive Director, Global Fund for Aids, TB and Malaria (Sands, 2020). See also 'Why the HIV epidemic is not over' (www.who.int/news-room/spotlight/why-the-hiv-epidemic-is-not-over).

[24] See, for example, MSF (2018).

[25] Overweening concentration on epidemic disease displaces a more integrated concept of human health, suppressing attention to a range of issues from maternal mortality, through the absurdly titled 'neglected tropical diseases' to noncommunicable conditions and the global scourge of poor mental health. I asked a senior health official in Kinshasa on one occasion what his top three priorities were. He answered: "Family health, vaccines and malnutrition." When I asked him what his budget was spent on, he smiled and answered: "AIDS, TB and malaria."

[26] The Review Committee on the Function of the International Health Regulations on Pandemic Influenza (H1N1), 2011 concluded: 'Although WHO has a broad mandate to share urgent information on public-health events, [it] usually obtains agreement first from the affected State Party. The process of consulting with States Parties may delay posting on the EIS [Event Information System]. There is an inherent tension between WHO's obligation to inform other States Parties and the affected State Party's interest in avoiding potential social

and economic consequences' (IHR Review Committee, 2011: 54). In 2015 the Ebola Interim Assessment Panel, appointed by the WHO Director General to examine the organisation's performance during the 2014 outbreak in West Africa, noted a deliberate intention by the states most affected by the outbreak to delay their own government-issued reports while denying outbreak reports from non-state sources (see, for example, Davies, 2020).

[27] Following the 2003 SARS outbreak, an attempt led by high-income countries to revise the IHR, authorising greater access to affected countries under enforceable multilateral mandate was viewed as an attempt to contravene norms of national integrity and sovereignty and the move was rejected. During the renegotiation of the IHR between 2005 and 2007, the idea of 'pre-emption' advanced by high-income countries – allowing punitive action on states performing poorly on global health reporting requirements – was rejected by the majority of other states. When Portugal attempted to introduce the language of 'global health security' as overriding other legal provisions in the draft text of a multilateral consultation on influenza viruses and benefit-sharing, it was rejected by a group of emerging economies including Brazil, Thailand and India as unendorsed language (Aldis, 2008; see, for example, Shashikant, 2007; Rushton, 2010).

[28] 'World leaders urge for global treaty to protect countries from pandemic', 30 March 2021: "[To] build a more robust international health architecture ... lead[ing] to more mutual accountability and shared responsibility, transparency and cooperation ... to improve alert systems, data-sharing, research and local, regional and global production and distribution of medical and public health counter-measures such as vaccines, medicines, diagnostics and personal protective equipment" (WHO, 2021). The Independent Panel for Pandemic Preparedness and Response called for a 'high-level global council on health threats' and a global platform to support development and distribution of drugs, vaccines and medical supplies (see, for example, G20 High Level Independent Panel on Financing the Global Commons for Pandemic Preparedness and Response, 2021; Independent Panel for Pandemic Preparedness and Response, 2021).

[29] Including, *inter alia*:

- The Working Group on Strengthening WHO's Health Emergencies Preparedness and Response and a 'Group of Friends' of Solidarity for Global Health Security.
- The G7 Therapeutics and Vaccines Clinical Trials Charter.
- The 'Europe Horizon' EU-Africa partnership to support research and deployment of new pandemic technologies.
- The European Commission Health Emergency Preparedness and Response Authority 'incubator' to advance understanding of pathogen variants, vaccine adaptation and clinical trials, and the partnership between European and African Centres for Disease Control focusing on surveillance capacity and harmonisation of disease intelligence between the continental regions.
- The 'EU-FAB' Initiative on emergency production of vaccines and drugs in Europe.
- The European Investment Bank platform for private sector investment in health security and resilience on the African continent.
- The German Vaccine Production Task Force and financing for a new WHO Global Hub for Pandemic and Epidemic Intelligence based in Berlin focused on epidemic surveillance, intelligence and data analytics.
- Canadian investment in domestic mRNA vaccine production capacity.
- A UK-sponsored International Pandemic Preparedness Partnership to accelerate development of vaccines, therapeutics and diagnostics.
- The Australian Centre for Disease Preparedness focusing on animal and human disease protection and biosecurity responses.

- Germany's One Health Research, Education and Outreach Centre in Africa (OHRECA) at the International Livestock Research Institute.
- France's PREZODE (PREventing ZOonotic Diseases Emergence) to detect and prevent emerging zoonoses.
- The UK–US partnership on Epidemic Forecasting and Outbreak Analysis.
- The joint Australian/Japanese initiative supporting ASEAN's Centre for Public Health Emergencies and Emerging Diseases to strengthen cross-border surveillance and contact tracing, the South Korean Support Group for Global Infectious Diseases Response and the Northeast Asia Cooperation Initiative for Infectious Disease Control and Public Health.

See, for example, Hemm and Johnson (2021).

[30] The 'panopticon', developed in the 18th century, was a new model of prison design. Promoted by Jeremy Bentham, its annular architecture rendered all prisoners permanently visible to a single, central guard station, creating a new kind of relationship of knowledge and control between captor and captive (see, for example, Foucault, 1975).

[31] 'First, SARS-CoV-2 thrived on inequality. There is no serious discussion about the way this virus exploited deep disparities across societies and why attacking these disparities must be part of preparedness planning. Second, COVID-19 is a disease that normalised inequity – for testing, vaccines, and now antivirals. There is no sense of urgency to advance equity. And third, COVID-19 is a zoonotic disease. There is no recognition that preventing a pandemic means redefining the relationship between humans, wildlife, and the viruses that pass among us' (Horton, 2022: 1853).

12

The risk society

As societies modernise, the landscape of risk becomes ever more complex. What were once thought of as low-probability/high-impact events like nuclear war, biological terrorism, environmental catastrophe or pandemic disease[1] merge with more localised perceptions of social instability, criminal disorder and cultural decline, compounded by the daily pressures of increasingly precarious economic subsistence, eventually forming a framework whose actuarial probabilities are incalculable to the individual. Our growing demand for security becomes, in the end, rooted in the sense of being permanently insecure; our appetite for safety progressively rationalising the surrender of individual agency, ceding local autonomy in favour of top-down, state-centralised protection (Beck, 1992; Ekberg, 2007; Furedi, 2008; Kaldor, 2018).

The evolution of health security focuses, similarly, on the defensive control of diseases by enhancing centralised capacity to monitor and manage the interaction between population and pathogen; investing in hard enforcement capacity to exercise disciplinary control over citizens rather than engaging with communities to leverage the power of social cohesion and collective public action on which sustainable security is based (Cialdini and Goldstein, 2004).[2]

The Global Health Security Index (GHSI), launched in 2019, is designed to assess countries' pandemic preparedness.[3] Its metrics, though, privilege technical functions – of surveillance, detection and biomedical response – over softer dimensions of the citizen-state relationship such as trust in government, density of civil society, or quality of health communication networks (Mahajan, 2021). Measures relating to 'biosecurity and safety' weight the index in favour of high-income countries. Emphasis on institutional capability – in surveillance and laboratory systems, epidemiological and clinical workforce, as well as wider conditions of poverty and political instability – skew ranking in favour of more developed regions, offering false comfort to higher-scoring high-income countries and a greater latitude for enforcement in lower-scoring poorer states (Abbey et al, 2020; Razavi et al, 2020). In 2019, the US and UK topped the GHSI league table of pandemic readiness.

In the event, though, GHSI ranking had little to do with how COVID was managed. In an analysis of 100 countries with complete data for the first wave of the COVID pandemic, a higher GHSI score was associated with greater rates of infection; and no correlation was found between GHSI position and rate of population testing (Aitken et al, 2020). In the end, the US, at the top of the index, led the world in rates of COVID cases – its formidable arsenal of technological and pharmaceutical capabilities hobbled by simpler but less measurable failures of political leadership, coherent healthcare and public faith in systems of governance.[4]

The sociology of disease

A fundamental problem with the contemporary paradigm of health security is that it values urgency of technical capability over depth of social engagement, seeking – acutely in the context of large-scale pandemic outbreaks – to operationalise sophisticated systems of surveillance and intervention but failing to engage with the more nuanced sociological relationship between people and their pathogens.

Diseases have personality, social character – a combination of, on one hand, transmissibility, severity and amenability to treatment and, on the other, popular perceptions of the threat they entail, mingling narratives of physical causation with moral attribution of responsibility. Each pathogen forges a new epidemiological, biomedical and social relationship with its human host, inspiring new forms of scientific and social knowledge, its profile shaping the way it is perceived, the extent of public demand for intervention, and the level of tolerance for resulting control measures (Fee and Fox, 1988; Baum et al, 1997; O'Manique, 2005).[5]

Unless strategies for health security are carefully tailored to the sociological profile of an emerging disease, the impact of control measures will be at best partial and at worst lethally counterproductive (Bardosh et al, 2020). Imposing control on disjointed communities risks effects which are ultimately exclusive and divisive, delivering a version of security which is unstable, unsustainable and often incrementally oppressive. Where outbreak controls attempt to close down high-value cultural practices without adequate dialogue, compliance will likely be limited, and where enforced will provoke suspicion, anger and ultimately violence (Crouse Quinn and Kumar, 2014); where pandemic interventions are invoked without accounting for social and economic functions critical to survival among poor households, a simple cost-benefit analysis – in which poor families are necessarily expert – will easily justify resistance; where government proclaims a health emergency among communities accustomed to generations living on the societal margin, the uptake of alarm may be expected to be muted at best; where it advises more stringent health practices among people whose access to wider medical care has, over decades, been a grim lottery of high cost and poor service, such advice is likely to be met with scepticism at best.

Where pathogens exploit pre-existing faultlines of social inequality, manifesting aggressively in marginalised groups, a hard model of top-down securitisation oriented to responsibilising and managing identity and behaviour can feed narratives of blame, exacerbating fragmentation, legitimising stigmatisation, and creating in the public mind a confused combination of complacency and fear fatal to the cohesion and cooperation on which genuine security depends; where security measures fail to engage with underlying social dynamics, their effects will likely be inequitable and weakly effective. The four epidemic vignettes making up the body of this chapter illustrate some common problems with the hard model of health security.

HIV/AIDS

HIV/AIDS occupies a unique position in the annals of global health security – the archetypal modern plague and the pandemic that never quite was.[6] With its capacity for years-long latency, evasive genetic mutation and powerfully suppressive social stigma, HIV presented a challenge to the urgent timeline of the health security paradigm. The response, over four decades, follows a telling arc: from overwhelming policy ambivalence shaped by the perception of HIV as a modest risk confined to marginal economic regions or social groups;[7] through rapidly escalating attention and finance, dominated by high-income countries gripped by a dawning sense of HIV's potential to undermine political stability within societies and economic interaction between them; culminating finally in a renewed decline in interest and money as effective antiretroviral therapies became sufficiently widely available to ensure protection for mainstream social groups, converting the disease – for those with the wherewithal to access treatment – from fatal infection to chronic condition.

From the early 1980s – notwithstanding a growing coalition of citizen and civil society movements demanding action – an insidious articulation of HIV with notions of social deviancy limited perception of mainstream risk, weakening the incentives for public policy engagement. From China and India to South Africa and Brazil, AIDS was widely framed as a problem of foreigners, aliens and morally marginalised minorities (Solomon and Ganesh, 2002; Gauri and Lieberman, 2004; Yan Zhong, 2005).[8] In the US, media messaging was dominated by public reassurance for the mainstream majority, interspersed with short bursts of alarm as the suspicion of wider population spread started to emerge (Colby and Cook, 1991; Singhal and Rogers, 2003).

As the epidemic grew, policy pronouncements in wealthy countries – focusing on high-risk behaviours but grounded in a strategy of universalising fear – led to fragmented public understanding and multiplying narratives of origin, causation, infection and responsibility, interweaving scientific fact with folk interpretation, empirical reflections on exposure and risk with spiritual fears of pollution and death (Ford and Quam, 1987; Bishop et al,

1991). Around the world, ambiguous and contradictory communications fed widespread uncertainty, resulting in high levels of support for mass enforcement measures including quarantine and criminalisation – and an unsurprising upsurge in stigma and widely legitimised public hostility to those viewed as responsible (Kathleen and Field, 1988; Allard, 1989; Nelkin et al, 1991; Ramasubban, 1998; Gostin, 2001; Herek et al, 2002; Ekstrand et al, 2012).[9]

During the 1990s, with compelling global evidence of mainstream (for which read heterosexual) spread, communication focusing on social and behavioural change largely concentrated on modification to sexual relations – primarily abstinence, delayed sexual activity and condom use – with limited realistic attention to the inequality in gendered power through which those relations are played out.[10] Social change, in any case, was progressively overshadowed by an emphasis on individual viral status – on 'voluntary testing and counselling', the necessary informational basis on which roll-out of newly developed therapeutic treatments could be planned (Taggart et al, 2021). Confidence in pharmaceutical intervention quickly dominated major AIDS funding strategies to the extent that treatment came to be viewed as the most efficient route to prevention – biomedical management of the virus gradually marginalising change in the social, political, economic and cultural drivers of infection (Figure 12.1) (Fee and Krieger, 1993; Siplon, 2002; Seckinelgin, 2007; Whitacre, 2021).[11]

Figure 12.1: President's Emergency Plan for AIDS Relief (PEPFAR) expenditure by technical area, 2005–2011

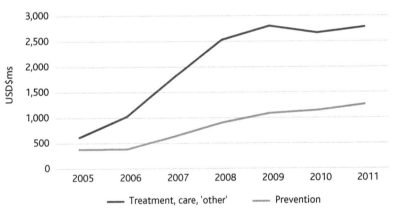

Source: Author's calculations[12]

The global response to HIV/AIDS was, in many ways in the end, an unprecedented expression of technical, pharmaceutical and financial power (Fauci and Eisinger, 2018).[13] But it is one whose disproportionate attention to a single disease drastically skewed wider investment in comprehensive public health; one which focused, first, on the exceptionalisation and containment of marginal risk groups and then on protecting the mainstream from risk rooted in and arising from social marginality; one which substituted pharmaceutical control for the harder task of building social resilience, failing to engage with the underlying social structures, relations and attitudes that create and sustain HIV risk and impact in disempowered and marginalised communities – addicts and substance abusers, men who have sex with men, gay and transgender people, migrants and immigrants, Africans, women (Daniel and Parker, 1993).

Forty years into the global pandemic, as effective therapy mitigates its existential threat to society, AIDS starts to sink once more below the horizon of a health security issue, as if the job is done. But the security with which we are left is an incomplete one. It is a security for the majority achieved without the inconvenience of challenging or disrupting the inequitable social norms that created the marginal communities of risk in the first place – communities still afflicted by stigma and discrimination, now hardening in many parts of the world into newly emboldened restrictive policies and laws, sustaining their exposure to risk, impeding their access to treatment and care, loading them anew with the burden of social and economic exclusion consequent on being positive (Earnshaw et al, 2013; Grossman and Stangl, 2013; Stockton et al, 2018; Sullivan et al, 2020).[14]

Zika

With a primary mortality rate close to zero and comparatively mild symptoms, Zika is an unusual candidate for global health security. First identified in primates in Uganda in 1947, Zika has been associated with sporadic outbreaks in humans in Africa and Asia but, prior to 2016, had attracted only limited attention as one of the class of arboviruses which includes the considerably more lethal dengue and chikungunya (Harris et al, 2016). In October 2015, however, following a rash of children born with microcephaly in and around Pernambuco, northeastern Brazil, the country declared a national emergency. By February 2016, WHO had agreed a public health emergency of international concern (PHEIC). Over the course of the year, between 400,000 and 1.3 million cases of Zika were recorded across South, Central and North America.

In the immediate instance, the Zika emergency appears to have been prompted not so much by what was known about the virus but by what was not – an unnerving lacuna in the centres of global health policy as to what the outbreak meant, what it presaged: the parameters of syndromic interaction between infection and birth defect, and the degree of risk to the pregnant mother and baby in that interaction; uncertainty compounded by a disease vector which moved swiftly, widely and quietly (Maurice, 2016; Kelly et al, 2020; Oliveira et al, 2020).[15] There is every reason to support an emergency global intervention which seeks to clarify the potential effect of a particular virus on public health. But the short timeframe of the Zika emergency – declared over within nine months of its start – suggests priority given to the process of data gathering and diagnostic analysis, resolving the shortfall in epidemiological knowledge, over more grounded investment in mitigating local effect (McCloskey and Endericks, 2017).

On the ground, in affected countries, the emergency was enacted through public policy actions which sought to securitise two principal threats: mosquitoes and women – one constituted as the source of disease, the other as the source of its effect. Primary prevention focused on environmental intervention, advocating enhanced domestic hygiene and removal of standing water, complemented by neighbourhood fumigation, to reduce insects and bites – the familiar model of sanitising poor communities in the absence of any more structural improvement in the material conditions of urban and periurban poverty.[16] More problematically, the securitisation of Zika was sought through modification in the reproductive behaviour of women – the socioeconomically marginal rendered as biologically culpable.[17] It was an emergency which instrumentalised women – advocating urgent changes to sexual activity and family planning – without acceding to the profound social, economic, political and cultural constraints placed on their agency (Davies and Bennett, 2016; Jamrozik and Selgelid, 2018). It was an emergency in which women – and more particularly poor women of colour – were simultaneously constituted as victim of the vector and vector of the effect (Wenham et al, 2019; Wenham, 2021).

The health security response to Zika was mandated through global processes seemingly carried on far from the immediacy of the lives of the most affected. It was implemented through sterile interventions visited upon communities rich with gendered inequality and profound poverty. The period of the emergency may well have been sufficient to secure global knowledge *about* Zika but fell far short of the time it takes to challenge norms of gender and reproduction through which it operates, shifting the dial in favour of more equitable action. The implicitly punitive focus on reproduction – exacerbating potential for gendered conflict while failing to strengthen meaningful access to female control – seems more likely to have nourished than alleviated the extensive pre-existing fragility of rights and inequality of power.

Ebola

Ebola is the stuff of nightmares. First identified in 1976 around an eponymous river in Central Africa, Ebolavirus disease had, until recently, confined itself within isolated rural African localities, killing its dead-end human host sufficiently rapidly to limit long-distance transmissibility – its propensity for the *grand guignol* rendering it for much of the last 50 years a kind of *Heart of*

Darkness horror happening somewhere over there, to be witnessed but not intruded upon. In 2014, all that changed.

In December 2013, an 18-month-old boy from a Guinean village was identified as the index case of a new Ebolavirus disease outbreak. This time, though – capitalising on the increasingly dense social linkages of West Africa's economic development – Ebola made it to the city, spreading to Conakry by mid-March of the following year, and from there tearing down the customary cultural, familial and commercial arteries of the Mano River Basin to neighbouring Liberia and Sierra Leone by July. Two and a half years after the first case was discovered, the outbreak ended with more than 28,600 cases and 11,325 deaths.

For around five months from confirmation of initial reports, the international community – spearheaded by the WHO's Geneva headquarters – appeared to vacillate (Philips and Markham, 2014).[18] It was only in August that the WHO's Director-General, Margaret Chan, secured a PHEIC declaration. Warily eyeing the prospect of societal collapse and state failure in one of Africa's most unstable regional patchworks of national and ethnic identity, the UN Security Council issued a resolution on 18 September declaring Ebola 'an international threat to peace and security' (Security Council Resolution 2177 – UNSCR). The day after, operational control of the international response was removed from WHO and placed under a newly established 'UN Mission for Emergency Ebola Response', answerable to the Department of Peacekeeping rather than the coordinating office for humanitarian affairs.[19] After a lethargic start, action accelerated. Stung perhaps by the prospect of infections spreading towards the wealthy world,[20] mobilisation took an emphatically militarised form, landing heavily on affected localities and drawing on a conventional suite of technical controls inadequately tailored to the complex social factors through which their efficacy would be mediated.[21]

In a context characterised by chronically poor governance and deep and persistent poverty, hard lockdown measures with limited preparatory communication provoked fear and anger. Public infection control, administered by frightening cohorts of bright yellow biohazard-clad aliens, turned the potential for crucial public engagement into fear and evasion (Kamradt-Scott et al, 2015; Marais et al, 2015; Woodall, 2016; Wenham, 2017). Families' efforts to secure assistance from local health facilities quickly turned ugly – health systems dilapidated over years of conflict and disinvestment resulting in poorly resourced and insanitary clinics becoming, themselves, centres of transmission, further degrading already fragile trust in public services and in government viewed as accountable (Heymann et al, 2015; Hasan et al, 2019).

A combination of public health advisories and behavioural enforcement attempted to mitigate disease transmission by modifying social interaction, without adequately understanding or addressing the underlying drivers and incentives of local practice – restricting geographical mobility during periods of agricultural trading critical to households' income, food security and survival; reconfiguring intricate mourning, preparation and burial practices as processes of incineration for the purposes of poorly understood infection control; and proscribing unprotected sex – a matter of highly gendered decision-making – for a minimum 12 months after infection. Supporting these complex socioeconomic, cultural and behavioural interventions, an estimated 0.03 per cent of the total West African Ebola spend was allocated to anthropological research.[22]

The Ebola pandemic has been represented as a failure at all levels. This is perhaps a little indiscriminate. The outbreak was, in the end, contained, stimulating remarkable development of therapeutic medicines and new vaccines. The real failure of the intervention was to seek to securitise the population in order to control the pathogen, rather than seeking to manage the outbreak by enhancing popular agency; to try to overlay security, through the imposition of hard controls on people rather than to work through communities to engender meaningful security from within – the failure to design intervention through a grounded understanding of the risk–benefit calculus of poor households whose incentives to survive, to gather food, to sustain trading relations, to care for one another, to maintain community weighed heavily against sterile and uncomprehending public notices and infection prevention measures issued with the menace of underlying violence (Sanders et al, 2015; Southall et al, 2017; Horton, 2019).

In the end, superimposing punitive security restrictions, through the prism of public health, on conditions of population poverty and fragmentary healthcare produced some needed short-run disease control outcomes, but with very limited sustainable effect. The communities left behind were scarred by the experience – scarring which weakens rather than strengthening the structural tissue of cohesive social development which lasting health security requires.

COVID

Shortly before Christmas 2019, Chinese epidemiologists picked up a cluster of cases of 'pneumonia of unknown cause' in Wuhan, Hubei Province.[23] On New Year's Day 2020, the WHO initiated an incident management support team, and by 10 January had issued technical guidelines on detection, testing and management of cases, based on prior knowledge of SARS and MERS. Next day, China shared the genetic sequence of the new coronavirus; eight days after that, its human-to-human transmissibility was confirmed. On 22 January, the WHO's Emergency Committee failed to reach consensus on the threat presented by COVID under the IHR. Eight days later, following a period of epidemiological – and doubtless political – reflection, COVID was declared, on 30 January, a PHEIC.

The global awakening to COVID-19 was comparatively agile – early incidence captured quickly in China's sophisticated system of socio-epidemiological surveillance, briefly blocked by the political architecture of information control between local level and Beijing, and then tracked with progressively detailed analysis as it spread westwards into high-income country health systems. The global response, by contrast, was chaotic – combining astonishingly rapid scientific collaboration in diagnostics, vaccinology and treatment and an equally startling collapse in the political coherence of transnational action, undermined by multiple, splintering national strategies, few paying much attention to WHO's nominal leadership, science or advice (Griffin, 2020; Sauer et al, 2021).

The brutal genius of COVID-19 was to concentrate its destructive force on groups at the margins of economic society – its propensity to seek out and exploit the fault-lines of social inequality in intersecting conditions of age, minority ethnicity, pre-existing morbidity and poverty creating an existential threat to individuals within certain groups, but a more ambiguous risk at the level of population as a whole.[24] COVID attacked the weak but left the younger and more economically active predominantly intact. A miasma of empirical uncertainty in the initial phase of the pandemic – likely transmission and lethality of the new virus, scope for prophylaxis and therapeutics, practicability of mass social control measures – was compounded by complex political and moral trade-offs beyond the scope of the epidemiological science: between protecting the vulnerable minority and preserving majority rights, between the needs of society's elderly and the needs of its young, between blocking transmission and mitigating disease, between short-term preservation of individual human life and long-run defence of collective economic function (Van Dooren and Noordegraaf, 2020).

Virtually all countries, with some degree of variation, adopted hard control measures in the initial phase of COVID spread.[25] But over time, two distinct streams of national COVID security strategy emerged: countries which opted for what might be called the 'unity model' – coopting the whole population from the outset in a collective endeavour dedicated to viral suppression;[26] and countries which pursued a 'utilitarian model' – involving the continuous calibration and recalibration of competing interests reflected in repeated shifts in the composition of control measures and commensurately confused public communication. Between the two, the unity model performed comparatively well in terms of infection and mortality; the utilitarian model was distinctly less successful (Bellazzi and Boyneburgk, 2020; Peisah et al, 2020; Balakrishnan, 2021; Bambino Geno Tai et al, 2021; Gostin, 2021; Huizar et al, 2021; Matilla-Santander et al, 2021; Vearey et al, 2021).[27] The question is what may account for the difference?

Trust – between people in communities, between citizens and their government – is fundamental to the efficacy of mass public health interventions (Blair et al, 2017; Han et al, 2021; Pagliaro et al, 2021; Schmelz, 2021).[28] Where securitisation of COVID was presented as a series of trade-offs – especially in societies with high or rising levels of social inequality – trust between groups whose interests were construed as competitive was undermined, trust in government duly fragmenting in multiple contesting narratives of risk and responsibility. Loss of trust within countries undermined the coherence of domestic security strategies. Divergent and contradictory national approaches – intensified by an increasingly ugly vaccine contest – undermined global coherence enabling a series of repeating outbreak waves facilitating viral mutation and resulting in a massive rise in cases of the omicron variant in early 2022 (Figure 12.2).

There will likely be no formal end to COVID – the disease simply cycling down through genetic waves exchanging, with luck, increased transmissibility for diminishing virulence, as immune systems adapt and social systems calm.[29] But the long-term of this coronavirus – as its credentials as security emergency are watered down by governments and publics equally keen to resume a more normal life – is likely to settle into an endemic rhythm of intermittent incidence, prominently among the dispossessed, clinically vulnerable, socially marginal and poor (Newton, 2020; Ritchie et al, 2020; Stawicki et al, 2020).

Conclusion

Pandemic diseases change society. How we propose to secure ourselves from them is fundamental to the nature of that change. Where health security is enacted as a kind of militaristic defence against external attack – imposed top-down on unremediated inequalities without attention to the internal societal dynamics by which threat is converted into risk and thence managed – it can worsen socioeconomic, political and cultural fractures, undermining the very social coherence on which disease control depends. Health security which relies on technical capability – surveillance, quarantine, detention, mass vaccination – can promote a citizen–state relationship based on the extension of power rather than creation of resilience, on obedience rather than trust – undervaluing the potential of communities to innovate in the face of hazard, diminishing people's sense of agency, constituting them as part of the problem rather than solution, and encroaching on core rights of freedom, democratic participation and equity (Mason et al, 2015).[30]

Building relationships of trust between people and their governing institutions may well be the Holy Grail of 'good governance' (Lalot et al, 2021). But it takes time. As an outbreak escalates, credible communication – transparent presentation of information and genuine dialogue on choices

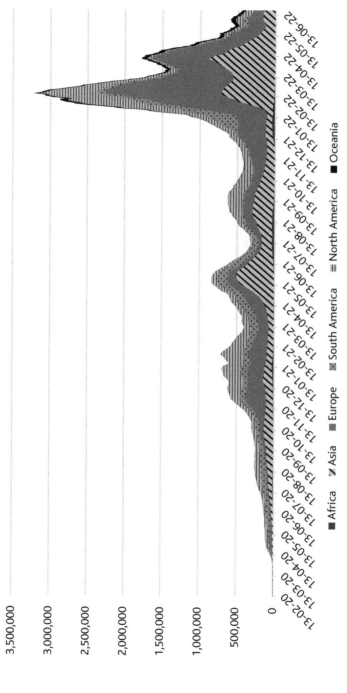

Figure 12.2: Confirmed COVID-19 cases, rolling 7-day average, by global region, February 2020 to June 2022

Source: JHU CSSE COVID-19 Data/Our World in Data

and trade-offs – is key to securing public compliance with necessary social controls. If trust – manifested in equitable local welfare, for example in the form of reliable, accessible healthcare – is not in place before the onset of a public health emergency, it will not be effectively established in the fog of war, and it will likely be further degraded as a result of poor pandemic management (Lal et al, 2021). What appears clear is that good governance is itself a vital health security strategy. And that if trust is, truly, a determinant of health security, then the radically different pandemic pathways experienced by different countries were already mapped out years before COVID-19 ever considered making the interspecies leap.

Two roads diverged in a wood

National responses to COVID lent heavily on the language of war, justifying an extraordinary expansion of government authority, and shifting the balance of power between citizen and state (Wæver, 1995; Chapman and Miller, 2020; Kirk and McDonald, 2021).[31] Executive fiat was extended directly through mass lockdowns, border closures, powers of detention, mandatory quarantine and enhancement of state surveillance and biosecurity – but also indirectly through much wider changes in the permissible range of economic activity, in commercial enterprise, employment conditions, in public service entitlements and in rights – of assembly, speech, representation and protest (Matthewman and Huppatz, 2020; Luehrmann and Rooney, 2021).[32]

There are two principal ways forward from the pandemic, transitioning once again from wartime to peace. One is to use the experiences of COVID securitisation to build an understanding of what we lost and, from this, what we must recover, preserve and better value. The other is, more cynically, to capitalise on processes of securitisation, to open up new spaces for the extension of state control allied with a reduction in what one might call human-centred social development and governmental accountability for its delivery.

COVID opened up a new front in the competition between democratic and autocratic governance and the values attached by each regime type to security. China's comparatively successful early pandemic exploited an extensive pre-existing architecture of hard public controls, expanding population techno-surveillance capabilities – ramping up big data, cloud computing and artificial intelligence through new public–private operations – and reaffirming the massive ubiquity of the state in the lives of individuals, households and neighbourhoods (Sun et al, 2021).[33] As the beacon of global liberalism, America's terrible COVID experience, by contrast, invites an uncomfortable comparison between the virtues of democracy and the comparative advantages of the autocratic alternative (Mechler et al, 2020; Cassani, 2021; Chang, 2021; Dentico, 2021; Huang, 2021).

A question hangs over how this contest will play out in the post-COVID world (as we will see in the next chapter). Through the pandemic, China has engaged in robust narrative-building – constructing a successful COVID experience to validate regime legitimacy and influence in global and multilateral institutions – celebrating unitary party autocracy as a more effective provider of population safety than its democratic peers.[34] On past performance, the chances that China will seek more aggressively to promote its domestic system as contender for global dominance remain modest (if quietly growing).[35] As, and possibly more likely, liberal democracies may find themselves jealously eyeing the COVID efficacy of some authoritarian nations – and to start to wonder as COVID subsides whether there might be some advantage in moderating their own model of liberalism to preserve some of the political and fiscal opportunities those more autocratic governments appear to have enjoyed under the justifying nomenclature of 'security' (Edgell et al, 2021).

All governments, whatever they say, value an ability to surveil their populations. Surveillance was key to managing COVID and is at the heart of preparations for the next global event (Greitens, 2020; Morgan et al, 2021). An obvious post-COVID question is how far democratic governments will be tempted to leave on the constitutional books an expanded licence to monitor citizens, quietly bedding this down as part of the much-feted 'new normal' (Lin et al, 2020; *The Economist*, 2022). Surveillance, though, is just one entry point to a larger suite of societal control capabilities. Expansion of mandatory access to personalised data during COVID accelerated the shifting boundaries of individual privacy creating new risks at the intersection between citizen rights, state welfare and private sector interest.[36] Digitisation of individual disease monitoring links, relatively seamlessly, with broader commercial functions in health insurance, doubtless improving calculation of risk and allocation of benefit but at the same time expanding the space for more disciplinary functions – contractual exclusions refusing cover for pre-existing conditions, for genetic inheritance and, ultimately, for behaviours associated with particular illnesses.

Meanwhile, the pandemic enabled much wider changes in the social and economic interaction between citizens and government – notably in the provision of core social services in health, education and justice. The virtualisation of core public sector provision – particularly in access to healthcare and education – may have created valuable lessons and opportunities in a more cost-efficient model of service delivery, converting securitising pandemic necessity into a new post-COVID model of public entitlement and state accountability. There is no question that remote forms of working can enhance service provision and uptake in some instances, but they also shrink the space for direct human interaction – in the clinic, the classroom, the courthouse – with the potential to diminish the depth of people's participation, impede regulatory oversight, and worsen inequality among the digitally excluded (Chellaiyan et al, 2019; Dodoo et al, 2021).[37] One may wonder how far democratic governments will be tempted to rationalise a new, streamlined 'hybrid' public sector model, invoking the convenience of virtual delivery to camouflage cost-cutting policy choices, appealing in the pandemic's debt-laden aftermath (Hargreaves, 2021). In the end, we may see in the post-COVID economy, an expansionary approach to digital infrastructure accompanied by a contractionary approach to the scope and depth of public services (Metinsoy, 2021).

To what extent will this post-COVID security society – opening up personal data to state and commercial interests; shifting to online interaction depleting the vital if hard-to-define qualities of face-to-face contact; narrowing the statutory range of rights and equity in healthcare, education and employment; degrading transparency and due diligence in government procurement processes; subjecting our freedoms to discretionary change in public security rules – be properly subject to public scrutiny and deliberative evaluation? To what extent, following the classical concept of security, will scrutiny be curtailed – not actively (as in the autocratic context) but through a chilling effect justified by ourselves to ourselves, drawing on the experience of pandemic, to consent to a security paradigm necessarily released from its social and political context and from the norms of liberal governance (Dalby, 1990).[38]

Notes

[1] Prior to the irrefutability of climate change, COVID and the bizarre nuclear tilt in Putin's Ukraine venture.

[2] Although there is a much wider field of health security studies, this chapter focuses on 'health security' in the context of human security, as duty of care owed by governments and international partners to defend populations from serious health threats like pandemics (see, for example, Rushton and Youde, 2015).

[3] GHSI is an initiative of the Nuclear Threat Initiative and the Johns Hopkins Center for Health Security Homepage – GHS Index. While independent and additional to the Joint External Evaluation mandated under the IHR, the two systems share much in terms of emphasis of indicators.

[4] Perhaps surprisingly, America was ranked top again in the GHSI 2021. See https://www.ghsindex.org/wp-content/uploads/2021/12/2021_GHSindexFullReport_Final.pdf; see also Yong (2022).

[5] Through history, diverse pandemic diseases have provoked quite different social responses. For example, pathogens with higher case fatality appear to incur less scapegoating, while diseases with higher mortality rate among children, and less consensus on causation, are associated with greater stigma and propensity for social fragmentation (Jedwab et al, 2021).

[6] Although widely described as a pandemic, HIV/AIDS is more formally classed as a 'global epidemic'. HIV/AIDS predates the 2005 revision of IHR which created the category 'public health emergency of international concern'.

[7] Epitomised in the primitive '4-Hs' categorisation: 'homosexuals, haemophiliacs, Haitians and heroin users'.

[8] In 1993, I recall seeing a billboard hoarding in Yunnan, southwest China – then central to the spread of HIV/AIDS into China from southeast Asia, which read: 'AIDS – 不用担心' ('AIDS – don't worry'). Twelve years after the first case was reported in India, with an

estimated three million cases, official government documents described HIV in India as 'in its early stages' (NACO, 1996).

9   In the early 1980s, one in three Americans believed AIDS was as contagious as the common cold. By the end of the decade, the same proportion supported some level of quarantine for those infected with HIV. In Canada support for coercive measures to control the epidemic was strongest among those with most intense perception of public susceptibility, disease severity and incurability. In India, misconceptions regarding transmission fed rising popular support for mandatory testing for marginalised groups and coercive policies for people and families living with HIV.

10 In 2017, unsafe sex was the leading factor related to HIV/AIDS mortality, with young females (15–19) most exposed. See 'HIV/AIDS', Our World in Data (https://ourworldindata.org/hiv-aids).

11 PEPFAR is one of the largest single-source financial contributions in the history of the global AIDS response, established in 2003 by George W Bush. The annual allocation rose sharply between 2004 and 2010 from USD$2.2 billion to USD$6.5 billion, levelling off thereafter. PEPFAR's original legislative authorisation, the Leadership Act, stipulated a minimum 70 per cent of funds to be spent on curative and palliative care, with 20 per cent assigned to prevention – of which at least one-third was to be spent on abstinence, monogamy, fidelity and delay of sexual debut. See 'The U.S. President's Emergency Plan for AIDS Relief (PEPFAR)', KFF (www.kff.org/global-health-policy/fact-sheet/the-u-s-presidents-emergency-plan-for-aids-relief-pepfar/).

12 Based on Committee on the Outcome and Impact Evaluation of Global HIV/AIDS Programs Implemented Under the Lantos-Hyde Act of 2008; Board on Global Health; Board on Children, Youth, and Families; Institute of Medicine (2013) *Evaluation of PEPFAR*, Washington DC: National Academies Press. Available at: www.ncbi.nlm.nih.gov/books/NBK207 014/

13 In 1982, the median survival time for someone diagnosed with HIV in the US was between one and two years. In 2018, life expectancy for an HIV-positive person in their 20s receiving ART is around 53 years. In the last quarter-century, AIDS-related mortality worldwide has been cut in half (Eisinger and Fauci, 2018).

14 In late 2021, 38 million people around the world were living with HIV – in 2020, another 1.5 million were infected (5,500 women aged 15–24 every week). Two-thirds of infections occurred in sub-Saharan Africa. One in six infected people are unaware of their status. Twenty-seven per cent of people living with HIV were not on treatment. DGHT-HIV-Factsheet.pdf (cdc.gov).

15 The declaration by WHO on 23 July 2022 of monkeypox as a PHEIC may, to some extent, have been shaped by a similar concern – a nasty viral infection for long endemic and ignored in poorer regions, starting to spread rapidly in high-income settings through poorly understood forms of social interaction and network, and heavily concentrated among men who have sex with men, raising issues of marginality and discrimination in understanding and engaging with the outbreak. See, for example, 'WHO Director-General declares the ongoing monkeypox outbreak a Public Health Emergency of International Concern', www.who.int/europe/news/item/23-07-2022-who-director-general-declares-the-ongoing-monkeypox-outbreak-a-public-health-event-of-international-concern

16 Reminiscent of the Global Malaria Eradication Programme launched in 1955 and abandoned in 1969 – combining over-confidence in the new vector control capability

promised by indoor Dichlorodiphenyltrichloroethane (DDT) spraying and the apparently unforeseen 'refractory behaviour' of humans and mosquitoes. The global spread of diseases including zika, dengue and chikungunya is closely linked to the scale of poorly governed urbanisation, inequitable labour and employment conditions, food insecurity and exclusion from basic health and education services (see Bardosh, 2020).

17 WHO's interim advice offered this: 'Women who wish to discontinue their pregnancy should receive accurate information about their options to the full extent of the law, including harm reduction where the care desired is not readily available' (WHO, 2016: 1). This is right in theory but challenging for women in contexts where abortion is criminalised or subject to extreme religious and cultural disapprobation, appropriate care is scarce and expensive, incidence of unsafe termination widespread, and consequences of abortion potentially violent.

18 WHO has come in for much criticism over the handling of West Africa's Ebola outbreak. Some of this is doubtless merited – but much of it is not. WHO was, to an extent, simply doing what it has been constructed and financed to do. Progressive reduction in member states' voluntary contributions have forced the global health leader to make unconscionable choices about what to pay for and what to cut. Emergency response was the loser. Moreover, as the 'servant of its membership', WHO's capacity to lead normative international action has always been severely hampered by the political preferences of its regions – in this case the reticence of affected governments to invoke an economically crippling public health emergency before they absolutely had to. By May 2014, WHO had deployed to West Africa the largest contingent of field epidemiologists in its history.

19 'UN Mission for Ebola Emergency Response (UNMEER)', Global Ebola Response (https://ebolaresponse.un.org/un-mission-ebola-emergency-response-unmeer).

20 The virus would reach in Dallas, Texas by the end of September. www.cdc.gov/vhf/ebola/history/2014-2016-outbreak/cumulative-cases-graphs.html

21 Dr Joanne Liu, Medecins sans Frontieres, 'United Nations special briefing', 2 Sept. 2014: 'Many of the Member States represented here today have invested heavily in biological threat response. You have a political and humanitarian responsibility to immediately utilize these capabilities in Ebola-affected countries. To curb the epidemic, it is imperative that States immediately deploy civilian and military assets with expertise in biohazard containment.' http://www.doctorswithoutborders.org/news-stories/speechopen-letter/united-nations-special-briefing-ebola. In both Liberia and Sierra Leone, the outbreak management chain of command swung between military and health agencies. In Sierra Leone, emergency response leadership migrated from a Presidential Task Force, through a Ministry of Health Emergency Operations Centre, to a National Ebola Response Centre under the authority of the Ministry of Defence. Both the US and the UK deployed significant military contingents in support respectively of Liberia (2,900 personnel) and Sierra Leone (750).

22 In mid-2021, social sciences comprised around 13 per cent of research funding for COVID (see, for example, Abramowitz, 2020; UKCDR and GloPID-R, 2020).

23 https://bfpg.co.uk/2020/04/covid-19-timeline/

24 The estimated case fatality rate for COVID-19 is around 1.6 per cent. The case fatality rate for SARS was 9.5 per cent and for MERS a little over 34 per cent; Ebola and Marburg disease both average around 50 per cent, killing every other case.

25 By mid-April 2020, 80 per cent of countries had imposed some form of containment and lockdown measures.

[26] Noting the long-run problems with the zero-COVID strategy making indefinite suppression almost certainly impossible and, in the end, counterproductive to recovery.

[27] The 'unity' model would include, for example, China, Singapore, South Korea, Hong Kong, Taiwan, New Zealand and Australia; the 'utilitarian': the US, the UK, India and Brazil. It is, of course, a flawed taxonomy, struggling to account for many countries occupying the large intervening policy space, from Germany, the Netherlands and Sweden to Russia and the Philippines, complicated by large differences in state capacity and access to vaccines – but it may help in pointing to the larger division in the political drivers shaping overall COVID security thinking (see, for example, Mao and Illmer, 2021).

[28] Trust is complex. It can protect against disease as people adopt protective measures on behalf of others and it can enhance compliance with official instructions and social controls. But it can also increase transmission and mortality in early pandemic onset as people's confidence in one another undermines the perceived necessity of distancing. On the whole, though, COVID has shown, once again, the importance of trust – between people in communities and between citizens and their government – as a key dimension of societal security.

[29] Bearing in mind that while it is reasonable to hope for genetic mutation in viruses which follow a path of falling lethality, the non-linear nature of variation does not by any means guarantee this (Reynolds et al, 2022).

[30] The Global Polio Eradication Initiative, stalled between 2015 and 2021 in Pakistan and Afghanistan, is the archetypal example of an extraordinarily effective technical vaccination programme blocked by deep socioeconomic and political factors fragmenting cohesive society and engendering rationalities of resistance.

[31] Between 16 and 22 March 2020, Emmanuel Macron announced six times, "We are at war"; Boris Johnson invoked the powers of "wartime government"; Giuseppe Conte said, "Italians are fighting in the trenches"; Donald Trump tweeted "I want all Americans to understand: we are at war with an invisible enemy"; and Scott Morrison declared, "We are at war with this virus, and all Australians are enlisted to do the right thing" (see Engberg-Pedersen, 2020; Haddad, 2020).

[32] Under cover of emergency conditions, COVID legitimised significant changes in the scope of public services – restricting access to justice, limiting judicial oversight, reducing employment and labour protections, relaxing training requirements for healthcare workers, reducing educational provision and increasing class sizes. In the US, 397 regulations, largely relating to labour rights, were waived in the fight against COVID. By April 2020, 84 countries had enacted emergency laws extending executive privilege over other branches of government (see, for example, *Financial Times*, 2020; Magri, 2020; Šeško, 2021).

[33] China's leading COVID strategy (防控, 'fangkong' or 'prevention and control') is the same language used to describe its national model of policing, social control and regime stability (Greitens, 2020).

[34] 'Since the outbreak of COVID-19 in Wuhan, under the strong leadership of the Communist Party of China and the Chinese government, the Chinese people have united as one, fully brought to bear the strengths of the socialist system with Chinese characteristics, through tenacious efforts and enormous sacrifice, we achieved the initial stage victory against the epidemic. This not only effectively protects the safety and health of the Chinese people, but also greatly boosts the confidence of people around the world

in overcoming the epidemic. China has played an indispensable and unparalleled role in safeguarding the lives and health of people around the world' (Zhao, 2020).

35 Xinhua News (2018).

36 Contact-tracing apps, as well as public registration and online access protocols have blurred the divide between compulsory inclusion and personal choice, narrowing individuals' ability to protect their data from government and commercial organisations (Rana et al, 2021). In China, protest against restrictive banking controls is reported to have been deterred when authorities changed protesters' digital health status from green to red, cutting off their access to a range of public services (Tham, 2022).

37 Take, for example, the establishment of 'Nightingale Courts' borrowing from the COVID-19 construction of Nightingale Hospitals in the UK in the early phase of the pandemic. Nightingale Courts supplanted an earlier scheme to expand the role of non-jury trials. The new courts were promoted by the government to accelerate processing of a large and growing backlog of cases created at least in part by deep cuts to legal aid which provided access to justice for poorer households. Nightingale Courts were contextualised by expansion of video technology for remote hearings, legislation to expand the power of lower level magistrates to enact longer sentences, as well as legislation criminalising a broadening spectrum of rights to public protest. All of this, contextualised, in early 2022, by the announcement of a 'Brexit Freedom' bill designed to facilitate the extraction of UK law from EU provisions, including in key areas of labour rights and environmental protection, without the oversight of primary legislation.

38 See, for example, Gebrekidan (2020).

PART V

Democracy

13

All for one

Until quite recently, the world's future looked decidedly democratic. Between 1972 and 2018, accelerating after the fall of the Soviet Union in 1990, the proportion of democratic countries rose from 25 to 62 per cent – more than half the population of the planet, for the first time in history, living in some form of popular participatory government – or, to put it another way, substantially fewer people living under overtly despotic rule (Figure 13.1) (IDEA, 2019).

Figure 13.1: Democracies versus nondemocracies, global, 1800–2016

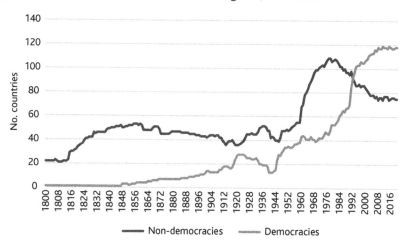

Source: Our World in Data Democracy – Our World in Data (ourworldindata.org)

Since the turn of the millennium, however – and acutely in the last decade – we have seen a reversal in that process (Maerz et al, 2020; Boese et al, 2021; Larry, 2022). This involves not just a deceleration in the conversion of oppressive regimes or the reversion of newly reforming governments to older ways, but also deterioration in the quality of established democracies – the level of executive, judicial and administrative standards they espouse and, perhaps correspondingly, the depth of popular faith in the democratic model on which their legitimacy depends. In 1980, almost half of the world's democracies were classed as 'high-performing'. By 2018 this had fallen to around one in five.[1]

If there is a democratic crisis, it is one which is epitomised by the slow-growing confrontation between America and China.[2] But what is the nature of the crisis? To what extent is it a genuine clash of political civilisations; to what extent the distressed construction of Western countries fearing the loss of global ascendancy; and to what extent is it simply democracy bending under the weight of its own contradictions – the growing disconnect, fuelled by climbing inequality, between constitutional ideal and popular reality?[3]

We are, without doubt, seeing a resurgence of authoritarian rhetoric in some of the world's most powerful democracies – from America and Brazil to India and Turkey. And we are seeing stalled democratic reform and reversion to policy-by-diktat in significant parts of Latin America, Eastern Europe and Central Asia. How, then, to respond? Assuming that, in a crude sense, democracy is preferable to autocracy – not least with respect to matters of bodily integrity and psychosocial dignity – how are we to reaffirm the value of democratisation?

Part of the problem is that while a rhetorical idealisation of democracy has long been enthusiastically promulgated around the world, its practical characteristics – how it works and what it must and cannot do – remain rather less well defined (Lührmann et al, 2018). What exactly *is* a democracy? What does it need to be and do to qualify, and thus what expectations can be leveraged on nations seeking entry to the democratic club?

From the primitive collectives of hunter-gatherer society to the Chinese People's Democratic Dictatorship and the post-war dominance of the American archetype – what is claimed under the banner of democracy incorporates a remarkably broad array of forms and practices (Linz and Valenzuela, 1994; Costa et al, 2017). The 'third wave' of democratisation, particularly after 1989, was without question excitingly wide in geographical and demographic scale, but it was arguably rather shallow in depth. Most countries in the post-war period honour at least the theatre of electoral process. Some of them do so, though, more in the traditions of pantomime.

It cannot go unnoticed that many of the world's most advanced democracies have, over time, also been those most active in the oppression and exploitation of other less militarily robust or economically developed parts of the world. There is doubtless some scope for forensic historiographical debate about the helps and harms of colonial occupation. But there is a weight of evidence that these global interactions were generally speaking unsought, often violent, and ultimately rejected. Since then, waves of clandestine and overt military intervention in other people's polities, notably by the US, cast further shade on the bona fides of the democratic offer.

If democracy is predicated on one thing above others, it is, surely, on the maximisation of meaningful popular participation (Hyland, 1995; Parvin,

2018). Yet as societies modernise, becoming more administratively complex, direct citizen engagement in decision-making has generally yielded in favour of indirect representative models, with increasingly professionalised political classes elected to facilitate the preferences of their constituencies. As democracies mature, power drifts upwards. Delegates become detached from their base, driven by short-term re-electoral strategy over long-term public good, frequently coopted to narrower ideological and economic constituencies seeking the invaluable imprimatur of political legitimacy (Allen et al, 2019; López and Dubrow, 2020).[4] Electoral process, progressively refined into a minimalist cycle of sporadic voter activation interspersed by long periods of frustrated passivity, drain the model of its most vital credential – belief in the instrumental power of the vote (see, for example, UNDP, 2004). A growing sense of individual powerlessness transforms the electoral act from positive participation to residual expression of disenfranchised disenchantment.

There is no question that open elections are a necessary condition of the democratic state. But it is increasingly clear that they are, on their own, insufficient. If democracy comprises two principal functions – popular deliberation and policy decision-making – over the last century, the latter has come to dominate over the former; the core virtue of democratic society viewed as the momentary power entailed to voters through electoral process, once every few years, while the depth and content of public participation within which such electoral moments should sit, has dwindled (Goenaga, 2022).

Health and democracy

The link between democracy and health seems self-evident. On the face of it, democracy comes with the offer of a longer life. In 2015, average life expectancy in the 36 countries with a Liberal Democracy Index score of 0.7 or higher was 72 years; all 21 countries with life expectancy below 60 scored under 0.55 (Figure 13.2) (Coppedge et al, 2018). Although the relationship between democratic governance and economic growth remains ambiguous, democracies have higher average government health spending, lower levels of violence and corruption, and a better track record on provision of universal health coverage (Altman and Castiglioni, 2009; Jetter et al, 2015; Kolstad and Wiig, 2016; Templin et al, 2021).[5]

Democratic societies tend to protect media freedom and accountability of government to popular appraisal. Greater freedom of information in democracies should, in theory, encourage the elevation to power of relatively honest leaders, with more testable credentials for competence, while ensuring that government is less able to conceal and more galvanised to act on large-scale population health threats (Safaei, 2006).[6] Fair electoral processes, in principle, incentivise contesting candidates to promise – and possibly deliver – healthier socioeconomic conditions and life-saving care services (Marx et al, 2022).

Figure 13.2: Life expectancy at birth and Liberal Democracy Index, 2015

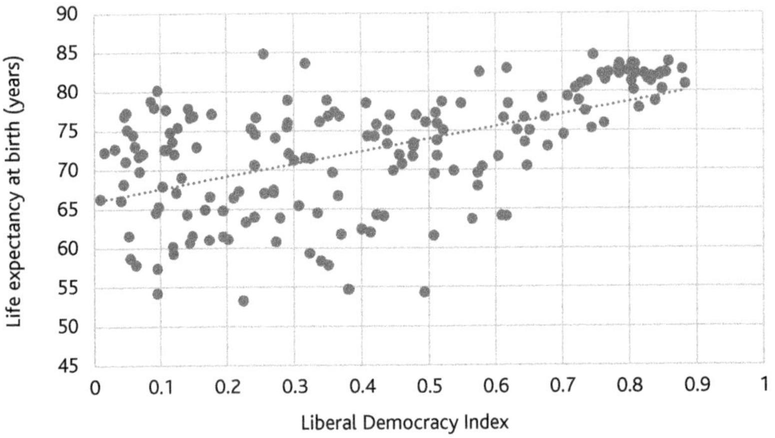

Source: Our World in Data Life expectancy vs. liberal democracy, 2019 (ourworldindata.org)[7]

Democracy is positively associated with political and economic stability, higher levels of human capital and, to some extent, greater government capacity – all of which feed better conditions for health, although benefits tend to gravitate towards higher-income groups as influence is captured by those with greater socioeconomic and political capital (Helliwell, 1994; Gerring et al, 2005; Ross, 2006; Doucouliagos and Ulubaşoğlu, 2008).[8] Loss of democracy can dramatically worsen provision of healthcare, as well as wider public welfare and development opportunities contributory to population health (Wigley et al, 2020). In contested autocracies, withdrawal of life-critical services may be weaponised to weaken popular resistance.[9]

But regime types are neither homogeneous nor historically static. Latin American nations can claim deeper historical democratic roots than their Asian counterparts dating, at least in formal terms, to post-colonial independence from the late 18th century on. Yet while the quality of democratic institutions in Latin America is considered greater, performance on measures of equitable social and economic development – key inputs to the practical functioning of the democratic principle – is better in Asia (Whitehead, 2002). A version of the Preston Curve adapted to reflect democratic and autocratic states in the early 1980s shows the extremes of democratic superiority and poorer autocratic performance, but also a mingling of regime type and health outcome around the elbow of the curve (Figure 13.3) (Besley and Kudamatsu, 2006, 2008; Burroway, 2016).

Figure 13.3: The Preston Curve by democratic and autocratic regime, 1982

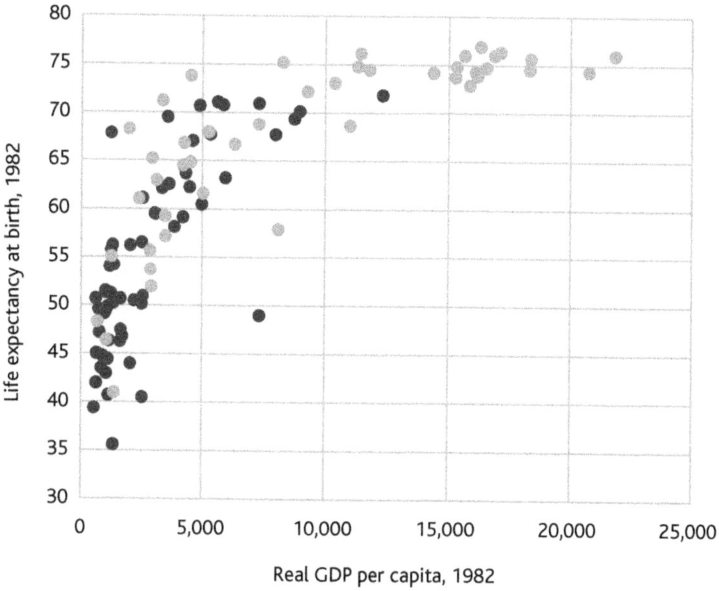

Note: light grey = democracy; dark grey = autocracy.

Source: Besley and Kudamatsu (2006)[10]

Between 1950 and 1980, autocratic regimes including Indonesia, South Korea, Thailand, Syria, Iraq, Togo, Gabon, Ecuador, Peru, Poland and Romania channelled economic growth into increased investment for social development and health with significant positive effect (Kudamatsu, 2007; Patterson and Veenstra, 2016). In the last three decades, nondemocracies including Ethiopia, Rwanda, Uganda and Myanmar have shown striking examples of political leadership and some genuinely impressive results in advancing maternal, neonatal and under-five child survival.[11]

Authoritarian states which are rooted in socialist traditions tend to perform better than other autocracies on inclusive services and public health, as do nondemocracies which manage to evolve relatively efficient mechanisms for selecting and deselecting leaders (Miller, 2015; Pieters et al, 2016; Cassani, 2017).[12] Autocratic regimes, less reliant on plural political constituencies, may be more able than their fledgling developing country democratic counterparts to resist processes of globalisation, imposing external conditions on fiscal policy and trade openness associated with compromised welfare and health sector spending (Bergh and Nilsson, 2010; Mackenbach et al, 2013; Welander et al, 2015; Agha et al, 2021).[13]

None of this implies that autocracy is somehow the preferable regime option. Oppressive governance and arbitrary control over individual rights and community freedoms corrode psychological welfare and psychosocial cohesion. They diminish the equitable availability of informational and material resources necessary for investment in public goods and the individual forces of aspiration and achievement. The absence of citizen checks on executive decision-making, regardless of its relation to decisional efficiency, is simply unacceptable.

But it suggests that more is at stake in shaping population health than a crude demarcation of 'democratic' and 'autocratic'; that it is not the simple present form of a regime – defined primarily by multi-party elections – that shapes its effect on human health. It is, rather, the quality of governance as it develops over time – the gradual process of institutional evolution, prioritising and sequencing social, economic and institutional dimensions of change, and in particular the willingness to confront structural inequality, furnishing people equitably with a basket of essential developmental public goods – that shapes health and human well-being.

There may well be a long-run positive relationship between democracy and health – and this interaction may get stronger over time. But it is a relationship whose dynamics are far from clear-cut. There is little argument that democracy is, in the end, the better option for satisfactory social existence. But the argument is sadly diminished if democracy is posed in vague aspirations revolving around a two-dimensional theatre of stale electoral formalism, political camouflage for an economic liberalism which tolerates inequality at levels which, in the end, undermine public faith in participatory politics (Kim and Kroeger, 2018; Wang et al, 2019).

Famine and feast

India and China – two Asian giants comparable in population – emerged almost simultaneously, in 1947 and 1949, into the newly forged freedoms of independent nationhood (Dummer and Cook, 2008). Accepting difference in ethnic composition and colonial history, the way these behemoths evolved is one of the great natural experiments in the comparative interaction of civilisation, state and human welfare: the largest democracy in the world facing off against its most populous autocracy, contrasting cultures of ideology and political economy separated only by the high Himalaya.

At Independence, India was, by volume of output, the seventh largest industrial nation in the world (Desai, 2003). China, by contrast, was a chronically poor, predominantly peasant economy emerging from decades of governmental dysfunction, invasion and cripplingly violent civil war. Yet, over subsequent decades, China saw a remarkable uplift in its population health – an effect which cannot simply be attributed to economic

Figure 13.4: China and India: GDP per capita and infant mortality rate, 1950–2010

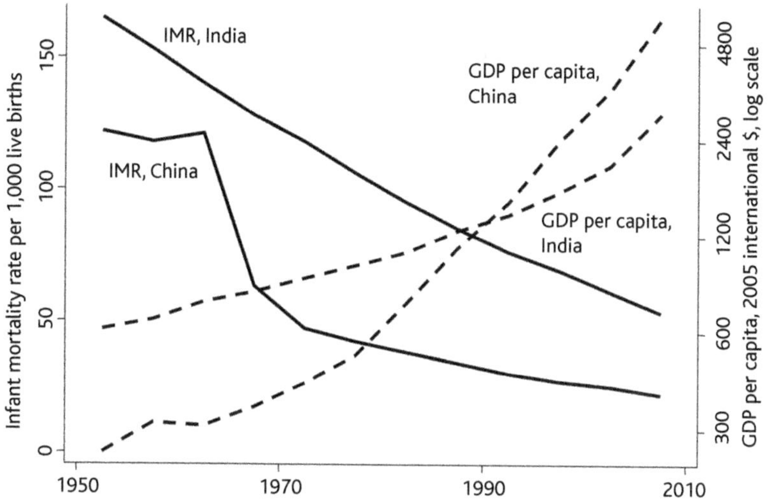

Source: Deaton (2013)

transformation; a steep reduction in infant mortality pre-dating the surge in GDP growth following Deng Xiaoping's market reforms after 1979 (Figure 13.4) (Deaton, 2006, 2013). India remains engaged meanwhile in a grinding struggle for the health of its children and families.

What accounts for the difference? One approach to answering this question is to argue that the face value of an authoritarian system in China is simply superior in promoting population welfare to the democratic system in India. An alternate approach is to look at the sociocultural terrain out of which the two systems of governance have grown.

During much of the modern period from the establishment of the Qing Dynasty in the mid-17th century, China pursued an isolationist path, hedged in by perceived or actually hostile external forces, feeding a powerful domestic discourse of internal cohesion and productive self-sufficiency. India, by contrast, was a patchwork of imperial and princely territories engaged in complex outward networks of collaboration and contest with European colonialists whose strategies of occupation mixed direct military control with administration via traditional hierarchies of local power offering compliance for status and survival.

India's colonial history is one of multiple weakly institutionalised states subject to external manipulation, sclerotic customary politics and fractious relations of religion, caste and class eternally pulling apart, most literally and violently with partition. China, over the same time, reflects an array of dynastic, ethnic and topographical localities riven, no doubt, by periods of chaos and renewal, but seeming constantly to reform according to the gravitational logic of a cultivated cultural homogeneity and the political narrative of a unitary civilisation-state (see, for example, Arne Westad, 2012).

China's communist revolution uprooted the foundational hierarchies of its society (while adopting, in the main, an impressively nuanced approach to the preservation of popular Confucian culture). Its nascent autocracy was built on a radical, if violent, break with the past, epitomised by the massive programme of land redistribution forming both part of Mao's strategy for consolidating revolutionary rural support and the process of agricultural collectivisation and experimental egalitarianism following victory in 1949. India's independence was founded on and managed through deep-rooted, largely unreconstructed traditions of political class and rigid caste hierarchy which, underpinning and compromising the formal democratic process, rendered real change in the egregious conditions of social and economic inequality much harder to challenge or change. '[I]f in China land reform was comparatively straightforward in equalising land ownership across the country, in India it was a maze of socioeconomic, political, regional, and hierarchical complexities' (Lin, 2015).[14]

There may be many things to regret about the changes in post-revolutionary China, and in the contemporary state of Beijing's approach to human rights. But it is hard to repudiate the effect of its new politics – of reformation in basic social relations on, for example, the question of gender and the emancipatory impact of revolution on the role of women (Figure 13.5).[15] In India, the power of patriarchy remained, by comparison, stolidly, fatally in place. In 2019, China's Gender Inequality Index score was 0.168. while India's was 0.488 (see, for example, UNDP, 2019).

Over the last 40 years, rates of economic growth in India and China have been positive (Figure 13.6). China has been ahead of India, but both have generated positive increase in national resources. Yet during this time China has consistently outpaced India, often by degrees of magnitude, in a range of major human development metrics.

In 2010–2011, China's literacy rate was around 95 per cent for men and women. In India around one in five boys and one in three girls over age seven could not read (World Bank, 2013; Lin, 2015). In the most recent year of measurement, the prevalence of child underweight in China was 2.4 per cent (2013); in India it was 33.4 per cent (2017).[16] In 2018, India had the highest absolute level of under-five mortality in the world (882,000). In the same period, China saw 142,000 child deaths.[17]

Both India and China struggle to accumulate the human capital necessary for national development – one blocked by the inability of democracy to

Figure 13.5: Women's political participation index by selected country/region, 1950–2018

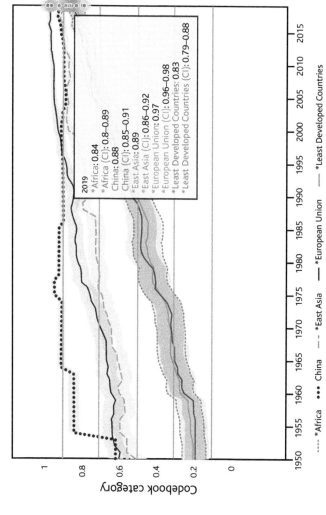

Highcharts.com V-Dem data version 10.0
Source: Coppedge et al (2022)[18]

Figure 13.6: Gross domestic product growth rate (annual percentage change), India and China, 1960–2020

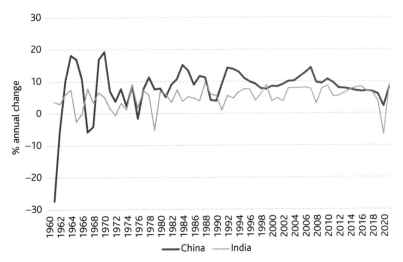

Source: World Bank[19]

overcome local power systems and rentier control of value, the other by the artificial constraints placed on individual dynamism by collective goals. The problem is not one of a zero-sum choice – between the democratic and the autocratic way – but rather of sequencing. While China seeks to harness the will of the people to the central state, India attempts to balance the function of the state on a diffused and inequitable mosaic of localised constituencies. In either case, the willingness of people to invest trust in what government asks of them is the key – both to democratic legitimacy and, ultimately, the survival of autocratic rule.

In the current period, Indians are, in principle, considerably freer than their Chinese counterparts to choose the life paths they wish to pursue. But they are too often fundamentally hobbled in the ability, equitably, to acquire the capabilities necessary to engage successfully in that pursuit. Energetic national programmes of basic education and skills building in China, by contrast, have engendered significant uplift in population capacities and a corresponding level of popular credence in the worth of the Beijing regime, in spite of its oppressive forms. A persistent failure in the same functions of state–citizen relationship in India fundamentally undermines the bona fides of government, fractured and coopted along deep trenches of opaque process, byzantine rule, parochial loyalty and steep inequality.[20]

By emphasising its role in the universalisation of equitable basic provision, the Chinese system may have achieved an advantage over the chaotic, creative, but enduringly inequitable pluralism of India (Grupe and Rose, 2010; Mok and Kang, 2019). What seems clear is that there is an interanimation over time between trust in government based on the state's ability to provide basic protections, and the state's willingness to trust its people to manage their lives along heterogeneous lines of ideological preference and individual identity.

The Chinese regime's ability to engender and sustain public trust – key to the credibility and implementation of its policies – is well noted (Zhengxu, 2005; Zhong and Zhan, 2021). But it is a trust, compared with other regimes, marked by particular features. The general trend for people to trust local more than central government appears reversed in China – Chinese communities cleaving more to the centralised ideal of the state than to its more material (and often rather imperfect) local manifestations – a state of affairs in which conformity to the higher-level appeal of a national development project may be relatively robust even in the face of localised dissatisfaction.[21] Unlike many country contexts, where trust in government declines as you move up the socioeconomic distribution, in China trust appears to increase among the wealthier and more educated (though this may be time-limited) (Wu and Wilkes, 2018).[22]

The hardiness of Indian democracy, in the face of a massive capacity for social and political turbulence, is often constituted as little short of miraculous. This is a fair point. But it may be that that hardiness is precisely the result of a democratic model rooted in, rather than challenging, the structural inequities of Indian society and the vast array of countervailing interests served by a perpetuation of the old ways – a low-cohesion agglomeration of antique powers and marginalisations preserved through formal political, electoral and judicial institutions too easily coopted by residual elites (Mitra, 2019).[23] In a comparison of the Chinese and Indian experience of political regime and health, it is less the case that autocracy triumphs and rather more, perhaps, that democracy in this instance has failed to confront the forces of inequality by which public engagement in cohesive progress is blocked.

There are, of course, many reasons to admire India's democratic movement towards social and economic freedom. And there are, equally, many reasons to criticise China's failure in political enfranchisement.[24] But on the bare evidence of population health and social welfare, China's distributional approach to livelihood capabilities has produced benefits which India struggles, still, to approximate. That the beneficence of the early years of the Chinese revolution have matured into inequity and inhumane control is not in dispute; nor that India, at its best, displays extraordinary social and economic creative energy. But it is hard to defend the condition of India on the grounds of its democratic credential in comparison with China's on the grounds of its democratic failure.

Conclusion

To be clear, there are intuitive and elementary reasons to prefer democracy over autocracy. Anyone who thinks the current assault on democratic norms is a passing problem or a matter of righteous Western comeuppance should consider the alternatives. Anyone who looks to an autocratic fantasy of achieving greater levels of efficiency should reflect on the costs borne by populations around the world, in the modern period, who labour under the arrogance of an immovable social and administrative elite. But if the aim is to reaffirm democratic norms, to restore public credence in the superiority of democratic government, perhaps we need to re-engage more critically with what we mean by 'democracy', and what we expect from it.

Above all, we need a much stronger emphasis on the value of local participation beyond the sterile formality of the periodic vote; to invest more heavily in the local level of democratic practice and deliberative dialogue – combining, without romanticising either, the vibrancy of Indian pluralism with the equity-enforcing instincts of the Chinese model; building systems of governance which encourage people to believe that they are meaningfully involved, that they are part of a larger collective project (Cohen, 2009; Lima, 2019; Mathonnat and Minea, 2019; McGuire, 2020; Prah Ruger, 2020).

Movements in local participatory governance have been growing since the 1960s, successfully engaged on issues directly bearing on people's lived reality and the quality of their community – municipal and district budget setting and oversight; housing development and urban planning, land use and allocation; governance of common resources like forests; collective welfare programmes in irrigation, water use and sanitation; urban and periurban waste disposal; educational options, provision and access; and community policing and security among others – all of them powerful determinants of health (Koonings, 2004; Baiocchi, 2005; Heller et al, 2007; Bherer, 2010; Montambeault, 2015; Balbim, 2016). National and regional consultative processes have convened around issues such as international development and environmental goals (Bherer et al, 2016; Eckersley, 2020; Willis et al, 2022).

In the aftermath of the COVID pandemic, public health offers real, tangible opportunities for local engagement – from debating future measures for effective disease control, through defining the scope of publicly funded healthcare services (or the essential content of 'basic healthcare packages'), as well as monitoring delivery of services, to weighing the pros and cons of taxing foods and drinks associated with poor health and chronic disease (Daniels and Sabin, 2002; Persad, 2019). Grounded in the urgent realities and realisations bequeathed to us by COVID-19, health constitutes a fertile terrain in which to re-establish credible democratic practice, in particular linking local dialogue with national policy formation.

Democracy and disease

It has become something of a convention that democracy had a worse pandemic than autocracy. While democracies were putting their boots on, autocracies were nailing down the furniture and laying in supplies for the lockdown. While democratic systems struggled to formulate, agree and affirm pandemic controls in appropriate legislation, autocracies simply imposed unilateral restrictions, radiating authoritative restrictions on population mobility and activating dense human and technological networks of contact tracing, isolation and quarantine (Engler et al, 2021; Economist Intelligence Unit, 2022). These, though, are characterisations. Many autocratic countries had a parlous pandemic. Some democratic countries managed COVID extraordinarily well (see, for example, Cassan and Van Steenvort, 2021). It is nonetheless the case that in the early stages of the pandemic, democracies ranked by constitutional commitment to freedom experienced higher rates of disease transmission (Figure 13.7) (Karabulut et al, 2021).[25]

This leads to the perplexing conclusion that if the apotheosis of democracy is to facilitate freedom of choice, then the higher the quality of a democratic regime, the higher its rate of COVID infection – that the hallmark of true democracy is its willingness to sacrifice pandemic protection on the altar of personal preference.

The notion that autocracy may be more effective than democracy in confronting crisis was given something of a boost by the way the pandemic played out. The idea, as it goes, is that autocratic regimes are able to take decisive, comprehensive action and to enforce emergency measures, unfettered by the requirements of public consultation and social compliance. The downside, though, is that they have built-in tendencies to distort and, as necessary, suppress information flows, such that the quality of raw data and the aggregative power of popular pressure are absent from the decision-making process. Democracies, meanwhile, actively foster informational transparency and so are better at detecting and understanding crisis, but are ill-equipped to take action, beholden to often complex 'rule-of-law' processes.

The idea of an autocratic advantage in crisis management only really applies if crisis is viewed as a one-off event – one in which immediacy of action is at a premium considerably in advance of other values. If, however, we conceptualise crisis more realistically as an iterative feature of the societal life-cycle – the periodic, sometimes violent reversal to which progress is almost invariably subject – the autocratic advantage quickly deteriorates. In the midst of an ongoing emergency, once having taken the wrong path – as a result of poor information or compromised decisional rationality – autocratic regimes may be less inclined (and less pressurised) to review action and change course, potentially compounding initial misdirection. In the aftermath, autocracies have limited incentives to learn from current crisis in order to prepare better for the next.

Figure 13.7: Freedom House 'Total Democracy' score and COVID-19 infection rate for 128 countries, December 2020

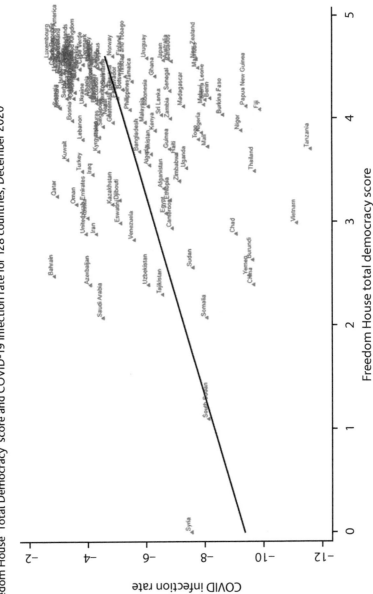

Source: Karabulut et al (2021)

If crisis is approached as a repeating phenomenon, democracy regains the edge – more likely, comparatively, to invest in the transparent review of past crisis management in order to refine future strategy; and more likely to allow for or actively promote public engagement and debate in determining the viability of such strategy (see, for example, Mackenbach and McKee, 2013). If openness to empirical scrutiny is a defining feature of adaptive crisis management over time, failure to exploit this capability condemns autocracies at best to an unpredictable blend of efficacy and error, their first-blush advantage compromised, over time, by an unstable attitude to data, information, transparency and truth.[26] There is no doubt that some autocratic countries did well in the last pandemic. But the net insight may be that democracies are, in fact, the preferable regime type to deal with crises we have yet to encounter over the long course of our coming history (see, for example, McCann and Tisch, 2021).

In the aftermath of COVID, two things appear clear. One is that the pandemic provided an extraordinary opportunity for democracy to reassert itself through the active promotion of citizen participation, dialogue and debate – broadening and deepening the role of lay voices in scientific and policy forums, not to achieve perfect consensus but to elicit and valorise public perspectives (Pearse, 2020; Stasavage, 2020; Brocard et al, 2021; Norheim et al, 2021; Afsahi et al, 2022).[27] The other is that many democracies appear to be busily failing to avail themselves of this opportunity. This is not the comparative inefficacy of democracy confronted with its sleeker autocratic peers. It is the endogenous failure of democracy to keep faith with its own essential premise.

Notes

[1]   In 2021, 36 per cent of the world's population lived in autocratising regimes; 3 per cent lived in countries moving the other way towards democracy (IDEA, 2019; Boese et al, 2022).

[2]   On 9 December 2021, Joe Biden convened an emergency global summit, announcing that the competition between democracy and autocracy was approaching 'an inflection point in history'.

[3]   John Adams to John Taylor, 17 December, 1814: "Remember, democracy never lasts long. It soon wastes, exhausts and murders itself. There never was a democracy yet that did not commit suicide."

[4]   Embodied in the 'revolving door' between electoral, bureaucratic and private sector interests and jobs.

[5]   Between 1972 and 2001, democracies in Latin America did better than nondemocracies in supporting human development, infant mortality and life expectancy (Altman and Castiglioni, 2009).

[6]   Although this can also work the other way as access to public information in the context of high or rising social inequality leads to worsening self-reported health (see, for example, Gugushvili and Reeves, 2021).

7   The Liberal Democracy Index is produced by the 'Varieties of Democracy' (V-Dem) project at the University of Gothenburg. The index is based on a qualitative and quantitative assessment of elections and suffrage rights; freedom of expression and association; equality before the law; and judicial and legislative constraints on the executive. It is measured in a continuous scale where more democratic regimes obtain higher scores.

8   Democracies have better survival rates for noncommunicable conditions like cardiovascular disease and cancer but do no better than autocracies on communicable diseases such as HIV/AIDS and malaria as well as diabetes and mental illness – pointing to a range of economic, technological, political and institutional factors complicating the interaction between democracy/autocracy and population health (Bollyky et al, 2019).

9   Personal observation in Taleban-led Afghanistan and Myanmar following the military coup in 2021.

10   Copyright American Economic Association; reproduced with permission of the *American Economic Review*.

11   Between 2000 and 2015, Rwanda achieved one of the fastest rates of child mortality reduction in history. Each of these countries, in its own, way, subsequently falling away from its most promising path.

12   See, for example, Bollyky et al (2019).

13   Under the influence of globalisation, democracies founded on common law principles, with greater flexibility to respond to public concerns, appear to produce better health than those built on civil law, where scope for responsiveness is more constrained.

14   States in northern India where colonial tax was collected through the *zamindari* (local powerbroking) system map onto areas of the country with the highest contemporary rates of malnutrition. Further south and west, the alternate practice of gathering tax directly from households (the *ryotwari* system) broke the stranglehold of local power structures leading to forms of agrarian land-holding and development associated with lower levels of malnutrition today (Lin, 2015).

15   As historian Maurice Meisner says, even accounting for the horrors and crimes of the Chinese revolution, 'few events in world history have done more to better the lives of more people' (Meisner, 1999).

16   Between 1959 and 1961, China experienced one of the worst famines in human history – a result of Mao's appallingly misjudged Great Leap Forward. At a conservative estimate, over three years around 30 million people died. Convention asserts that post-Independence India has never been exposed to similar catastrophic starvation – protected by the irrepressibility of information flow in democratic society. Yet over the last 70 years, even in the context of the Green Revolution, India's children have suffered far more than their Chinese peers from the devastating consequences of chronic undernutrition. In 2016, India's burden of chronic malnutrition was 12 times higher than China's. In 2017, malnutrition was the leading cause of child mortality in every single Indian state, contributing to almost two-thirds of under-five deaths across the country.

17   In 2019, China's per capita GDP was USD$10,551 compared with India's USD$1,928; Chinese life expectancy stood at 76.91 compared with India's 69.66; China's HDI was 0.761 against India's 0.645 (UNICEF, 2019). Between 1990 and 2018, China's under-five mortality rate fell from 54 per 1,000 live births to 9; India's from 129 to 37. In 2018, the lifetime risk to a woman of dying in childbirth was 1 in 2,100 in China and 1 in 290 in India. In early 2022, China had registered 3.43 COVID-19 deaths per million population;

India's rate was 355.89 (see, for example, UNICEF, 2019; see also Country comparison China vs India Human Development Index 2022 (countryeconomy.com).

[18] Pemstein et al (2022) Coppedge, M., Gerring, J., Knutsen, CH., Lindberg, S., Teorell, J., Alizada, et al (2022) 'V-Dem [Country–Year/Country–Date] Dataset v12' Varieties of Democracy (V-Dem) Project. https://doi.org/10.23696/vdemds22. Pemstein, D., Marquardt, K., Tzelgov, E., Wang, YT., Medzihorsky, J., Krusell, J., et al (2022) 'The V-Dem Measurement Model: La-tent Variable Analysis for Cross-National and Cross-Temporal Expert-Coded Data'. V-Dem Working Paper No. 21. 7th edition. University of Gothenburg: Varieties of Democracy Institute.

[19] Available at: GDP growth (annual %) – China, India, Data (worldbank.org)

[20] Indian democracy appears not much better than Chinese autocracy in protecting marginal populations from state expropriation of land, often for commercial development purposes (Ong, 2020).

[21] Although a catastrophic collapse in real estate markets in China might significantly alter this. In the early 1990s, I lived and worked in central China. Locally, the turbulence following Tiananmen Square in 1989, translated into both excitement about potential change in what was viewed as deeply repressive local government, seamlessly fitted within a tenacious faith in continuing credibility of the national Chinese state.

[22] In 2014, one-third of Indian respondents said they believe people, in general, could be trusted – compared with two-thirds of respondents in China (a rate almost exactly the same as that in Sweden). Proportion of people agreeing with the statement: 'most people can be trusted'. (Source: 'Trust', Our World in Data, https://ourworldindata.org/trust.)

[23] In 2021 the Freedom House survey downgraded India from free to 'partially free' democracy. In 2020, the V-Dem Institute classed India as an 'electoral autocracy'. Since 2014 India has fallen 26 places in the Economist Intelligence Unit's Democracy Index, joining the group of 'flawed democracies'. Available at: 'India reveres its democracy, but the room for dissent is shrinking', *New Statesman* (Kaur, R., 15 December 2021).

[24] Not least the extensive rights infringements and population control measures implemented in the Xinjiang Autonomous Region – an area whose geographic exposure westwards into central Asia has made it, throughout the history of the People's Republic, the subject of anxiety and periodic suppression by Beijing.

[25] Although case fatality was lower in advanced economies. It is unclear, too, whether it is autocracy itself that accounts for lower rates of infection, or omitted variables such as comparatively youthful populations (Cassan and Van Steenvort, 2021). According to one analysis, 'stronger democracies are slower to react in the face of the pandemic' (see, for example, Sebhatu et al, 2020).

[26] And, as it turns out, COVID data misreporting in autocratic regimes increases as the pandemic progresses compared with democratic regimes (Adam and Tsarsitalidou, 2022).

[27] During the pandemic, the 'Task Force on Life and the Law' established by then New York State Governor, Mario Cuomo, in 1985 to offer independent oversight on questions of health, medicine, ethics and law was, it is reported, nowhere to be seen (see, for example, Nuffield Council on Bioethics, 2020; Fins, 2021; Honigsbaum, 2022).

PART VI

Truth

14

Who counts?

Methods of quantitative measurement are the foundation of scientific modernity; systems of classification are the basis of political power. Somewhere between the two lies truth. From prehistoric systems of sheep-counting to the mapping of the human genome, our sense of self and social order is yoked to an instinct to enumerate the world around us – to tally, to classify, to analyse, to understand (Nassir Ghaemi, 2009). It has been suggested that '[t]he only sound way to appraise the state of the world is to count' (Pinker and Mack, 2014). To which estimably concise proposition, the only appropriate answer is, yes; but count what? How? For what purpose? And who decides?[1]

Take people. Enumerating the size and composition of a population has been central to processes of state formation and the projection of government power from Han China to modern Europe. But while numbers may be gathered, their significance remains highly contested – from the fight for birth registration in marginal communities[2] to the bitter struggles over census methodology – in countries from Afghanistan to America – disputing numerical superiority, geographical control, national identity and political power; or the contestation over population itself as societal necessity or existential species threat (Rosen, 1958; Glass and Eversley, 1965; Livi-Bacci, 1992; Kertzer et al, 2001; Todres, 2003; Lundberg et al, 2008; Carr-Hill, 2013; Visoka and Gjevori, 2013; Strmic-Pawl et al, 2018; McMichael and Weber, 2021).[3]

The idea of truth is, in any case, something of a fallacy – the eternally imperfect reconciliation of perception and reality (Ramsey, 1927). From Plato to Nietzsche, via Heisenberg and Schrödinger,[4] we encounter time and again fundamental limits in our ability to define the reality we inhabit, finding ourselves suspended probabilistically somewhere between accuracy and error (von Mises, 1957). It is, perversely, in the realm of concept that we are closest to capturing that reality. But as we convert concept into language, language into speech and speech into the endless nuance of human interaction, our ability to agree the truth of things – in particular what we owe one another as members of a common society – fragments (Wittgenstein, 1953; Levi-Strauss, 1955; Gard, 2011).

In the last decade, intensifying in the shadow of populist narratives and proliferating social media, we have heard much about 'fake news', a 'war on truth' and the ascendance of a 'post-truth world' (Jacobson and Mackey, 2019; Dobson, 2020). This, though, is perhaps a little overdone. Truth has always been elusive. In the social sciences we have, for some time now, immersed ourselves in the swirling uncertainties of the postmodern turn; in natural science, we are permanently either hypothetically ahead or experimentally behind truth. The trick is not whether in some implausibly immanent sense we can claim, finally, to have laid our hands on its finished form, but rather how we orient ourselves to truth in its continual state of becoming.

If the basic processes of truth remain largely intact, perhaps it is our appetite that has changed; that, having traversed a long history of kowtowing first to the primitive icons of traditional authority, then to the suffocating diktat of modern bureaucracy – and found the benefits of both wanting – we have emerged into a new world dominated by the demand for charismatic leadership offering revelatory solutions to the complicated business of modern life (Weber, 1922). People in regions across the world seem to have decided they no longer enjoy truths which feel imposed, borrowed or shared. They want, instead, truths which are personalised and wholly owned – nipped, tucked, tailored and delivered day and night to our hermetically sealed bubbles of prejudice and preference; the legacy, perhaps, of a neoliberal model which renders information a poorly regulated consumption commodity.[5]

The last 20 years have seen an industrial revolution in information technology – a *tsunami* of untestable ways of being and knowing and an unprecedented emptying out of our inner selves into the public ether. It is not that truth has changed – simply that it has become more difficult to pick out in an expanded landscape of competing possibilities. Social media doubtless bear some responsibility, supplying intimations of informational infallibility while nourishing us with the entrails of an eviscerated society. But the appetite for alternative facts does not equate with a demand for untruth. It looks rather more like a conscious stratagem among the left behind of globalisation, spurred by an increasing sense of powerlessness, to reacquire some semblance of dignity and control – the satisfactions of individual dissent over the benefits of common knowledge. It is not truth that has slipped away from us, but we who have allowed the delicate fabric of a shared will to believe – to privilege collective credence over individual inclination – to weaken and decay (Cosentino, 2020).

In 1938, at the 6th National Congress of the Chinese Communist Party, Chairman Mao urged his comrades to "seek truth from facts".[6] For all his faults, Mao had, it seems, rather a subtle sense of 'fact' and 'truth'; that one is derived from the other, and that neither is absolute; that truth reveals itself progressively and continuously and so must carry in itself the permanent admission of fallibility (Feyerabend, 1975; Aldemer, 1985; Atkins, 1995). Up to a point, truth liberates and unifies; beyond that point, it divides and imprisons. Viewed as absolute, static and universal, as George Orwell observed, truth is the preferred tool of totalitarian oppression, religious intolerance and ideological violence. Viewed as a process, however, it is arguably the only meaningful pursuit we have; the necessary basis – recognising both spiritual and scientific modes of inquiry – on which human society is made possible. That 'truth' is out there is, for all pragmatic purposes, not worth doubting. That we fail continuously quite to reach or grasp it is the problem at hand.

Health as truth?

Patterns of disease distribution tell us much about the physical world of pathogens – but they tell us even more about the social world through which those pathogens move. In India in 2006, Muslims constituted roughly 16 per cent of the population but around 70 per cent of cases of poliomyelitis (Figure 14.1) (Hussain et al, 2015).[7] This is unlikely to have been the result of a viral fondness for Islamic bodies. Polio infection was, rather, mapping deeper tensions – of religious identity, economic status and political power – fracturing Indian society of the time. Whilst acquiring hard data through sophisticated systems of surveillance was key to identifying patterns of physical transmission,

Figure 14.1: Poliomyelitis in India, 2003–2004

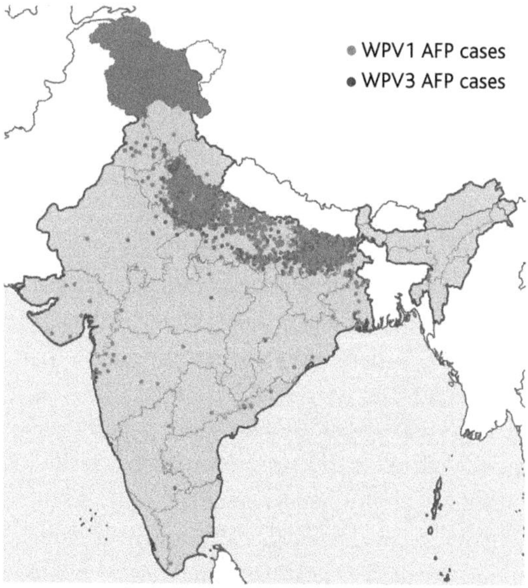

Source: WHO HQ/Global Polio Eradication Initiative (2004)

it was the political interpretation of those data – shaped by fiercely contested visions of epidemiological meaning, social causation and responsibility – that determined the scope of policy responses, and their impact on the human world.[8]

As a matter of definition, health is satisfyingly binomial. At the end of the day you either are, or you are not, dead (Shiffman, 2014; Nay and Barre-Sinoussi, 2022). Hippocrates believed that medicine was the archetype of scientific knowledge – the human body offering a unique combination of empirical information and ethical imperative. Over a long history, ideas of medicine and health have evolved an ecosystem of interlinking taxonomies bridging conceptual and practical, practical and social, social and moral – of anatomy, pathophysiology and pharmacology, diagnostics and disease, evidence and ethics, prevention and cure: a nuanced heuristic by which to gauge the condition of our bodies and the state of our society.

It is a history, though, characterised by tension between the intuitions of rationalism and the stricter requirements of empirical proof – whittling away, over centuries, grand monistic theories of causation towards more granular analysis of physical effect, from macrosocial notions of *qi* and *humor* to the microbiological world of spike proteins and neurotransmitters (Shryock 1969; Atwood, 2003; Gillett, 2006; Cook, 2010; van den Tweel and Taylor, 2010).[9] In the process, in keeping with the precepts of modernity, we have tilted towards empiricism as the surer route to objective knowledge – the idea that truth is discoverable independent of its social context – cleaving to the idea of experimental testability, the emergence of 'evidence-based medicine' and the apotheosis of the randomised control trial (RCT) (Jackson, 1932; Hill, 1937; Cochrane, 1972; Holmes et al, 2006).

A fundamental premise of RCTs is that the distorting influence of social values and the bias they introduce can largely be stripped out of the experimental process, allowing us to demonstrate with maximum objectivity the true nature of an intervention's effect, whether in pharmaceutical treatment or social policy. The problem here is not that independence or objectivity is undesirable – but that it is very hard to achieve. RCTs are considerably more vulnerable to distortions of design, implementation and interpretation than their reputation often allows (Deaton and Cartwright, 2018; Wieringa et al, 2018; Ravallion, 2020). Findings achieved in strenuously controlled settings are notoriously hard to replicate in the scaled-up world of untrammelled reality. And, in the end, the assertion of results as definitive can misrepresent as scientifically certified policy choices which are necessarily plural, social and political.

The intention of the RCT is unimpeachable – but as a research tool not an article of faith. The practical and ethical costs of trying to outlaw social messiness through the ritual purification of the RCT may, in the end, outweigh benefits – which, in the nature of the methodology, tend in any case to be quantitatively modest between treatment and non-treatment groups. If ideas of truth are progressively detached from historical experience and political context they cease to serve the purposes of public knowledge, removed to an elite sphere within which policy is increasingly invisible to the people whose lives they shape.

The earth from space

The post-war period saw a sharp acceleration of exchange between nations, raising the possibility of constructing new frameworks of global knowledge beyond the irregularity of countries and cultures – a single vision of collective humanity, subordinating questions of political value under the imprimatur of technological objectivity (see Figure 14.2) (Broome and Quirke, 2015).[10] Health, combining rich traditions of empiricism and matters of universal human value, offered a potent field of global knowledge mapping new medical capabilities onto our most urgent needs (Mahajan, 2019).[11]

Figure 14.2: 'Earthrise', 1968

From the 1960s, a plethora of 'summary population measures' emerged forming the building blocks of a global architecture of health information, integrating traditional measurement of mortality and longevity with estimations of the physical quality of people's lives prior to death.[12] Of all the indicators, the quality-adjusted life year (QALY) and the disability-adjusted life year (DALY) are probably the most widely used and influential (Sredl, 2011; Voigt and King, 2017). The QALY was developed in the 1960s and 1970s to help quantify the economic utility of emerging medical treatments, primarily in advanced economies, providing a notionally objective rationale by which policy makers could allocate resources to healthcare technologies as wealthy, ageing societies sought ever more costly biomedical intervention (MacKillop and Sheard, 2018). The DALY was developed in the 1980s with a focus on low-income developing countries – initially part of the World Bank's 'Global Burden of Disease' (GBD) study, designed to generate more nuanced understanding of the combined impact on poor economies of mortality and non-fatal illness (Cookson et al, 2021).[13]

Over the last three decades, the GBD has grown into probably the most extensive body of global health data in history – becoming, in the process, both repository and arbiter of the truth of human health to many global institutions and governments, and anathema to those who question its veracity or repudiate its articulation of physical needs with economic value (Adams, 2016). There is no particularly valid reason to reject systems of ranking and economic evaluation, especially where interventions flowing from them rely on public investment. But there are good reasons to challenge such approaches where they distort, misrepresent – or simply fail to encapsulate – reality (Woods et al, 2016; Gold and Muennig, 2002).

For one thing, comparative estimation of illnesses may be viewed as pitting one human experience against another, types of disease and disability arranged competitively in ways which can further disadvantage groups already normatively marginalised.[14] Aggregation of preference across populations, generating an average of 'what people want', may fail to reflect divergent values and aspirations of individuals, families and communities, desensitising attention to distributional justice, and risking the depoliticisation of issues which deserve active public debate (Scott, 2008; Drummond et al, 2009; Pettitt et al, 2016).[15]

Ranking methodologies are generally based on public preference surveys, using hypothetical trade-off games. Such games, though, tend to underplay psychological framing – the extent of people's health literacy, their ability to estimate societal averages from local experience, their different levels of risk tolerance, and the degree by which they discount the value of the future. Applied in poor communities, trade-off games struggle to account for external conditions – of poverty in income, assets, social capital and choice – which shape the way we formulate expectation (Trautmann et al, 2021). As a result, estimates of the relative burden of different diseases differ substantially depending on the measure used and the status of the people you ask (Field and Gold, 1998; Gold et al, 2002; Polinder et al, 2012).[16] Questions of methodology are compounded, however, by more fundamental weaknesses in the raw material of information – the extent to which global data systems are able to capture grounded reality in parts of the world where human life is often poorly enumerated.

The GBD draws on multiple sources – civil registration, national health information systems and population surveys, supported by peer-reviewed and grey research literature and overseen by thematic expert advisory groups. It is a solid edifice of checks and balances in a world hampered by incomplete fact. But each source is, in its own way, fallible (Torrance, 1986; Gold et al, 2002; Chan, 2012). Global health research and publication tends to be weighted in favour of high-income country perspectives. Population surveys tend to be sporadic, retrospective and reliant on the variability of verbal autopsy and human recall. Most critically, the quality of official data is widely questionable, acutely in poorer, less institutionally developed countries – among government agencies occupied by more pressing issues of politics, poverty and survival, drawing on local health information systems struggling to manage huge volumes of often paper-based recording while crushed under the weight of frontline service demands (Voigt and King, 2014; Wyber et al, 2015; Zuboff, 2015; Tichenor and Sridhar, 2019).[17]

The geography of meaning

The GBD constitutes what is, very likely, a largely accurate aggregate view of the world. But truth is not simply a question of accuracy, and aggregation tends to obscure important local diversity (see, for example, Lee, 2015). Truth may not be relative, but it is certainly relational – its use-value changing from one context to another, shaped by the material circumstances in which it is deployed. This is not, of course, to suggest that facts may be viewed as differently factual in different places. Rather that the practical significance of knowledge – its potential to serve society – changes as it moves between geographical and institutional levels, from global to national to local. From the polished conference PowerPoint on maternal mortality to the management of an obstructed labour in a remote rural clinic, the utility of our truths depends on the degree to which they are generated and applied within the meaningful range of people's lives and the resources available to operationalise them.

The construction of a global architecture of health knowledge – however magnificent in form – 'dis-locates' truth, leaving obscured in its palatial foundations a fragmented, partial, incomplete reality on the ground where people live and die, draining energy out of the critical local processes of information, analysis, knowledge and debate through which lived society comes to know and act on itself; assiduously hoovering up primary data and moulding them, through arcane computational processes into what is without question an unprecedentedly comprehensive vision of the human world but one which is abstracted from that world in a kind of ethereal epistemological domain of knowing (Horton, 2013; Mathers, 2020).[18]

Health data are more than units of meaning which, in the right order, form facts. They are a manifestation of the relationship – political, technological, clinical, social – between citizen and state, a form of currency between community and health centre, between patient and doctor, between doctor and nurse, between clinician and administrator. In health, failures of recording, registration and documentation – in the community, the clinic, the local hospital and local government – reflect more than simply administrative oversight; they represent unresolved weaknesses in the social and institutional interactions that make up the developmental premise of the 'good society'; the way we, in a literal sense, are able to evaluate – and then value – one another; how our needs are recognised (or not) and the quality of statutory and social relations through which those needs are or are not met.

Gaps and distortions in the local landscape of health information tell us about more than just the absence of enumeration (Power, 2004). They tell us about relationships of knowledge, hierarchy, value and power – where primary data recording falls to underpaid clerical staff and undervalued nurses and midwives hard-pressed by other duties and too often disempowered in owning the meaning and utility of the data they are asked to collect; where underinvestment in technological capacity and clinical training limit diagnostic capability resulting in the enumeration of diseases more aligned to global taxonomies than local reality; where the nature of mortality itself is shaped by the uncertain interaction between social and medical notions of risk, value and loss;[19] where local actors harvest information to feed upward to central governments increasingly inclined to fashion a national epidemiological picture to fit international goals and financing incentives.

The problem with the global model of aggregate health information is not that it is in some respect fatally flawed. It is not.[20] The problem is that it risks overemphasising truth in the world above while leaving truth incomplete, fragmented and underutilised in the world below; that the weight of a superdominant truth eventually steamrolls over local processes of inquiry, investigation and enumeration – processes which are vital to the creation of knowledge in forms which are rooted in local realities of social value as they change and evolve.

Terra incognita

Systems of knowledge tend to reflect status quo society – the amalgam of an evidenced past and an uncertain future, as they meet and merge in the political present. Systems of health information, especially as they aggregate communities and countries, tend to privilege metrics which enable continuity with what came before, to ensure coherent construction of trend over time. The result, though, is a picture of global health which is disciplinarily biomedical and socially conservative, which struggles to incorporate changing social values, offering a vision of the future bound unhelpfully to an understanding of the past.

The International Classification of Diseases (ICD) is possibly one of the driest documents you will ever read, and probably the most substantial document defining the physical make-up of modern society – the ultimate taxonomy of the physiological truths of the human condition. Originally agreed in 1900, the ICD has been through ten further revisions, roughly one per decade.[21] Over this time, each new iteration has been a struggle between the powerful instinct to maintain historical continuity over recognition of social change – the canon of authorised biomedical knowledge confronted by emerging social interpretations of physical values, their function and dysfunction (Bowker, 1996).

What is included in the ICD has been the subject of vigorous contest between the interests of continuity and the imperatives of change: from resistance to the inclusion of poor-country diseases as authority for classification shifted from European colonial powers through the League of Nations to the notional universality of the UN system; through the physiological definition of the start of life, grounded in differing religious and cultural worldviews; to the assignment of cause of death, in cases of co-morbidity, oriented to factors most amenable to technological intervention, most relevant to economic formation (for example industrial accidents) or to the exclusion of effects (like domestic violence) constituted as outside the purview of the state.[22]

Taxonomies like the GBD and ICD offer an invaluable opportunity to extend and expand our understanding of global health. But they may also, in their nature, exclude or suppress conditions of being which bridge between physical classification and social norm as the demarcation between the two changes – matters such as those of sexuality, gender and identity, of mental health, of ageing; conditions which, as countries overcome infectious disease and noncommunicable illness, will become the new frontiers in what it means to live a life of health and well-being; but conditions, too, which embody great challenge in the intersection between biomedical and social interpretations.[23]

The incorporation of disability in the GBD unquestionably expanded our understanding of mental health at the centre of human suffering where before there had been little more than an uncomfortable global silence. Yet action remains limited – partly the effect of scarce clinical resources, acutely in low- and middle-income countries, but also continuing legal, institutional, clinical and social ambivalence about what we mean by mental illness, where the boundaries lie between idiosyncrasy and disorder, and about the efficacy, necessity and validity of pharmaceutical and non-pharmaceutical interventions – all rooted in the abiding influence of stigma and shame.

While the social demarcations of identity rights defined by sex and gender have become subject to widening challenge in the last four decades, most enumerative exercises – from scientific research to public census, legal process and social policy – remain firmly anchored in the stolid binary notion of definitively 'male' and 'female' types (Sundby, 1999; Cislaghi et al, 2020; Weber et al, 2021). The informational infrastructure which authorises our empirical understanding of sex and gender does not support, or actively constrains, the necessary breadth of debate about the increasingly nuanced experiences of gender and the possibilities of individual being – our concepts of identity indentured to a backward-looking vision of sex, while our daily experience blurs – to the point of destruction – the conventional boundaries of that vision (see, for example, Carpenter, 2021; Chamberlain and Lyons, 2022).

Within the next hundred years, it is quite possible that our dyadic view of sex, gender and identity will be viewed as a quaint if perplexingly two-dimensional historical artefact. But the ways in which we approach knowing this in the interim will determine to a significant extent the degree to which change will be a matter of constructive learning or of bitterly contested truths.

Conclusion

Health offers a unique domain in which objective needs, technical capabilities and social values merge. We are making extraordinary advances in our ability to support population health, and equally impressive strides in the way those advances can be measured. The potential of health to act as an arbiter of our progress – from local to global levels – is vast. But we fail to substantiate that potential if we allow our physical well-being to be posed as disembodied, elite knowledge snatched from us in upward-oriented bureaucratic or proprietarily opaque processes and visited back on us in ways which are increasingly unresponsive to the changing values of the lives we lead.

As we navigate the grey areas between physical and social identity, the architecture of global health data – properly imagined – offers a fertile space in which to capture new and emerging concepts, rendering them open to structured contestation, and monitoring the distance between empirical tradition and the lived reality of the social world as it evolves; to create a quantitative language within which qualitatively new social forms can find their articulation; to create a framework within which the inevitable personal, public and ethical struggles over the meaning of markers of physical and social identity, like gender, can be managed through a more structured pattern of signifiers and a more open field of epistemological debate. Over the last half century, we have developed an extraordinarily sophisticated capability in global health measurement. But if it floats over the world's multiple and complex realities, imposing a form of order, of truth which we are unable to recognise, it betrays the nature of health as social meaning.

We are all, in the end, researchers in the nature and quality of our lives – in the interaction between the physical and social conditions we occupy.[24] We are making extraordinary progress in illuminating the physical properties of the natural and human worlds. But when the empirical is posed as independently sovereign – stripping out social meaning, ideological interpretation, group interest and personal experience – it risks creating a monopoly hold on knowledge, undermining the essentially political process through which the physical facts of our lives are transformed into the social truths of our individual and collective existence. Truth – as it is embodied in patterns of health, disease and death around the world – fails if it becomes detached from the ground in which it grows or undermines the necessary forces of contestation through which it evolves.

COVID: truth and trust

COVID-19 has been widely construed as the first 'post-truth' pandemic (Parmet and Paul, 2020; Shelton, 2020; Formighieri Giordani et al, 2021; Kwok et al, 2021; Nally, 2022; Prasad, 2022).[25] This may, though, be mainly a matter of over-excited labelling. What is clear is that COVID-19 placed our notions of truth in an awkward position – beset by proliferating distrust and rippling counter-narratives, flamboyantly outré accounts, of conspiracy and confection by the deep state, a demented confabulation of virus, 5G and creeping Chinese imperialism, of exotic treatments and quack remedies (Hunt, 2020; Adalberto, 2021; Gutenschwager, 2021).

What fuels these narratives is not so much their wide credence among the majority, but their appeal to the mass and social media business model for whom straightforward, thoughtful questioning is simply less commercially attractive than sinister theory and the inflation of polarising audience bubbles – sometimes the product of malign interests but mainly amplified by a yen for sensation among the swelling ranks of the disempowered and disenchanted (Keidl and Melamed, 2020). In a sense, the clamorous noise of pandemic 'post-truth' is the inevitable, and wholly predictable, consequence of late-stage modernity – the democratisation of knowledge and the fragmentation of authority (Farr, 2003). You cannot spend decades urging people to individualise every aspect of their lives and then express horrified surprise when they insist on individualising their truth settings.[26]

COVID-19 has been described as an 'infodemic'[27] – a painful coinage constituting knowledge (and its distortions) as if naturally occurring agents (Venkataramakrishnan, 2020). But information does not simply happen to us – it is what we choose and create, the currency of our social and political relations. If COVID is characterised by anything relating to the question of truth, it is in the slow-motion car crash between reasonable public questioning and grotesquely under-powered political response. The objective facts of COVID were, in the early pandemic, clouded by high levels of uncertainty in the science of the disease and significant variation in the dynamics of its impact – of disease severity, from asymptomatic transience to rapid deterioration and death or crippling 'long COVID'; of tragic personal experience diluted by disputed estimates of population risk (Jewell et al, 2020);[28] outlandish therapies – from gargling garlic to ingesting bleach – facing off against the real-time struggle of frontline clinicians to find effective treatments for a mounting cohort of desperately unwell patients; the unparalleled speed of vaccine development itself provoking questions of pharmaceutical transparency; complex statistical evidence of vaccine efficacy further complicated by commercial competition and an unprecedented differentiation of antigen 'brands', undermining generalised vaccine confidence in the face of inevitable, but in the interim unscalable, adverse events, for products which remained, in any case, unavailable in the initial instance to a large part of the world.

In the UK, wavering government posture frozen for weeks in the pandemic's headlights – between 'letting it rip' to build an illusory herd immunity and stopping COVID dead through society-wide lockdown – fed a seemingly endless back-and-forth between scientific and policy communities about the evidence for control measures, from the monstrous imposition of face masks to the degree of aerosol and fomite transmission and the metrical specificity of effective social distancing; vacillating cycles of lockdown imposition and easing, swapping epidemiological logic for economic imperative, emanating through multiple streams of political, official and public health communication horribly mangling the intelligibility of rules whose margins of interpretability required high levels of essentially voluntary public understanding and self-restraint.

The post-truth problem of the COVID-19 pandemic was a failure of governance.[29] Much institutional energy was invested in mounting what might be viewed as a rather cynical daily theatre of crisis communication – the *mise-en-scène* splicing slides of scientific data with policy pronouncement as if epistemologically coterminous; government seeking to camouflage its policy choices – its inability to choose, and its luckless choices – under a cloak of scientific objectivity; political and scientific leaders, shoulder to awkward shoulder, locked in a joint enterprise interweaving clarity and obfuscation.[30] The political attempt to coopt 'science' as independent justification for policy choice may well, in the long run, be the most toxic legacy of the COVID pandemic.[31]

Truth is the product of scientific investigation mediated by social and economic values and processed through political confrontation and public debate. Popular post-pandemic notions – that we should hereafter have more science in politics or, conversely, that we should accept the inevitable politicisation of science – reflect the necessary tension between the two communities (Carney and Bennett, 2014; Fuller, 2020).[32] Transparency is key – both in the clear distinction between what is known and what not, and the demarcation between scientific knowledge and political choice (Sarmiento et al, 2021). Transparency, though, depends on active public scrutiny, itself dependent on populations adequately engaged in their communities and society. High and rising rates of social and economic inequality – radically different experiences of security and insecurity, inclusion and exclusion, of access to essential public health, medical and social care services, in household reserves of financial, material and social capital by which to manage the immediate and long-run impacts of lockdown – fundamentally erode the collective rationality of shared truths, and the practical ability of households to comply with what those truths require.

Notes

[1] There is a (likely apocryphal) account by Michel Foucault of an ancient Chinese imperial taxonomy of animals, discovered in a translator's text and described by Jorge Luis Borges in his 1942 essay 'El idioma analítico de John Wilkins'. In the fictitious encyclopaedia, animals are divided into: '(a) belonging to the Emperor (b) embalmed (c) tame (d) suckling pigs (e) sirens (f) fabulous (g) stray dogs (h) included in the present classification (i) frenzied (j) innumerable (k) drawn with a very fine camelhair brush (l) *et cetera* (m) having just broken the water pitcher (n) that from a long way off look like flies'. Borges' example points to the potential for chaos, not to say absurdity, in attempting to create hierarchical order by allocating social meaning to the physical world – what belongs to whom, and why – without reference to some kind of objective method (see Foucault, 1970: xv).

[2] In 2019, one in four children under five years old around the world did not officially exist (see UNICEF, 2019).

[3] In 1960, global fertility was 200 per cent of global mortality. Between 1975 and 1977, India declared a national emergency during which eight million citizens were subjected to sterilisation, many of them forcibly. By the mid-1970s, the American aid budget was wholly dominated by investments in family planning.

[4] Respectively, Werner Heisenberg's uncertainty principle, that we cannot know with complete accuracy both the position and momentum of a particle; and Erwin Schrödinger's thought experiment in which a cat sealed in a box with a phial of poison which breaks when radioactivity from randomly decaying atomic material is detected may be considered, until observed as one or the other, to be simultaneously alive and dead (see, for example, Schrödinger, 1935).

[5] The irony being that, given the impossible effort and inefficiency of eight billion individual knowledge systems, people disavowing centralised truth are obliged to re-form in smaller epistemic communities the price of admission to which is, all too often, the adoption of an aggressive credulousness.

[6] 'Shi shi qiu shi' (实事求是). This admirable, if opaque, pragmatism was revived by Premier Deng Xiaoping after 1978 as a central ideological platform of 'socialism with

Chinese characteristics' – the daring reformist attempt to incorporate market economics within China's socialist political system. Deng's strategy was to 'cross the river by feeling for stones' – in essence shaping policy truths on the basis of their empirical effect, but allowing that this may change, sometimes radically, over time.

[7] See, for example, the tight clustering of polio infections in the poorest Indian states of Uttar Pradesh and Bihar, with some of the country's largest Muslim populations, in the early 2000s (see Figure 14.1).

[8] At the time, reference to differential exposure among Muslim communities was viewed as politically unacceptable in the context of the then-dominant Hindu nationalist Bharatiya Janata Party administration in Delhi [personal observation]. It was decided that infected communities should be described as 'underserved' – their exposure to disease reconfigured as one of healthcare access and vaccine acceptance rather than religious identity and socioeconomic exclusion.

[9] American Medical Association Transactions. Philadelphia, 1851.

[10] A vision epitomised in 'Earthrise' taken from the Apollo 8 mission by William Anders (NASA, 1968; Figure 14.2). British astronomer Fred Hoyle noted that '[o]nce a photograph of the earth, taken from outside, is available, a new idea as powerful as any in history will be let loose'.

[11] In 2013, Bill Gates compared the development of global health metrics with the invention of steam power (see Bill & Melinda Gates Foundation, 2013).

[12] From the 'health-adjusted life year' (HALY), 'health-adjusted life expectancy' (HALE) and 'health-related quality of life' (HRQL), through 'quality-adjusted life expectancy or years' (QALE/QALY), 'years of healthy life' (YHL) to disability-adjusted life years (DALY) and 'disability-free life expectancy' (DFLE) among others.

[13] The QALY and DALY articulating rather neatly the two faces of global health – the extension of viable life in the rich world and the mitigation of avoidable death in the poor. Both systems use a 0–1 scoring system – but where a QALY score of 1 denotes perfect health, a DALY score of 1 constitutes being dead. The GBD was initially input to the World Bank's 1993 World Development Report. It is now managed by the Institute for Health Metrics and Evaluation.

[14] Such that 'on average, society judges a year with blindness to be preferable to a year with paraplegia, and a year with paraplegia to be preferable to a year with unremitting unipolar major depression' (Mathers et al., 2001).

[15] Comparative estimates of necessity and cost may make sense in the context of countries with universal healthcare, they are arguably less helpful in systems of care – reflective of much of the world – which are fragmented, inequitable and inaccessible.

[16] 'Willingness to pay' (WTP) is a popular way of assessing how much people value different health states thus guiding policy options, by assessing how much individuals would sacrifice in money terms to avoid indisposition or death. Aside from the obvious question about how this works across households with wildly different levels of wealth, different evaluative methods generate widely differing results (McDougall et al, 2020). In one survey, hypothetical WTP was 3.2 times higher than actual WTP. One of the best, if possibly most misunderstood, examples of imputed economistic inhumanity is the 'value of statistical life' (VSL) (Balmford et al, 2019; Sweis, 2022). In some respects, rather an innocuous proposition (an actuarial estimate of how much

additional wage people would require to assume extra risk), VSL has been accused of being (or at least sounding) rather callous, bordering on unethical (Cameron, 2010). Part of the problem, perhaps, is that VSL appears to be methodologically comfortable concluding that, based on World Bank income data, the lifetime value of one Bermudan is approximately that of 400 Rwandans (USD$18.2 million versus USD$45,000) (Viscusi and Masterman, 2017).

[17] In 2016, in the GBD's five-star 'cause of death' data quality rating, 20 out of 22 countries in Western Europe scored 4–5 stars; of 46 countries in sub-Saharan Africa, 26 scored one star and 16 none (Naghavi et al, 2019). One response to this – reflecting our new faith in big data – is to repair incomplete reality through increasingly sophisticated statistical remodelling backed by astounding capabilities in supercomputing; to manage 'garbage codes', data gaps and black holes through processes of plausible redistribution and imputation. The results are nothing if not impressive. The GBD offers global policy makers and time-poor, need-rich developing countries a structured way of framing health and deriving evidence-based priorities for action through a methodology notionally transferrable from one part of the world to another. This kind of massive data processing, we are told, will lead to a better understanding of who we are and what we need as individuals and as societies. But it does so without, perhaps, adequate transparency or public engagement around the question: better for whom, and according to what? The uses of big data – the policy choices it supports – require coherent, transparent governance. There is a distinct risk that the collective technological, statistical and computational power of a fragmentary landscape of public and private global health actors will ultimately displace WHO's mandated global authority while at the same time overwhelming under-resourced but governmentally vital national information systems (see, for example, Coyle, 2019; see also Clinton and Sridhar, 2017; Pastorino et al, 2019; Shiffman and Shawar, 2020; Supriya and Chattu, 2021; Thomason, 2021).

[18] Not unlike the island of Laputa in Swift's *Gulliver's Travels* – populated by an intellectual elite with a penchant for mathematics living in splendid magnetic levitation above the world over which they rule.

[19] Recording of mortality is weak in many developing countries – and continues to be problematic in the wealthier world. Standardised hospital mortality methodologies were the subject of bitter argument in the UK in the early 2000s; in Myanmar, hospital registers are littered with the final entry 'signed and left', denoting cases where parents prefer for cultural reasons to bring a yet-living child home, probably but not certainly to die; the opprobrium attached to mothers dying in some developing countries, under the pressure of global goals, results in maternal deaths around the time of birth being reassigned to other less sensitive causes, distorting our ability, in quite wide geographies, accurately to understand the risk women bear in childbirth; stillbirth is still significantly under-reported globally, the combined effect of clinical practice and cultural norm.

[20] The same argument applies to emerging forms of artificial intelligence – that they are technically valid, with a high level of potential to contribute to decision-making – but that their value remains rooted in the extent to which they embody social and political objectives which are transparently agreed and monitored.

[21] ICD-11 was endorsed through the 72nd World Health Assembly on 25 May 2019 and came into effect on 1 January 2022.

[22] The preface to the 5th ICD, in 1938, notes: 'the Conference endeavoured to make no changes in the contents ... so that statistics based on the successive Lists should be as comparable as possible, and employees of the registration and statistical services of the

different countries should have their habits of work changed as little as possible. Many possible improvements in matters of form and order were abandoned in order to achieve this practical object' (League of Nations, 1938, p. 947 in Bowker, 1996).

[23] See, for example, WHO (2001), Summerfield (2012), Patel (2014), Balon et al (2016) and *Lancet* (2017).

[24] As Rudolph Virchow noted: 'Medicine is a social science and politics is nothing else but medicine on a large scale.'

[25] Pandemics, like other catastrophic events, have for much of human history been accompanied by 'alternative' explanations, cod philosophies and quack remedies. Perhaps COVID, though, is the first pandemic experienced in the context of fully globalised systems of communication, markets and governance.

[26] Reminiscent of Captain Renault in *Casablanca*, on collecting his winnings at Rick's café: "I am shocked … *shocked* … to discover that gambling is going on in here."

[27] WHO Director-General Tedros Adhanom Ghebreyesus at the Munich Security Conference, 2020. 'An infodemic is too much information including false or misleading information in digital and physical environments during a disease outbreak. It causes confusion and risk-taking behaviours that can harm health. It also leads to mistrust in health authorities and undermines the public health response.' See also, Debanjan and Meena, 2021; Infodemic (who.int).

[28] See, for example, India's challenge to WHO's mortality estimates, Concerns With Method, Says India On Report Of "Stalling" WHO COVID Report (ndtv.com), 17 April 2022.

[29] 'That so many advanced countries with highly capable science advisory ecosystems had failures and were unable to act wisely and early is astounding' (William Colglazier, 9 April 2020).

[30] For a shameful *post-hoc* attempt to rewrite the history of the UK government's pandemic decision-making – the political seeking to frame the scientific as culpable – see former Chancellor Rishi Sunak's comments in Nelson (2022).

[31] In 2021, doctors were the most trusted of the world's many professions, closely followed by scientists and teachers. Least trusted were government ministers, advertising executives and politicians. Trying to force the two extremes into a single credible voice is likely to be problematic at best. IPSOS Global Trustworthiness Index, 12 October 2021. Global Trustworthiness Index 2021 (ipsos.com).

[32] "We need science to have the same power as economics in political decisions and policy-making" (Patrick Vallance, UK Chief Science Officer, 12 October 2021).

Conclusion: crisis redux

Crisis is an ambiguous construct – part menace, part hope; open as much to the possibility of catharsis as of catastrophe. Our sense of crisis may be framed by the acute moment of onset, but it is defined by the way we respond – how societies react in the short term, absorbing and distributing impact and, perhaps more importantly, how in the aftermath we learn and adapt.

Because the current cluster of calamities is hardly new. It is the contemporary iteration of a long historical timeline. Economic collapse, global pestilence, war – we have been here before. Today, though, there are two important differences. First, the crises from which this book proceeds are all now subsidiary to and linked, directly or indirectly, with a planetary emergency whose scale and imminence are no longer open to doubt. Second, we are as never before in history, possessed of the knowledge, wealth, technological expertise and – at least in principle – global interconnectedness with which to fashion an effective response. In other words, we have every reason to do better, and little choice.

There is a third and, I think, defining factor shaping our prospects of charting a way forward from COVID – and it is the extent to which we choose to do something serious about inequality. Because the idea of crisis discussed in this book is not so much the particular instance of profligate finance or raging pandemic or even climate emergency. It is the quieter, subtler failure in the structural mechanisms through which such systemic breakdown is handled; the underlying slow-burn collapse in relations between people in communities, between citizens and their government, and between governments globally; the disintegration of faith in the shared values which have brought us to this point and which we will need to draw on, revisit – and perhaps radically redefine – as we navigate our way out.

The suggestion of a crisis in liberal values is not to imply their wholesale rejection. It is, rather, to challenge the dominant influence of a particular neoliberal philosophy through which they are interpreted (Fukuyama, 2022); to rebalance the relentless, mindless concentration on individual and market as the indispensable correlates of social meaning; to re-socialise the liberal premise in a form which recognises its values as fundamentally relational; to demonstrate the necessarily collective dimensions through which liberalism is itself made possible. Nor is the idea of crisis to deny progress – but rather to challenge the speciousness of facile optimism just as of dogged pessimism, the hallmarks of polarising political discourse untethered from the obligations of evidence and balance (Dember et al, 1989; Hecht, 2013).[1]

Over the last 250 years, we have covered a volatile terrain of hopes and fears – evolving layer upon layer of complexity as 'developed' and 'developing' regions have merged in a single globalising enterprise, weaving a marvellous tapestry of competing theoretical model and empirical argument: of triumphal Enlightenment positivism and anti-imperial rage (Fanon, 1961; Pinker, 2018); of demographic gloom and irrepressible technological cornucopianism (Malthus, 1798; Simon, 1981; Galor, 2022); of iron laws of economic decay and hopeful hypotheses of unbounded growth (Singer, 1975; Romer, 1990); of confidence and critique in the cultural probity and empirical effectiveness of international development (Escobar, 1995; Sachs, 2005; Easterly, 2006).

There is much in the present world for which we should be profoundly thankful and of which we can be justly proud. Our progress has been truly breath-taking. We have covered an enormous distance, sharply rising in a stunning sequence of short historical bursts over the last three centuries. The revelations of the Enlightenment and everything that has followed in scientific discovery and the application of reason constitute, without doubt, a grand speciating moment – mapping earth, sea and sky; exploring and quantifying the physical universe, the dynamics of human society, the genome, the microbiome, the nanosphere and the magical properties of the quantum world; establishing common principles of government, law and exchange; forming a global community of nations embodying a shared faith in the rule of law through multiple multilateral platforms of encounter and engagement; advancing democratic norms and confronting autocratic brutality; mitigating absolute economic poverty and creating unprecedented wealth; spurring fields of technological and medical discovery confronting our morbidities and mortality, harnessing infectious and chronic diseases, unravelling genetic causation, disseminating treatments and driving down avoidable suffering (Deaton, 2013).

But there is failure too – failure whose gravity is exactly commensurate with the scale of our widely advertised success. It is, at heart, a failure of universality; a failure to confront, comprehensively, the disequalising forces of hierarchy from local to global; to fight much – much – harder for an equitable engagement, within countries and between them, in common access to the extraordinary capabilities we appear able to engender; a willful political failure, galvanised around narratives which harp on justice while repudiating the notion of equality, to enact the fundamental truth of common human entitlement.

In the last decade or so – perhaps as an intuitive response to a deepening global malaise – there has been something of a resurgence of optimistic thinking, repudiating the endlessly bleak arguments of doom-saying sociologists and environmentalists and their unappealing habit of mauling, so the story goes, the liberal hand that feeds the very intellectual freedoms they enjoy. But it is an optimism which subordinates wickedly problematic dynamics of population, resource and inequality to the imputedly superior forces of intellectual rationalism and the magical power of apparently unlimited technological innovation; an optimism which merges a unifying Enlightenment past with a shining global future, swatting away the aggregate problems of international scarcity and overconsumption, while delicately overstepping the messy realities of a present whose management – now, today – is defined by increasingly contested political questions of equity, distribution and justice (see, for example, Rosling, 2018; Galor, 2020; Gates, 2020; Pinker, 2021).

COVID has made the case with brutal clarity. COVID-19 evoked the very best and the very worst of human behaviour – from individual and community to governmental and global. The pandemic was the logical environmental outcome of our rapacious economic appetite – penetrating ecologies driven alike by grinding poverty and the endless search for commercial gain, while critical public health controls were diluted to the point of inefficacy by an irrational over-attachment to the overriding importance of economic function. COVID illuminated deeply unequal systems of identity and value by which our societies are riven – while communities, as people and professionals, responded with extraordinary acts of cooperation, kindness and sacrifice. We conquered COVID – technically at least – through unprecedented intellectual openness and scientific collaboration before sequestrating our discoveries in iron-clad property law and bullying monopoly power. As we look ahead, we are already drawing up new architectures of global health security shaped by the technological superiority of North over South – framed in a maze of systems of surveillance and control operationalised over the heads of the mass of people, from one continent to another, on whose willingness to work together our future security will ultimately depend.

COVID was not simply a crisis of health. It was a crisis of trust between people and government, of communication between science and the state, between evidence and policy, between nations in a world struggling to retain its global coherence. The point, surely, as we emerge into a post-COVID world, is to not to resume our prior partialities – the preferences for one narrative over another – but rather to apply as scrupulously as possible a dispassionate analysis; to promote transparent, balanced and properly nuanced public debate. Not to offer spurious solutions but to ask better questions – about where we are going right, and where we are going wrong. To re-state the premises shaping the choices we will make and – at least as importantly – the manner in which we propose to make them (Kharas, 2019; see also Roser and Nagdy, 2014).

First, that while there is no doubt economic growth is a powerful driver of human progress, it is better understood as a social tool than a sacred commandment, modifiable according to its provable utility over time – that the value of growth changes as we pursue it, the balance shifting from strongly positive to ambiguous at best and environmentally catastrophic at worst; that as we get richer, the contribution of growth to our life expectancy declines and the risk it poses to our survival grows; that growth on its own does not guarantee us a better or healthier life and that the benefit of GDP depends on a quality of political governance – achievable to a large degree independently of economic wealth – which channels national resources equitably into vital public goods; that growth and health are not tradable options in a zero-sum game, but aspects of a single societal process; that, in the end, a new approach, conditioning ourselves to lower rates of growth accompanied by more muscular redistribution, merging health and wealth as facets of a single strategy for human development makes more sense epidemiologically, environmentally and economically.

Second, that if freedom is foundational to the idea of being human, its characterisation as essentially or even primarily individual is inadequate in concept and corrosive in practice. It is little good being told repeatedly by politicians, media pundits and advertising hoardings that we are free, that our choices are uniquely our own, whilst the material space within which we are able meaningfully to choose is shrinking, hemmed in by increasingly concentrated systems of political and commercial power; that while freedom is appealing in the narrative of heroic individual autonomy, that autonomy is itself illusory – a political narrative fostered by interests opposed to the regulation of harmful practices in employment and commerce, to the inherent collectivism of the state, and to the redistribution of wealth; that the security of collective social action is the foundation in which meaningful autonomy grows and that the absolute assertion of individual freedom undermines critical collective functions on which social progress is founded; that there is a deeper freedom to be found in interdependence embodied in universal entitlement to essential public goods and services – a statutory protection which liberates individuals from the arbitrary jeopardy of randomly adverse events, freeing them to engage more confidently in entrepreneurial enterprise, whether commercial or social.

Third, that while the idea of social justice remains philosophically murky it is, or should be, clear that current levels and trends in inequality, within countries and between them, cannot remotely be construed as just; that the systematic nature of inequality, reproduced generation after generation along the same old lines of identity and status, gives the lie to 'opportunity' as the primary mechanism of juster life chances; that remediation of misery at the bottom of the social and economic distribution, whether in income terms or access to basic care services, is inadequate even to the simplest notion of justice; that chasing physiological longevity through a biomedical model of healthcare – like the attempt to mitigate endless ecological exploitation through technological manipulation – will bankrupt us all in the medium term, but not before opening up grotesque new dimensions of biologically inscribed inequity.

That change in the conditions for one part of society requires change in the conditions of social hierarchy itself and that justice defined by the status quo will fail, therefore, to supply the more radical change that entrenched inequality requires; that as inequality divides communities, the better and worse off increasingly hermetically sealed off from one another, critical mechanisms of mutual understanding and dialogue deteriorate towards dysfunction; that a serious commitment to fostering justice on the demand side will require much more active policy – to reverse the ghettoisation of wealthy and poor neighbourhoods, to mitigate the progressive sequestration of different communities in their own bubbles of gated and excluded difference; to shape the physical spaces of society, creating engagement across the classical demarcations of class, caste, race, ethnicity and socioeconomic status, leveraging in particular the immense power of education and schools, housing and neighbourhood through which children grow and learn.

Fourth, that though security is now a dominant discourse shaping national and global policy, we have yet to agree where true security is to be found; that an emphasis on the 'hard' security of enforcement undervalues the longer-run 'soft' security of public compliance and is, in the absence of community resilience, likely to end up unsustainably repressive; that security overlaid on top of long historical experience of inequality and exclusion undermines, rather than building, the social cohesion on which public safety depends; that a model of global health security which perpetuates a North–South division, barely concealing the protectionist instincts of the wealthy world over poorer regions construed primarily as source of risk, simply revisits a model of international relations as outdated in principle as it is inefficient in practice – forfeiting the enormous gains available from a more open field of genuinely global collaboration and partnership.

Fifth, that although democracy is, for all sorts of reasons, the better prospect compared with authoritarian alternatives, its badge of superiority, predicated on the increasingly threadbare practice of skeletal electoral formalism, is starting to lose the credibility on which it lives or dies; that the restoration of the democratic idea will require more than simply stamping and re-stamping its rhetorical virtue on increasingly alienated electorates;

that the perception of a growing gap in power between policy making elites and the lived lives of the majority renders the notion of democratic choice increasingly unconvincing; that larger systems of democratic decision-making need to be re-rooted in local systems of engagement, deliberation and dialogue, protected and promoted through meaningful decentralisation of political and fiscal power balanced by robust national and global systems of accountability.

Sixth, that although our comprehension of the world is advancing at ever-increasing speed – with astonishing discoveries in field after disciplinary field – the conversion of 'fact' into 'truth' depends on the quality of interaction between scientific and political communities, on the openness of dialogue between the two and the transparency of public process by which empirical evidence is converted into policy choice; that perceptions of inequality corrode popular will to believe, and to invest credence in governmental pronouncements whose authority is founded on the premise of truthfulness; that over-reliance on quantitative data stripped of social context can generate overconfident policy knowledge separated from the realities through which its utility is shaped; that the use-value of truth changes according to the geographical and socioeconomic context in which it is applied, as different levels of resource determine the range of people's choices and reframe the rationalities by which they choose; that a global architecture of information may make the world appear more ordered and amenable to management but that it is knowledge generated within the local range of people's lives, and embodied in local systems of meaning, that informs and shapes their relations to one another, the mutual obligations and forms of interaction on which a productive and progressive society may be built.

As we emerge from the COVID pandemic and prepare for the crises to come, the next decade will be characterised by escalating complexity in the social, economic, technological, demographic and environmental forces shaping our prospects for progress – prospects which are, increasingly clearly, defined by interdependence within societies and between them. Yet while we invest in the hardware of crisis management – in hi-tech innovation and capabilities of control – we remain chronically underinvested in the societal software on which the efficacy of those technological and bureaucratic systems relies; on our ability to act collectively, to trust one another, and our government representatives, and to work together. At the heart of this problem lies the unreconciled question of inequality – occupying a kind of superordinate position in social organisation, a 'source-code' corruption in the operating system of societies, capable of undermining the functionality of all its other basic values.

For much of the post-war period, gathering pace after 1980, a dominant caucus of governments, policy makers, academics and media have advocated tolerance for inequality or acceptance, at least, of its necessary existence – explicitly or implicitly – as the inevitable counterpart to economic growth, the fundamental expression of a free society, and the manifestation of natural justice. We know now, though, that inequality is nothing of the sort – that inequality blocks and distorts growth, that inequality constitutes perhaps the last great barrier to genuine individual freedom, that inequality corrodes the necessary mechanisms of security, the foundational plausibility of democracy and the utility of truth – the coordinates on which coherent, consensual, productive and peaceful social progress relies. The COVID pandemic has accentuated these observations from country to country across the world, opening up a moment rich in potential for transformation. The question is whether we will, collectively, profit from that moment.

Note

[1] In a letter written from his prison cell in 1929, Gramsci calls optimism and pessimism 'vulgar, banal moods'.

Postscript: crisis in the UK

On 5 September 2022, following the disgraced departure of Boris Johnson, Liz Truss – a marginal Cabinet member widely disparaged for lack of discernible talent – assumed the duties of Prime Minister announcing a 'bold new plan' for revitalising the country's economic performance. She would last 49 days, becoming both the shortest-lived PM in UK history and one of its most spectacularly incompetent.

On the 23rd of the same month, close ally and newly minted Chancellor Kwasi Kwarteng delivered a poorly trailed 'fiscal event', unaccompanied by the customary institutional oversight designed to offer independent confidence to capital markets wary of unfunded economic promises. On one hand, the Truss–Kwarteng plan aimed, quite reasonably, to shield households from sharply rising fuel bills consequent, in part, on the Ukraine invasion and Russian gas diplomacy, but also on long-standing UK failure to invest in a coherent, sustainable domestic energy security strategy. The cap, conservatively estimated to cost north of €115 billion, was to be funded through national debt rather than the alternative, unappealing to the presiding Conservative administration, of a windfall tax on excess energy company profits.

But their plan was much larger in scale. Promoted as a recipe for unleashing growth, it went to war on tax, viewed two-dimensionally as a dead-weight imposition on individual enterprise. Increases in corporate and capital gains tax, planned to replenish national coffers battered by pandemic spending, were rescinded. And new cuts to taxable income were announced both at the base and the top rate. The plan was received in the international markets, for want of a better term, like a bucket of cold sick – an economically illiterate attempt to revive discredited notions of 'trickle-down' wealth generation liberated from the ethical and practical concerns of distributive efficiency, and imbued with so aggressive an uninterest in the problem of inequality as to be unappealing even to the fabled rapacity of global capital (Dearden, 2022; Ghitis, 2022).

Although much attention was directed at Truss and Kwarteng's economic prospectus, this itself was only one component of a wider attempt to shift social, political and environmental policy further towards an individualist paradigm of small-state libertarianism – quietly smothering advanced 'white paper' policy work on health inequalities, and disavowing or disappearing public health strategies on obesity, smoking and exercise (Campbell, 2022; Wise, 2022); accelerating – needlessly and dangerously – the Brexit promise to strip some 2,500 EU laws, including vital provisions on environmental protection and labour rights, out of newly recovered (if illusory) Britannic legislative sovereignty; rolling back obligations to international aid withdrawing further from a meaningful role in global humanitarianism; throwing commitments on climate action – the bedrock of all other meaningful policy – sharply into reverse or relegated to the ambiguous status of 'policy under review';[1] and subjecting tiresome public rights to protest these processes to unprecedented restriction through new powers of judicial, policing and public control.[2]

This remarkable interlude was presented, in the aftermath, as a moment of madness – the fever-dream of a pair of unhinged ideological outliers.[3] It was nothing of the sort. The Truss–Kwarteng moment was, rather, the logical extension of a gradual rightwards shift in the normative centre of political discourse over the last 40 years – a shift effected through cycles of economic crisis and response, from the oil shocks of the late 1970s and the ascendance of neoliberalism through New Labour's astonishingly effective pivot to market-led liberalism and the 2008 financial crash into a decade of post-crash austerity deepening the wounds of left-behind regional disadvantage which turned, in the end, with understandable if self-defeating Brexit savagery on the smugly insulated and apparently ineffectual progressive values of metro- and ultimately cosmopolitan elites (Isaac, 2022).

With the support of increasingly concentrated global media protective of commercial interests, we have seen over four decades the gradual consolidation of a political consensus, a set of fundamental policy truths, based on the pragmatic electoral calculus of what the imaginary voter values and what the market will bear, progressively adopted and endorsed as orthodoxy by mainstream left and right alike – of government as necessary but undesirable actor, the state to be minimised where possible and its roles passed over to the market to define and deliver; of economic policy as subject first and foremost to the approval of international markets;[4] of national debt as the mark of fiscal incontinence, to be driven down everywhere and always irrespective of other costs; of tax as an affront to economic liberty, disliked by markets and voters alike – an embarrassing necessity to be approached only ever minimally and reluctantly; of regulation as intrusion – the dead hand of red tape on the animal energies of the individual unbound and the unfettered firm; of labour as a flexible commodity rather than a collective good; and of welfare as compassion rather than entitlement – the casually limitable discretionary generosity of those who naturally have towards those who deservingly do not.[5]

Within hours of Kwarteng's maiden mini-budget, sterling had dropped to an historic low against the US dollar and yields on UK debt (including the supposedly oak-solid 30-year gilts) had moved sharply upwards increasing the cost of national borrowing and collapsing the anticipated fiscal headroom for medium- to long-term investment.[6] Kwarteng was sacked. Truss soon followed.

Compounded by the economic echoes of COVID and the global aftershocks of the Ukrainian invasion, the impact of the Truss–Kwarteng intervention was immediate and severe – an administration wrestling with badly dented international credibility and an estimated GBP£55–60 billion hole in public finance going forward (*Financial Times*, 2022); a country facing some of the worst employment conditions in the post-pandemic OECD and the possible prospect of a long and bitter recession; households struggling with sharply rising living costs in fuel, housing and food against a backdrop of already-inadequate wage and welfare payments further undermined by escalating levels of inflation and interest (Crook, 2022; Nelson, 2022); and, at the heart of it all, a population's health, for the first time in a hundred years, going backwards – bucking the basic assumption that our life chances should improve generation after generation, corroding the fabric of individual well-being and community cohesion – the foundations of a stable, engaged citizenry – and feeding a self-reinforcing spiral of economic and social decline (BMA, 2022; *Lancet Public Health*, 2022).

Yet, confronted by this 'polycrisis', in late 2022 we found ourselves earnestly preparing to invoke the same old response – at its centre, the immovable imperative of reacquiring market confidence by reducing debt and deficit, accompanied by modest and deeply reluctant increases in tax (Booth, 2022; Elliott, 2022; Foy et al, 2022; *The Telegraph*, 2022) – and demanding, therefore, yet another return to austerity: the 'eye-wateringly difficult decisions' flagged by incoming Chancellor Jeremy Hunt, echoing George Osborne's incessant mantra of 'hard choices' a decade earlier;[7] assiduously hacking away at the very roots of sustainable social welfare and long-run infrastructural investment on which genuine revival depends.

This response – the kneejerk reversion to austerity – reveals not simply a failure to learn. It embodies a profound constraint on what we collectively believe to be politically and economically learnable (Lansley, 2021; Hutton, 2022). Austerity balances the books on the backs of the poor. And it does not work (McKee et al, 2012; Ball et al, 2013; Ortiz et al, 2015; Giles, 2020; Stiglitz and Welsbrot, 2022). It exacerbates inequality and corrodes not just the welfare of the population but its cohesion, its sense of a common purpose, its ability and willingness to commit to forms of social cooperation and economic production on which our common wealth depends.

We need, in the coming period, to divest ourselves of this consensual straitjacket, to revisit the values underpinning our response to socioeconomic crisis, drawing on the experience of COVID – to challenge the shibboleths of a profoundly incomplete liberal orthodoxy: to celebrate, instead of demonising, the value of taxation as the source of essential common societal goods; to recognise that national economies are not like credit cards to be 'maxed out' and that indebtedness can be virtuous when dedicated to strategic investment in human, social and infrastructural development; that capital seeks the returns that credible long-run investment supplies – and that such returns diminish in a nation consigned to disinvestment and decay (Van Reenan, 2015; Bell, 2022); that, therefore, a programme of post-crisis renewal founded on optimising tax and debt revenues can be the basis of robust but positive negotiation between the sovereign state and the market, rather than one of irreconcilably conflicting interests or abject subordination.

Rebuilding an equitable social infrastructure of public goods is the indispensable basis of post-crisis renewal – in health, childcare and early child development, in inclusive academic and technical education linked to credible employment pathways and labour rights beyond the minimum wage zero-hour model, in affordable, decent housing and sustainable transport – delivered where possible through properly financed local government. At the heart of that renewal must be an unconditional commitment to protect and invest in people as the primary resource of meaningful social development; not through the increasingly common careless processes of outsourced third-party sub-contracting, offering cookie-cutter interventions in 'transitional training' giving minimal aid to workforces struggling with profound experiences of social and economic change; but recognising that it is through real, publicly led investment programmes in a nation's human potential that we can bring together in a single coherent strategic proposition the values of economic productivity, human rights and health.

Sebastian Taylor
London, June 2023

Notes

[1] The popular 'Environmental Land Management Scheme', designed to replace the EU's monumentally inefficient Common Agricultural Policy, threatened with reassessment; the promised removal of 570 regulatory agreements on environmental protection from the UK statute book – a proposition so toxic it brought together in unprecedentedly angry advocacy the Royal Society for the Protection of Birds and the National Trust among others; the promise to extend and accelerate licensing for North Sea fossil fuel extraction, and to reduce regulatory thresholds on shale-gas fracking; and the farcical to-and-fro vacillation of UK leaders on whether or not to turn up to COP27. See, for example, Retained EU Law (Revocation and Reform) Bill (https://www.gov.uk/gov ernment/publications/retained-eu-law-revocation-and-reform-bill-2022-impact-assess ment); UNISON National (https://www.unison.org.uk/news/2022/10/the-retained-eu-law-bill-an-attack-on-working-women); Helm, 2022.

2   See, for example, Public Order Bill – JUSTICE.

3   Albeit supported over a number of years by a range of comparatively extreme right-wing thinktanks.

4   A disciplinary relationship learnt over time, not least through the devaluation of sterling in 1967, the 1976 IMF bailout, the Exchange Rate Mechanism debacle in 1992 and the overwhelming prioritisation of national debt and deficit reduction after the 2008 crash.

5   This is not to suggest that there are no policy differences between – and indeed within – parties, but rather than such differences, for example on forms and levels of taxation, are themselves captured within a broader orthodoxy that tax is, of its nature, undesirable. Over time, the assumption that tax is unappealing to voters shapes electoral manifestos, which in turn shape policy agendas, which feed back into public understanding of what government should look like. And so the cycle of confirmation bias turns (Bell, 2010; Evans and Dirk de Graaf, 2013; Brandenburg and Johns, 2014; English et al, 2016; Temple et al, 2016; Azzolini and Evans, 2021).

6   In October 2022, yields for ten-year bonds remained elevated a month after the fiscal event was announced, significantly above where they had been in August (*The Economist*, 2022).

7   Choices arguably somewhat harder for poor households struggling to shoulder their impact than for the comparatively comfortable politicians issuing them. The 'horrible decisions' trailed by Jeremy Hunt prior to the autumn statement appeared to include, as if equivalent, increasing tax on those earning over £125,000 a year and cutting welfare payments to households living on a few hundred pounds a month.

References

Preface

Beckett, A. (2019) 'The Age of Perpetual Crisis', *The Guardian*, 17 December. Available at: www.theguardian.com/society/2019/dec/17/decade-of-perpetual-crisis-2010s-disrupted-everything-but-resolved-nothing

Ipsos Global Advisor (2022) 'Earth Day 2022: Public Opinion on Climate Change'. Available at: www.ipsos.com/sites/default/files/ct/news/documents/2022-04/Ipsos%20-%20Global%20Advisor%20-%20Earth%20Day%202022%20-%20Release%201.pdf

Zevin, A. (2022) 'Gradualism's Prophet', *New Left Review*, 135, May/June.

Introduction: health and civilisation

Achebe, C. (1999) 'Africa is People', *The Massachusetts Review*, 40(3), 313–321.

Andersen, R. (1997) 'The Eye and its Diseases in Ancient Egypt', *Acta Ophthalmologica Scandinavica*, 75, 338–344.

Bailin, M. (2007) *The Sick Room in Victorian Literature: The Art of Being Ill*, Cambridge University Press.

Barro, R. and Ursua, J. (2009) 'Pandemics and Depressions', *Wall Street Journal*, 5 May.

Bekker, L.G., Ratevosian, J., Spencer, J., Piot, P. and Beyrer, C. (2019) 'Governance for Health: The HIV Response and General Global Health', *Bulletin of the World Health Organization*, 97(3), 170–170A.

Berryman, J. (2012) 'Motion and Rest: Galen on Exercise and Health', *The Lancet*, 380(9838), 210–211.

Bewell, A. (2003) *Romanticism and Colonial Disease*, Johns Hopkins University Press.

Biasin, G.P. (2014) *Literary Diseases: Theme and Metaphor in the Italian Novel*, University of Texas Press.

Boadle, A., Brown, T. and Orr, B. (2016) 'US, Brazil Researchers Join Forces to Battle Zika Virus', *Reuters*, 18 February.

Bogousslavsky, J. and Dieguez, S. (eds) (2013) *Literary Medicine: Brain Disease and Doctors in Novels, Theater and Film*, Karger.

Brainerd, E. and Siegler, M. (2002) 'The Economic Effects of the 1918 Influenza Epidemic', CEPR Discussion Papers 3791.

Bray, R. (1996) *Armies of Pestilence: The Impact of Disease on History*, Barnes Noble.

Buse, K., Tlou, S. and Poku, N. (2018) 'Global Health Disruptors: HIV/AIDS'. *British Medical Journal*. Available at: https://blogs.bmj.com/bmj/2018/11/26/global-health-disruptors-aids/

Carrick, P. (2001) *Medical Ethics in the Ancient World*, Georgetown University Press.

Cawthorn, K. (2008) *Becoming Female: The Male Body in Greek Tragedy*, Bloomsbury.

CDC (2019) '2009 H1N1 Pandemic'. Available at: www.cdc.gov/flu/pandemic-resources/2009-h1n1-pandemic.html

Chin, A., Simon, G., Anthamatten, P., Kelsey, K., Crawford, B. and Weaver, A. (2020) 'Pandemics and the Future of Human-Landscape Interactions', *Anthropocene*, 31: 100256.

Choy, H. (ed) (2016) *Discourses of Disease: Writing Illness, the Mind and the Body in Modern China*, Brill.

Christ, C. (1976) 'Aggression and Providential Death in George Eliot's Fiction', *NOVEL: A Forum on Fiction*, 9(2), 130–140.

The Economist (2019) 'Measuring the 1%', 29 November.

Elliot, L. (2020) 'IMF Estimates Global Covid Cost at $28tn in Lost Output', *The Guardian*, 13 October. Available at: www.theguardian.com/business/2020/oct/13/imf-covid-cost-world-economic-outlook

European Centre for Disease Prevention and Control (2021) 'Geographical Distribution of Confirmed MERS-CoV Cases by Country of Infection and Year'. Available at: www.ecdc.europa.eu/en/publications-data/geographical-distribution-confirmed-mers-cov-cases-country-infection-and-year-15

Fee, E. and Krieger, N. (1993) 'Understanding AIDS: Historical Interpretations and the Limits of Biomedical Individualism', *American Journal of Public Health*, 83(10), 477–1486.

Feierman, S. and Janzen, J. (eds) (1992) *The Social Basis of Health and Healing in Africa*, University of California Press.

Frank, M., Moll, F., Leissner, J. and Bergdolt, K. (2008) 'The Great Plague: Pandemics can Change History', *Journal of Urology*, 179(4), 311.

G20 High Level Independent Panel on Financing the Global Commons for Pandemic Preparedness and Response (2021) *A Global Deal for Our Pandemic Age*. Available at: www.pandemic-financing.org

Gilbert, S. and Green, C. (2021) *Vaxxers: A Pioneering Moment in Scientific History*, Hodder & Stoughton.

Glasser, B. and Irvine, S. (2017) *Medicinema: Doctors in Films*, CRC Press.

Grigsby, B. (2003) *Pestilence in Medieval and Early Modern English Literature*, Routledge.

Hakola, O. and Kivistö, S. (eds) (2014) *Death in Literature*, Cambridge Scholars Publishing.

Haldar, J. (1992) *Development of Public Health in Buddhism*, Indological Book House.

Harper, G. and Moor, A. (eds) (2005) *Signs of Life: Cinema and Medicine*, Wallflower Press.

Healy, M. (2011) *Fictions of Disease in Early Modern England: Bodies, Plagues and Politics*, Palgrave.

Honigsbaum, M. (2013) *A History of the Great Influenza Pandemics: Death, Panic & Hysteria, 1830–1920*, Tauris.

Horton, R. and Lo, S. (2015) 'Planetary Health: A New Science for Exceptional Action', *The Lancet*, 386(10007), 1921–1922.

Howell, K. (2004) *God's Two Books: Copernican Cosmology and Biblical Interpretation in Early Modern Science*, Notre Dame Press.

Hutcheon, L. and Hutcheon, M. (1996) *Opera: Desire, Disease, Death*, University of Nebraska Press.

Johnson, B. (2018) *Shakespeare, Madness and Threatened Identities*. Available at: https://medium.com/@johnsonbrook247/shakespeare-madness-and-threatened-identities-597149ce79a8

Jones, K., Patel, N., Levy, M., Storeygard, A., Balk, D., Gittleman, J. et al (2008) 'Global Trends in Emerging Infectious Diseases', *Nature*, 451(7181), 990-U4.

Kaplan, M. (1987) 'Implications of Individualism in Public Health Policy', *Journal of Economic Issues*, 21(1), 349–356.

Lawlor, C. (2006) *Consumption and Literature: The Making of the Romantic Disease*, Palgrave Macmillan.

Lawlor, C. and Suzuki, A. (2012) 'The Disease of Self: Representing Consumption 1700–1830', *Bulletin of the History of Medicine*, 74(1), 458–494.

Lendik, L.S., Chan, M.Y., Renganathan, S. and Yap, N.T. (2017) 'Metaphor and the Representations of Health and Illness among the Semai Indigenous Community in Malaysia', *Gema Online Journal of Language Studies*, 17(4), 61–83.

Leslie, C. and Young, A. (eds) (1992) *Paths to Asian Medical Knowledge*, University of California Press.

Lu, D. (2013) 'Influence of I-Ching (Yijing, or the Book of Changes) on Chinese Medicine, Philosophy and Science', *Acupuncture & Electrotherapeutics Research*, 38(1–2), 77–133.

Milanovic, B. (2020) 'The First Global Event in the History of Humankind', *Social Europe*, 7 December. Available at: www.socialeurope.eu/the-first-global-event-in-the-history-of-humankind

Mitchell-Boyask, R. (2008) *Plague and the Athenian Imagination: Drama, History and the Cult of Asclepius*, Cambridge University Press.

Ngalamulume, K. (2017) 'Health, Medicine, and the Study of Africa', in T. Spear (ed) *Oxford Bibliographies in African Studies*, Oxford University Press.

Norridge, Z. (2013) *Perceiving Pain in African Literature*, Palgrave Macmillan.

Novillo-Corvalán, P. (ed) (2015) *Latin American and Iberian Perspectives on Literature and Medicine*, Routledge.

Nunn, J. (1996) *Ancient Egyptian Medicine*, University of Oklahoma Press.

O'Callaghan, B. and Murdock, E. (2021) 'Are We Building Back Better? Evidence from 2020 and Pathways to Inclusive Green Recovery Spending', Global Recovery Observatory, Oxford University Economic Recovery Project & UN Environment Program.

Ohnuki-Tierney, E. (1984) *Illness and Culture in Contemporary Japan: An Anthropological View*, Cambridge University Press.

Ormand, K. (ed) (2012) *A Companion to Sophocles*, Blackwell Publishing.

Pett, S. (2018) 'Reading, Writing, Rashness: Virginia Woolf's On Being Ill and the Contemporary Illness Account', *Literature and Medicine*, 37(1), 26–66.

Porter, D. (1990) *Health, Civilization and the State: A History of Public Health from Ancient to Modern Times*, Routledge.

Reddy, M. (2012) 'Psychotherapy: Insights from the *Bhagavad Gita*', *Indian Journal of Psychological Medicine*, 34(1), 100–104.

Rothfield, L. (1992) *Vital Signs: Medical Realism in Nineteenth-Century Fiction*, Princeton University Press.

Roy, A. (2020) 'The Pandemic is a Portal', *Financial Times*, 3 April. Available at: www.ft.com/content/10d8f5e8-74eb-11ea-95fe-fcd274e920ca

Sahlas, D. (2001) 'Functional Neuroanatomy in the Pre-Hippocratic Era: Observations from the *Iliad* of Homer', *Neurosurgery*, 48(6), 1352–1357.

Saini, A. (2016) 'Physicians of Ancient India', *Journal of Family Medicine and Primary Care*, 5(2), 254–258.

Sánchez-Blake, E. and Kanost, L. (2015) *Latin American Women and the Literature of Madness: Narratives at the Crossroads of Gender, Politics and the Mind*, Macfarland & Co.

Soni, R. (1976) 'Buddhism in Relation to the Profession of Medicine', in D.W. Millard (ed) *Religion and Medicine*, SCM Press, vol 3, pp 135–151.

Sontag, S. (2001) *Illness as Metaphor and AIDS and Its Metaphors*, Picador.

Tatem, A. (2020) 'Pandemic Acceleration'. Available at: https://blog.geog raphydirections.com/2020/07/02/pandemic-acceleration/

Taylor, S. (2012) *Beyond the Health Governance Gap: Maternal Newborn and Child Health in South Sudan* [unpublished], World Vision/IDL Group. Available at: www.researchgate.net/publication/326913734_Beyond_the_Health_ Governance_Gap_Maternal_newborn_and_child_health_in_South_Sudan

Tosh, W. (2016) 'Shakespeare and Madness', *Discovering Literature: Shakespeare & Renaissance*. Available at: www.bl.uk/shakespeare/articles/shakespeare-and-madness

van Bergeijk P. (2021) 'Economic Preparation for the Next Pandemic', *VOX/CEPR*. Available at: https://cepr.org/voxeu/columns/economic-preparation-next-pandemic

Vrettos, A. (1995) *Somatic Fictions: Imagining Illness in Victorian Culture*, Stanford University Press.

Wellner, K. (2010) 'A History of Embryology (1959), by Joseph Needham', *Embryo Project Encyclopedia*. Available at: http://embryo.asu.edu/handle/ 10776/2031

WHO (World Health Organization) (2008) *The Final Report of the Commission on Social Determinants of Health*, WHO. Available at: www.who.int/social_ determinants/thecommission/finalreport/en/

WHO (2018) 'Ten Threats to Global Health in 2019'. Available at: www. who.int/emergencies/ten-threats-to-global-health-in-2019

WHO (2022) 'COVID-19 Weekly Epidemiological Update Edition 103', 3 August, WHO. Available at: www.who.int/publications/m/item/weekly-epidemiological-update-on-covid-19---3-august-2022

WHO/Global Preparedness Monitoring Board (2019) *A World at Risk: Annual Report on Global Preparedness for Health Emergencies*, World Health Organization.

Woolf, V. (1926) *On Being Ill*, Criterion.

World Bank/WHO (2019) 'Pandemic Preparedness Financing: Global Update', September.

Crisis: a timeline

Akinyemi, J.O., Adebowale, A.S., Bamgboye, E.A. and Ayeni, O. (2015) 'Child Survival Dynamics in Nigeria: Is the 2006 Child Health Policy Target Met?', *Nigerian Journal of Health Science*, 15, 18–26.

Algan, Y., Papaioannou, E., Passari, E. and Guriev, S. (2018) 'The European Trust Crisis and the Rise of Populism', EBRD Working Paper No. 208, https://ssrn.com/abstract=3128274

Alston, P. (2018) 'Report of the Special Rapporteur on Extreme Poverty and Human Rights on His Mission to the United States of America', Human Rights Council 38th Session, 18 June–6 July 2018, Agenda item 3: 'Promotion and protection of all human rights, civil, political, economic, social and cultural rights, including the right to development.'

Alvaredo, F., Chancel, L., Piketty, T., Saez, E. and Zucman, G. (2018) *World Inequality Report*. Available at: https://wir2018.wid.world/part-4.html

Alvarez, S., Rubin, J., Thayer, M., Baiocchi, G. and Laó-Montes, A. (eds) (2017) *Beyond Civil Society: Activism, Participation, and Protest in Latin America*, Duke University Press.

Andreouli, E. (2019) 'Cosmopolitan Brexiteers, or when "European" Means Inward-Looking', *LSE Blogs*. Available at: https://blogs.lse.ac.uk/brexit/2019/06/05/cosmopolitan-brexiteers-or-when-european-means-inward-looking/

Arias, E. (2014) 'United States Life Tables, 2009', *National Vital Statistics Reports*, 62(7), 6 January.

Aronowitz, S. (2006) *Left Turn: Forging a New Political Future*, Routledge.

Bacchetta, M. and Jansen, M. (eds) (2011) 'Making Globalisation Socially Sustainable', International Labour Organization and World Trade Organization. Available at: www.wto.org/english/res_e/booksp_e/glob_soc_sus_e.pdf#page=250

Barnichon, R., Matthes, C. and Ziegenbein, A. (2018) 'The Financial Crisis at 10: Will We Ever Recover?' *FRBSF Economic Letter*, 13 August.

Batory, A. and Svensson, S. (2019) 'The Use and Abuse of Participatory Governance by Populist Governments', *Policy & Politics*, 47(2), 227–244.

Bourquin, P., Joyce, R. and Norris Keiller, A. (2020) 'Living Standards, Poverty and Inequality in the UK', Institute for Fiscal Studies. Available at: https://ifs.org.uk/publications/living-standards-poverty-and-inequality-uk-2020

Brand, U. and Sekler, N. (2009) 'Postneoliberalism: Catch-all Word or Valuable Analytical and Political Concept? Aims of a Beginning Debate', *Development Dialogue*, 51, January.

Brown, K. and Bērziņa-Čerenkova, U.A. (2018) 'Ideology in the Era of Xi Jinping', *Journal of Chinese Political Science*, 23, 323–339.

Brubaker, R. (2018) 'The New Language of European Populism: Why "Civilization" Is Replacing the Nation'. Available at: https://scholar.ss.ucla.edu/wp-content/uploads/sites/6/2018/02/The-New-Language-of-European-Populism-Foreign-Affairs-final.pdf

Cahill, D., Cooper, M., Konings, M. and Primrose, D. (eds) (2018) *The SAGE Handbook of Neoliberalism*, SAGE.

Calvert, J. and Arbuthnott, G. (2021) *Failures of State: The Inside Story of Britain's Battle with Coronavirus*, HarperCollins.

Cárdenas, M., Kharas, H. and Henao, C. (2015) 'Latin America's Global Middle Class: A Preference for Growth over Equality', in J. Dayton-Johnson (ed) *Latin America's Emerging Middle Classes*, Palgrave Macmillan, pp 51–69.

Carroll, W. and Sapinski, J. (2010) 'The Global Corporate Elite and the Transnational Policy-Planning Network, 1996–2006: A Structural Analysis', *International Sociology*, 25(4).

Choudry, A. and Kapoor, D. (2013) *NGOization: Complicity, Contradictions and Prospects*, Zed Books.

Cooper, H. and Szreter, S. (2021) *After the Virus: Lessons from the Past for a Better Future*, Cambridge University Press.

Cribb, J. and Johnson, P. (2018) '10 Years On: Have We Recovered from the Financial Crisis?'. Available at: www.ifs.org.uk/publications/13302

Durant, R., Fiorino, D. and O'Leary, R. (eds) (2004) *Environmental Governance Reconsidered: Challenges, Choices, and Opportunities*, MIT Press.

Edmonds, T. (2010) 'Financial Crash Timeline', House of Commons Briefing Paper, no. 04991, 12 April. Available at: https://researchbriefings.files.parliament.uk/documents/SN04991/SN04991.pdf

Energy Information Agency (2006) *Annual Energy Review*, US/Energy Information Agency. Available at: www.eia.doe.gov

Erixon, F. and Razeen, S. (2010) 'Trade, Globalisation and Emerging Protectionism since the Crisis', ECIPE Working Paper, No. 02/2010, European Centre for International Political Economy (ECIPE), Brussels.

Erixon, F., Sally, R., Kharas, H. and Gertz, G. (2010) 'The New Global Middle Class: A Cross-Over from West to East', Wolfensohn Center for Development at Brookings; draft version of Chapter 2 in C. Li (ed) *China's Emerging Middle Class: Beyond Economic Transformation*, Brookings Institution Press.

Ferragina, E. and Arrigoni, A. (2016) 'The Rise and Fall of Social Capital: Requiem for a Theory?', *Political Studies Review*, 15(3), 355–367.

Feusatl, R. (2018) 'Powerless Arguments: Demagogue and Populist Language', *The Progressive Post*. Available at: https://progressivepost.eu/special-coverage/powerless-arguments-demagogue-and-populist-language

Frank, R. (2007) *Falling Behind: How Rising Inequality Harms the Middle Class*, University of California Press.

Frankfurt, H. (2005) *On Bullshit*, Princeton University Press.

Fukuyama, F. (1992) *The End of History and the Last Man*, Free Press.

Giddens, A. (1998) *The Third Way*, Polity Press.

Gideon, J. and Porter, F. (2016) 'Challenging Gendered Inequalities in Global Health: Dilemmas for NGOs', *Development & Change*, 47(4), 782–797.

Ginn, J. (2013) 'Austerity and Inequality: Exploring the Impact of Cuts in the UK by Gender and Age', *Research on Ageing and Social Policy*, 1(1), 28–53.

Gozgor, G. and Ranjan, P. (2017) 'Globalisation, Inequality and Redistribution: Theory and Evidence', *The World Economy*, 40(12), 2704–2751.

Griffith-Jones, S. and Ocampo, J. (2009) 'The Financial Crisis and its Impact on Developing Countries', Working Paper, No. 53, International Policy Centre for Inclusive Growth (IPC-IG), Brasilia.

Haas, E. (2007) 'False Equivalency: Think Tank References on Education in the News Media', *Peabody Journal of Education*, 82(1), 63–102.

Ham, C. (2021) 'The UK's Poor Record on COVID-19 is a Failure of Policy Learning', *British Medical Journal*, 372, n284.

Hines, A. (2017) 'How to Understand the Language of Political Populism', *The Conversation*. Available at: http://theconversation.com/how-to-understand-the-language-of-political-populism-74903

Hosseinpoor, A., Bergen, N., Schlotheuber, A., Gacic-Dobo, M., Hansen, P., Senouci, K. et al (2016) 'State of Inequality in Diphtheria-Tetanus-Pertussis Immunisation Coverage in Low-Income and Middle-Income Countries: A Multicountry Study of Household Health Surveys', *Lancet Global Health*, 4, e617–626.

Hunston, S. (nd) 'Donald Trump and the Language of Populism'. Available at: www.birmingham.ac.uk/research/perspective/donald-trump-language-of-populism.aspx

IDEA (Institute for Democratic and Electoral Assistance) (2016) 'Europe's Steep Decline in Voter Turnout in Elections Brings Down Global Average'. Available at: www.idea.int/news-media/media/europes-steep-declince-voter-turnout-elections-brings-down-global-average

International IDEA (nd) 'Voter Turnout Database'. Available at: www.idea.int/data-tools/data/voter-turnout

Kharas, H. (2017) 'The Unprecedented Expansion of the Global Middle Class: An Update', Global Economy & Development Working Paper 100, February, Brookings Institute.

Klassen, S. (2016) 'What to Do about Rising Inequality in Developing Countries?', PEGNet Policy Brief, No. 5/2016.

Kyle, J. and Gultchin, L. (2018) 'Populists in Power Around the World', Tony Blair Institute for Global Change. Available at: https://institute.global/insight/renewing-centre/populists-power-around-world

Lakner, C. and Milanovic, B. (2013) *Global Income Distribution: From the Fall of the Berlin Wall to the Great Recession*, World Bank.

Leatherby, L. (2017) 'Five Charts Show Why Millennials are Worse Off Than Their Parents', *Financial Times*, 29 August. Available at: www.ft.com/content/e5246526-8c2c-11e7-a352-e46f43c5825d

Lensink, R. (1996) *Structural Adjustment in Sub-Saharan Africa*, Longman.

Lobo, L. and Shah, J. (eds) (2015) *The Trajectory of India's Middle Class: Economy, Ethics and Etiquette*, Cambridge Scholars Publishing.

Lupton, R., Burchardt, T., Hills, J., Stewart, K. and Vizard, P. (eds) (2016) *Social Policy in a Cold Climate: Policies and Their Consequences Since the Crisis*, Policy Press.

Mahler, V. and Jesuit, D. (2014) 'Electoral Turnout and State Redistribution: A Cross-National Study of Fourteen Developed Countries', *Political Research Quarterly*, 67(2).

McElwee, S. (2015) 'The Income Gap at the Polls', *Politico*, 7 January. Available at: www.politico.com/magazine/story/2015/01/income-gap-at-the-polls-113997

Milanovic, B. (2016) *Global Inequality: A New Approach for the Age of Globalization*, Harvard University Press.

Muntaner, C. and Lynch, J. (2002) 'Social Capital, Class, Gender and Race Conflict, and Population Health: An Essay Review of *Bowling Alone*'s Implications for Social Epidemiology', *International Journal of Epidemiology*, 31(1), 261–267.

Mustapha, S. (2014) 'What Lessons can we Learn from the 1980s and 1990s Debt Crises for Developing Countries and How are Today's Conditions Similar, How are they Different?' Economic and Private Sector Professional Evidence and Applied Knowledge Services, Overseas Development Institute.

Niño-Zarazúa, M., Roope, L. and Tarp, F. (2017) 'Global Inequality: Relatively Lower, Absolutely Higher', *The Review of Income and Wealth*, 63(4), 661–684.

Noam, E. (ed) (2015) *Who Owns the World's Media? Media Concentration and Ownership Around the World*, Oxford University Press.

O'Reilly, K. (2011) '"We Are Not Contractors": Professionalizing the Interactive Service Work of NGOs in Rajasthan, India', *Economic Geography*, 87(2), 207–226.

Ostry, J., Loungani, P. and Furceri, D. (2016) 'Neoliberalism: Oversold?', International Monetary Fund, *Finance & Development*, June.

Our World in Data (nd) Available at: https://ourworldindata.org/

Oxenford, M. (2018) 'The Lasting Effects of the Financial Crisis Have Yet to Be Felt', Chatham House, 12 January. Available at: www.chathamhouse.org/expert/comment/lasting-effects-financial-crisis-have-yet-be-felt

Palmer, J. (2017) 'The Resistible Rise of Xi Jinping', *Foreign Policy*, 19 October. Available at: https://foreignpolicy.com/2017/10/19/the-resistible-rise-of-xi-jinping/

Peck, M. (2014) 'The Time America almost Invaded OPEC', *Nationalinterest.org*, 10 April.

Pinker, S. (2018) *Enlightenment Now: The Case for Reason, Science, Humanism, and Progress*, Viking.

Putnam, R. (2000) *Bowling Alone: The Collapse and Revival of American Community*, Simon & Schuster.

Rachman, G. (2022) *The Age of the Strongman: How the Cult of the Leader Threatens Democracy Around the World*, Bodley Head.

Rakesh, K. (2020) 'A Global Middle Class Is More Promise than Reality', in C. Suter, S. Madheswaran and B.P. Vani (eds) *The Middle Class in World Society: Negotiations, Diversities & Lived Experiences*, Routledge.

Ravallion, M. (2018) 'Inequality and Globalization: A Review Essay', *Journal of Economic Literature*, 56(2), 620–642.

Rifkin, J. (1995) *The End of Work: The Decline of the Global Labor Force and the Dawn of the Post-Market Era*, GP Putnam's & Sons.

Roderick, A. (2014) 'Beyond the Financial Crisis: The Sustainable Development Goals and the Need for a Grand Bargain between Sustainability and Development', Sheffield Political Economy Research Institute's 2014 Annual Conference, 'The Global Contours of Growth & Development Beyond the Crisis'.

Rosling, H. (2018) *Factfulness*, Sceptre.

Salamon, L., Anheier, H., List, R., Toepler, S. and Sokolowski, S. (1999) 'Global Civil Society: Dimensions of the Non-Profit Sector', The Johns Hopkins Nonprofit Sector Series, The Johns Hopkins Center for Civil Society Studies, Baltimore.

Smaje, C. (2018) 'The Great Convergence?', *Resilience*, 28 May. Available at: www.resilience.org/stories/2019-05-28/the-great-convergence/

Stewart, F. (2011) 'Horizontal Inequalities as a Cause of Conflict: A Review of CRISE Findings', Background Paper, World Development Report 2011, World Bank.

Equality Trust, The (nd) 'How has Inequality Changed? Development of UK Income Inequality'. Available at: www.equalitytrust.org.uk/how-has-inequality-changed

UN (2015) 'The Millennium Development Goals Report, 2015'. Available at: www.un.org/millenniumgoals/2015_MDG_Report/pdf/MDG%202015%20rev%20(July%201).pdf

UN Environment Programme (2020) *Preventing the Next Pandemic: Zoonotic Diseases and How to Break the Chain of Transmission*. Available at: https://wedocs.unep.org/bitstream/handle/20.500.11822/32316/ZP.pdf?sequence=1&isAllowed=y

UNESCAP (2018) 'Global Financial Crisis: Flashback and Flashforward for Asia and the Pacific'. Available at: www.unescap.org/blog/global-financial-crisis-flashback-and-flashforward-asia-and-the-pacific

Wolff, E. (2010) 'Rising Profitability and the Middle-Class Squeeze', *Science & Society*, 74, 429–449.

Woolf, S and Schoomaker, H. (2019) 'Life Expectancy and Mortality Rates in the United States, 1959–2017', *Journal of the American Medical Association*, 322(20), 1996–2016.

World Bank (1980) *World Development Report*, World Bank.

World Bank (2009) 'The Economic Crisis and the Millennium Development Goals'. Available at: http://www.worldbank.org/en/news/feature/2009/04/24/the-economic-crisis-and-the-millennium-development-goals

World Bank (2021) 'The Global Economy: On Track for Strong but Uneven Growth as COVID-19 Still Weighs', World Bank.

Chapter 1: Growth, wealth and health

Amirkhalkhali, S. and Dar, A. (2019) 'Trade Openness, Factor Productivity, and Economic Growth: Recent Evidence from OECD Countries (2000–2015)', *Applied Econometrics and International Development*, 19–1, 5–14.

Arora, S. (2001) 'Health, Human Productivity, and Long-Term Economic Growth', *The Journal of Economic History*, 61(3), 699–749.

Baker, P. (2008) 'On the relationship between economic growth and health improvements: Some lessons for health-conscious developing countries', *Radical Statistics*, 98, 26.

Balabanova, D., Mills, A., Conteh, L., Akkazieva, B., Banteyerga, H., Dash, U. et al (2013) 'Good Health at Low Cost 25 Years On: Lessons for the Future of Health Systems Strengthening', *The Lancet*, 381(9883), 2118–2133.

Barro, R. (1996) *Health and Economic Growth*, Mimeo.

Biciunaite, A. (2014) 'Economic Growth and Life Expectancy: Do Wealthier Countries Live Longer?', *Euromonitor*. Available at: https://blog.euromonitor.com/economic-growth-and-life-expectancy-do-wealthier-countries-live-longer/

Bloom, D. and Canning, D. (2007) 'Commentary: The Preston Curve 30 Years On: Still Sparking Fires', *International Journal of Epidemiology*, 36(3), 498–499.

Bloom, D., Canning, D. and Sevilla, J. (2004) 'The Effect of Health on Economic Growth: A Production Function Approach', *World Development*, 32(1), 1–13.

Bloom, D., Kuhn, M. and Prettner, K. (2018) 'Health and Economic Growth', *Economic and Finance*. Available at: https://oxfordre.com/economics/economics/view/10.1093/acrefore/9780190625979.001.0001/acrefore-9780190625979-e-36

Broadberry, S. and Wallis, J. (2017) 'Growing, Shrinking, and Long-run Economic Performance: Historical Perspectives on Economic Development', *NBER Working Paper* no 23343.

Carroll, C. and Summers, L. (1991) 'Consumption Growth Parallels Income Growth: Some New Evidence', in B. Douglas Bernheim and J Shoven (eds) *National Saving and Economic Performance*, University of Chicago Press.

Chen, W.Y. (2016) 'Health Progress and Economic Growth in the USA: The Continuous Wavelet Analysis', *Empirical Economics*, 50(3), 831–855.

Clark, A., Frijters, P. and Shields, M. (2008) 'Relative Income, Happiness, and Utility: An Explanation for the Easterlin Paradox and Other Puzzles', *Journal of Economic Literature*, 46(1), 95–144.

Cole, W. (2019) 'Wealth and Health Revisited: Economic Growth and Wellbeing in Developing Countries, 1970 to 2015', *Social Science Research*, 77, 45–67.

Costanza, R., Kubiszewski, I., Giovannini, E., Lovins, H., McGlade, J., Pickett, K. et al (2014) 'Development: Time to Leave GDP Behind', *Nature*, 505(7483), 283–285.

Coyle, D. (2017) 'GDP: A Brief but Affectionate History', *Quarterly Journal of Austrian Economics*, 20(1).

Cutler, D., Deaton, A. and Lleras-Muney, A. (2006) 'The Determinants of Mortality', *Journal of Economic Perspectives*, 20(3), 97–120.

Czapinski, J. (2013) 'The Economics of Happiness and Psychology of Wealth', MPRA Paper No. 52897, University of Finance and Management in Warsaw.

D'Acci, L. (2011) 'Measuring Well-Being and Progress', *Social Indicators Research*, 104, 47–65.

Davis, K. (1956) 'The Amazing Decline of Mortality in Underdeveloped Areas', *American Economic Review*, 46(2), 305–318.

Deaton, A. (2010) 'Understanding the Mechanisms of Economic Development', *Journal of Economic Perspectives*, 24(3), 3–16.

Deaton, A. (2013) *The Great Escape: Health, Wealth and the Origins of Inequality*, Princeton University Press.

De Long, B. (1998) 'Estimates of World GDP, One Million BC – Present', UC Berkeley, 10–11.

Dickinson, E. (2011) 'GDP: A Brief History', *Foreign Policy*. Available at: https://foreignpolicy.com/2011/01/03/gdp-a-brief-history/

Diener, E., Kahneman D. and Helliwell, J. (2010) *International Differences in Well-Being*, Oxford University Press.

Easterlin, R. (1974) 'Does Economic Growth Improve the Human Lot? Some Empirical Evidence', in P. David and M. Reder (eds) *Nations and Households in Economic Growth*, Academic Press, pp 89–125.

Eggoh, J., Houeninvo, H. and Sossou, G.A. (2015) 'Education, Health and Economic Growth in African Countries', *Journal of Economic Development*, 40(1), 93–111.

Fine, B. (2000) 'Critical Survey. Endogenous Growth Theory: A Critical Assessment', *Cambridge Journal of Economics*, 24(2), 245–265.

Fogel, R. (1994) 'Economic Growth, Population Theory, and Philosophy: The Bearing of Long-Term Processes on the Making of Economic Policy', *American Economic Review*, 84(3), 369–395.

Foley, D., Michl, T. and Tavani, D. (eds) (2019) *Growth and Distribution*, 2nd edn, Harvard University Press.

Frenk, J. (2004) 'Health and the Economy: A Vital Relationship', OECD Observer No 243.

Friedman, B. (2006) 'The Moral Consequences of Economic Growth', *Society*, 43(2), 15–22.

Gallup, J. and Sachs, J. (2000) 'The Economic Burden of Malaria', Center for International Development Working Paper 52, Harvard University.

Garcia, J., Narvil, J. and Oh, S. (2016) 'Modern Day Evaluation of the Preston Curve: The Relationship Between Life Expectancy and Income', Georgia Tech Library. Available at: https://smartech.gatech.edu/bitstream/handle/1853/56046/relationship_between_life_expectancy_and_income.pdf

Georgiadis, G., Pineda, J. and Rodríguez, F. (2010) 'Has the Preston Curve Broken Down?', Human Development Research Paper 2010/32, United Nations Development Programme.

Haines, A. and Heath, I. (2000) 'Joining Together to Combat Poverty: Everybody Welcome and Needed', *BMJ Quality & Safety*, 9(1).

Haldane, A. (2018) 'Ideas and Institutions: A Growth Story'. Available at: www.bankofengland.co.uk/-/media/boe/files/speech/2018/ideas-and-institutions-a-growth-story-speech-by-andy-haldane

Inglehart, R. (1996) 'The Diminishing Utility of Economic Growth: From Maximizing Security toward Maximizing Subjective Well-being', *Critical Review*, 10(4), 509–531.

Jamison, D.T., Lau, L.J. and Wang J. (1998) 'Health's Contribution to Economic Growth, 1965–1990', WHO, *Health, Health Policy and Health Outcomes: Final Report*, Health and Development Satellite WHO Director-General Transition Team, WHO, pp 61–80.

Jardine, L. (1996) *Worldly Goods: A New History of the Renaissance*, Macmillan.

Jetter, M., Laudage, S. and Stadelmann, D. (2019) 'The Intimate Link Between Income Levels and Life Expectancy: Global Evidence from 213 Years', *Social Science Quarterly*, 100(4), 1387–1403.

Jorgenson, D. (1991) 'Productivity and Economic Growth', in E. Berndt and J. Triplett (eds) *Fifty Years of Economic Measurement: The Jubilee of the Conference on Research in Income and Wealth*, University of Chicago Press, pp 19–118.

Jorgenson, D. (2018) 'Production and Welfare: Progress in Economic Measurement', *Journal of Economic Literature*, 56(3), 867–919.

Kenny, C. and Williams, D. (2001) 'What Do We Know About Economic Growth? Or, Why Don't We Know Very Much?', *World Development*, 29(1), 1–22.

King, M. (2016) *The End of Alchemy: Money, Banking and the Future of the Global Economy*, Norton.

King, M. and Kay, J. (2020) *Radical Uncertainty: Decision-Making for an Unknowable Future*, Little, Brown Book Group Ltd.

Knight, J. and Gunatilaka, R. (2011) 'Does Economic Growth Raise Happiness in China?' *Oxford Development Studies*, 39(1), 1–24.

Kocherlakota, N. and Yi, K.M. (1996) 'A Simple Time-Series Test of Endogenous vs Exogenous Growth Models: An Application to the United States', *The Review of Economics and Statistics*, 78(1), 126–134.

Lange, G.M., Wodon, Q. and Carey, K. (2018) *The Changing Wealth of Nations 2018: Building a Sustainable Future*, World Bank.

Lange, S. and Vollmer, S. (2017) 'The Effect of Economic Development on Population Health: A Review of the Empirical Evidence', *British Medical Bulletin*, 121, 47–60.

Lutz, W. and Kebede, E. (2018) 'Education and Health: Redrawing the Preston Curve', *Population & Development Review*, 44(2), 343–361.

Mankiw, N. (2014) *Principles of Macroeconomics*, Cengage Learning.

Mauss, I.B., Tamir, M., Anderson, C.L. and Savino, N.S. (2011) 'Can Seeking Happiness Make People Unhappy? Paradoxical Effects of Valuing Happiness', *Emotion*, 11(4), 807–815.

Mayer, D. (2001) 'The Long-Term Impact of Health on Economic Growth in Latin America', *World Development*, 29(6), 1025–1033.

McNeill, J.R. (2000) *Something New Under the Sun: An Environmental History of the Twentieth-Century World*, W.W. Norton & Company.

Meer, J., Miller, D. and Rosen, H. (2003) 'Exploring the Health–Wealth Nexus', *Journal of Health Economics*, 22(5), 713–730.

Meldrum, M. (2000) 'A Brief History of the Randomized Controlled Trial: From Oranges and Lemons to the Gold Standard', *Understanding Clinical Trials*, 14(4), 745–760.

Morawetz, D. (1977) 'Twenty-five Years of Economic Development, 1950–1975', World Bank report 10098, World Bank.

Morikawa, M. (2019) 'Uncertainty in Long-Term Macroeconomic Forecasts: Ex-post Evaluation of Forecasts by Economics Researchers', Discussion Paper 19804, Research Institute of Economy, RIETI.

Mustafa, G., Rizov, M. and Kernohan, D. (2017) 'Growth, Human Development, and Trade: the Asian Experience', *Economic Modelling*, 61, 93–101.

Oishi, S. and Kesebir, S. (2015) 'Income Inequality Explains Why Economic Growth Does Not Always Translate to an Increase in Happiness', *Psychological Science*, 26(10), 1630–1638.

Prados de la Escosura, L. (2019) 'Human Development in the Age of Globalisation', Instituto Figuerola, Universidad Carlos III, Working Paper 19-04.

Preston, S. (1975) 'The Changing Relation between Mortality and Level of Economic Development', *Population Studies: A Journal of Demography*, 29(2), 231–248.

Pritchett, L. and Summers, L. (1993) 'Wealthier is Healthier', World Development Report Policy Research Working Papers, World Bank.

Ranis, G., Stewart, F. and Ramirez, A. (2000) 'Economic Growth and Human Development', *World Development*, 28(2), 197–219.

Ravallion, M. (2018) 'Should the Randomistas (Continue to) Rule?' Center for Global Development Working Paper 492, August (updated January 2019).

Rosendo Silva, F., Simões, M. and Sousa Andrade, J. (2018) 'Health Investments and Economic Growth: A Quantile Regression Approach', *International Journal of Development Issues*, 17(2), 220–245.

Rubinstein, A. (2012) *Economic Fables*, Open Books Publishing.

Sabatini, F. (2014) 'The Relationship between Happiness and Health: Evidence from Italy', *Social Science & Medicine*, 114, 178–187.

Schmelzer, M. (2016) *The Hegemony of Growth: The OECD and the Making of the Economic Growth Paradigm*, Cambridge University Press.

Schumpeter, J. (1952) *Ten Great Economists: From Marx to Keynes*, George Allen & Unwin Ltd.

Sedlacek, T. (2011) *Economics of Good and Evil: The Quest for Economic Meaning from Gilgamesh to Wall Street*, Oxford University Press.

Sen, A. (1999) *Development as Freedom*, Oxford University Press.

Smil, V. (2019) *Growth: From Microorganisms to Megacities*, MIT Press.

Steffen, W., Broadgate, W., Deutsch, L., Gaffney, O. and Ludwig, C. (2015) 'The Trajectory of the Anthropocene: The Great Acceleration', *The Anthropocene Review*, 2(1), 81–98.

Subramanian, S.V., Kim, D. and Kawachi, I. (2005) 'Covariation in the Socioeconomic Determinants of Self-Rated Health and Happiness: A Multivariate Multilevel Analysis of Individuals and Communities in the USA', *Journal of Epidemiology & Community Health*, 59, 664–669.

Szreter, S. (2003) 'The Population Health Approach in Historical Perspective', *American Journal of Public Health*, 93(3), 421–431.

Tapper, J. (2022) 'Rich Countries That Let Inequality Run Rampant Make Citizens Unhappy, Study Finds', *The Guardian*, 17 April. Available at: www.the guardian.com/inequality/2022/apr/17/rich-countries-that-let-inequality-run-rampant-make-citizens-unhappy

Taylor, S. (2009) 'Wealth, Health and Equity: Convergence and Divergence in Late-20th Century Globalisation', *British Medical Bulletin*, 91, 29–48.

Tett, G. (2013) 'An Interview with Alan Greenspan', *Financial Times*, 25 October. Available at: www.ft.com/content/25ebae9e-3c3a-11e3-b85f-00144feab7de

Veblen, T. (1909) 'The Limitations of Marginal Utility', *Journal of Political Economy*, 620–636.

Veenhoven, R. (2008) 'Healthy Happiness: Effects of Happiness on Physical Health and the Consequences for Preventive Health Care', *Journal of Happiness Studies*, 9, 449–469.

Wang, J., Jamison, D., Bos, E., Preker, A. and Peabody, J. (1999) *Measuring Country Performance on Health: Selected Indicators for Countries*, World Bank.

Wheelan, C. (2010) *Naked Economics: Undressing the Dismal Science*, Norton & Co.

WHO (World Health Organization) (1980) 'Sixth Report on the World Health Situation', WHO. Available at: https://apps.who.int/iris/handle/10665/44199

Wiles, P. (1956) 'Growth Versus Choice', *Economic Journal*, 66(262), 244–255.

Zhao, R. (2019) 'Technology and Economic Growth: From Robert Solow to Paul Romer', *Human Behaviour & Emerging Technology*, 1, 62–65.

Chapter 2: Health, development, capital and trade
Alleyne, G., Binagwaho, A., Haines, A., Jahan, S., Nugent, R., Rojhani, A. and Stuckler, D. on behalf of The Lancet NCD Action Group (2013) 'Embedding Non-Communicable Diseases in the Post-2015 Development Agenda', *The Lancet*, 381(9866), 566–574.

Alston, P. (2020) 'The Parlous State of Poverty Eradication: Report of the Special Rapporteur on Extreme Poverty and Human Rights', Human Rights Council, forty-fourth session, 15 June–3 July 2020. Available at: https://chrgj.org/wp-content/uploads/2020/07/Alston-Poverty-Report-FINAL.pdf

Arndt, C., McKay, A. and Tarp, F. (eds) (2016) *Growth and Poverty in Sub-Saharan Africa*, Oxford University Press.

Asongu, S. (2014) 'A Brief Clarification to the Questionable Economics of Foreign Aid for Inclusive Human Development', African Governance and Development Institute (AGDI) Working Paper WP/28/14.

Baldacci, E., Cui, Q., Clements, B. and Gupta, S. (2004) 'Social Spending, Human Capital, and Growth in Developing Countries: Implications for Achieving the MDGs', International Monetary Fund Working Paper WP/04/217.

Barlow, P., McKee, M., Basu, S. and Stuckler, D. (2017) 'The Health Impact of Trade and Investment Agreements: A Quantitative Systematic Review and Network Co-Citation Analysis', *Global Health*, 13, 13.

Barlow, P., Labonté, R., McKee, M. and Stuckler, D. (2019) 'WHO Response to WTO Member State Challenges on Tobacco, Food and Beverage Policies', *Bulletin of the World Health Organization*, 97, 846–848.

Beaglehole, R. and Yach, D. (2003) 'Globalisation and the Prevention and Control of Non-Communicable Disease', *The Lancet*, 362(9387), 903–908.

Blouin, C., Chopra, M. and van der Hoeven, R. (2009) 'Trade and Social Determinants of Health', *The Lancet*, 373(9662), 502–507.

Botev, J., Égert, B., Smidova, Z. and Turner, D. (2021) 'Human Capital in OECD Countries: A New Measure and its Policy Drivers', VoxEU CEPR, 6 January. Available at: https://cepr.org/voxeu/columns/human-capital-oecd-countries-new-measure-and-its-policy-drivers

Bourgignon, F., Benassy-Quere, A., Dercon, S., Estache, A., Gunning, J.W., Kanbur, R. et al (2010) 'The Millennium Development Goals: An Assessment', in R. Kanbur and M. Spence (eds) *Equity and Growth in a Globalising World*, International Bank for Reconstruction and Development/World Bank.

Chang, K. and Ying, Y.H. (2006) 'Economic Growth, Human Capital Investment, and Health Expenditure: A Study of OECD Countries', *Hitotsubashi Journal of Economics*, 47(1), 1–16.

Di Cesare, M., Khang, Y.H., Asaria, P., Blakely, T., Cowan, M., Farzadfar, F. et al (2013) 'Inequalities in Non-Communicable Diseases and Effective Responses', *The Lancet*, 381(9866), 585–597.

Easterly, W. (2001) 'The Lost Decades: Developing Countries' Stagnation in Spite of Policy Reform 1980–1998', *Journal of Economic Growth*, 6, 135–157.

Elson, D. (2005) 'Unpaid Work, the Millennium Development Goals, and Capital Accumulation', Conference on Unpaid Work and the Economy: Gender, Poverty, and the MDGs, 1–3 October.

FAO, IFAD, UNICEF, WFP and WHO (2018) *The State of Food Security and Nutrition in the World 2018: Building Climate Resilience for Food Security and Nutrition*, FAO.

Frey, D.F. (2017) 'Economic growth, full employment and decent work: the means and ends in SDG 8', *The International Journal of Human Rights*, 21: 8, 1164–1184.

Frenk, J. (2010) 'The Global Health System: Strengthening National Health Systems as the Next Step for Global Progress', *PLoS Medicine*, 7(1), e1000089.

Friel, S. and Jamieson, L. (2019) 'Political Economy, Trade Relations and Health Inequalities: Lessons from General Health', *Community Dental Health*, 36, 152–156.

Fukuda-Parr, S. (2017) *Millennium Development Goals: Ideas, Interests and Influence*, Routledge.

Ghislandi, S., Sanderson, W. and Scherbov, S. (2019) 'A Simple Measure of Human Development: The Human Life Indicator', *Population and Development Review*, 45(1), 219–233.

Gopinathan, U., Watts, N., Lefebvre, A., Cheung, A., Hoffman, S. and Røttingen, J.A. (2019) 'Global Governance and the Broader Determinants of Health: A Comparative Case Study of UNDP's and WTO's Engagement with Global Health', *Global Public Health*, 14(2), 175–189.

Gostin, L. and Taylor, A. (2008) 'Global Health Law: A Definition and Grand Challenges', *Public Health Ethics*, 1(1), 53–63.

Gostin, L. and Sridhar, D. (2014) 'Global Health and the Law', *New England Journal of Medicine*, 370, 1732–1740.

Gostin, L., DeBartolo, M. and Katz, R. (2017) 'The Global Health Law Trilogy: Towards a Safer, Healthier, and Fairer World', *The Lancet*, 390(10105), 1918–1926.

Hearne, S. (2022) 'The Pandemic Shows We Have Set the CDC Up to Fail', *The Hill*, 19 February.

Horton, R. (2015) 'Why the Sustainable Development Goals will Fail', *The Lancet*, 383(9936), 2196.

Kabeer, N. (2015) 'Gender Equality, the MDGs and the SDGs: Achievements, Lessons and Concerns', *LSE Blogs*. Available at: blogs.lse.ac.uk/southasia/2015/10/05/gender-equality-the-mdgs-and-the-sdgs-achievements-lessons-andconcerns/

Kaldor, J. (2018) 'Food Reformulation for NCD Prevention: Regulatory Options and Potential Barriers', *QUT Law Review*, 18(1), 76–95.

Kaye, D. (1992) 'Proof in Law and Science', *Jurimetrics*, 32(3), 313–322.

Kniess, J. (2018) 'Tobacco and the Harms of Trade', *The Journal of Political Philosophy*, 0(0), 1–11.

Labonté, R. (2020) 'Neoliberalism 4.0: The Rise of Illiberal Capitalism. Comment on "How Neoliberalism Is Shaping the Supply of Unhealthy Commodities and What This Means for NCD Prevention"', *International Journal of Health Policy & Management*, 9(4), 175–178.

Labonté, R. and Sanger, M. (2006) 'Glossary of the World Trade Organization and Public Health: Part 1', *Journal of Epidemiology & Community Health*, 60, 655–661.

Labonté, R., Mohindra, K. and Lencucha, R. (2011) 'Framing International Trade and Chronic Disease', *Globalization and Health*, 7(21).

Lange, S. and Vollmer, S. (2017) 'The Effect of Economic Development on Population Health: A Review of the Empirical Evidence', *British Medical Bulletin*, 121, 47–60.

Loewe, M. and Rippin, N. (2015) *The Sustainable Development Goals of the Post-2015 Agenda: Comments on the OWG and SDSN Proposals*. Available at: https://ssrn.com/abstract=2567302

Mackintosh, M. and Tibandebage, P. (2016) *Health as a Productive Sector: Integrating Health and Industrial Policy*, Economic and Social Research Foundation (ESRF).

Magnusson, R. (2019) 'Noncommunicable Diseases and Global Health Politics', in C. McInnes, K. Lee and J. Youde (eds) *The Oxford Handbook of Global Health Politics*, Oxford University Press.

Marks-Sultan, G., Tsai, F., Anderson, E., Kastler, F., Sprumont, D. and Burris, S. (2016) 'National Public Health Law: A Role for WHO in Capacity-Building and Promoting Transparency', *Bulletin of the World Health Organization*, 94(7), 534–539.

McArthur, J. and Rasmussen, K. (2018) 'Change of Pace: Accelerations and Advances during the Millennium Development Goal Era', *World Development*, 105, 132–143.

McBride, B., Hawkes, S. and Buse, K. (2019) 'Soft Power and Global Health: The Sustainable Development Goals (SDGs) Era Health Agendas of the G7, G20 and BRICS', *BMC Public Health*, 19, 815.

McKinsey (2014) 'McKinsey: Obesity Costs Global Society 2.0 Trillion a Year'. Available at: www.consultancy.uk/news/1078/mckinsey-obesity-costs-global-society-20-trillion-a-year

Melamed, C., Higgins, K. and Sumner, A. (2010) 'Economic Growth and the MDGs', ODI Briefing Paper No 60.

Mitchell, A. and Voon, T. (2011) 'Implications of the World Trade Organization in Combating Non-Communicable Diseases', *Public Health*, 125(12), 832–839.

Nandi, P. and Shahidullah, S.M. (eds) (1998) *Globalization and the Evolving World Society*, Brill.

Niaz Asadullah, M. and Savoia, A. (2018) 'Poverty Reduction during 1990–2013: Did Millennium Development Goals Adoption and State Capacity Matter?', *World Development*, 105, 70–82.

Nilsson, M., Griggs, D. and Visbeck, M. (2016) 'Map the Interactions between Sustainable Development', *Nature*, 534, 320–322.

Nissanke, M. and Ndulo, M. (eds) (2017) *Poverty Reduction in the Course of African Development*, Oxford University Press.

Nugent, R. and Feigl, A. (2007) 'Where Have All the Donors Gone? Scarce Donor Funding for Non-Communicable Diseases', Working Paper 228, Center for Global Development.

OECD (nd) 'Creditor Reporting System'. Available at: https://stats.oecd.org/Index.aspx?DataSetCode=crs1

Obersteiner, M., Walsh, B., Frank, S., Havlík, P., Cantele, M., Liu, J. et al (2016) 'Assessing the Land Resource–Food Price Nexus of the Sustainable Development Goals', *Science Advances*, 2(9).

Ogundari, K. and Awokuse, T. (2018) 'Human Capital Contribution to Economic Growth in Sub-Saharan Africa: Does Health Status Matter More than Education?', *Economic Analysis and Policy*, 58, 131–140.

O'Laughlin, B. (2016) 'Pragmatism, Structural Reform and the Politics of Inequality in Global Public Health', *Development and Change*, 47(4), 686–711.

Osborn, D., Cutter, A. and Ullah, F. (2015) 'Universal Sustainable Development Goals: Understanding the Transformational Challenge for Developed Countries', Report of a Study by Stakeholder Forum, May.

Popkin, B., Corvalan, C. and Grummer-Strawn, L. (2020) 'Dynamics of the Double Burden of Malnutrition and the Changing Nutrition Reality', *The Lancet*, 395(10297), 65–74.

Pradhan, P., Costa, L., Rybski, D., Lucht, W. and Kropp, J. (2017) 'A Systematic Study of Sustainable Development Goal (SDG) Interactions', *Earth's Future*, 5(11), 1169–1179.

Price, D., Pollock, A. and Shaoul, J. (1999) 'How the World Trade Organization is Shaping Domestic Policies in Health Care', *The Lancet*, 354(9193), 1889–1892.

Rostow, W. (1959) 'The Stages of Economic Growth', *The Economic History Review*, New Series, 12 (1), 1–16.

Ruckert, A., Ciurlia, D., Labonté, R., Lencucha, R., Drope, J., Nhamo, N. et al (2022) 'The Political Economy of Tobacco Production and Control in Zimbabwe: A Document Analysis', *Canadian Institutes of Health Research*.

Sachs, J. (2005) 'Achieving the Millennium Development Goals: The Case of Malaria', *New England Journal of Medicine*, 352(2), 115–117.

Sachs, J. (2012) 'From Millennium Development Goals to Sustainable Development Goals', *The Lancet*, 379(9832), 2206–2211.

Sachs, J., Schmidt-Traub, G., Kroll, C., Durand-Delacre, D. and Teksoz, K. (2017) 'SDG Index and Dashboards Report 2017', Bertelsmann Stiftung and Sustainable Development Solutions Network (SDSN).

Saltman, R., Bankauskaite, V. and Vrangbæk, K. (eds) (2007) *Decentralisation in Health Care: Strategies and Outcomes*, McGraw Hill Open University Press.

Schiermeier, Q. (2019) 'Carbon Markets Shape Agenda at UN Climate Summit', *Nature*, 576(7785), 17–18.

Singer, H.W. (1989) 'The 1980s: A Lost Decade – Development in Reverse?', in H.W. Singer and S. Sharma (eds) *Growth and External Debt Management*, Palgrave Macmillan, pp 46–56.

Spaiser, V., Scott, K., Owen, A. and Holland, R. (2019) 'Consumption-based Accounting of CO2 Emissions in the Sustainable Development Goals Agenda', *International Journal of Sustainable Development & World Ecology*, 26(4), 282–289.

Stein, F. (2018) 'Human Capital and Global Health', Global Health Governance Programme. Available at: www.academia.edu/37995687/Human_Capital_and_global_health

Stein, F. and Sridhar, D. (2019) 'Back to the Future? Health and the World Bank's Human Capital Index', *British Medical Journal*, 367, I5706.

Taylor, S. (2015) 'A Political Economy of International Health: Understanding Obstacles to Multilateral Action on Non-Communicable Disease', *Global Health Governance*, 9(1), 75–91.

Taylor, S. (2018) 'Global Health – Meaning What?', *British Medical Journal Global Health*, 3: e000843.

Thomas, B. and Gostin, L. (2013) 'Tackling the Global NCD Crisis: Innovations in Law and Governance', *Law, Medicine & Ethics*, 41(1), 16–27.

Thow, A., Jones, A., Hawkes, C., Ali, I. and Labonté, R. (2018) 'Nutrition Labelling is a Trade Policy Issue: Lessons from an Analysis of Specific Trade Concerns at the World Trade Organization', *Health Promotion International*, 33(4), 561–571.

Toebes, B. (2015) 'International Health Law: An Emerging Field of Public International Law', *Indian Journal of International Law*, 55, 299–328.

UNDP (1990) *Human Development Index (HDI)*. Available at: http://hdr.undp.org/en/content/human-development-index-hdi

UN Millennium Project (2005) *Investing in Development: A Practical Plan to Achieve the Millennium Development Goals*, New York.

van Bergeijk, P. and van der Hoeve, R. (eds) (2019) *Sustainable Development Goals and Income Inequality*, Edward Elgar.

Vandemoortele, J. (2011) 'The MDG Story: Intention Denied', *Development & Change*, 42(1), 1–22.

Venkat Narayan, K., Ali, M. and Koplan, J. (2010) 'Global Noncommunicable Diseases: Where Worlds Meet', *New England Journal of Medicine*, 363, 1196–1198.

Walls, H., Smith, R., Cuevas, S. and Hanefeld, J. (2019) 'International Trade and Investment: Still the Foundation for Tackling Nutrition Related Non-Communicable Diseases in the Era of Trump?', *British Medical Journal*, 365, l2217.

WHO (World Health Organization) (2011) 'Summary Report of the Discussions at the Round Tables of the High-Level Panel on the Control and Prevention of Non-Communicable Diseases', WHO.

WHO (2013) 'Political Declaration of the High-level Meeting of the General Assembly on the Control and Prevention of Noncommunicable Diseases', WHO. Available at: http://apps.who.int/gb/ebwha/pdf_files/WHA66/A66_R10-en.pdf

WHO (2015) 'Health in 2015: from Millennium Development Goals to Sustainable Development Goals', WHO.

WHO/UNICEF (2022) *Progress on WASH in Health Care Facilities 2000–2021: Special Focus on WASH and Infection Prevention and Control (IPC)*, WHO and UNICEF.

World Bank (2016) 'Global Monitoring Report 2015/2016: Development Goals in an Era of Demographic Change', World Bank.

WTO/WHO (2002) 'WTO Agreements & Public Health: A Joint Study by the WTO and WHO Secretariat'. Available at: www.wto.org/english/res_e/booksp_e/who_wto_e.pdf

Chapter 3: 'They go on because they have begun'

Allen, L., Williams, J., Townsend, N., Mikkelsen, B., Roberts, N. and Foster, C. et al (2017a) 'Socioeconomic Status and Non-Communicable Disease Behavioural Risk Factors in Low-Income and Lower-Middle-Income Countries: A Systematic Review', *Lancet Global Health*, 5(3), e277–e289.

Allen, T., Murray, K., Zambrana-Torrelio, C. et al (2017b) 'Global Hotspots and Correlates of Emerging Zoonotic Diseases', *Nature Communications*, 8, 1124.

Arredondo, A., Azar, A. and Recaman, A. (2018) 'Challenges and Dilemmas on Universal Coverage for Non-Communicable Diseases in Middle-Income Countries: Evidence and Lessons from Mexico', *Globalization and Health*, 14(89).

Asante, A., Price, J., Hayen, A., Jan, S. and Wiseman, V. (2016) 'Equity in Health Care Financing in Low- and Middle-Income Countries: A Systematic Review of Evidence from Studies Using Benefit and Financing Incidence Analyses', *PLoS One*, 11(4).

Barroso, A., Chaves, C., Martins, F. and Castelo Branco, M. (2016) 'On the Possibility of Sustainable Development with Less Economic Growth: A Research Note', *Environment, Development and Sustainability*, 18(5), 1399–1414.

Bernstein, A., Ando, A., Loch-Temzelides, T., Vale, M., Li, B., Li, H.Y. et al (2022) 'The Costs and Benefits of Primary Prevention of Zoonotic Pandemics', *Science Advances*, 8(5).

Blasco-Fontecilla, H. (2014) 'Medicalization, Wish-Fulfilling Medicine, and Disease Mongering: Toward a Brave New World?', *Revista Clínica Española*, 214(2), 104–107.

Borowy, I. and Schmelzer, M. (eds) (2017) *History of the Future of Economic Growth: Historical Roots of Current Debates on Sustainable Degrowth*, Routledge.

Brunner, E. (2020) *The Planet, Economic Growth and Ourselves Post-Pandemic: Health Trends in Rich Countries*, UCL Lunchtime Lecture, 28 May.

Buchholz, W. and Sandler, T. (2021) 'Global Public Goods: A Survey', *Journal of Economic Literature*, 59(2), 488–545.

Chiavacci, D. and Hommerich, C. (2017) *Social Inequality in Post-growth Japan*, Routledge.

Cifuentes-Faura, J. (2021) 'Circular Economy and Sustainability as a Basis for Economic Recovery Post-COVID-19', *Circular Economy & Sustainability*, 2, 1–7.

Curry, N., Castle-Clarke, S. and Hemmings, N. (2018) 'What Can England Learn From the long-Term Care System in Japan?', Nuffield Trust.

Daly, H. (2008) 'Towards a Steady-State Economy', essay commissioned by the Sustainable Development Commission, UK.

Davies, A., Keeble, E., Bhatia, T. and Fisher, E. (2016) 'Focus On: Public Health and Prevention', The Health Foundation and Nuffield Trust.

Eisenmenger, N., Pichler, M., Krenmayr, N., Noll, D., Plank, B., Schalman, E. et al (2020) 'The Sustainable Development Goals Prioritize Economic Growth Over Sustainable Resource Use: A Critical Reflection on the SDGs from a Socio-Ecological Perspective', *Sustainability Science*, 15, 1101–1110.

Ekins, P. (1993) '"Limits to Growth" and "Sustainable Development": Grappling with Ecological Realities', *Ecological Economics*, 8(3), 269–288.

Ferguson, J. (1999) 'Curative and Population Medicine: Bridging the Great Divide', *Neuroepidemiology*, 18, 111–119.

Frankel, M. (2003) 'Inheritable Genetic Modification and a Brave New World: Did Huxley Have It Wrong?', *The Hastings Centre Report*, 33(2), 31–36.

Gmeinder, M., Morgan, D. and Mueller, M. (2017) 'How Much Do OECD Countries Spend on Prevention?', OECD Health Working Paper No 101.

Gostin, L. (2021) *Global Health Security: A Blueprint for the Future*, Harvard University Press.

Gostin, L. and Katz, R. (2016) 'The International Health Regulations: The Governing Framework for Global Health Security', *Milbank Quarterly*, 94(2), 264–313.

Hargrove, A., Qandeel, M. and Sommer, J. (2019) 'Global Governance for Climate Justice: A Cross-National Analysis of CO_2 Emissions', *Global Transitions*, 1, 190–199.

Hensher, M., Tisdell, J., Canny, B. and Zimitat, C. (2020) 'Health Care and the Future of Economic Growth: Exploring Alternative Perspectives', *Health Economics, Policy & Law*, 15(4), 419–439.

Hirsch, F. (1976) *The Social Limits to Growth*, Harvard University Press.

IMF (2019) Available at: www.imf.org/external/np/exr/facts/mdg.htm

IMF (2022) *World Economic Outlook: Gloomy and More Uncertain*, IMF. Available at: www.imf.org/en/Publications/WEO/Issues/2022/07/26/world-economic-outlook-update-july-2022

Jackson, T. (2019) 'The Post-Growth Challenge: Secular Stagnation, Inequality and the Limits to Growth', *Ecological Economics*, 156, 236–246.

Jakovljevic, M. and Getzen, T. (2016) 'Growth of Global Health Spending Share in Low and Middle Income Countries', *Frontiers of Pharmacology*, 7(21).

Jamison, D.T., Summers, L.H., Alleyne, G., Arrow, K., Berkley, S., Binagwaho, A. et al (2013) 'Global Health 2035: A World Converging within a Generation', *The Lancet*, 382(1921), 1898–1955.

Jones, C. (2016) 'Life and Growth', *Journal of Political Economy*, 124(2).

Khan, M. and Munira, S. (2021) 'Climate Change Adaptation as a Global Public Good: Implications for Financing', *Climatic Change*, 167, 50.

Krugman, P. (2020) 'The Case for Permanent Stimulus', *Vox EU*, 10 March. Available at: https://voxeu.org/article/case-permanent-stimulus

Kwame Morgan, A., Aberinpoka Awafo, B. and Quartey, T. (2021) 'The Effects of COVID-19 on Global Economic Output and Sustainability: Evidence from Around the World and Lessons for Redress', *Sustainability: Science, Practice and Policy*, 17(1), 77–81.

Le Billon, P., Lujala, P., Singh, D., Culbert, V. and Kristoffersen, B. (2021) 'Fossil Fuels, Climate Change, and the COVID-19 Crisis: Pathways for a Just and Green Post-Pandemic Recovery', *Climate Policy*, 21(10), 1347–1356.

Lee, K. and Piper, J. (2020) 'The WHO and the COVID-19 Pandemic', *Global Governance: A Review of Multilateralism and International Organizations*, 26(4), 523–533.

Loh, E., Zambrana-Torrelio, C., Olival, K., Bogich, T., Johnson, C., Mazet, J., Karesh, W. and Daszak, P. (2015) 'Targeting Transmission Pathways for Emerging Zoonotic Disease Surveillance and Control', *Vector-Borne and Zoonotic Diseases*, 15(7), 432–437.

Luyten, J., Kessels, R., Goos, P. and Beutels, P. (2015) 'Public Preferences for Prioritizing Preventive and Curative Health Care Interventions: A Discrete Choice Experiment', *Value in Health*, 18(2), 224–233.

Malmaeusa, J.M. and Alfredsson, E. (2017) 'Potential Consequences on the Economy of Low or No Growth: Short and Long Term Perspectives', *Ecological Economics*, 134, 57–64.

Manstetten, R., Kuhlmann, A., Faber, M. and Frick, M. (2021) 'Groundwork for Social-Ecological Transformations: The Social Contract, Global Governance and the Meaning of Time. Constructive Criticism of the WBGU Report World in Transition – a Social Contract for a Great Transformation', ZEW Discussion Paper No 21–043.

Marmot, M. and Bell, R. (2019) 'Social Determinants and Non-Communicable Diseases: Time for Integrated Action', *British Medical Journal*, 364, l251.

McDermott, J. and Grace, D. (2012) 'Agriculture-Associated Disease: Adapting Agriculture to Improve Human Health', in S. Fan and R. Pandya-Lorch (eds) *Reshaping Agriculture for Nutrition and Health*, International Food Policy Research Institute.

McMichael, A. (1993) *Planetary Overload: Global Environmental Change and the Health of the Human Species*, Cambridge University Press.

Meadows, D., Randers, J. and Meadows, D. (2005) *The Limits to Growth: The 30-Year Update*, Earthscan.

Meadows, D., Meadows, D., Randers, J. and Behrens, W. (1972) *The Limits to Growth*, Potomac Associates.

Meckling, J. and Allan, B. (2020) 'The Evolution of Ideas in Global Climate Policy', *Nature Climate Change*, 10, 434–438.

Middleton, R. (2000) *The British Economy since 1945*, Palgrave Macmillan.

Miranda, J., Kinra, S., Casas, J., Davey Smith, G. and Ebrahim, S. (2008) 'Non-Communicable Diseases in Low- and Middle-Income Countries: Context, Determinants and Health Policy', *Tropical Medicine & International Health*, 13(10), 1225–1234.

Napolitano Ferreira, M., Elliott, W., Golden Kroner, R., Kinnaird, M., Prist, P., Valdujo, P. and Vale, M. (2021) 'Drivers and Causes of Zoonotic Diseases: An Overview', *Parks*, 27 (Special Issue), 15–24.

NHE (nd) 'NHE Fact Sheet'. Available at: www.cms.gov/research-statistics-data-and-systems/statistics-trends-and-reports/nationalhealthexpenddata/nhe-fact-sheet

Nordhaus, W. and Tobin, J. (1972) 'Is Growth Obsolete?', in *Economic Research: Retrospect and Prospect*, NBER, vol 5, pp 1–80.

OECD (nd) 'Health Expenditure'. Available at: www.oecd.org/els/health-systems/health-expenditure.htm#:~:text=This%20is%20as%20a%20result,2022%2C%20updated%20in%20November%202022.

OECD (2019) Available at: www.oecd.org/economy/going-for-growth/

Papanicolas, I., Woskie, L. and Jha, A. (2018) 'Health Care Spending in the United States and Other High-Income Countries', *Journal of the American Medical Association*, 319(10), 1024–1039.

Parrique, T., Barth, J., Briens, F. and Spangenberg, J. (2019) *Decoupling Debunked: Evidence and Arguments against Green Growth as a Sole Strategy for Sustainability*, a study edited by the European Environment Bureau EEB.

Pascual, U., Balvanera, P., Christie, M., Baptiste, B., González-Jiménez, D., Anderson, C. et al (eds) (2022) 'Summary for Policymakers of the Methodological Assessment of the Diverse Values and Valuation of Nature of the Intergovernmental Science-Policy Platform on Biodiversity and Ecosystem Services', IPBES Secretariat.

Petrovic, D., de Mestral, C., Bochud, M., Bartley, M., Kivimäki, M., Vineis, P. et al (2018) 'The Contribution of Health Behaviors to Socioeconomic Inequalities in Health: A Systematic Review', *Preventive Medicine*, 113, 15–31.

Polanyi, K. (1944) *The Great Transformation*, Farrar Rinehart.

Quirke, V. and Gaudilliere J.P. (2008) 'The Era of Biomedicine: Science, Medicine, and Public Health in Britain and France after the Second World War', *Medicine and History*, 52(4), 441–452.

Robertson, B. and Mousavian, M. (2022) *The Carbon Capture Crux: Lessons Learned*, Institute for Energy Economics and Financial Analysis, September. Available at: www.IEEFA.org

Saito, K. (2020) *Hitashinsei no Shihonron* [*Capital in the Anthropocene*], Shueisha.

Saker, L., Lee, K., Cannito, B., Gilmore, A. and Campbell-Lendrum, D. (2004) 'Globalisation and Infectious Diseases: A Review of the Linkages', UNICEF/UNDP/World Bank/WHO Special Program for Research and Training in Tropical Diseases, TDR/SDR/SEB/ST 04.2.

Salata, C., Calistri, A., Parolin, C. and Palu, G. (2019) 'Coronaviruses: A Paradigm of New Emerging Zoonotic Diseases', *Pathogens and Disease*, 77(9), 1–5.

Samb, B., Desai, N., Nishtar, S., Mendis, S., Bekedam, H., Wright, A. et al (2010) 'Prevention and Management of Chronic Disease: A Litmus Test for Health-Systems Strengthening in Low-Income and Middle-Income Countries', *The Lancet*, 376(9754), 1785–1797.

Skidelsky, R. (2009) *Keynes: The Return of the Master*, Allen Lane.

Smil, V. (2019) *Growth: From Microorganisms to Megacities*, MIT Press.

Stringhini, S., Sabia, S., Shipley, M., Brunner, E., Nabi, H., Kivimaki, M. et al (2010) 'Association of Socioeconomic Position with Health Behaviors and Mortality', *Journal of the American Medical Association*, 303(12), 1159–1166.

Taherzadeh, O. (2021) 'Promise of a Green Economic Recovery Post-Covid: Trojan Horse or Turning Point?', *Global Sustainability*, 4, E2.

Taleb, N. (2007) *Black Swan: The Impact of the Highly Improbable*, Allen Lane.

Tanaka, H., Toyokawa S., Tamiya, N. and Takahashi, H., Noguchi, H. and Kobayashi, Y. (2017) 'Changes in Mortality Inequalities across Occupations in Japan: A National Register Based Study of Absolute and Relative Measures, 1980–2010', *BMJ Open*, 7, e015764

UN (2019) *The Sustainable Development Goals Report*, UN.

Victor, P. (2010) 'Questioning Economic Growth', *Nature*, 468, 370–371.

Wang, F., Wang, J.D. and Huang, Y.X. (2016) 'Health Expenditures Spent for Prevention, Economic Performance, and Social Welfare', *Health Economics Review*, 6, 45.

Weiss, T, and Wilkinson, R. (2018) 'The Globally Governed: Everyday Global Governance', *Global Governance*, 24(2)(April–June), 193–210.

Wendimagegn, N. and Bezuidenhout, M. (2019) 'Integrating Promotive, Preventive, and Curative Health Care Services at Hospitals and Health Centers in Addis Ababa, Ethiopia', *Journal of Multidisciplinary Healthcare*, 12, 243–255.

WHO (World Health Organization) (2017) *Towards Universal Health Coverage: Thinking Public. Overview of Trends in Public Expenditure on Health (2000–2014)*, WHO.

World Bank (2021) *The Global Economy: On Track for Strong but Uneven Growth as COVID-19 Still Weighs*. Available at: www.worldbank.org/en/news/feature/2021/06/08/the-global-economy-on-track-for-strong-but-uneven-growth-as-covid-19-still-weighs

World Bank (2022a) Available at: www.worldbank.org/en/publication/global-economic-prospects

World Bank (2022b) 'Is a Global Recession Imminent?'. Available at: www.worldbank.org/en/research/brief/global-recession#:~:text=Although%20these%20forecasts%20do%20not,recession%20in%20the%20near%20future

Wu, T., Perrings, C., Kinzig, A., Collins, J.P., Minteer, B.A. and Daszak, P. (2017) 'Economic Growth, Urbanization, Globalization, and the Risks of Emerging Infectious Diseases in China: A Review', *Ambio*, 46(1), 18–29.

Xu, K., Soucat, A., Kutzin, J., Brindley, C., Vande Maele, N., Touré, H. et al (2018) 'Public Spending on Health: A Closer Look at Global Trends', WHO/HIS/HGF/HF Working Paper/18.3, WHO.

Yusuf, S., Wood, D., Ralston, J. and Srinath Reddy, K. (2015) 'The World Heart Federation's Vision for Worldwide Cardiovascular Disease Prevention', *The Lancet*, 386(9991), 399–402.

Chapter 4: The nature of freedom

Allison, H. (1990) *Kant's Theory of Freedom*, Cambridge University Press.

Arendt, H. (1961) *Between Past and Future*, Faber & Faber.

Arendt H. (1966–1967) *A Lecture*. Available at: https://lithub.com/never-before-published-hannah-arendt-on-what-freedom-and-revolution-really-mean/

Azétsop, J. (2016) 'Epidemiological Research, Individualism, and Public Health', *New Directions for Catholic Social and Political Research*, 26, 35–52.

Azétsop, J. and Rennie, S. (2010) 'Principlism, Medical Individualism, and Health Promotion in Resource-Poor Countries: Can Autonomy-Based Bioethics Promote Social Justice and Population Health?', *Philosophy, Ethics and Humanities in Medicine*, 5(1). Available at: www.peh-med.com/content/5/1/1

Bauman, Z. (2000) *Liquid Modernity*, Polity.

Becker, G. (1981) *A Treatise on the Family*, Harvard University Press.

Berlin, I. (1969) *Four Essays on Liberty*, Oxford University Press.

Berlin, I. (2002) *Freedom and Its Betrayal: Six Enemies of Human Liberty*, Princeton University Press.

Brown, B. and Baker, S. (2012) *Responsible Citizens: Individuals, Health and Policy under Neoliberalism*, Anthem Press.

Campus, A. (1987) *Marginal Economics*, Palgrave.

Chandler, D. (2013) 'Where is the Human in Human-Centred Approaches to Development? A Critique of Amartya Sen's "Development as Freedom"', *The Biopolitics of Development*, 16, 67–86.

Charvet, J. and Kaczynska-Nay, E. (2008) *The Liberal Project & Human Rights: The Theory and Practice of a New World Order*, Cambridge University Press.

Crowder, G. (2004) *Isaiah Berlin: Liberty and Pluralism*, Polity.

Da Silva, M. (2020) 'The Complex Structure of Health Rights', *Public Health Ethics*, 13(1), 99–110.

De Jong, M., Collins, A. and Plüg, S. (2019) '"To be healthy to me is to be free": How Discourses of Freedom are used to Construct Healthiness among Young South African Adults', *International Journal of Qualitative Studies on Health and Well-being*, 14(1).

Desmond, M. (2019) 'In Order to Understand the Brutality of American Capitalism, You Have to Start on the Plantation', *The 1619 Project/New York Times Magazine*. Available at: www.nytimes.com/interactive/2019/08/14/magazine/slavery-capitalism.html

Elsayed-Ali, S. (2019) 'On the Future of Human Rights', CCDP 2019–008. Harvard Kennedy School/Carr Center for Human Rights Policy.

Figes, O. (2002) *Natasha's Dance: A Cultural History of Russia*, Penguin Books.

Foner, E. (1998) *The Story of American Freedom*, Norton.

Fox, A. and Mason Meier, B. (2009) 'Health as Freedom: Addressing Social Determinants of Global Health Inequities through the Human Right to Development', *Bioethics*, 23(2), 112–122.

Franco, P. (1999) *Hegel's Philosophy of Freedom*, Yale University Press.

Friedman, M. (1962) *Capitalism and Freedom*, University of Chicago Press.

Gallie, W. (1955) 'Essentially Contested Concepts', *Proceedings of the Aristotelian Society*, LVI(X), 167–198.

Gasper, D. (2020) 'Amartya Sen, Social Theorizing and Contemporary India', International Institute of Social Studies, Working Paper No 658.

Gourevitch, A. and Robin, C. (2020) 'Freedom Now', *Polity*, 52(3), 384–398.

Graf, G. and Schweiger, G. (2014) 'Poverty and Freedom', *Human Affairs*, 24(2), 258–268.

Hertel, S. and Minkler, L. (eds) (2007) 'Economic Rights: The Terrain', *Economic Rights: Conceptual Measurement and Policy Issues*, 1(1).

Howard-Hassmann, R. (1995) *Human Rights and the Search for Community*, Routledge.

Hunt, P. (1993) 'Reclaiming Economic, Social and Cultural Rights', *Waikato Law Review*, 141.

Hurst, J.W. (1956) *Law and the Conditions of Freedom in the Nineteenth-Century United States*, University of Wisconsin Press.

Hyland, T. (1988) 'Values and Health Education: A Critique of Individualism', *Educational Studies*, 14(1), 23–31.

Ioana, C. (2014) 'The Intersection of Economic, Social, and Cultural Rights and Civil and Political Rights', in E. Riedel, G. Giacca and C. Golay (eds) *Economic, Social, and Cultural Rights in International Law. Contemporary Issues and Challenges*, Oxford University Press, pp 448–472.

Kalantry, S., Getgen, J. and Arrigg Koh, S. (2010) 'Enhancing Enforcement of Economic, Social, and Cultural Rights Using Indicators: A Focus on the Right to Education in the ICESCR', *Human Rights Quarterly*, 32, 253–310.

Kapczynski, A. (2019) 'The Right to Medicines in an Age of Neoliberalism', *Humanity*, 10(1), 79–107.

Korich, M. (2017) 'The Ambivalence of Freedom', Goethe Institut. Available at: www.goethe.de/en/kul/ges/eu2/fre/21228192.html

Krause, S. (2005) 'Two Concepts of Liberty in Montesquieu', *Perspectives on Political Science*, 34(2), 88–96.

Krause, S. (2015) *Freedom Beyond Sovereignty: Reconstructing Liberal Individualism*, University of Chicago Press.

Locke, J. (1689) *An Essay Concerning Human Understanding*, Edw. Mory.

Macdonald, C. and Hoffman, S. (eds) (2010) *Rousseau and Freedom*, Cambridge University Press.

MacGilvray, E. (2011) *The Invention of Market Freedom*, Cambridge University Press.

Mackenzie, C. (2008) 'Relational Autonomy, Normative Authority and Perfectionism', *Journal of Social Philosophy*, 39(4), 512–533.

Malinowski, B. (1947) *Freedom and Civilization*, George Allen & Unwin.

McCorquodale, R. (ed) (2003) *Human Rights*, Ashgate.

Mill, J.S. (1860) *On Liberty*, 2nd edn, John W Parker & Son.

Millis Simons, S. (1950) 'Point Four: A Global Attack on Poverty', *Social Work*, 31(1), 9–15.

Montesquieu, C. (1748) *De L'esprit des Lois*, Barrillot et Fils.

Neumann, F. (1953) 'The Concept of Political Freedom', *Columbia Law Review*, 53(7), 901–935.

Oksala, J. (2005) *Foucault on Freedom*, Cambridge University Press.

Paterson, T. (1973) 'Foreign Aid under Wraps: The Point Four Program', *The Wisconsin Magazine of History*, 56(2), 119–126.

Prakash, G. (1996) 'Colonialism, Capitalism and the Discourse of Freedom', *International Review of Social History*, 41, 9–25.

Rockefeller, N. (1951) 'Widening Boundaries of National Interest', *Foreign Affairs*, 29(4), 523–538.

Rose, N. (1998) *Inventing Our Selves: Psychology, Power, and Personhood*, Cambridge University Press.

Rose, N. (1999) *Powers of Freedom: Reframing Political Thought*, Cambridge University Press.

Rudanko, J. (2012) *Discourses of Freedom of Speech: From the Enactment of the Bill of Rights to the Sedition Act of 1918*, Palgrave Macmillan.

Schlesinger, A. (1949) *The Vital Center: The Politics of Freedom*, Houghton Mifflin.

Sen, A. (1987) 'Freedom of Choice: Concept and Content', Alfred Marshall Lecture at the annual meeting of the European Economic Association, Copenhagen, 22 August, World Institute for Development Economics Research of the United Nations University.

Sen, A. (1999) *Development as Freedom*, Anchor Books.

Sen, A. (2010) 'Why Health Equity?', in R. Hofrichter and R. Bhatia (eds) *Tackling Health Inequities Through Public Health Practice: Theory to Action*, 2nd edn, Oxford University Press.

Stanley, A. (1998) *From Bondage to Contract: Wage Labor, Marriage, and the Market in the Age of Slave Emancipation*, Cambridge University Press.

Steiner, H., Alston, P. and Goodman, R. (2008) *International Human Rights in Context: Law, Politics, Morals*, 3rd edn, Oxford University Press.

Stewart, D. (2004) 'Justiciability of Economic, Social, and Cultural Rights: Should there be an International Complaints Mechanism to Adjudicate the Rights to Food, Water, Housing, and Health?' *American Journal of International Law*, 462–515.

Streissler, E. (ed) (1969) *Roads to Freedom: Essays in Honour of Friedrich A von Hayek*, Routledge.

Taylor, C. (1984) 'Foucault on Freedom and Truth', *Political Theory*, 12(2), 152–183.

Tiedermann, F. (ed) (2006) *Adorno T. History and Freedom: Lectures 1964–1965*, Polity.

Udehn, L. (2001) *Methodological Individualism: Background, History and Meaning*, Routledge.

Urbina, D. and Ruiz-Villaverde, A. (2019) 'A Critical Review of Homo Economicus from Five Approaches', *American Journal of Economics and Sociology*, 78(1), 63–93.

Villa, D. (2008) *Public Freedom*, Princeton University Press.

William J Gibbons (1953) 'The Point Four Program and Our Responsibilities to Underdeveloped Areas', *Review of Social Economy*, 11(1), 31–43.

Chapter 5: The vaccine society

Allen, J. and Allen, R. (1986) 'From Short Term Compliance to Long Term Freedom: Culture-Based Health Promotion by Health Professionals', *American Journal of Health Promotion*, 1(2).

Baumgaertner, B., Carlisle, J.E. and Justwan, F. (2018) 'The Influence of Political Ideology and Trust on Willingness to Vaccinate', *PLoS ONE*, 13(1).

Benin, A., Wisler-Scher, D., Colson, E., Shapiro, E. and Holmboe, E. (2006) 'Qualitative Analysis of Mothers' Decision-Making About Vaccines for Infants: The Importance of Trust', *Pediatrics*, 117(5), 1532–1541.

Blundell, R., Costa Dias, M., Joyce, R. and Xu, X. (2020) 'COVID-19 and Inequalities', *Fiscal Studies*, 41, 291–319.

Bonner, A. (ed) (2022) *COVID-19 and Social Determinants of Health: Wicked Issues and Relationalism*, Policy Press.

Bowleg, L. (2020) 'We're Not All in This Together: On COVID-19, Intersectionality, and Structural Inequality', *American Journal of Public Health*, 110(7), 917.

Brownlie, J. and Howson, A. (2006) '"Between the demands of truth and government": Health Practitioners, Trust and Immunisation Work', *Social Science & Medicine*, 62(2), 433–443.

Buttenheim, A., Joyce, C., Ibarra, J., Agas, J., Feemster, K., Handy, L., et al (2020) 'Vaccine Exemption Requirements and Parental Vaccine Attitudes: An Online Experiment', *Vaccine*, 38(11), 2620–2625.

Colgrove, J. and Samuel, S. (2022) 'Freedom, Rights, and Vaccine Refusal: The History of an Idea', *American Journal of Public Health*, 112, 234–241.

Dew, K. and Donovan, S. (2020) 'Vaccines, Polarising Divides and the Role of Public Health', *Critical Public Health*, 30(1), 1–3.

Doherty, M., Buchy, P., Standaert, B., Giaquinto, C. and Prado-Cohrs, D. (2016) 'Vaccine Impact: Benefits for Human Health', *Vaccine*, 34(52), 6707–6714.

Dube, E., Gagnon, D., Macdonald, N. and the SAGE Group on Vaccine Hesitancy (2015) 'Strategies Intended to Address Vaccine Hesitancy: Review of Published Reviews', *Vaccine*, 33(34), 4191–4203.

Dudley, M., Halsey, N., Omer, S., Orenstein, W., O'Leary, S., Limaye, R. and Salmon, D. (2020) 'The State of Vaccine Safety Science: Systematic Reviews of the Evidence', *Lancet Infectious Diseases*, 20(5), e80–e89.

Earl, E. (2005) 'The Victorian Anti-Vaccination Movement', *The Atlantic*, 15 July.

Ecclestone-Turner, M. and Upton, H. (2021) 'International Collaboration to Ensure Equitable Access to Vaccines for COVID-19: The ACT-Accelerator and the COVAX Facility', *The Milbank Quarterly*, 99(2), 426–449.

Figueiredo, A., Simas, C., Karafillakis, E., Paterson, P. and Larson, H. (2020) 'Mapping Global Trends in Vaccine Confidence and Investigating Barriers to Vaccine Uptake: A Large-Scale Retrospective Temporal Modelling Study', *The Lancet*, 396(10255), P898–908.

Flanigan, J. (2014) 'A Defense of Compulsory Vaccination', *HEC Forum*, 26, 5–25.

Gellin, B. (2020) 'Why Vaccine Rumours Stick: And Getting Them Unstuck', *The Lancet*, 396(10247), 303–304.

Giubilini, A. and Savulescu, J. (2019) 'Vaccination, Risks, and Freedom: The Seat Belt Analogy', *Public Health Ethics*, 12(3), 237–249.

Gostin, L., Hodge, J., Bloom, B., El-Mohandes, A., Fielding, J., Hotez, P. et al (2020) 'The Public Health Crisis of Underimmunisation: A Global Plan of Action', *Lancet Infectious Diseases*, 20(1), e11–e16.

Gowda, C. and Dempsey, A. (2013) 'The Rise (and Fall?) of Parental Vaccine Hesitancy', *Human Vaccines & Immunotherapeutics*, 9(8), 1755–1762.

Gray, J. (2013) *The Silence of Animals: On Progress and other Modern Myths*, Farrar, Straus & Giroux.

Greenwood, B. (2014) 'The Contribution of Vaccination to Global Health: Past, Present and Future', *Philosophical Transactions of the Royal Society London Series B Biological Sciences*, 369(1645), 1–9.

Grzybowski, A., Patryn, R., Sak, J. and Zagaja, A. (2017) 'Vaccination Refusal: Autonomy and Permitted Coercion', *Pathogens and Global Health*, 111(4), 200–205.

Hobson-West, P. (2003) 'Understanding Vaccination Resistance: Moving Beyond Risk', *Health, Risk & Society*, 5(3), 273–283.

Hoffman, J. (2020) 'Measles Deaths Soared Worldwide Last Year, as Vaccine Rates Stalled', *New York Times*, 12 November. Available at: www.nytimes.com/2020/11/12/health/measles-deaths-soared-worldwide-last-year-as-vaccine-rates-stalled.html

Hooper, E. (1999) *The River: A Journey to the Source of HIV and AIDS*, Little Brown & Company.

Hosseinpoor, R., Bergen, N., Schlotheurber, A., Gacic-Dobo, M., Hansen, P., Senouci, K. et al (2016) 'State of Inequality in Diphtheria-Tetanus-Pertussis Immunisation Coverage in Low-Income and Middle-Income Countries: A Multi-Country Study of Household Health Surveys', *Lancet Global Health*, 4(9), e617–e626.

Iriart, J. (2017) 'Autonomia individual *vs.* proteção coletiva: a não-vacinação infantil entre camadas de maior renda/escolaridade como desafio para a saúde pública', *Caderna de Saúde Pública*, 33(2).

Jacobson, R., St. Sauver, J., Griffin, J., MacLaughlin, K. and Finney Rutten, L. (2020) 'How Health Care Providers Should Address Vaccine Hesitancy in the Clinical Setting: Evidence for Presumptive Language in Making a Strong Recommendation', *Human Vaccines & Immunotherapeutics*, 16(9), 2131–2135.

Jarrett, C., Wilson, R., O'Leary, M., Eckersberger, E. and Larson, H. (2015) 'Strategies for Addressing Vaccine Hesitancy: A Systematic Review', *Vaccine*, 33(34), 4180–4190.

Jit, M., Hutubessy, R., Png, M.E., Sundaram, N., Audimulam, J., Salim, S. et al (2015) 'The Broader Economic Impact of Vaccination: Reviewing and Appraising the Strength of Evidence', *BMC Medicine*, 13, 209, 1–9.

Johnson, S. (2022) 'Warnings of Global Child Health Crisis as Tens of Millions Miss Vaccinations', *The Guardian*, 15 July. Available at: www.theguardian.com/global-development/2022/jul/15/warnings-of-global-child-health-crisis-as-tens-of-millions-miss-vaccinations

Kennedy, J. (2019) 'Populist Politics and Vaccine Hesitancy in Western Europe: An Analysis of National-Level Data', *The European Journal of Public Health*, 29(3), 512–516.

Kennedy, J. (2020) 'Vaccine Hesitancy: A Growing Concern', *Pediatric Drugs*, 22, 105–111.

Korna, L., Böhm, R., Meier, N. and Betsch, C. (2020) 'Vaccination as a Social Contract', *PNAS*, 117(26), 14890–14899.

Kraaijeveld, S. (2020) 'Vaccinating for Whom? Distinguishing between Self-Protective, Paternalistic, Altruistic and Indirect Vaccination', *Public Health Ethics*, 13(2), 190–200.

Larson, H., Clarke, R., Jarrett, C., Eckersberger, E., Levine, Z., Schulz, W. et al (2018) 'Measuring Trust in Vaccination: A Systematic Review', *Human Vaccines & Immunotherapeutics*, 14(7), 1599–1609.

Lee, C. (2020) 'The Constitutionality of Mandatory Vaccinations: Eliminating Exemptions', *Journal of Biosecurity, Biosafety and Biodefense Law*, 11(1).

Lee, C., Whetten, K., Omer, S., Pan, W. and Salmon, D. (2016) 'Hurdles to Herd Immunity: Distrust of Government and Vaccine Refusal in the US, 2002–2003', *Vaccine*, 34(34), 3972–3978.

Lewin, S., Austvoll-Dahlgren, A., Glenton, C. and Munabi-Babigumira, S. (2014) 'Interventions Aimed at Communities to Inform and/or Educate about Early Childhood Vaccination', *Cochrane Database of Systematic Reviews*, 11.

McCoy, C. (2017) 'Anti-Vaccination Beliefs don't Follow the Usual Political Polarization', *The Conversation*, 23 August. Available at: http://the conversation.com/anti-vaccination-beliefs-dont-follow-the-usual political-polarization-81001

McCoy, C.A. (2020) 'The Social Characteristics of Americans Opposed to Vaccination: Beliefs about Vaccine Safety versus Views of U.S. Vaccination Policy', *Critical Public Health*, 30(1), 4–15.

Mooney, G. (2020) 'How to Talk About Freedom During a Pandemic', *The Atlantic*, 19 May.

Navin, M. (2016) *Values and Vaccine Refusal*, Routledge.

Nnaji, C., Owoyemi, A., Amaechi, U., Wiyeh, A., Ndwandwe, D. and Wiysonge, C. (2021) 'Taking Stock of Global Immunisation Coverage Progress: The Gains, the Losses and the Journey Ahead', *International Health*, 13(6), 653–657.

Nyhan, B., Reifler, J., Richey, S. and Freed, G. (2014) 'Effective Messages in Vaccine Promotion: A Randomized Trial', *Pediatrics*, 133(4), e835–e842.

Olterman, P. (2020) 'Europe's COVID Predicament: How Do You Solve a Problem Like the Anti-Vaxxers?', *The Guardian*, 24 May.

Patryn, R. and Zagaja, A. (2016) 'Vaccinations: Between Free Will and Coercion', *Human Vaccines & Immunotherapeutics*, 12(8), 2204–2205.

Paules, C., Marston, H. and Fauci, A. (2019) 'Measles in 2019: Going Backward', *New England Journal of Medicine*, 380, 2185–2187.

Pierik, R. (2018) 'Mandatory Vaccination: An Unqualified Defence', *Journal of Applied Philosophy*, 35(2), 381–398.

Reich, J. (2016) *Calling the Shots: Why Parents Reject Vaccines*, New York University Press.

Remy, V., Zollner, Y. and Heckmann, U. (2015) 'Vaccination: The Cornerstone of an Efficient Healthcare System', *Journal of Market Access & Health Policy*, 3(1).

Roth, F., Nowak-Lehmann, F. and Otter, T. (2011) 'Has the Financial Crisis Shattered Citizens' Trust in National and European Government Institutions?' CEPS Working Document No 343/February.

Roush, S., Murphy, T. and the Vaccine-Preventable Disease Table Working Group (2007) 'Historical Comparisons of Morbidity and Mortality for Vaccine-Preventable Diseases in the United States', *Journal of the American Medical Association*, 298(18), 2155–2163.

Silverman, R. and May, T. (2001) 'Private Choice versus Public Health: Religion, Morality, and Childhood Vaccination Law', *Margins*, 505.

Streefland, P. (2001) 'Public Doubts about Vaccination Safety and Resistance against Vaccination', *Health Policy*, 55(3), 159–172.

Tacke, T., Madgavkar, A. and Kotz, H. (2020) 'The Covid-19 Crisis: Exposing Underlying Vulnerabilities in Social Contracts'. Available at: https://voxeu.org/article/exposing-underlying-vulnerabilities-social-contracts

Tafuri, S., Martinelli, D., Prato, R. and Germinario, C. (2011) 'From the Struggle for Freedom to the Denial of Evidence: History of the Anti-Vaccination Movements in Europe', *Annali di Igiene: Medicina Preventiva e di Comunita*, 23(2), 93–99.

Taylor, S., Mahmud, K., Muhammad, A., Akpala, O., Morry, C., Feek, W. and Ogden, E. (2017) 'Understanding Vaccine Hesitancy: A Survey of Polio Eradication Non-Compliance at Household and Community Level in Northern Nigeria', *Vaccine*, 35(47), 6438–6443.

Tull, K. (2019) 'Vaccine Hesitancy: Guidance and Interventions', K4D, 27 September. Available at: https://opendocs.ids.ac.uk/opendocs/bitstream/handle/20.500.12413/14747/672_Vaccine_Hesitancy.pdf?sequence=1&isAllowed=y; https://wellcome.ac.uk/reports/wellcome-global-monitor/2018

Varoufakis, Y. (2020) *Another Now*, Bodley Head.

Walkinshaw, E. (2011) 'Mandatory Vaccinations: The International Landscape', *Canadian Medical Association Journal*, 183(16).

Watson, O., Barnsley, G., Toor, J., Hogan, A., Winskill, P. and Ghani, A. (2022) 'Global Impact of the First Year of COVID-19 Vaccination: A Mathematical Modelling Study', *Lancet Infectious Diseases*, S1473–3099(22)00320–6.

Williamson, L. and Glaab, H. (2018) 'Addressing Vaccine Hesitancy Requires an Ethically Consistent Health Strategy', *BMC Medical Ethics*, 19(84).

Chapter 6: The freedom to fail
Adom, T., De Villiers, A., Puoane, T. and Kengne, A.P. (2020) 'School-Based Interventions Targeting Nutrition and Physical Activity, and Body Weight Status of African Children: A Systematic Review', *Nutrients*, 12(1), 95.

Alageel, S., Gulliford, M.C., McDermott, L. and Wright, A. (2017) 'Multiple Health Behaviour Change Interventions for Primary Prevention of Cardiovascular Disease in Primary Care: Systematic Review and Meta-Analysis', *BMJ Open*, 7, e015375.

Allen, L., Nicholson, B., Yeung, B. and Goiana da Silva, F. (2020) 'Implementation of Non-Communicable Disease Policies: A Geopolitical Analysis of 151 Countries', *Lancet Global Health*, 8(1), e50–e58.

Anderson, P., Chisholm, D. and Fuhr, D. (2009) 'Effectiveness and Cost-Effectiveness of Policies and Programmes to Reduce the Harm Caused by Alcohol', *The Lancet*, 373(9682), 2234–2246.

Arnott, B., Rehackova, L., Errington, L., Sniehotta, F., Roberts, J. and Araujo-Soares, V. (2014) 'Efficacy of Behavioural Interventions for Transport Behaviour Change: Systematic Review, Meta-Analysis and Intervention Coding', *International Journal of Behavioral Nutrition and Physical Activity*, 11(133).

Ayer, A. (1972) *Philosophical Essays*, Palgrave Macmillan.

Bartlett, O. (2018) 'Power, Policy Ideas and Paternalism in Non-Communicable Disease Prevention', *European Law Journal*, 24(6), 474–489.

Bartlett, O. and Garde, A. (2015) 'The EU Platform and EU Forum: New Modes of Governance or a Smokescreen for the Promotion of Conflicts of Interest?', in A. Alemanno and A. Garde (eds) *Regulating Lifestyle Risks: The EU, Alcohol, Tobacco and Unhealthy Diets*, Cambridge University Press, pp 283–308.

Bellian, R. (2019) 'Food Deserts in Urban Areas', *The Downtown Review*, 6(1). Available at: https://engagedscholarship.csuohio.edu/tdr/vol6/iss1/1

Boddington, P. (2010) 'Dietary Choices, Health, and Freedom: Hidden Fats, Hidden Choices, Hidden Constraints', *The American Journal of Bioethics*, 10(3), 43–44.

Brown, G., Yamey, G. and Wamala, S. (2014) *The Handbook of Global Health Policy*, John Wiley & Sons.

Brownell, K., Kersh, R., Ludwig, D., Post, R., Puhl, R., Schwartz, M. and Willett, W. (2010) 'Personal Responsibility and Obesity: A Constructive Approach to a Controversial Issue', *Health Affairs*, 29(3), 379–387.

Byrne, M. (2019) 'Increasing the Impact of Behavior Change Intervention Research: Is There a Role for Stakeholder Engagement?', *Health Psychology*, 38(4), 290–296.

Champion, K., Parmenter, B., McGowan, C., Spring, B., Wafford, Q.E. and Gardner, L. (2019) 'Effectiveness of School-Based eHealth Interventions to Prevent Multiple Lifestyle Risk Behaviours among Adolescents: A Systematic Review and Meta-Analysis', *Lancet Digital Health*, 1(5), e206–e221.

Chater, N. and Loewenstein, G. (2022) 'The i-Frame and the s-Frame: How Focusing on Individual-Level Solutions Has Led Behavioral Public Policy Astray'. Available at SSRN: https://ssrn.com/abstract=4046264

Childress, J., Faden, R., Gaare, R., Gostin, L., Kahn, J., Bonnie, R. et al (2002) 'Public Health Ethics: Mapping the Terrain', *Journal of Law, Medicine & Ethics*, 30, 170–178.

Clark, J. (2014) 'Medicalization of Global Health 3: The Medicalization of the Non-Communicable Diseases Agenda', *Global Health Action*, 7: 10.3402/gha.v7.24002.

Clark, P. (2019) '"Problems of Today and Tomorrow": Prevention and the National Health Service in the 1970s', *Social History of Medicine*, 33(3), 981–1000.

Coggon, J. (2018) 'The Nanny State Debate: A Place Where Words Don't Do Justice', Faculty of Public Health.

Conly, S. (2013) 'Coercive Paternalism in Health Care: Against Freedom of Choice', *Public Health Ethics*, 6(3), 241–245.

Cradock, K., ÓLaighin, G., Finucane, F., Gainforth, H., Quinlan, L. and Martin Ginis, K. (2017) 'Behaviour Change Techniques Targeting Both Diet and Physical Activity in Type 2 Diabetes: A Systematic Review and Meta-Analysis', *International Journal of Behavioral Nutrition and Physical Activity*, 14(18), 1–17.

Crawford, R. (2006) 'Health as a Meaningful Social Practice', *Health*, 10(4), 401–420.

de Lacy-Vawdon, C., Vandenberg, B. and Livingstone, C.H. (2022) 'Recognising the Elephant in the Room: The Commercial Determinants of Health', *BMJ Global Health*, 7, e007156.

Eikemo, T., Huijts, T., Bambra, C., McNamara, C., Stornes, P. and Balaj, M. (2016) 'Social Inequalities in Health and their Determinants: Topline Results from Round 7 of the European Social Survey', *European Social Survey*, Topline Series 6.

FAO, IFAD, UNICEF, WFP and WHO (2020) *The State of Food Security and Nutrition in the World 2020: Transforming Food Systems for Affordable Healthy Diets*, FAO. Available at: https://doi.org/10.4060/ca9692en

Fooks, G.J., Smith, J., Lee, K. and Holden, C. (2017) 'Controlling Corporate Influence in Health Policy Making? An Assessment of the Implementation of Article 5.3 of the World Health Organization Framework Convention on Tobacco Control', *Global Health*, 13, 12, 1–20.

Gilmore, A., Savell, E. and Collin, J. (2011) 'Public Health, Corporations and the New Responsibility Deal: Promoting Partnerships with Vectors of Disease?', *Journal of Public Health*, 33(1), 2–4.

Global Nutrition Report (2020) Available at: https://globalnutritionreport.org/reports/2020-global-nutrition-report/introduction-towards-global-nutrition-equity/

Gostin, L. and Wiley, L. (eds) (2008) *Public Health Law: Power, Duty, Restraint*, Millbank.

Gostin, L. and Gostin, K. (2009) 'A Broader Liberty: J. S. Mill, Paternalism and the Public's Health', *Public Health*, 123, 214–221.

Heller, O., Somerville, C., Suzanne Suggs, L., Lachat, S., Piper, J., Aya Pastrana, N. et al (2019) 'The Process of Prioritization of Non-Communicable Diseases in the Global Health Policy Arena', *Health Policy and Planning*, 34(5), 370–383.

Holman, D., Lynch, R. and Reeves, A. (2018) 'How Do Health Behaviour Interventions Take Account of Social Context? A Literature Trend and Co-Citation Analysis', *Health: An Interdisciplinary Journal for the Social Study of Health, Illness and Medicine*, 22(4), 389–410.

InterAcademy Partnership (2018) Available at: www.interacademies.org/sites/default/files/publication/iap_fnsa_global_web_complete_28nov.pdf

Kaldor, J. (2018) 'What's Wrong with Mandatory Nutrient Limits? Rethinking Dietary Freedom, Free Markets and Food Reformulation', *Public Health Ethics*, 11(1), 54–68.

Kass, N. (2001) 'An Ethics Framework for Public Health', *American Journal of Public Health*, 91, 1776–1782.

Kaur, R. (2020) 'Has Modi Finally Met His Match in India's Farmers?', *The Guardian*, 10 December. Available at: www.theguardian.com/commentis free/2020/dec/10/modi-indias-farmers-government-factory-corporations

Kriznik, N., Kinmonth, A., Ling, T. and Kelly, M. (2018) 'Moving Beyond Individual Choice in Policies to Reduce Health Inequalities: The Integration of Dynamic with Individual Explanations', *Journal of Public Health*, 40(4), 764–775.

Lencucha, R. and Thow, A. (2019) 'How Neoliberalism Is Shaping the Supply of Unhealthy Commodities and What This Means for NCD Prevention', *International Journal of Health Policy Management*, 8(9), 514–520.

Levy, N. (2018) 'Responsibility as an Obstacle to Good Policy: The Case of Lifestyle Related Disease', *Journal of Bioethical Inquiry*, 15, 459–468.

Lund, T., Sandoe, P. and Lassen, J. (2011) 'Attitudes to Publicly Funded Obesity Treatment and Prevention', *Obesity*, 19(8), 1580–1585.

Marmot, M. and Bell, R. (2019) 'Social Determinants and Non-Communicable Diseases: Time for Integrated Action', *British Medical Journal*, 365(1), 10–12.

McCrabb, S., Lane, C., Hall, A., Milat, A., Bauman, A., Sutherland, R., Yoong, S. and Wolfenden, L. (2019) 'Scaling-Up Evidence-Based Obesity Interventions: A Systematic Review Assessing Intervention Adaptations and Effectiveness and Quantifying the Scale-Up Penalty', *Obesity Reviews*, 20(7), 964–982.

McGill, R., Anwar, E., Orton, L., Bromley, H., Lloyd-Williams, F., O'Flaherty, M. et al (2015) 'Are Interventions to Promote Healthy Eating Equally Effective for All? Systematic Review of Socioeconomic Inequalities in Impact', *BMC Public Health*, 15, 457, 1–15.

Modi, R. and Cheru, F. (eds) (2013) *Agricultural Development and Food Security in Africa: The Impact of Chinese, Indian and Brazilian Investments*, Zed Books.

Murray, J., Brennan, S., French, D., Patterson, C., Kee, F. and Hunter, R. (2017) 'Effectiveness of Physical Activity Interventions in Achieving Behaviour Change Maintenance in Young and Middle-Aged Adults: A Systematic Review and Meta-Analysis', *Social Science & Medicine*, 192, 125–133.

Nelson Allen, L. (2017) 'Financing National Non-Communicable Disease Responses', *Global Health Action*, 10(1).

Nugent, R. (2019) 'Noncommunicable Diseases and Climate Change: Linked Global Emergencies', based on the University College London-Lancet Annual Global Health Lecture, London UK, 29 April.

Oosterveen, E., Tzelepis, F., Ashton, L. and Hutchesson, M. (2017) 'A Systematic Review of eHealth Behavioral Interventions Targeting Smoking, Nutrition, Alcohol, Physical Activity and/or Obesity for Young Adults', *Preventive Medicine*, 99, 197–206.

Owens, J. and Cribb, A. (2013) 'Beyond Choice and Individualism: Understanding Autonomy for Public Health Ethics', *Public Health Ethics*, 6(3), 262–271.

Pearce, N., Ebrahim, S., McKee, M., Lamptey, P., Barreto, M., Matheson, D. et al (2014) 'The Road to 25×25: How Can the Five-Target Strategy Reach its Goal?' *Lancet Global Health*, 2(3), e126–e128.

Popay, J., Whitehead, M. and Hunter, D. (2010) 'Injustice is Killing People on a Large Scale – But What is to be Done about It?', *Journal of Public Health*, 32(2), 148–149.

Resnik, D. (2010) 'Trans Fat Bans and Human Freedom', *The American Journal of Bioethics*, 10(3), 27–32

Schrecker, T. and Taler, V. (2017) 'How to Think about Social Determinants of Health: Revitalizing the Agenda in Canada', in I. Bourgeault, R. Labonté, C. Packer and V. Runnels (eds) *Population Health in Canada: Issues, Research, and Action*, Canadian Scholars.

Seitz, K. and Martens, J. (2017) 'Philanthrolateralism: Private Funding and Corporate Influence in the United Nations', *Global Policy*, 8(S5), 46–50.

Sell, S. and Williams, O. (2020) 'Health under Capitalism: A Global Political Economy of Structural Pathogenesis', *Review of International Political Economy*, 27(1), 1–25.

Shaw, K.M., Theis, K.A., Self-Brown, S., Roblin, D.W. and Barker, L. (2016) 'Chronic Disease Disparities by County Economic Status and Metropolitan Classification, Behavioral Risk Factor Surveillance System', *Prevention of Chronic Diseases*, 13, 160088.

Standing, G. (2011) 'Behavioural Conditionality: Why the Nudges Must be Stopped – an Opinion Piece', *Journal of Poverty and Social Justice*, 19(1), 27–38.

Steele, S., Ruskin, G. and Stuckler, D. (2020) 'Pushing Partnerships: Corporate Influence on Research and Policy via the International Life Sciences Institute', *Public Health Nutrition*, 23(11), 2032–2040.

Tangcharoensathien, V., Chandrasiri, O., Kunpeuk, W., Markchang, K. and Pangkariya, N. (2019) 'Addressing NCDs: Challenges from Industry Market Promotion and Interferences', *International Journal of Health Policy Management*, 8(5), 256–260.

Taylor, S. (2015) 'A Political Economy of International Health: Understanding Obstacles to Multilateral Action on Non-Communicable Disease', *Global Health Governance*, 9(1), 75–91.

Templin, T., Cravo Oliveira Hashiguchi, T., Thomson, B., Dieleman, J. and Bendavid, E. (2019) 'The Overweight and Obesity Transition from the Wealthy to the Poor in Low- and Middle-Income Countries: A Survey of Household Data from 103 Countries', *PLoS Medicine*, 16(11).

Toomey, E., Hardeman, W., Hankonen, N., Byrne, M., McSharry, J., Matvienko-Sikar, K. et al (2020) 'Focusing on Fidelity: Narrative Review and Recommendations for Improving Intervention Fidelity within Trials of Health Behaviour Change Interventions', *Health Psychology and Behavioral Medicine*, 8(1), 132–151.

Traverso-Yepez, M. and Hunter, K. (2016) 'From "Healthy Eating" to a Holistic Approach to Current Food Environments', *SAGE Open*, 1–9.

Vandevijvere, S. and Kraak, V. (2019) 'Future Directions to Prevent Obesity within the Context of the Global Syndemic', *Obesity Reviews*, 20(S2), 3–5.

Varkevisser, R., van Stralen, M., Kroeze, W., Ket, J. and Steenhuis, I. (2019) 'Determinants of Weight Loss Maintenance: A Systematic Review', *Obesity Reviews*, 20(2), 171–211.

Varman, R. and Vikas, R. (2007) 'Freedom and Consumption: Toward Conceptualizing Systemic Constraints for Subaltern Consumers in a Capitalist Society', *Consumption Markets & Culture*, 10(2), 117–131.

Wiist, W. (2010) *The Bottom Line or Public Health: Tactics Corporations Use to Influence Health and Health Policy, and What We Can Do to Counter Them*, Oxford University Press.

Chapter 7: The dead hand of care
Allcott, H., Boxell, L., Conway, J., Gentzkow, M., Thaler, M. and Yang, D. (2020) 'Polarization and Public Health: Partisan Differences in Social Distancing during the Coronavirus Pandemic'. Available at: http://web.stanford.edu/~gentzkow/research/social_distancing.pdf

Almgren, G. (2018) *Health Care Politics, Policy, and Services*, 3rd edn, Springer Publishing.

Armstrong, H. (2001) 'Social Cohesion and Privatization in Canadian Health Care', *Canadian Journal of Law and* Society, 16(2), 65–81.

Barber, S., Lorenzoni, L. and Ong, P. (2019) *Price Setting and Price Regulation in Health Care: Lessons for Advancing Universal Health Coverage*, World Health Organization, Organisation for Economic Co-operation and Development.

Basu, S., Andrews, J., Kishore, S., Panjabi, R. and Stuckler, D. (2012) 'Comparative Performance of Private and Public Healthcare Systems in Low- and Middle-Income Countries: A Systematic Review', *PLoS Medicine*, 9(6), e1001244.

Bittner, R. (2019) 'What It Is to Be Free', in M. Welker (ed) *Quests for Freedom: Biblical, Historical, Contemporary*, 2nd edn, Cascade Books.

Blair, R., Morse, B. and Tsai, L. (2017) 'Public Health and Public Trust: Survey Evidence from the Ebola Virus Disease Epidemic in Liberia', *Social Science & Medicine*, 172, 89–97.

Brown, W. (1995) *States of Injury: Power and Freedom in Late Modernity*, Princeton University Press.

Busse, R., Blumel, M., Knieps, F. and Barnighausen, T. (2017) 'Statutory Health Insurance in Germany: A Health System Shaped by 135 Years of Solidarity, Self-Governance, and Competition', *The Lancet*, 390(10097), 882–897.

Cecilia Quercioli, C., Messina, G., Basu, S., McKee, M., Nante, N. and Stuckler, D. (2013) 'The Effect of Healthcare Delivery Privatisation on Avoidable Mortality: Longitudinal Cross-Regional Results from Italy, 1993–2003', *Journal of Epidemiology and Community Health*, 67(2), 132–138.

Charvet, J. (1981) *A Critique of Freedom and Equality*, Cambridge University Press.

Chuang, Y., Chuang, K. and Yang, T. (2013) 'Social Cohesion Matters in Health', *International Journal of Equity in Health*, 12(87), 1–12.

Coarasa, J., Das, J., Gummerson, E. and Bitton, A. (2017) 'A Systematic Tale of Two Differing Reviews: Evaluating the Evidence on Public and Private Sector Quality of Primary Care in Low- and Middle-Income Countries', *Globalization and Health*, 13(24).

Culyer, A. (2014) 'Social Values in Health and Social Care', Background Paper, Commission on the Future of Health and Social Care in England. Available at: www.kingsfund.org.uk/sites/default/files/media/commission-background-paper-social-values-health-social-care.pdf

Dayrit, M. and Mendoza, R. (2020) 'Social Cohesion vs COVID-19', 18 March. Available at: https://ssrn.com/abstract=3555152

De Costa, A. and Diwan, V. (2007) '"Where is the public health sector?": Public and Private Sector Healthcare Provision in Madhya Pradesh, India', *Health Policy*, 84(2–3), 269–276.

Devereaux, P., Heels-Ansdell, D., Lacchetti, C., Haines, T., Burns, K., Cook, D. et al (2004) 'Payments for Care at Private for-Profit and Private Not-for-Profit Hospitals: A Systematic Review and Meta-Analysis', *Canadian Medical Association Journal*, 170(12).

Dougherty, C. (1992) 'The Excesses of Individualism: For Meaningful Healthcare Reform, the United States Needs a Renewed Sense of Community', *Health Progress*, 73(1), 22–28.

The Economist (2008) 'Health Care in China: Losing Patients', 21 February.

EXPH (Expert Panel on Effective Ways of Investing in Health) (2015) 'Report on Investigating Policy Options regarding Competition among Providers of Health Care Services in EU Member States', 7 May. Available at: 008_competition_healthcare_providers_en_0.pdf

Flavin, P., Pacek, A.C. and Radcliff, B. (2014) 'Assessing the Impact of the Size and Scope of Government on Human Well-Being', *Social Forces*, 92(4), 1241–1258.

Gaynor, M., Propper, C. and Seiler, S. (2016) 'Free to Choose? Reform, Choice and Consideration Sets in the English National Health Service', *American Economic Review*, 106(11), 3521–3557.

Gille, F., Smith, S. and Mays, N. (2015) 'Why Public Trust in Health Care Systems Matters and Deserves Greater Research Attention', *Journal of Health Services Research & Policy*, 20(1), 62–64.

Gilson, L. (2003) 'Trust and the Development of Health Care as a Social Institution', *Social Science & Medicine*, 56(7), 1453–1468.

Gilson, L., Lehmann, U. and Schneider, H. (2017) 'Practicing Governance towards Equity in Health Systems: LMIC Perspectives and Experience', *International Journal of Equity in Health*, 16, 171.

Goodair, B and Reeves, A. (2022) 'Outsourcing Health-Care Services to the Private Sector and Treatable Mortality Rates in England, 2013–20: An Observational Study of NHS Privatisation', *Lancet Public Health*, 7, e638–46.

Hanson, K., Gilson, L., Goodman, C., Mills, A., Smith, R. and Feachem, R. et al (2008) 'Is Private Health Care the Answer to the Health Problems of the World's Poor?', *PLoS Medicine*, 5(11), e233.

Herrera, C.A., Rada, G., Kuhn-Barrientos, L. and Barrios, X. (2014) 'Does Ownership Matter? An Overview of Systematic Reviews of the Performance of Private For-Profit, Private Not-For-Profit and Public Healthcare Providers', *PLoS ONE*, 9(12), e93456.

Heymann, D.L., Chen, L., Takemi, K., Fidler, D., Tappero, J., Thomas, M. et al (2015) 'Global Health Security: The Wider Lessons from the West African Ebola Virus Disease Epidemic', *The Lancet*, 385, 1884–1901.

IFC Global Private Health Conference (2019) 'Disrupting the Present, Building the Future: Embracing Innovation to Deliver Results', 27–28 March, Miami, Florida.

Independent Panel for Pandemic Preparedness & Response (2021) *COVID-19: Make it the Last Pandemic*.

Jamison, D., Yamey, G., Beyeler, N. and Wadge, H. (2016) 'Investing in Health: The Economic Case', Report of the WISH Investing in Health Forum 2016.

Janzen, J. (1978) 'The Comparative Study of Medical Systems as Changing Social Systems', *Social Science & Medicine*, 12, 121–129.

Jeffrey, B., Walters, C., Kylie, E., Jeffrey, B., Walters, C., Ainslie, K. et al (2020) 'Anonymised and Aggregated Crowd Level Mobility Data from Mobile Phones', Imperial College London.

Karsten, S. (1995) 'Health Care: Private Good vs. Public Good', *The American Journal of Economics and Sociology*, 54(2), 129–144.

Kawachi, I. and Berkman, L. (2000) 'Social Cohesion, Social Capital, and Health', in L. Berkman and I. Kawachi (eds) *Social Epidemiology*, Oxford University Press.

Lagarde, M. and Palmer, N. (2009) 'The Impact of Contracting Out on Health Outcomes and Use of Health Services in Low and Middle-Income Countries', *Cochrane Database of Systematic Reviews*, 4.

Light, D.W. (2003) 'Universal Health Care: Lessons from the British Experience', *American Journal of Public Health*, 93(1), 25–30.

MacCallum, G. (1967) 'Negative and Positive Freedom', *Philosophical Review*, 76, 312–334.

Mackintosh, M. and Koivusalo, M. (eds) (2005) *Commercialization of Health Care: Global and Local Dynamics and Policy Responses*, Palgrave Macmillan.

Mackintosh, M., Channon, A., Karan, A., Selvaraj, S., Cavagnero, E. and Zhao, H.W. (2016) 'What is the Private Sector? Understanding Private Provision in the Health Systems of Low-Income and Middle-Income Countries', *The Lancet*, 388(10044), 596–605.

Mahase, E. (2020) 'Covid-19: Was the Decision to Delay the UK's Lockdown over Fears of "Behavioural Fatigue" based on Evidence?', *British Medical Journal*, 370, m3166.

Mahnkopf, B. (2008) 'Privatisation of Public Services in the EU: An Attack on Social Cohesion and Democracy', *Work Organisation, Labour & Globalisation*, 2(2), 72–84.

Marten, R. (2019) 'How States Exerted Power to Create the Millennium Development Goals and How this Shaped the Global Health Agenda: Lessons for the Sustainable Development Goals and the Future of Global Health', *Global Public Health*, 14(4).

Matharu, H. (2020) 'Johnson's Suggestion that "Freedom-Loving" Britain has a Death Wish May Be his Greatest Insight', *Financial Times*, 22 September.

Montagu, D., Anglemyer, A., Tiwari, M., Drasser, K., Rutherford, G., Horvath, T. et al (2011) 'Private versus Public Strategies for Health Service Provision for Improving Health Outcomes in Resource-Limited Settings', Global Health Sciences, University of California.

Morgan, R. and Waters, H. (2016) 'Performance of Private Sector Health Care: Implications for Universal Health Coverage', *The Lancet*, 388(10044), 606–612.

Musgrove, P. (1996) 'Public and Private Roles in Health: Theory and Financing Patterns', International Bank of Reconstruction and Development/ World Bank.

Muthukrishna, M. (2020) 'Long Read: Cultural Evolution, Covid-19, and Preparing for What's Next', *LSE Blogs*, 22 April. Available at: https://blogs.lse.ac.uk/businessreview/2020/04/22/long-read-cultural-evolution-covid-19-and-preparing-for-whats-next/

Nambiar, D. and Mander, H. (2017) 'Inverse Care and the Role of the State: The Health of the Urban Poor', *Bulletin of the World Health Organization*, 95(2), 152–153

Novignon, J. and Lawanson, A. (2017) 'Health Expenditure and Child Health Outcomes in Sub-Saharan Africa', *African Review of Economics and Finance*, 9(1), 96–121.

Novignon, J., Olakojo, S. and Nonvignon, J. (2012) 'The Effects of Public and Private Health Care Expenditure on Health Status in Sub-Saharan Africa: New Evidence from Panel Data Analysis', *Health Economics Review*, 2, 22, 1–8.

O'Laughlin, B. (2016) 'Pragmatism, Structural Reform and the Politics of Inequality in Global Public Health', *Development & Change*, 47(4), 686–711.

Odendaal, W., Ward, K., Uneke, J., Uro-Chukwu, H., Chitama, D., Balakrishna, Y. and Kredo, T. (2018) 'Contracting Out to Improve the Use of Clinical Health Services and Health Outcomes in Low- and Middle-Income Countries', *Cochrane Database of Systematic Reviews*, 4.

Oliu-Barton, M., Pradelski, B., Aghion, P., Artur, P., Kickbusch, I. and Lazarus, J. (2021) 'SARS-CoV2 Elimination, not Mitigation, Creates Best Outcomes for Health, the Economy, and Civil Liberties', *The Lancet*, 397(10291), 2234–2236.

Oxfam (2009) 'Blind Optimism', Briefing Paper, February. Available at: https://policy-practice.oxfam.org.uk/publications/blind-optimism-challenging-the-myths-about-private-health-care-in-poor-countries-114093

Partanem, A. (2017) 'The Fake Freedom of American Health Care', *New York Times*, 18 March.

Pascoe, J. and Stripling, M. (2020) 'Surging Solidarity: Reorienting Ethics for Pandemics', *Kennedy Institute of Ethics Journal*. Available at: https://kiej.georgetown.edu/tag/covid-19/

Petrou, P., Samoutis, G. and Lionis, C. (2018) 'Single-Payer or a Multipayer Health System: A Systematic Literature Review', *Public Health*, 163, 141–152.

Prah Ruger, J. (2020) 'Social Justice as a Foundation for Democracy and Health', *British Medical Journal*, 371, m4049.

Samek, R. (1981) 'Justice as Ideology: Another Look at Rawls', *The Canadian Bar Review*, 59.

Schieber, G. and Poullier, J.-P. (1989) 'Overview of International Comparisons of Health Care Expenditures', *Health Care Financing Review*, 1–7.

Schmidtz, D. and Pavel, C. (eds) (2018) *The Oxford Handbook of Freedom*, Oxford University Press.

Srivastan, R. and Shatrugna, V. (2012) 'Political Challenges to Universal Access to Healthcare', *Economic and Political Weekly*, XLVII(8), 61–63.

Stephen, J. (1874) *Liberty, Equality, Fraternity: Three Brief Essays*, 2nd edn, Smith, Elder & Co.

Storeng, K., Prince, R. and Mishra, A. (2019) 'The Politics of Health Systems Strengthening', in J. Parker and J. Garcia (eds) *Routledge Handbook on the Politics of Global Health*, Routledge.

Sudhir, A. and Ravallion, M. (1993) 'Human Development in Poor Countries: On the Role of Private Incomes and Public Services', *Journal of Economic Perspectives*, 7(1): 133–150.

Tang, S., Meng, Q., Chen, L., Bekedam, H., Evans, T. and Whitehead, M. (2008) 'Tackling the Challenges to Health Equity in China', *The Lancet*, 372, 1493–1501.

Tibandebage, P. and Mackintosh, M. (2005) 'The Market Shaping of Charges, Trust and Abuse: Health Care Transactions in Tanzania', *Social Science & Medicine*, 61(7), 1385–1395.

Torchia, M., Calabrò, A. and Morner, M. (2015) 'Public–Private Partnerships in the Health Care Sector: A Systematic Review of the Literature', *Public Management Review*, 17(2), 236–261.

Turcotte-Tremblay, A., Spagnolo, J., De Allegri, M. and Ridde, V. (2016) 'Does Performance-Based Financing Increase Value for Money in Low- and Middle-Income Countries? A Systematic Review', *Health Economic Review*, 6(30), 1–18.

UK/House of Parliament (2021) *Coronavirus: Lessons Learned to Date*. Sixth Report of the Health and Social Care Committee and Third Report of the Science and Technology Committee of Session 2021–22, 21 September.

UK Scientific Advisory Group for Emergencies (SAGE) (2020) *Potential Impact of Behavioural and Social Interventions on an Epidemic of Covid-19 in the UK*, 9 March. Available at: www.gov.uk/government/publications/potential-impact-of-behavioural-and-social-interventions-on-an-epidemic-of-covid-19-in-the-uk-9-march-2020

Wadge, H., Roy, R., Sripathy, A., Prime, M., Carter, A., Fontana, G. et al (2017) 'Evaluating the Impact of Private Providers on Health and Health Systems', Imperial College London.

Welzel, C. (2013) *Freedom Rising: Human Empowerment and the Quest for Emancipation*, Cambridge University Press.

Wenham, C., Katz, R., Birungi, C., Boden, L., Ecclestone-Turner, M. and Gostin, L. et al (2019) 'Global Health Security and Universal Health Coverage: From a Marriage of Convenience to a Strategic, Effective Partnership', *BMJ Global Health*, 4, e001145.

West-Oram, P. (2013) 'Freedom of Conscience and Health Care in the United States of America: The Conflict Between Public Health and Religious Liberty in the Patient Protection and Affordable Care Act', *Health Care Analysis*, 21, 237–247.

Whetten, K., Leserman, J., Whetten, R., Ostermann, J., Thielman, N., Swartz, M. and Stangl, D. (2006) 'Exploring Lack of Trust in Care Providers and the Government as a Barrier to Health Service Use', *American Journal of Public Health*, 96(4), 716–721.

Wu, J. and Mao, Y. (2017) 'Liberty in Health Care: A Comparative Study Between Hong Kong and Mainland China', *The Journal of Medicine and Philosophy: A Forum for Bioethics and Philosophy of Medicine*, 42(6), 690–719.

Chapter 8: The poverty of justice

Alfani, G. (2019) 'Wealth and Income Inequality in the Long Run of History', in C. Diebolt and M. Haupert (eds) *Handbook of Cliometrics*, 2nd edn, Springer.

Alfani, G. (2020) 'Epidemics, Inequality and Poverty in Preindustrial and Early Industrial Times', Stone Center on Socioeconomic Inequality, Working Paper Series No 23.

Alkire, S. (2002) 'Dimensions of Human Development', *World Development*, 30(2), 181–205.

Alvaredo, F., Chancel, L., Piketty, T., Saez, E. and Zucman, G. (2018) *World Inequality Report*. Available at: https://wir2018.wid.world/

Assouad, L., Chancel, L. and Morgan, M. (2018) 'Extreme Inequality: Evidence from Brazil, India, the Middle East, and South Africa', *AEA Papers and Proceedings*, 108, 119–123.

Balasubramanian, S., Kumar, R. and Loungani, P. (2021) 'Sustaining India's Growth Miracle Requires Increased Attention to Inequality of Opportunity', *CEPR Policy Portal*. Available at: https://voxeu. org/article/sustaining-india-s-growth-miracle-requires-increased-attention-inequality-opportunity

Bandyopadhyay, S. (2017) 'The Absolute Gini is a More Reliable Measure of Inequality for Time Dependent Analyses (Compared with the Relative Gini)', Queen Mary University of London, 1 June.

Bloome, D. (2014) 'Racial Inequality Trends and the Intergenerational Persistence of Income and Family Structure', *American Sociological Review*, 79(6), 1196–1225.

Bourguignon, F., Bénassy-Quéré, A., Dercon, S., Estache, A., Gunning, J.W., Kanbur, R. et al (2009) 'Millennium Development Goals at Midpoint: Where Do We Stand and Where Do We Need to Go?', Directorate General for Development of the European Commission, European Report on Development.

Brown, J.M. (2019) 'Relational Equality and Disability Injustice', *Journal of Moral Philosophy*, 16(3), 327–357.

Buchanan, A., Cole, T. and Keohane, R. (2009) 'Justice in the Diffusion of Innovation', *The Journal of Political Philosophy*, 19(3), 306–332.

Chelstowski, A. (2012) 'Individualism, Environmentalism and Social Change', *Perspectives*, 4(1), No 12.

Choules, K. (2007) 'The Shifting Sands of Social Justice Discourse: From Situating the Problem with "Them," to Situating it with "Us"', *Review of Education, Pedagogy, and Cultural Studies*, 29(5), 461–481.

Christiansen, C. and Jensen, S. (2019) 'Histories of Global Inequality: Introduction', in C. Christiansen and S. Jensen (eds) *Histories of Global Inequality*, Palgrave Macmillan.

Coffey, D., Deshpande, A., Hammer, J. and Spears, D. (2019) 'Local Social Inequality, Economic Inequality, and Disparities in Child Height in India', *Demography*, 56, 1427–1452.

Cohen, G. (2008) *Rescuing Justice and Equality*, Harvard University Press.

Commission on Social Mobility (2018) 'Social Mobility Barometer: Public Attitudes to Social Mobility in the UK', December.

Cornia, A. and Martorano, B. (2012) 'Development Policies and Income Inequality in Selected Developing Regions, 1980–2010', UNCTAD Discussion Paper, 12 December.

Criado Perez, C. (2019) *Invisible Women: Exposing Data Bias in a World Designed for Men*, Chatto.

Curtiss, K. and Choo, E. (2020) 'Indigenous Populations: Left Behind in the COVID-19 Debate', *The Lancet*, 395(10239), 1753.

de Barros, R., Ferreira, F., Vega, J. and Chanduvi, J. (2009) *Measuring Inequality of Opportunities in Latin America and the Caribbean*, World Bank.

Della Porta, D., Andretta, M., Calle, A., Combes, H., Eggert, N., Giugni, M. et al (2007) *Global Justice Movement: Cross-National and Transnational Perspectives*, Paradigm Publishers.

De Stefano, V. (2019) '"Negotiating the Algorithm": Automation, Artificial Intelligence and Labour Protection', *Comparative Labor Law & Policy Journal*, 41(1).

Detels, R., Gulliford, M., Abdool Karim, Q. and Chuan Tan, C. (eds) (2015) *Oxford Textbook of Global Public Health*, 6th edn, Oxford University Press.

Development Initiatives (2019) 'Poverty Trends: Global, Regional and National, Factsheet', December 2019. Available at: https://devinit.org/resources/poverty-trends-global-regional-and-national/

De Zwart, P. (2019) *The Global History of Inequality*, IRSH 64, 309–323, Paper, Internationaal Instituut voor Sociale Geschiedenis.

Dickens, C. (1848) *Dombey and Son*, Bradbury & Evans.

Easterly, W. (2007) 'Inequality Does Cause Underdevelopment: Insights from a New Instrument', *Journal of Development Economics*, 84(2), 755–766.

The Economist (2020) 'The Grim Racial Inequalities behind America's Protests', 3 June.

Eyal, N., Hurst, S., Norheim, O. and Wikler, D. (2013) *Inequalities in Health: Concepts, Measures, and Ethics*, Oxford University Press.

Feinberg, J. (1974) 'Noncomparative Justice', *The Philosophical Review*, 83(3), 297–338.

Feinstein, L. (2003) 'Inequality in the Early Cognitive Development of British Children in the 1970 Cohort', *Economica*, 70(277), 73–97.

Fischer, A. (2018) *Poverty as Ideology: Rescuing Social Justice from Global Development Agendas*, Zed Books.

Foa, R., Klassen, A., Slade, M. and Collins Rand, A. (2020) 'The Global Satisfaction with Democracy Report 2020', Centre for the Future of Democracy.

Förster, M. (2012) 'Divided We Stand: Why Inequality Keeps Rising', OECD Social Policy Division Press Conference, 22 March, Budapest, Európa Kávéház.

Freedom House (2020) *Freedom in the World*. Available at: https://freedomhouse.org/sites/default/files/2020-03/FINAL_FIW_2020_Abridged.pdf

Freistein, K. and Mahlert, B. (2016) 'The Potential for Tackling Inequality in the Sustainable Development Goals', *Third World Quarterly*, 37(12), 2139–2155.

Funjika, P. and Gisselquist, R. (2020) 'Social Mobility and Inequality between Groups', UNU/WIDER Working Paper 2020/12.

Galbraith, J.K. (2016) *Inequality: What Everyone Needs to Know*, Oxford University Press.

Glaeser, E., Scheinkman, J. and Shleifer, A. (2003) 'The Injustice of Inequality', *Journal of Monetary Economics*, 50, 199–222.

Gledhill, J. (2012) 'Rawls and Realism', *Social Theory and Practice*, 38(1), 55–82.

Goda, T. (2016) 'Global Trends in Relative and Absolute Income Inequality', *Ecos de Economía*, 20(42), 46–69.

Greenberg, J. and Cohen, R. (eds) (1982) *Equity and Justice in Social Behavior*, Academic Press.

Grigoryev, L. and Pavlyushina, V. (2019) 'Relative Social Inequality in the World: Rigidity against the Economic Growth, 1992–2016', *Russian Journal of Economics*, 5, 46–66.

Gugushvili, A., Reeves, A. and Jarosz, E. (2020) 'How Do Perceived Changes in Inequality Affect Health?' *Health & Place*, 62, 102276.

Guo, S., Lin, X., Coicaud, J.M., Gu, S., Gu, Y., Liu, Q. et al (2019) 'Conceptualizing and Measuring Global Justice: Theories, Concepts, Principles and Indicators', *Fudan Journal of the Humanities and Social Sciences*, 12, 511–546.

Harsanyi, J. (1980) 'Can the Maximin Principle Serve as a Basis for Morality? A Critique of John Rawls's Theory', *American Political Science Review*, 69(2), 594–606.

Hernández, A., Ruano, A., Marchal, B., San Sebastian, M. and Flores, W. (2017) 'Engaging with Complexity to Improve the Health of Indigenous People: A Call for the Use of Systems Thinking to Tackle Health Inequity', *International Journal of Equity in Health*, 16, 26.

Hirschmann, N. (2008) *Gender, Class, and Freedom in Modern Political Theory*, Princeton University Press.

Hoff, K. and Pandey, P. (2004) 'Belief Systems and Durable Inequalities: An Experimental Investigation of Indian Caste', World Bank/Pennsylvania State University.

Jain-Chandra, S., Khor, N., Mano, R., Schauer, J., Wingender, P. and Zhuang, J. (2018) 'Inequality in China – Trends, Drivers and Policy Remedies', IMF Working Paper WP/18/127. Available at: www.imf.org/en/Publications/WP/Issues/2018/06/05/Inequality-in-China-Trends-Drivers-and-Policy-Remedies-45878

Jolliffe, D. and Beer Prydz, E. (2021) 'Societal Poverty: A Relative and Relevant Measure', *The World Bank Economic Review*, 35(1), 180–206.

Kanbur, R. and Vines, D. (2000) 'The World Bank and Poverty Reduction: Past, Present and Future', in C. Gilbert and D. Vines (eds) *The World Bank: Structure and Policies*, Cambridge University Press, pp 87–107.

Kanbur, R. and Spence, M. (2010) 'Equity and Growth in a Globalizing World', Washington DC: World Bank. Available at: https://doi.org/10.1596/978-0-8213-8180-9

Kanbur, R. and Wagstaff, A. (2014) 'How Useful is Inequality of Opportunity as a Policy Construct?' World Bank/IBRD.

Kaplinsky, R. (2005) *Globalization, Poverty and Inequality: Between a Rock and a Hard Place*, Polity Press.

Khandaker, K. and Narayanaswamy, L. (2020) *The Unbearable Whiteness of International Development: The SDGs and Decolonial Feminisms*, Ghent Centre for Global Studies.

Klasen, S. (2016) 'What to do about Rising Inequality in Developing Countries?' PEGNet Policy Brief, No. 5/2016, Kiel Institute for the World Economy (IfW), Poverty Reduction, Equity and Growth Network (PEGNet).

Koplenig, A. (2017) 'The Impact of Lacking Metadata for the Measurement of Cultural and Linguistic Change using the Google Ngram Data Sets: Reconstructing the Composition of the German Corpus in Times of WWII', *Digital Scholarship in the Humanities*, 32(1), 169–188.

Korinek, A. and Stiglitz, J. (2017) 'Artificial Intelligence and its Implications for Income Distribution and Unemployment', NBER Working Paper 24174.

Kuznets, S. (1955) 'Economic growth and income inequality', *American Economic Review*, 45(1): 1–28.

Legatum Institute (2019) *Global Prosperity Index*.

Li, S., Sato, H. and Sicular, T. (eds) (2013) *Rising Inequality in China: Challenges to a Harmonious Society*, Cambridge University Press.

Lopez, G. (2022) 'A Hotter World', *New York Times*, 3 June.

Lucas, J. (1972) 'Justice', *Philosophy*, 47(181), 229–248.

Major, L.E. and Machin, S. (2018) *Social Mobility and its Enemies*, Pelican.

Matsuda, M. (1986) 'Liberal Jurisprudence and Abstracted Visions of Human Nature: A Feminist Critique of Rawls' Theory of Justice', *New Mexico Law Review*, 613.

McGill Centre for Human Rights and Legal Pluralism, International Disability Alliance and DICARP (2022) Status Report on Disability Inclusion in National Climate Commitments and Policies, June. Available at: www.internationaldisabilityalliance.org/sites/default/files/drcc_status_report_english_0.pdf

McIntosh, K., Moss, E., Nunn, R. and Shambaugh, J. (2020) 'Examining the Black-White Wealth Gap', Brookings Institute. Available at: www.brookings.edu/blog/up-front/2020/02/27/examining-the-black-white-wealth-gap/

Meshelski, K. (2019) 'Amartya Sen's Nonideal Theory', *Ethics & Global Politics*, 12(2), 31–45.

Milanovic, B. (2015) 'Global Inequality of Opportunity: How Much of Our Income Is Determined by Where We Live?', *Review of Economics and Statistics*, 97(2), 452–460.

Milanovic, B. (2016) *Global Inequality: A New Approach for the Age of Globalization*, Harvard University Press.

Milanovic, B. (2018) 'What is Happening with Global Inequality?', *Global Policy*, 13 November.

Mir Ahad Saeed, K., Osmani, S. and Collins, D. (2022) 'Calculating the Cost and Financing Needs of the Basic Package of Health Services in Afghanistan: Methods, Experiences, and Results', *Global Health: Science and Practice*, 10(4).

Moellendorf, E. (2009) 'Global Inequality and Injustice', *Journal of International Development*, 21, 1125–1136.

Moore, M. (2014) 'Reconstituting Labour Market Freedom: Corporate Governance and Collective Worker Counterbalance', *Industrial Law Journal*, 43(4), 398–428.

Mosse, D. (2010) 'A Relational Approach to Durable Poverty, Inequality and Power', *The Journal of Development Studies*, 46(7), 1156–1178.

Munoz Boudet, A.M., Bhatt, A., Azcona, G., Yoo, J. and Beegle, K. (2021) 'A Global View of Poverty, Gender, and Household Composition', Policy Research Working Paper No. 9553, World Bank. Available at: https://openknowledge.worldbank.org/handle/10986/35183

Munsaka, E. and Charnley, H. (2013) '"We do not have chiefs who are disabled": Disability, Development and Culture in a Continuing Complex Emergency', *Disability & Society*, 28(6), 756–769.

Nagel, T. (2005) 'The Problem of Global Justice', *Philosophy and Public Affairs*, 33(2), 113–147.

Narayan, A., Van der Weide, R., Cojocaru, A., Lakner, C., Redaelli, S. and Mahler, D. et al (2018) *Fair Progress? Economic Mobility across Generations around the World*, World Bank.

Nussbaum, M. and Glover, J. (1995) *Women, Culture, and Development: A Study of Human Capabilities*, Clarendon Press.

OECD (2019) *Health for Everyone? Social Inequalities in Health and Health Systems*, OECD Health Policy Studies.

Oishi, S., Kesebir, S. and Diener, E. (2011) 'Income Inequality and Happiness', *Psychological Science*, 22(9), 1095–1100.

Okin, S. (2005) '"Forty acres and a mule" for Women: Rawls and Feminism', *Politics, Philosophy & Economics*, 4(2), 233–248.

Philips, A. (2004) 'Defending Equality of Outcome', LSE Research Online. Available at: http://eprints.lse.ac.uk/533/1/equality_of_outcome.pdf

Piketty, T. (2013) *Capital in the 21st Century*, Harvard University Press.

Piketty, T. (2020a) *Capital & Ideology*, Belknap Press.

Piketty, T. (2020b) 'Global Inequalities: Where Do We Stand', *Le Monde*, 17 November. Available at: www.lemonde.fr/blog/piketty/2020/11/17/global-inequalities-where-do-we-stand/

Platt, L. and Zuccotti, C. (2021) 'Social Mobility & Ethnicity', The Deaton Review of Inequality, Institute for Fiscal Studies. Available at: https://ifs.org.uk/inequality/wp-content/uploads/2021/06/Social-mobility-and-ethnicity.pdf

Pogge, T. (1989) *Realizing Rawls*, Cornell University Press.

Präg, P. and Gugushvili, A. (2020) 'Intergenerational Social Mobility and Self-Rated Health in Europe', August 2020. Available at: https://doi.org/10.31235/osf.io/5tk4z

Qureshi, Z. (2020) *Tackling the Inequality Pandemic: Is there a Cure?* Brookings Institute, 17 November.

Raphael, D. (2001) *Concepts of Justice*, Oxford University Press.

Ravallion, M. (2017) 'Inequality and Globalization: A Review Essay', *Journal of Economic Literature*, 56(2), 620–642.

Rawls, J. (1971) *A Theory of Justice*, revised edn, 1999, Harvard University Press.

Rawls, J. (1999) *The Law of Peoples*, Harvard University Press.

Reis, H. (1984) 'The Multidimensionality of Justice', in R. Folger (ed) *The Sense of Injustice: Critical Issues in Social Justice*, Springer, pp 25–61.

Sachs, J. (2017) 'Globalization: In the Name of Which Freedom?' *Humanistic Management Journal*, 1, 237–252.

Salomon, M. (2013) 'From NIEO to Now and the Unfinishable Story of Economic Justice', *International and Comparative Law Quarterly*, 62(1), 31–54.

Samek, R. (1981) 'Justice as Ideology: Another Look at Rawls', *The Canadian Bar Review*, 59.

Sandel, M. (1998) *Liberalism and the Limits of Justice*, 2nd edn, Cambridge University Press.

Scheidel, W. (2017) *The Great Leveller: Violence and the History of Inequality from the Stone Age to the Twenty-First Century*, Princeton University Press.

Seguino, S. (2016) 'Global Trends in Gender Equality', *Journal of African Development*, 18(1), 9–30.

Sen, A. (2009) *The Idea of Justice*, Belknap, Harvard University Press.

Sen, K. (2019) 'Social Mobility in Developing Countries: Research and Policy Gaps', *UNU-WIDER blogs*, November. Available at: www.wider.unu.edu/publication/social-mobility-developing-countries

Shannon, G., Jansen, M., Williams, K., Cáceres, C., Motta, A., Odhiambo, A. et al (2019) 'Gender Equality in Science, Medicine, and Global Health: Where are We at and Why Does It Matter?', *The Lancet*, 393(10171), 560–569.

Shepelak, N. and Alwin, D. (1986) 'Beliefs about Inequality and Perceptions of Distributive Justice', *American Sociological Review*, 51(1), 30–46.

Simson, R. (2018) 'Mapping Recent Inequality Trends in Developing Countries', LSE International Inequalities Institute Working Paper 24.

Stoner, A. and Melathopoulos, A. (2015) *Freedom in the Anthropocene: Twentieth-Century Helplessness in the Face of Climate Change*, Palgrave Macmillan.

Tavares, P. and Wodon, Q. (2018) *Ending Violence Against Women and Girls: Global and Regional Trends in Women's Legal Protection against Domestic Violence and Sexual Harassment*, World Bank.

UN (2020) 'The Parlous State of Poverty Eradication', Report of the Special Rapporteur on Extreme Poverty and Human Rights, Human Rights Council 44th Session, 15 June–3 July 2020.

UNDESA (2015) 'Concepts of Inequality', *Development Issues*, 1, 21 October.

UNDESA (2020a) *Inequality in a Rapidly Changing World*, World Social Report.

UNDESA (2020b) *World Social Report*, ch 1.

UNESCO (2014) *Global Justice as a Framework for Eliminating Poverty*, UNESCO/ISSC, 28–29 April.

UN Women (2015) *Progress of the World's Women 2015–2016: Transforming Economies, Realising Rights*. Available at: https://www.unwomen.org/en/digital-library/publications/2015/4/progress-of-the-worlds-women-2015#:~:text=%E2%80%9CProgress%20of%20the%20World's%20Women%202015%E2%80%932016%E2%80%9D%20brings%20together,make%20women's%20rights%20a%20reality

UN Women (2019) 'Redistribute unpaid work'. Available at: www.unwomen.org/en/news/in-focus/csw61/redistribute-unpaid-work#:~:text=From%20cooking%20and%20cleaning%2C%20to,combining%20paid%20and%20unpaid%20labour

van Bavel, B. (2016) *The Invisible Hand? How Market Economies have Emerged and Declined since AD 500*, Oxford University Press.

van Bavel, B. and Scheffer, M. (2021) 'Historical Effects of Shocks on Inequality: The Great Leveler Revisited', *Humanities and Social Science Communications*, 8, 76.

Vandemoortele, J. (2019) 'The Open-and-Shut Case against Inequality', *Development Policy Review*, Overseas Development Institute, November.

Vandergeest, P. and Marschke, M. (2020) 'Modern Slavery and Freedom: Exploring Contradictions through Labour Scandals in the Thai Fisheries', *Antipode*, 52(1), 291–315.

van der Vossen, B. and Brennan, J. (2018) *In Defense of Openness: Why Global Freedom Is the Humane Solution to Global Poverty*, Oxford University Press.

van Deurzen, I., van Oorschot, W. and van Ingen, E. (2014) 'The Link between Inequality and Population Health in Low- and Middle-Income Countries: Policy Myth or Social Reality?', *PLoS ONE*, 9(12), e115109.

Venkatasubramanian, V. (2017) *How Much Inequality Is Fair? Mathematical Principles of a Moral, Optimal and Stable Capitalist Society*, Columbia University Press.

Wang, G. (ed) (2018) *Global History and Migrations*, Routledge.

Wesley, E. and Peterson, F. (2017) 'Is Economic Inequality Really a Problem? A Review of the Arguments', *Social Science*, 6, 147.

Wilkinson, R. and Pickett, K. (2009) *The Spirit Level: Why More Equal Societies Almost Always Do Better*, Allen Lane.

Xu, Z. (2016) 'Essays on Fairness Preferences: An Experimental Approach', Dissertation, Texas A&M University.

Yang, D.T. (2002) 'What Has Caused Regional Inequality in China?', *China Economic Review*, 13, 331–334.

Young, M. (1958) *The Rise of the Meritocracy: 1870–2033*, Thames & Hudson.

Young, M. (1990) *Justice and the Politics of Difference*, Princeton University Press.

Young, M. (2001) 'Down with Meritocracy', *The Guardian*, 29 June.

Zhang, S. (2017) 'The Pitfalls of using Google Ngram to Study Language', *Wired*.

Chapter 9: Just health, just care

Abekah-Nkrumah, G. (2019) 'Trends in Utilisation and Inequality in the Use of Reproductive Health Services in Sub-Saharan Africa', *BMC Public Health*, 19, 1541, 1–15.

Abrishami, P. and Repping, S. (2019) '"Nurturing Societal Values in and Through Health Innovations": Comment on "What Health System Challenges Should Responsible Innovation in Health Address?"', *International Journal of Health Policy Management*, 8(10), 613–615.

Anand, S., Peter, F. and Sen, A. (eds) (2004) *Public Health, Ethics, and Equity*, Oxford University Press.

Arneson, R. (1989) 'Equality and Equal Opportunity for Welfare', *Philosophical Studies: An International Journal for Philosophy in the Analytic Tradition*, 56(1), 77–93.

Barasa, E., Kazungu, J., Nguhiu, P. and Ravishankar, N. (2021) 'Examining the Level and Inequality in Health Insurance Coverage in 36 Sub-Saharan African Countries', *BMJ Global Health*, 6, e004712.

Barker, H. (2020) 'Global Economic Inequality and Health', *Medicine, Conflict and Survival*, 36(4), 368–374.

Barreto, M. (2017) 'Health Inequalities: A Global Perspective', *Ciência Saúde Coletiva*, 22(7), 2097–2108.

Barros, A., Victora, C., França, C., da Silva, I., Amouzou, A. and Krasevec, J. (2018) 'Socioeconomic Inequalities Persist Despite Declining Stunting Prevalence in Low- and Middle-Income Countries', *Journal of Nutrition*, 148, 254–258.

Benfer, E.A. (2015) 'Health Justice: A Framework (and Call to Action) for the Elimination of Health Inequity and Social Injustice', *American University Law Review*, 65(2), 275–351.

Bhutta, Z.A., Siddiqi, S., Aftab, W., Siddiqui, F., Huicho, L. and Mogilevskii, R. et al (2020) 'What Will It Take to Implement Health and Health-Related Sustainable Development Goals?', *BMJ Global Health*, 5, e002963.

Boylan, M. (2004) *A Just Society*, Rowman & Littlefield.

Boyle, C.F., Levin, C., Hatefi, A., Madriz, S. and Santos, N. (2015) 'Achieving a "Grand Convergence" in Global Health: Modeling the Technical Inputs, Costs, and Impacts from 2016 to 2030', *PLoS ONE*, 10(10), e0140092.

Braveman, P., Arkin, E., Orleans, T., Proctor, D., Acker, J. and Plough, A. (2018) 'What is Health Equity?', *Behavioral Science & Policy*, 4(1), 1–14.

Casas-Zamora, J.A. and Ibrahim, S. (2004) 'Confronting Health Inequity: The Global Dimension', *American Journal of Public Health*, 94, 2055–2058.

Chalkidou, K., Glassman, A., Marten, R., Vega, J., Teerawattananon, Y. and Tritasavit, N. et al (2016) 'Priority-Setting for Achieving Universal Health Coverage', *Bulletin of the World Health Organization*, 94(6), 462–467.

CNDSS (2008) *As Causas Sociais das Iniqüidades em Saúde no Brasil*, Editora Fiocruz.

Cookson, R., Doran, T., Asaria, M., Gupta, I. and Parra Mujica, F. (2021) 'The Inverse Care Law Re-Examined: A Global Perspective', *The Lancet*, 397(10276), 828–838.

Cutler, D., Deaton, A. and Lleras-Muney, A. (2006) 'The Determinants of Mortality', *Journal of Economic Perspectives*, 20(3), 97–120.

Daniels, N. (1985) *Just Health Care*, Cambridge University Press.

Daniels, N. (2012) *Just Health: Meeting Health Needs Fairly*, Cambridge University Press.

Frankena, W. (1976) 'Some Beliefs about Justice', in J. Goodpaster (ed) *Perspectives on Morality*, University of Notre Dame Press.

Fritz, Z. and Cox, C. (2019) 'Conflicting Demands on a Modern Healthcare Service: Can Rawlsian Justice Provide a Guiding Philosophy for the NHS and Other Socialized Health Services?', *Bioethics*, 33(5), 609–616.

Gapminder (nd) 'Child Mortality Rate, Under Age Five'. Available at: www.gapminder.org/data/documentation/gd005/

Goalkeepers Report (2022) *The Future of Progress*, Bill & Melinda Gates Foundation. Available at: www.gatesfoundation.org/goalkeepers/downloads/2022-report/2022-goalkeepers-report_en.pdf

Global Burden of Disease (GBD) Health Financing Collaborator Network (2019) 'Past, Present, and Future of Global Health Financing: A Review of Development Assistance, Government, Out-of-Pocket, and Other Private Spending on Health for 195 Countries, 1995–2050', *The Lancet*, 393, 2233–2260.

Goesling, B. and Baker, D. (2008) 'Three Faces of International Inequality', *Research in Social Stratification and Mobility*, 26(2), 183–198.

Graham, H. (ed) (2009) *Understanding Health Inequalities*, Open University Press.

Grintsova, O., Maier, W. and Mielck, A. (2014) 'Inequalities in Healthcare among Patients with Type Diabetes by Individual Socio-Economic Status (SES) and Regional Deprivation: A Systematic Literature Review', *International Journal of Equity in Health*, 13(43), 1–14.

Holst, J. (2020) 'Global Health: Emergence, Hegemonic Trends and Biomedical Reductionism', *Globalization and Health*, 16, 42.

Hosseinpoor, A., Bergen, N., Schlotheuber, A., Gacic-Dobo, M., Hansen, P., Senouci, K., Boerma, T. and Barros, A. (2016) 'State of Inequality in Diphtheria-Tetanus-Pertussis Immunisation Coverage in Low-Income and Middle-Income Countries: A Multi-Country Study of Household Health Surveys', *Lancet Global Health*, 4, e617–26.

Jamison, D.T., Summers, L.H., Alleyne, G., Arrow, K.J., Berkley, S. et al (2013) 'Global Health 2035: A World Converging within a Generation', *The Lancet*, 382, 1898–1955.

Jamison, D., Alwan, A., Mock, C., Watkins, D., Adeyi, O., Anand, S. et al (2017) 'Universal Health Coverage and Intersectoral Action for Health: Key Messages from Disease Control Priorities', *The Lancet*, 391, 10125.

Kelleher, J. (2013) 'Real and Alleged Problems for Daniels's Account of Health Justice', *The Journal of Medicine and Philosophy: A Forum for Bioethics and Philosophy of Medicine*, 38(4), 388–399.

Kifle, H., Merga, B.T., Dessie, Y., Demena, M., Fekadu, G. and Negash, B. (2021) 'Inequality and Inequity in Outpatient Care Utilization in Ethiopia: A Decomposition Analysis of Ethiopian National Health Accounts', *Clinicoeconomics & Outcomes Research*, 13, 89–98.

Khan, A. (2015) 'Understanding Health Equity: Key Concepts, Debates and Developments in Canada', *Health Tomorrow*, 3, 76.

Kumar, S., Kumar, N. and Vivekadhish, S. (2016) 'Millennium Development Goals (MDGs) to Sustainable Development Goals (SDGS): Addressing Unfinished Agenda and Strengthening Sustainable Development and Partnership', *Indian Journal of Community Medicine*, 41(1), 1–4.

Lehoux, P., Roncarolo, F., Silva, H.P., Boivin, A., Denis, J.L. and Hebert, R. (2018) 'What Health System Challenges Should Responsible Innovation in Health Address? Insights from an International Scoping Review', *International Journal of Health Policy Management*, 8(2), 63–75.

Li, C., Yao, N.A. and Yin, A. (2018) 'Disparities in Dental Healthcare Utilization in China', *Community Dentistry & Oral Epidemiology*, 46, 576–585.

Liou, L., Joe, W., Kumar, A. and Subramanian, S. (2020) 'Inequalities in Life Expectancy: An Analysis of 201 Countries, 1950–2015', *Social Science & Medicine*, 253, 112964.

Lu, C., Cuartas, J., Fink, G., McCoy, D., Liu, K. and Li, Z. et al (2020) 'Inequalities in Early Childhood Care and Development in Low/Middle-Income Countries: 2010–2018', *BMJ Global Health*, 5, e002314.

Lynch, J. (2017) 'Reframing Inequality? The Health Inequalities Turn as a Dangerous Frame Shift', *Journal of Public Health*, 39(4), 653–660.

Malbon, E., Carey, G. and Meltzer, A. (2019) 'Personalisation Schemes in Social Care: Are They Growing Social and Health Inequalities?' *BMC Public Health* 19(805), 1–12.

McKeown, T., Record, R. and Turner, R. (1975) 'An Interpretation of the Decline of Mortality in England and Wales during the Twentieth Century', *Population Studies*, 29, 391–422.

Moscelli, G., Siciliani, L., Gutacker, N. and Cookson, R. (2018) 'Socioeconomic Inequality of Access to Healthcare: Does Choice Explain the Gradient?', *Journal of Health Economics*, 57, 290–314.

Mulyanto, J., Kringos, D.S. and Kunst, A.E. (2019) 'Socioeconomic Inequalities in Healthcare Utilisation in Indonesia: A Comprehensive Survey-Based Overview', *BMJ Open*, 9, e026164.

National Population Commission [Nigeria] and ICF (2019) *Nigeria Demographic and Health Survey 2018*.

Netter Epstein, W. (2021) 'A Legal Paradigm for the Health Inequity Crisis', *Journal of Law and the Biosciences*, forthcoming.

Nino-Zarazua, M. and Jorda, V. (2017) 'Global Inequality in Length of Life: 1950–2015', WIDER Working Paper 192/2017.

Norheim, O. and Asada, Y. (2009) 'The Ideal of Equal Health Revisited: Definitions and Measures of Inequity in Health Should be Better Integrated with Theories of Distributive Justice', *International Journal of Equity in Health*, 8(40), 1–9.

Nussbaum, M. (1999) *Sex and Social Justice*, Oxford University Press.

Nussbaum, M. (2000) *Women and Human Development: The Capabilities Approach*, New York: Cambridge University Press.

Nussbaum, M. (2011) 'Capabilities, Entitlements, Rights: Supplementation and Critique', *Journal of Human Development and Capabilities*, 12(1), 23–37.

O'Neill, O. (2002) 'Public Health or Clinical Ethics: Thinking beyond Borders', *Ethics and International Affairs*, 16(2), 35–45.

Our World in Data (nd) 'Child and Infant Mortality'. Available at: https://ourworldindata.org/child-mortality

Permanyer, I. and Smits, J. (2020) 'Inequality in Human Development across the Globe', *Population and Development Review*, 46(3), 583–601.

Petter Ottersen, O., Dasgupta, J., Blouin, C., Buss, P., Chongsuvivatwong, V., Frenk, J. et al (2014) 'The Political Origins of Health Inequity: Prospects for Change', *The Lancet-University of Oslo Commission on Global Governance for Health*, 383(9917), 630–667.

Plamondon, K., Bottorff, J., Susana Caxaj, C. and Graham, I. (2020) 'The Integration of Evidence from the Commission on Social Determinants of Health in the Field of Health Equity: A Scoping Review', *Critical Public Health*, 30(4), 415–428.

Prah Ruger, J. (2004) 'Health and Justice', *The Lancet*, 364(9439), 1075–1080.

Prah Ruger, J. and Kim, H. (2006) 'Global Health Inequalities: An International Comparison', *Journal of Epidemiology & Community Health*, 60, 928–936.

Pulok, M., Uddin, J., Enemark, U. and Hossin, M. (2018) 'Socioeconomic Inequality in Maternal Healthcare: An Analysis of Regional Variation in Bangladesh', *Health & Place*, 52, 205–214.

Rajan, S., Ricciardi, W. and McKee, M. (2020) 'The SDGs and Health Systems: The Last Step on the Long and Unfinished Journey to Universal Health Care?', *European Journal of Public Health*, 30(1), i28–i31.

Reed, A. and Chowkwanyun, M. (2012) 'Race, Class, Crisis: The Discourse of Racial Disparity and its Analytical Discontents', *Socialist Register*, 48, 149–175.

Reidpath, D. and Allotey, P. (2007) 'Measuring Global Health Inequity', *International Journal of Equity in Health*, 6, 16.

Restrepo-Méndez, M.C., Barros, A.J., Wong, K.L., Johnson, H., Pariyo, G. and França, G. et al (2016) 'Inequalities in Full Immunization Coverage: Trends in Low- and Middle-Income Countries', *Bulletin of the World Health Organization*, 94(11), 794–805B.

Rid, A. (2008) 'Just Health: Meeting Health Needs Fairly', *Bulletin of the World Health Organization*, 86(8).

Sachs, B. (2010) 'Lingering Problems of Currency and Scope in Daniels's Argument for a Societal Obligation to Meet Health Needs', *The Journal of Medicine and Philosophy: A Forum for Bioethics and Philosophy of Medicine*, 35(4), 402–414.

Sachs, J., Schmidt-Traub, G. and Lafortune, G. (2020) 'Speaking Truth to Power about the SDGs', SDSN Network Working Paper, 26 August.

Salamanca-Buentello, F. and Daar, A.S. (2021) 'Nanotechnology, Equity and Global Health', *Nature Nanotechnology*, 16, 358–361.

Sanders, D., Nandi, S., Labonté, R., Vance, C. and Van Damme, W. et al (2019) 'From Primary Health Care to Universal Health Coverage: One Step Forward and Two Steps Back', *The Lancet*, 394(10199), 619–621.

Satinsky, E., Fuhr, D., Woodward, A., Sondorp, E. and Roberts, B. (2019) 'Mental Health Care Utilisation and Access among Refugees and Asylum Seekers in Europe: A Systematic Review', *Health Policy*, 123(9), 851–863.

Schmidt-Traub, G. (2015) 'Investment Needs to Achieve the Sustainable Development Goals: Understanding the Billions and Trillions', Sustainable Development Solutions Network Working Paper Version 2.

Sen, A. (2010) 'Why Health Equity?', in R. Hofrichter and R. Bhatia (eds) *Tackling Health Inequities Through Public Health Practice: Theory to Action*, Oxford University Press.

Sen, A. (2015) 'Universal Health Care: The Affordable Dream', *Guardian*, 6 January. Available at: www.theguardian.com/society/2015/jan/06/-sp-universal-healthcare-the-affordable-dream-amartya-sen

Sen, A. (2017) 'Ethics and the Foundation of Global Justice', *Ethics & International Affairs*, 31(3), 261–270.

Shawky, S. (2020) 'Geography of Economic Disparities and Global Health Inequality', in R. Haring, I. Kickbusch, D. Ganten and M. Moeti (eds) *Handbook of Global Health*, Springer.

Steinbeis, F., Gotham, D., von Philipsborn, P. and Stratil, J. (2019) 'Quantifying Changes in Global Health Inequality: The Gini and Slope Inequality Indices Applied to the Global Burden of Disease Data, 1990–2017', *BMJ Global Health*, 4, e001500.

Stenberg, K., Hanssen, O., Tan-Torres Edejer, T., Bertram, M., Brindley, C., Meshreky, A. et al (2017) 'Financing Transformative Health Systems towards Achievement of the Health Sustainable Development Goals: A Model for Projected Resource Needs in 67 Low-Income and Middle-Income Countries', *The Lancet*, 5(9), E875–E887.

Szreter, S. (1992) 'Mortality and Public Health, 1815–1914', *Recent Findings of Research in Economic and Social Policy*, 14, 1–4.

Szreter, S. (2004) 'Industrialization and Health', *British Medical Bulletin*, 69(1), 75–86.

UN (2020) 'The Sustainable Development Goals Report'. Available at: https://unstats.un.org/sdgs/report/2020/The-Sustainable-Development-Goals-Report-2020.pdf

UNDP (2022) *Uncertain Times, Unsettled Lives: Shaping Our Future in a Transforming World*, Human Development Report 2021–22, United Nations. Available at: https://hdr.undp.org/content/human-development-report-2021-22

UNICEF (nd) 'Child Mortality'. Available at: https://data.unicef.org/topic/child-survival/under-five-mortality/

van Raalte, A., Sasson, I. and Martikaine, P. (2018) 'The Case for Monitoring Life-Span Inequality', *Science*, 362(6418).

Vega, W.A. and Sribney, W.M. (2017) 'Growing Economic Inequality Sustains Health Disparities', *American Journal of Public Health*, 107(10), 1606–1607.

Venkatapuram, S. (2011) *Health Justice: An Argument from the Capabilities Approach*, Polity Press.

Venkatapuram, S. (2019) 'Health Disparities and the Social Determinants of Health: Ethical and Social Justice Issues', in A. Mastroianni, J. Kahn and N. Kass (eds) *The Oxford Handbook of Public Health Ethics*, Oxford University Press, pp 266–276.

Victora, C., Vaughan, J.P., Barros, F.C., Silva, A.C. and Tomasi, E. (2000) 'Explaining Trends in Inequities: Evidence from Brazilian Child Health Studies', *The Lancet*, 356(9235), 1093–1098.

von dem Knesebeck, O., Vonneilich, N. and Kim, T.J. (2016) 'Are Health Care Inequalities Unfair? A Study on Public Attitudes in 23 Countries', *International Journal of Equity in Health*, 15, 61.

Vorisek, D. and Shu, Y.S. (2020) 'Understanding the Cost of Achieving the Sustainable Development Goals', Policy Research Working Paper 9146, World Bank Group.

WHO (World Health Organization) (nd) 'Children: Improving Survival and Well-Being'. Available at: www.who.int/news-room/fact-sheets/detail/children-reducing-mortality

WHO (2019) *Primary Health Care on the Road to Universal Health Coverage 2019*, Global Monitoring Report, WHO, World Bank.

WHO and International Bank for Reconstruction and Development/ World Bank (2017) 'Tracking Universal Health Coverage: 2017 Global Monitoring Report'.

WHO, UNICEF, UNFPA, World Bank Group and the United Nations Population Division (2015) *Trends in Maternal Mortality: 1990 to 2015*, WHO.

World Health Statistics (2018) *Monitoring Health for the SDGs*, WHO.

Yourkavitch, J., Burgert-Brucker, C., Assaf, S. and Delgado, S. (2018) 'Using Geographical Analysis to Identify Child Health Inequality in Sub-Saharan Africa', *PLoS ONE*, 13(8), e0201870.

Chapter 10: A kingdom of ends

Ahrens, L. (2019) 'Theorizing the Impact of Fairness Perceptions on the Demand for Redistribution', *Political Research Exchange*, 1(1), 1–17.

Aldama, A., Bicchieri, C., Freundt, J., Mellers, B. and Peters, E. (2021) 'How Perceptions of Autonomy Relate to Beliefs about Inequality and Fairness', *PLoS ONE*, 16(1).

Allen, L., Williams, J., Townsend, N., Mikkelsen, B., Roberts, N. and Foster, C. et al (2017) 'Socioeconomic Status and Non-Communicable Disease Behavioural Risk Factors in Low-Income and Lower-Middle-Income Countries: A Systematic Review', *Lancet Global Health*, 5, e277–e289.

Baker, P., Friel, S., Kay, A., Baum, F., Strazdins, L. and Mackean, T. (2018) 'What Enables and Constrains the Inclusion of the Social Determinants of Health Inequities in Government Policy Agendas? A Narrative Review', *International Journal of Health Policy Management*, 7(2), 101–111.

Barnett-Howell, Z., Watson, O.J. and Mobarak, A.M. (2021) 'The Benefits and Costs of Social Distancing in High- and Low-Income Countries', *Transcript of the Royal Society of Tropical Medicine & Hygiene*, 115(7), 807–819.

Bennett, J., Pearson-Stuttard, J., Kontis, V., Capewell, S., Wolfe, I. and Ezzati, M. (2018) 'Contributions of Diseases and Injuries to Widening Life Expectancy Inequalities in England from 2001 to 2016: A Population-Based Analysis of Vital Registration Data', *The Lancet*, 3(12), E586–E597.

Bergen, N., Ruckert, A., Abebe, L., Asfaw, S., Kiros, G., Mamo, A., Morankar, S., Kulkarni, M. and Labonté, R. (2021) 'Characterizing "Health Equity" as a National Health Sector Priority for Maternal, Newborn, and Child Health in Ethiopia', *Global Health Action*, 14(1), 1853386.

Berwick, D. (2020) 'The Moral Determinants of Health', *Journal of the American Medical Association*, 324(3), 225–226.

Bibby, J., Everest, G. and Abbs, I. (2020) 'Will COVID-19 be a watershed moment for health inequalities?' *The Health Foundation*, 7 May. Available at: www.health.org.uk/publications/long-reads/will-covid-19-be-a-watershed-moment-for-health-inequalities

Blacksher, E. (2012) 'Redistribution and Recognition: Pursuing Social Justice in Public Health', *Cambridge Quarterly of Healthcare Ethics*, 21(3), 320–331.

Bond, C. and Singh, D. (2020) 'More than a Refresh Required for Closing the Gap of Indigenous Health Inequality', *Medical Journal of Australia*, 212(5).

Brown, T.H., Richardson, L.J., Hargrove, T.W. and Thomas, C.S. (2016) 'Using Multiple-Hierarchy Stratification and Life Course Approaches to Understand Health Inequalities: The Intersecting Consequences of Race, Gender, SES, and Age', *Journal of Health and Social Behavior*, 57(2), 200–222.

Cha, S. and Jin, Y. (2020) 'Have Inequalities in All-Cause and Cause-Specific Child Mortality between Countries Declined across the World?', *International Journal of Equity in Health*, 19, 1.

Chandhoke, N. (2013) 'Realising Justice', *Third World Quarterly*, 34, 312.

Chandler, M. and Lalonde, C. (1998) 'Cultural Continuity as a Hedge against Suicide in Canada's First Nations', *Transcultural Psychiatry*, 35(2), 193–211.

Chetty, R., Jackson, M.O., Kuchler, T., Stroebel, J., Hendren, N. and Fluegge, R. et al (2022) 'Social Capital I: Measurement and Associations with Economic Mobility', *Nature*, https://doi.org/10.1038/s41586-022-04996-4

Cifuentes, M.P., Rodriguez-Villamizar, L.A., Rojas-Botero, M.L., Alvarez-Moreno, C.A. and Fernández-Niño, J.A. (2021) 'Socioeconomic Inequalities associated with Mortality for COVID-19 in Colombia: A Cohort Nationwide Study', *Journal of Epidemiology & Community Health*, 75, 610–615.

Clougherty, J.E., Souza, K. and Cullen, M.R. (2010) 'Work and its Role in Shaping the Social Gradient in Health', *Annals of the New York Academy of Sciences*, 1186, 102–124.

Counts, G.S. (1978) *Dare the Schools Build a New Social Order?* Southern Illinois University Press.

Crimmins, E. (2021) 'Recent Trends and Increasing Differences in Life Expectancy Present Opportunities for Multidisciplinary Research on Aging', *Nature Aging*, 1, 12–13.

Das-Munshi, J. and Thornicroft, G. (2018) 'Failure to Tackle Suicide Inequalities across Europe', *The British Journal of Psychiatry*, 212(6), 331–332.

Davenport, A., Farquharson, C., Rasul, I., Sibieta, L. and Stoye, G. (2020) 'The Geography of the COVID-19 Crisis in England', Institute for Fiscal Studies. Available at: https://ifs.org.uk/publications/geography-covid-19-crisis-england

Davidai, S. (2018) 'Why Do Americans Believe in Economic Mobility? Economic Inequality, External Attributions of Wealth and Poverty, and the Belief in Economic Mobility', *Journal of Experimental Social Psychology*, 79, 138–148.

Davidson, R., Mitchell, R. and Hunt, K. (2008) 'Location, Location, Location: The Role of Experience of Disadvantage in Lay Perceptions of Area Inequalities in Health', *Health & Place*, 14(2), 167–181.

Davies, M. (2022) 'COVID-19: WHO Efforts to Bring Vaccine Manufacturing to Africa are Undermined by the Drug Industry, Documents Show', *British Medical Journal*, 376, o304.

Davis, B. (2020) 'Discrimination: A Social Determinant of Health Inequities', *Health Affairs Blog*, 25 February.

Deveaux, M. (2018) 'Poor-Led Social Movements and Global Justice', *Political Theory*, 46(5), 698–725.

Dorling, D. (2015) *Injustice: Why Social Inequality Still Persists*, Policy Press.

Dwyer-Lindgren, L., Bertozzi-Villa, A., Stubbs, R.W., Morozoff, C., Mackenbach, J., van Lenthe, F. et al (2017) 'Inequalities in Life Expectancy among US Counties, 1980 to 2014: Temporal Trends and Key Drivers', *JAMA Internal Medicine*, 177(7), 1003–1011.

The Economist (2014) 'Why aren't the Poor Storming the Barricades?', 21 January.

Edsall, T. (2015) 'Why Don't the Poor Rise Up?' *New York Times*, 24 June.

Eikemo, T.A. and Øversveen, E. (2019) 'Social Inequalities in Health: Challenges, Knowledge Gaps, Key Debates and the Need for New Data', *Scandinavian Journal of Public Health*, 47(6), 593–597.

Ekström, A.M., Berggren, C., Tomson, G., Gostin, L., Friberg, P. and Petter Ottersen, O. (2021) 'The Battle for COVID-19 Vaccines Highlights the Need for a New Global Governance Mechanism', *Nature Medicine*, 27, 739–740.

Elgar, F.J., Pfortner, T.-K., Moor, I., De Clercq, B., Stevens, G.W. and Currie, C. et al (2015) 'Socioeconomic Inequalities in Adolescent Health 2002–2010: A Time-Series Analysis of 34 Countries Participating in the Health Behaviour in School-Aged Children Study', *The Lancet*, 385(9982), 2088–2095.

Elgar, F., Stefaniak, A. and Wohl, J. (2020) 'The Trouble with Trust: Time-Series Analysis of Social Capital, Income Inequality, and COVID-19 Deaths in 84 Countries', *Social Science & Medicine*, 263, 113365.

Embrett, M. and Randall, G. (2014) 'Social Determinants of Health and Health Equity Policy Research: Exploring the Use, Misuse, and Nonuse of Policy Analysis Theory', *Social Science & Medicine*, 108, 147–155.

Engebretsen, E., Gornitzka, A., Maassen, P. and Stolen, S. (2021) 'A Step Backwards in the Fight against Global Vaccine Inequities', *The Lancet*, 397(10268), 23–24.

Ewing, K. and Hendy, L. (2020) 'Covid-19 and the Failure of Labour Law: Part 1', *Industrial Law Journal*, 49(4), 497–538.

Fehr, E. and Fischbacher, U. (2000) *Third Party Punishment*, University of Zürich.

Fehr, E. and Schmidt, K. (2006) 'The Economics of Fairness, Reciprocity and Altruism: Experimental Evidence and New Theories', in *Handbook of the Economics of Giving, Altruism and Reciprocity*, 1/615–691. Elsevier.

Feinberg, M. and Willer, R. (2011) 'Apocalypse Soon? Dire Messages Reduce Belief in Global Warming by Contradicting Just-World Beliefs', *Psychological Science*, 22(1), 34–38.

Garthwaite, K. and Bambra, C. (2017) '"How the other half live": Lay Perspectives on Health Inequalities in an Age of Austerity', *Social Science & Medicine*, 187, 268–275.

Gillispie-Bell, V. (2021) 'The Contrast of Color', *Obstetrics & Gynecology*, 137(2), 220–224.

Gimpelson, V. and Treisman, D. (2018) 'Misperceiving Inequality', *Economics and Politics*, 30(1), 27–54.

Gkiouleka, A., Huijts, T., Beckfield, J. and Bambra, C. (2018) 'Understanding the Micro and Macro Politics of Health: Inequalities, Intersectionality & Institutions – a Research Agenda', *Social Science & Medicine*, 200, 92–98.

Goldin, I. (2021) 'COVID-19: How Rising Inequalities Unfolded and Why We Cannot Afford to Ignore It', *The Conversation*, 20 May. Available at: https://theconversation.com/covid-19-how-rising-inequalities-unfolded-and-why-we-cannot-afford-to-ignore-it-161132

Goodman, P. (2020) 'One Vaccine Side Effect: Global Economic Inequality', *New York Times*, 25 December.

Gottlieb, C., Grobovšek, J., Poschke, M. and Saltiel, F. (2021) 'Working from Home in Developing Countries', *VOX/CEPR*, 18 March. Available at: https://cepr.org/voxeu/columns/working-home-developing-countries

Goudarzi, S., Pliskin, R., Jost, J.T. and Knowles, E. (2020) 'Economic System Justification Predicts Muted Emotional Responses to Inequality', *Nature Communications*, 11, 383.

Graham, C. (2008) 'Happiness and Health: Lessons – and Questions – For Public Policy', *Health Affairs*, 27(1).

Graham, H. (2009) *Understanding Health Inequalities*, Open University Press.

Greenwood, M., de Leeuw, S. and Lindsay, N.M. (eds) (2018) *Determinants of Indigenous Peoples' Health*, 2nd edn, Canadian Scholars.

Hauser, O. and Norton, M. (2017) '(Mis)perceptions of Inequality', *Current Opinion in Psychology*, 18, 21–25.

Hecht, K., Burchardt, T. and Davis, A. (2022) 'Richness, Insecurity and the Welfare State', *Journal of Social Policy*, 1–22.

Heinemann, A. and Beegle, K. (2021) 'Gender and Safety Nets: Priorities for Building Back Better', World Bank.

Hernández, A., Ruano, A., Marchal, B., San Sebastián, M. and Flores, W. (2017) 'Engaging with Complexity to Improve the Health of Indigenous People: A Call for the Use of Systems Thinking to Tackle Health Inequity', *International Journal of Equity in Health*, 16, 26.

Hicken, M., Kravitz-Wirtz, N., Durkee, M. and Jackson, J. (2017) 'Racial Inequalities in Health: Framing Future Research', *Social Science & Medicine*, 199, 11–18.

Huber, D. (2017) *Exclusion by Elections: Inequality, Ethnic Identity, and Democracy*, Cambridge University Press.

International Institute for Population Sciences and ICF (2017) *National Family Health Survey* (NFHS-4), 2015–16.

Johnson, P., Joyce, R. and Platt, L. (2020) 'The IFS Deaton Review of Inequalities: A New Year's Message', Institute for Fiscal Studies, 2020. Available at: https://ifs.org.uk/inequality/wp-content/uploads/2021/01/IFS-Deaton-Review-New-Year-Message.pdf

Jost, J., Pelham, B., Sheldon, O. and Sullivan, B. (2003) 'Social Inequality and the Reduction of Ideological Dissonance on Behalf of the System: Evidence of Enhanced System Justification among the Disadvantaged', *European Journal of Social Psychology*, 33(1), 13–36.

Jost, J., Sapolsky, R. and Nam, H. (2018) 'Speculations on the Evolutionary Origins of System Justification', *Evolutionary Psychology*, 16(2), 1–21.

Kay, A. and Friesen, J. (2011) 'On Social Stability and Social Change: Understanding When System Justification Does and Does Not Occur', *Current Directions in Psychological Science*, 20(6), 360–364.

Kenworthy, L. and McCall, L. (2018) 'Inequality, Public Opinion and Redistribution', *Socio-Economic Review*, 6(1), 35–68.

King, N., Harper, S. and Young, M. (2013) 'Who Cares about Health Inequalities? Cross-Country Evidence from the World Health Survey', *Health Policy and Planning*, 28(5), 558–571.

Kluegel, J. and Smith, E. (1986) *Beliefs about Inequality: Americans' Views of What is and What Ought to be*, Routledge.

Knell, M. and Stix, H. (2017) 'Perceptions of Inequality', Oesterreichische Nationalbank, February.

Krieger, N. (2001) 'A Glossary for Social Epidemiology: Part II', *Journal of Epidemiology and Community Health*, 55(55), 693–700.

Krouse, H.J. (2020) 'COVID-19 and the Widening Gap in Health Inequity', *Otolaryngology – Head and Neck Surgery*, 163(1), 65–66.

Ku, H. and Salmon, T. (2013) 'Procedural Fairness and the Tolerance for Income Inequality', *European Economic Review*, 64, 111–128.

The Lancet (2020) 'Editorial: Taking Urgent Action on Health Inequities', *The Lancet*, 395(10225), 659, 29 February.

Leon, D. (2011) 'Trends in European Life Expectancy: A Salutary View', *International Journal of Epidemiology*, 40(2), 271–277.

Levin, A., Owusu-Boaitey, N., Pugh, S., Fosdick, B, Zwi, A., Malani, A. et al (2022) 'Assessing the Burden of COVID-19 in Developing Countries: Systematic Review, Meta-Analysis and Public Policy Implications', *BMJ Global Health*, 7, e008477.

Li, Z.H., Li, M.Q., Subramanian, V. and Lu, C.L. (2017) 'Assessing Levels and Trends of Child Health Inequality in 88 Developing Countries: From 2000 to 2014', *Global Health Action*, 10(1).

Lima, M. and Morais, R. (2015) 'Lay Perceptions of Health and Environmental Inequalities and their Associations to Mental Health', *Caderna de Saúde Pública*, 31(11).

Lucyk, K. and McLaren, L. (2017) 'Taking Stock of the Social Determinants of Health: A Scoping Review', *PLOS ONE*, 12(5), e0177306.

Lundberg O. (2020) 'Next Steps in the Development of the Social Determinants of Health Approach: The Need for a New Narrative', *Scandinavian Journal of Public Health*, 48(5), 473–479.

Lundell, H., Niederdeppe, J. and Clarke, C. (2013) 'Public Views About Health Causation, Attributions of Responsibility, and Inequality', *Journal of Health Communication*, 18(9), 1116–1130.

Luttig, M. (2013) 'The Structure of Inequality and Americans' Attitudes toward Redistribution', *Public Opinion Quarterly*, 77(3), 811–821.

Lynch, J. (2020) *Regimes of Inequality: The Political Economy of Wealth and Health*, Cambridge University Press.

Macchia, L., Plagnol, A. and Powdthavee, N. (2019) 'Why Do People Tolerate Income Inequality?' *Harvard Business Review*, November.

Macintyre, S., McKay, L. and Ellaway, A. (2005) 'Are Rich People or Poor People More Likely to be Ill? Lay Perceptions, by Social Class and Neighbourhood, of Inequalities in Health', *Social Science & Medicine*, 60(2), 313–317.

Macintyre, S., McKay, L. and Ellaway, A. (2006) 'Lay Concepts of the Relative Importance of Different Influences on Health: Are There Major Socio-Demographic Variations?', *Health Education Research*, 21(5), 731–739.

Mackenbach, J. (2019) *Health Inequalities: Persistence and Change in European Welfare States*, Oxford University Press.

Marchand, S., Wikler, D. and Landesman, B. (1998) 'Class, Health, and Justice', *The Millbank Quarterly*, 76(3), 449–467.

Marmot, M. (2015) 'The Health Gap: The Challenge of an Unequal World', *The Lancet*, 386(10011), 2442–2444.

Marmot, M. (2017) 'The Health Gap: Doctors and the Social Determinants of Health', *Scandinavian Journal of Public Health*, 45(7), 686–693.

Marmot, M. (2020) 'Health Equity in England: The Marmot Review 10 Years On', *British Medical Journal*, 368, m693.

Matheson, J., Patterson, J. and Neilson, L. (eds) (2020) *Tackling Causes and Consequences of Health Inequalities: A Practical Guide*, CRC Press.

McCartney, G., Popham, F., McMaster, R. and Cumbers, A. (2019) 'Defining Health and Health Inequalities', *Public Health*, 172, 22–30.

Miller, R. and Curran, E. (2021) 'World economy risks "dangerously diverging" even as growth booms', *Economic Times*, 4 April. Available at: https://economictimes.indiatimes.com/defaultinterstitial.cms

Nangwaya, A. and Truscello, M. (eds) (2017) *Why Don't the Poor Rise Up?* AK Press.

National Academies of Sciences, Engineering, and Medicine (NAS) (2015) *The Growing Gap in Life Expectancy by Income: Implications for Federal Programs and Policy Responses*, The National Academies Press.

Nature (2020) 'Editorial: The COVID Vaccine Challenges that Lie Ahead', 24 November. Available at: www.nature.com/articles/d41586-020-03334-w

Nedel, F. and Bastos, J. (2020) 'Whither Social Determinants of Health?', *Revista de Saude Publica*, 54, 15.

Noonan, L. and Smith, C. (2021) 'IMF warns on financial stability threat from vaccine shortages', *Financial Times*, 27 January. Available at: www.ft.com/content/1a4b40e3-2950-4c54-b9e6-8c2248502a12

Nutbeam, D. and Lloyd, J. (2021) 'Understanding and Responding to Health Literacy as a Social Determinant of Health', *Annual Review of Public Health*, 42, 159–173.

Olshansky, S.J., Antonucci, T., Berkman, L., Binstock, R.H., Boersch Supan, A., Cacioppo, J.T. et al (2012) 'Differences in Life Expectancy Due to Race and Educational Differences are Widening, and Many May Not Catch Up', *Health Affairs*, 31, 180313.

O'Neill, O. (2001) 'Agents of Justice', *Metaphilosophy*, 32(1/2), 182–189.

Ornstein, A. (2017) 'Social Justice: History, Purpose and Meaning', *Society*, 54, 541–548.

Oxfam (2020) 'Campaigners Warn that 9 out of 10 People in Poor Countries are Set to Miss Out on COVID-19 Vaccine Next Year', 9 December.

Paremoer, L., Paremoer, L., Nandi, S., Serag, H. and Baum, F. (2021) 'Covid-19 Pandemic and the Social Determinants of Health', *British Medical Journal*, 372, n129.

Payne, K. (2017) *The Broken Ladder: How Inequality Affects the Way We Think, Live, and Die*, Viking Press.

Popay, J., Bennett, S., Thomas, C., Williams, G., Gatrell, A. and Bostock, L. (2003) 'Beyond "Beer, Fags, Egg and Chips"? Exploring Lay Understandings of Social Inequalities in Health', *Sociology of Health and Illness*, 25(1), 1–23.

Popay, J., Whitehead, M., Ponsford, R., Egan, M. and Mead, R. (2020) 'Power, Control, Communities and Health Inequalities I: Theories, Concepts and Analytical Frameworks', *Health Promotion International*, daaa133.

Powers, M. and Faden, R. (2006) *Social Justice: The Moral Foundations of Public Health and Health Policy*, Oxford University Press.

Putland, C., Baum, F. and Ziersch, A. (2011) 'From Causes to Solutions: Insights from Lay Knowledge about Health Inequalities', *BMC Public Health*, 11, 67.

Sachs, J., Abdool Karim, S., Aknin, L., Allen, J., Brosbøl, K., Colombo, F. et al (2022) 'The Lancet Commission on Lessons for the Future from the COVID-19 Pandemic', *The Lancet*, S0140–6736(22)01585–9, https://doi.org/10.1016/

Samuels, D. (2015) 'Why Don't Voters Demand More Redistribution?', *Washington Post*, 5 June.

Sartawi, T. (2020) 'Poverty Reduction Strategies and Health Outcomes: Jordan as a Case Study', in I. Laher (ed) *Handbook of Healthcare in the Arab World*, Springer.

Sen, A. (2017) 'Ethics and the Foundation of Global Justice', *Ethics & International Affairs*, 31(3), 261–270.

Shepherd, C., Li, J. and Zubrick, S. (2012) 'Social Gradients in the Health of Indigenous Australians', *American Journal of Public Health*, 102, 107–117.

Silva, J. and Ribeiro-Alves, M. (2021) 'Social Inequalities and the Pandemic of COVID-19: The Case of Rio de Janeiro', *Journal of Epidemiology & Community Health*, 75(10).

Singh, G. (2021) 'Trends and Social Inequalities in Maternal Mortality in the United States, 1969–2018', *International Journal of Maternal and Child Health and AIDS*, 10(1), 29–42.

Singh, G.K. and Siahpush, M. (2014) 'Widening Rural-Urban Disparities in Life Expectancy, US 1969–2009', *American Journal of Preventive Medicine*, 46, e1929.

Singh, G.K., Daus, G.P., Allender, M., Ramey, C., Martin, E. and Perry, C. et al (2017) 'Social Determinants of Health in the United States: Addressing Major Health Inequality Trends for the Nation, 1935–2016', *International Journal of Maternal and Child Health and AIDS*, 6(2), 139–164.

Smith, K. and Anderson, R. (2018) 'Understanding Lay Perspectives on Socioeconomic Health Inequalities in Britain: A Meta-Ethnography', *Sociology of Health and Illness*, 40(1), 146–170.

Smith, K., Escobar, O. and Weakley, S. (2017) 'Lay Understandings of Health Inequalities and Potential Policy Responses – Comparing Data from a National Survey and Three Citizens' Juries'. Available at: https://www.scotpho.org.uk/media/1725/phins-2017-6-kat-smith.pdf

Strauss, D. and Wheatley, J. (2021) 'Vaccine delays risk more than halving global growth, World Bank warns', *Financial Times*, 6 January. Available at: www.ft.com/content/a9e10249-835c-4176-b46b-b891543140dc

Stroebe, K., Postmes, T. and Roos, C. (2019) 'Where Did Inaction Go? Towards a Broader and More Refined Perspective on Collective Actions', *British Journal of Social Psychology*, 58(3), 649–667.

Subbarao, D. (2021) 'Richer, and Poorer: Inequality will Continue to Scar the Economy Long after Covid Leaves Us', *Times of India*, 29 July.

Sundari Ravindran, TK. (2017) 'Commentary: Beyond the Socioeconomic in *The Health Gap*: Gender and Intersectionality', *International Journal of Epidemiology*, 46(4), 1321–1322.

Suzuki, E., Sharan, M. and Eduard Bos, E. (2012) 'Poverty and Health Monitoring Report', International Bank for Reconstruction and Development/World Bank.

Trump, K. (2020) 'When and Why is Economic Inequality Seen as Fair', *Current Opinion in Behavioral Sciences*, 34, 46–51.

von Andreas, M., Backett-Milburn, K. and Pavis, S. (1998) 'Perception of Health Inequalities in Different Social Classes, by Health Professionals and Health Policy Makers in Germany and in the United Kingdom', Veröffentlichungsreihe der Arbeitsgruppe Public Health Wissenschaftszentrum Berlin für Sozialforschung.

Whitehead, M. and Dahlgren, G. (2006) 'Concepts and Principles for Tackling Social Inequities in Health: Levelling Up, Part 1', WHO Collaborating Centre for Policy Research on Social Determinants of Health, University of Liverpool/WHO.

WHO (World Health Organization) (2008) *Closing the Gap in a Generation: Final Report of the Commission on Social Determinants of Health*, WHO.

WHO (2010) 'A Conceptual Framework for Action on the Social Determinants of Health', WHO.

WHO/AFRO (2021) 'Africa Faces Steepest COVID-19 Surge Yet', 24 June.

World Bank (2015) 'A Perceived Divide: How Indonesians Perceive Inequality and What They Want Done About It', November.

World Bank (2020) 'Assessing Country Readiness for COVID-19 Vaccines: First Insights from the Assessment Roll-Out', March. Available at: www.worldbank.org/en/topic/health/publication/assessing-country-readiness-for-covid19-vaccines-first-insights-from-the-assessment-rollout.print?cid=EXT_WBEmailShare_EXT

Chapter 11: War and peace

Aldis, W. (2008) 'Health Security as a Public Health Concept: A Critical Analysis', *Health Policy and Planning*, 23(6), 369–375.

Blinken, A.J. and Becerra, X. (2021) 'Strengthening Global Health Security and Reforming the International Health Regulations: Making the World Safer from Future Pandemics', *Journal of the American Medical Academy*, 326(13), 1255–1256.

Bobbitt, P. (2002) *The Shield of Achilles: War, Peace and the Course of History*, Penguin Books.

Brim, B. and Wenham, C. (2019) 'Pandemic Emergency Financing Facility: Struggling to Deliver on its Innovative Promise', *British Medical Journal*, 367, 5719.

Castillo-Salgado, C. (2010) 'Trends and Directions of Global Public Health Surveillance', *Epidemiologic Reviews*, 32(1), 93–109

Chandler, D. and Hynek, N. (2010) *Critical Perspectives on Human Security: Rethinking Emancipation and Power in International Relations*, Taylor & Francis.

Christie, R. (2010) 'Critical Voices and Human Security: To Endure, To Engage or To Critique?' *Security Dialogue*, 41(2), 169–190.

Commission on a Global Health Risk Framework for the Future (2016) *The Neglected Dimension of Global Security: A Framework to Counter Infectious Disease Crises*. Available at: http://nam.edu/GHRFreport

Commission on Human Security (2003) *Human Security Now: Protecting and Empowering People*, United Nations.

Davies, S. (2009) *Global Politics of Health*, Polity.

Davies, S. (2019) *Containing Contagion: The Politics of Disease Outbreaks in Southeast Asia*, Johns Hopkins University Press.

Davies, S. (2020) 'Reporting Disease Outbreaks in a World with No Digital Borders', in C. McInnes, K. Lee and J. Youde (eds) *The Oxford Handbook of Global Health Politics*, Oxford University Press, pp 512–529.

de Bengy Puyvallée, A. and Kittelsen, S. (2019) 'Disease Knows No Borders: Pandemics and the Politics of Global Health Security', in K. Bjørkdahl, and B. Carlsen (eds) *Pandemics, Publics, and Politics*, Palgrave Pivot, pp 59–73.

De Cock, K., Jaffe, H. and Curran, J. (2012) 'The Evolving Epidemiology of HIV/AIDS', *AIDS*, 26(10), 1205–1213.

De Waal, A. (2010) 'HIV/AIDS and the Challenges of Security and Conflict', *Perspectives: The Art of Medicine*, 375(9708), 22–23.

Dieleman, J., Haakenstad, A., Micah, A., Moses, M., Abbafati, C. and Acharya, P. (2018) 'Spending on Health and HIV/AIDS: Domestic Health Spending and Development Assistance in 188 Countries, 1995–2015', *The Lancet*, 391(10132), 1799–1829.

Duffield, M. (2001) 'Governing the Borderlands: Decoding the Power of Aid', *Disasters*, 25, 308–320.

Erikson, S. (2019) 'Faking Global Health', *Critical Public Health*, 29(4), 508–516.

Faria, N., Rambaut, A., Suchard, M., Baele, G., Bedford, T. and Ward, M. et al (2014) 'The Early Spread and Epidemic Ignition of HIV-1 in Human Populations', *Science*, 346, 6205, 56–61.

Feldbaum, H., Patel, P., Sondorp, E. and Lee, K. (2006) 'Global Health and National Security', *Medicine, Conflict and Survival*, 22(3), 192–198.

Financial Times (2020) 'World Bank Ditches Second Round of Pandemic Bonds', 5 July.

Foucault, M. (1975) *Surveiller et Punir*, Editions Gallimard.

G20 High Level Independent Panel on Financing the Global Commons for Pandemic Preparedness and Response (2021) *A Global Deal for Our Pandemic Age*. Available at: www.pandemic-financing.org

Gebresenbet, F. (2014) 'Securitisation of Development in Ethiopia: The Discourse and Politics of Developmentalism', *Review of African Political Economy*, 41(1), S64–S74.

Gilbert, M.T., Rambaut, A., Wlasiuk, G., Spira, T., Pitchenik, A. and Worobey, M. (2007) 'The Emergence of HIV/AIDS in the Americas and Beyond', *Proceedings of the National Academy of Sciences*, 104(47), 18566–18570.

Global Burden of Disease Health Financing Collaborator Network (2020) 'Health Sector Spending and Spending on HIV/AIDS, Tuberculosis, and Malaria, and Development Assistance for Health: Progress towards Sustainable Development Goal 3', *The Lancet*, 396, 693–724.

Gostin, L. (2021) *Global Health Security: A Blueprint for the Future*, Harvard University Press.

Grépin, K. (2015) 'International Donations to the Ebola Virus Outbreak: Too Little, too Late?' *British Medical Journal*, 350(h376).

Gronvall, G., Boddie, C., Knutsson, R. and Colby, M. (2014) 'One Health Security: An Important Component of the Global Health Security Agenda', *Biosecurity and Bioterror*, 12(5), 221–224.

Haq, M. (1995) 'New Imperatives of Human Security', *World Affairs: The Journal of International Issues*, 4(1), 68–73.

Hemm, A. and Johnson, Z. (2021) 'Breaking the "Cycle of Panic and Neglect": What Donor Countries are Doing to Prepare the World for the Next Pandemic', *Donor Tracker Insights*, 5 July. Available at: https://donor tracker.org/publications/breaking-cycle-panic-and-neglect-what-donor-countries-are-doing-prepare-world-next

Heymann, D. and Rodier, G. (2004) 'Global Surveillance, National Surveillance, and SARS', *Emerging Infectious Diseases*, 10(2), 173–175.

Hinton, E. (2015) 'Why We Should Reconsider the War on Crime', *Time*, 20 March. Available at: https://time.com/3746059/war-on-crime-history/

Hinton, E. (2017) *From the War on Poverty to the War on Crime: The Making of Mass Incarceration in America*, Harvard University Press.

HM Government (2008) *A Strong Britain in an Age of Uncertainty: The National Security Strategy*, The Stationery Office. Available at: https://assets.publishing.service.gov.uk/government/uploads/system/uploads/attachment_data/file/61936/national-security-strategy.pdf

Hoppe, H. (ed) (2003) *Myth of National Defense: Essays on the Theory and History of Security Production*, Mises Institute. Available at: https://mises.org/library/myth-national-defense-essays-theory-and-history-security-production

Horton, R. (2022) 'Offline: Bill Gates and the Fate of WHO', *The Lancet*, 399(10338), 1853.

Hsu, L. (2001) 'HIV Subverts National Security', UNDP South East Asia HIV and Development Program, Bangkok, Thailand.

Independent Panel for Pandemic Preparedness and Response (2021) *Covid-19. Make it the Last Pandemic.* Available at: https://theindependentpanel.rg/wp-content/ uploads/2021/05/COVID-19-Make-it-the-Last- Pandemic_final.pdf

International Crisis Group (2001) 'HIV/AIDS as a Security Issue', Report 1, 1 June.

Kirton, J. and Koch, M. (eds) (2021) *G7 UK The Cornwall Summit*, Pamphlet. GT Media London, the Global Governance Project.

Kirton, J. and Mannell, J. (2005) 'The G8 and Global Health Governance', G8 Research Group. Available at: http://www.g8.utoronto.ca/scholar/kirton2005/kirton_waterloo2005.pdf

Kiwan, D. (2019) 'Security and Development', in J. Midgley, R. Surender and L. Alfers (eds) *Handbook of Social Policy and Development*, Elgaronline.

Kuznetsova, L. (2020) 'COVID-19: The World Community Expects the World Health Organization to Play a Stronger Leadership and Coordination Role in Pandemics Control', *Frontiers in Public Health*, 8.

Kvartalnov, A. (2021) 'Indivisible Security and Collective Security Concepts: Implications for Russia's Relations with the West', *Central European Journal of International and Security Studies*, 15(3), 4–29.

Levich, J. (2015) 'The Gates Foundation, Ebola, and Global Health Imperialism', *The American Journal of Economics and Sociology*, 74(4), 704–742.

Luo, R.F. (2002) 'Understanding the Threat of HIV/AIDS', *Journal of the American Medical Association*, 288(13), 1649.

Malik, S.M., Barlow, A. and Johnson, B. (2021) 'Reconceptualising Health Security in Post-COVID-19 World', *BMJ Global Health*, 6, e006520.

McInnes, C. and Lee, K. (2006) 'Health, Security and Foreign Policy', *Review of International Studies*, 32(1), 5–23.

McInnes, C. and Rushton, S. (2013) 'HIV/AIDS and Securitisation Theory', *European Journal of International Relations*, 19(1), 115–138.

Medicins Sans Frontiers (MSF) (2018) 'UNAIDS Report Overlooks Significant Aspects of the Global HIV Response'. Available at: www.msf. org/unaids-report-overlooks-significant-aspects-global-hiv-response

Merson, M. (2006) 'The HIV/AIDS Pandemic at 25: The Global Response', *New England Journal of Medicine*, 354, 2414–2417.

National Intelligence Council/US Government (2000) *The Global Infectious Disease Threat and its Implications for the United States*, National Intelligence Estimate, Washington, DC United States Government Central Intelligence Agency.

Newby, G., Mpanju-Shumbusho, W. and Feacham, R. (2021) 'Global Health Security Requires Endemic Disease Eradication', *The Lancet*, 397(10280), 1163–1165.

New York Times (1998) 'AIDS Stalking Africa's Struggling Economies', *New York Times*, 15 November.

Nikogosian, H. and Kickbusch, I. (2021) 'The Case for an International Pandemic Treaty', *British Medical Journal*, 372, n527.

Patrick, S. (2020) 'When the System Fails', *Foreign Affairs*, 40.

Pepin, J. (2021) *The Origins of AIDS*, 2nd edn, Cambridge University Press.

Ruger, J. (2005) 'Democracy and Health', *QJM: An International Journal of Medicine*, 98(4), 299–304.

Rushton, S. (2010) 'AIDS and International Security in the United Nations System', *Health Policy and Planning*, 25(6), 495–504.

Rushton, S. (2011) 'Global Health Security: Security for Whom? Security from What?', *Political Studies*, 59(4), 779–796.

Sachs, J., Abdool Karim, S., Aknin, L., Allen, J., Brosbøl, K., Colombo, F. et al (2022) 'The Lancet Commission on Lessons for the Future from the COVID-19 Pandemic', *The Lancet*, S0140–6736(22)01585–9, https://doi.org/10.1016/

Sands, P. (2020) 'COVID-19 Must Transform The Definition Of Global Health Security', *The Global Fund*.

Schäferhoff, M., Chodavadia, P., Martinez, S., Kennedy McDade, K., Fewer, S. et al (2019) 'International Funding for Global Common Goods for Health: An Analysis Using the Creditor Reporting System and G-FINDER Databases', *Health Systems & Reform*, 5(4), 350–365.

Seidelmann, R. (2010) 'Old versus New Security: A Contribution to the Conceptual Debate', Center for Global Studies, University of Bonn, Discussion Paper 1 May.

Shashikant, S. (2007) 'WHO Meeting on Avian Flu Virus Ends with Draft Documents', *TWN Information Service on Health Issues*, Third World Network. Available at: http://www.twnside.org.sg/title2/health.info/twnhealthinfo041107.htm

Shrider, E., Kollar, M., Chen, F. and Semega, J. (2020) *US Census Bureau, Current Population Reports*, P60–273, Income and Poverty in the United States: 2020, US Government Publishing Office.

Sovacool, B. and Halfon, S. (2007) 'Reconstructing Iraq: Merging Discourses of Security and Development', *Review of International Studies*, 33(2), 223–243.

Stein, R. (2003) 'SARS Prompts WHO to Seek More Power to Fight Disease', *The Washington Post*, 18 May.

Stoeva, P. (2020) 'Dimensions of Health Security: A Conceptual Analysis', *Global Challenges*, 4, 1700003.

Šulović, V. (2010) 'Meaning of Security and Theory of Securitization', Belgrade Center for Security Policy, 5 October.

UNAIDS (2022) 'In Danger', UNAIDS Global AIDS Update 2022, Joint United Nations Programme on HIV/AIDS.

UNDP (1994) *Human Development Report: New Dimensions of Human Security*, UNDP. Available at: http://www.hdr.undp.org/en/content/human-development-report-1994

Verrecchia, R., Thompson, R. and Yates, R. (2019) 'Universal Health Coverage and Public Health: A Truly Sustainable Approach', *Lancet Public Health*, 4, E10–E11.

Wenham, C., Kavanagh, M., Torres, I. and Yamey, G. (2021) 'Preparing for the Next Pandemic', *British Medical Journal*, 373, n1295.

WHO (World Health Organization) (2007) *A Safer Future: Global Public Health Security in the 21st Century*, WHO.

WHO (2021) 'World leaders urge for global treaty to protect countries from pandemic', 30 March. Available at: www.who.int/news/item/30-03-2021-global-leaders-unite-in-urgent-call-for-international-pandemic-treaty

Zwierlein, C. (2018) 'Historicizing Environmental Security', *European Journal of Security Research*, 3, 1–13.

Zwierlein, C. and Graaf, B. (2013) 'Security and Conspiracy in Modern History', *Historical Social Research*, 38(1), 7–45.

Chapter 12: The risk society

Abbey, E.J., Khalifa, B.A., Oduwole, M.O., Ayeh, S.K., Nudotor, R.D., Salia, E.L. et al (2020) 'The Global Health Security Index is not Predictive of Coronavirus Pandemic Responses among Organization for Economic Cooperation and Development Countries', *PLoS ONE*, 15(10), e0239398.

Abramowitz, S. (2020) 'Epidemics (Especially Ebola)', *Annual Review of Anthropology*, 46, 421–445.

Aitken, T., Chin, K.L., Liew, D. and Ofori-Asenso, R. (2020) 'Rethinking Pandemic Preparation: Global Health Security Index (GHSI) is Predictive of COVID-19 Burden, but in the Opposite Direction', *Journal of Infection*, 81(2), 318–356.

Allard, R. (1989) 'Beliefs about AIDS as Determinants of Preventive Practices and of Support for Coercive Measures', *American Journal of Public Health*, 79(4), 448–452.

Balakrishnan, V. (2021) 'Impact of COVID-19 on Refugees and Migrants', *Lancet Infectious Disease*, 21(8), 1076–1077.

Bambino Geno Tai, D., Shah, A., Doubeni, C., Sia, I. and Wieland, M. (2021) 'The Disproportionate Impact of COVID-19 on Racial and Ethnic Minorities in the United States', *Clinical Infectious Diseases*, 72(4), 703–706.

Bardosh, K. (ed) (2020) *Locating Zika: Social Change and Governance in an Age of Mosquito Pandemics*, Routledge.

Bardosh, K., de Vries, D., Abramowitz, S., Thorlie, A., Cremers, L. and Kinsman, J. et al (2020) 'Integrating the Social Sciences in Epidemic Preparedness and Response: A Strategic Framework to Strengthen Capacities and Improve Global Health Security', *Global Health*, 16, 120.

Baum, A., Newman, S., Weinman, J., McManus, C. and West, R. (eds) (1997) *Cambridge Handbook of Psychology, Health and Medicine*, Cambridge University Press.

Beck, U. (1992) *Risk Society: Towards a New Modernity*, SAGE.

Bellazzi, F. and Boyneburgk, K. (2020) 'COVID-19 Calls for Virtue Ethics', *Journal of Law and the Biosciences*, 7(1), lsaa056.

Bishop, G., Alva, A., Cantu, L. and Rittiman, T. (1991) 'Responses to Persons with AIDS: Fear of Contagion or Stigma?', *Journal of Applied Social Psychology*, 21(23), 1877–1888.

Blair, R., Morse, B. and Tsai, L. (2017) 'Public Health and Public Trust: Survey Evidence from the Ebola Virus Disease Epidemic in Liberia', *Social Science & Medicine*, 172, 89–97.

Cassani, A. (2021) 'COVID-19 and the Democracy–Autocracy Freedom Divide: Reflections on Post-Pandemic Regime Change Scenarios', *Political Studies Review*, September 2021. doi:10.1177/14789299211047087.

Chang, Y.Y. (2021) 'The Post-Pandemic World: Between Constitutionalized and Authoritarian Orders – China's Narrative-Power Play in the Pandemic Era', *Journal of Chinese Political Science*, 26, 27–65.

Chapman, C. and Miller, D. (2020) 'From Metaphor to Militarized Response: The Social Implications of "we are at war with COVID-19": Crisis, Disasters, and Pandemics Yet to Come', *International Journal of Sociology and Social Policy*, 40(9/10), 1107–1124.

Chellaiyan, V.G., Nirupama, A.Y. and Taneja, N. (2019) 'Telemedicine in India: Where Do We Stand?', *Journal of Family Medicine & Primary Care*, 8(6), 1872–1876.

Cialdini, R.B. and Goldstein, N.J. (2004) 'Social Influence: Compliance and Conformity', *Annual Review of Psychology*, 55, 591–621.

Colby, D. and Cook, T. (1991) 'Epidemics and Agendas: The Politics of Nightly News Coverage of AIDS', *Journal of Health Politics, Policy & Law*, 16(2), 215–250.

Crouse Quinn, S. and Kumar, S. (2014) 'Health Inequalities and Infectious Disease Epidemics: A Challenge for Global Health Security', *Biosecurity and Bioterrorism: Biodefense Strategy, Practice, and Science*, 12(5), 263–273.

Dalby, S. (1990) 'American Security Discourse: The Persistence of Geopolitics', *Political Geography Quarterly*, 9(2), 171–188.

Daniel, H. and Parker, R. (1993) *Sexuality, Politics and AIDS in Brazil: In Another World?* Routledge.

Davies, S. and Bennett, B. (2016) 'A Gendered Human Rights Analysis of Ebola and Zika: Locating Gender in Global Health Emergencies', *International Affairs*, 92(5), 1041–1060.

Dentico, N. (2021) 'The Breathing Catastrophe: COVID-19 and Global Health Governance', *Development*, 64, 4–12.

Dodoo, J.E., Al-Samarraie, H. and Ibrahim Alzahrani, A. (2021) 'Telemedicine Use in Sub-Saharan Africa: Barriers and Policy Recommendations for Covid-19 and Beyond', *International Journal of Medical Informatics*, 151, 104467.

Earnshaw, V.A., Smith, L.R., Chaudoir, S.R., Amico, K.R. and Copenhaver, M.M. (2013) 'HIV Stigma Mechanisms and Well-Being among PLWH: A Test of the HIV Stigma Framework', *AIDS Behaviour*, 17(5), 1785–1795.

The Economist (2022) 'Welcome to the Era of the Hyper-Surveilled Office', 10 May. Available at: www.economist.com/business/welcome-to-the-era-of-the-hyper-surveilled-office/21809219

Edgell, A., Lachapelle, J., Lührmann, A. and Maerz, S. (2021) 'Pandemic Backsliding: Violations of Democratic Standards during Covid-19', *Social Science & Medicine*, 285, 114244.

Eisinger, R. and Fauci, A. (2018) 'Ending the HIV/AIDS Pandemic', *Emerging Infectious Diseases*, 24(3), 413–416.

Ekberg, M. (2007) 'The Parameters of the Risk Society: A Review and Exploration', *Current Sociology*, 55(3), 343–366.

Ekstrand, M., Bharat, S., Ramakrishna, J. and Heylen, E. (2012) 'Blame, Symbolic Stigma and HIV Misconceptions are Associated with Support for Coercive Measures in Urban India', *AIDS and Behavior*, 16(3), 700–710.

Engberg-Pedersen, A. (2020) 'COVID-19 and War as Metaphor', *boundary 2*. Available at: www.boundary2.org/2020/04/anders-engberg-pedersen-covid-19-and-war-as-metaphor/

Fauci, A. and Eisinger, R. (2018) 'PEPFAR – 15 Years and Counting the Lives Saved', *New England Journal of Medicine*, 378, 314–316.

Fee, E. and Fox, D. (eds) (1988) *AIDS: The Burdens of History*, University of California Press.

Fee, E. and Krieger, N. (1993) 'Understanding AIDS: Historical Interpretations and the Limits of Biomedical Individualism', *American Journal of Public Health*, 83(10), 1477–1486.

Financial Times (2020) 'Virus Lays Bare the Frailty of the Social Contract', 4 April. Available at: www.ft.com/content/7eff769a-74dd-11ea-95fe-fcd27 4e920ca

Ford, N. and Quam, M. (1987) 'AIDS Quarantine: The Legal and Practical Implications', *Journal of Legal Medicine*, 8(3), 353–396.

Furedi, F. (2008) 'Fear and Security: A Vulnerability-Led Policy Response', *Social Policy and Administration*, 42(6), 655–656.

Gauri, A.V. and Lieberman, E. (2004) 'AIDS and the State: The Politics of Government Responses to the Epidemic in Brazil and South', Presentation at the Annual Meetings of the American Political Science Association, Chicago, 2–5 September.

Gebrekidan, S. (2020) 'For Autocrats, and Others, Coronavirus Is a Chance to Grab Even More Power', *New York Times*, 30 March. Available at: www. nytimes.com/2020/03/30/world/europe/coronavirus-governments-power.html

Gostin, L. (2001) 'The Politics of AIDS: Compulsory State Powers, Public Health, and Civil Liberties', in U. Schüklenk (ed) *AIDS: Society, Ethics and Law*, Routledge, chapter 8.

Gostin, L. (2021) *Global Health Security: A Blueprint for the Future*, Harvard University Press.

Greitens, S. (2020) 'Surveillance, Security, and Liberal Democracy in the Post-COVID World', *International Organization*, 74(S1), E169–E190.

Griffin, S. (2020) 'Covid-19: Chaotic Decision Making and Failure to Communicate Undermined Government Response, Says Report', *British Medical Journal*, 371, m4940.

Grossman, C. and Stangl, A. (2013) 'Global Action to Reduce HIV Stigma and Discrimination', *Journal of the International AIDS Society*, 16, 18881.

Haddad, A. (2020) 'Metaphorical Militarisation: Covid-19 and the Language of War', 13 May. Available at: www.aspistrategist.org.au/metaphorical-militarisation-covid-19-and-the-language-of-war/

Han, Q., Zheng, B., Cristea, M., Agostini, M., Bélanger, J.J., Gützkow, B. et al (2021) 'Trust in Government regarding COVID-19 and its Associations with Preventive Health Behaviour and Prosocial Behaviour during the Pandemic: A Cross-Sectional and Longitudinal Study', *Psychological Medicine*, 1–11.

Hargreaves, A. (2021) 'Austerity and Inequality; or Prosperity for All? Educational Policy Directions beyond the Pandemic', *Education Research Policy & Practice*, 20, 3–10.

Harris, L., Silverman, N. and Marshall, M. (2016) 'The Paradigm of the Paradox: Women, Pregnant Women, and the Unequal Burdens of the Zika Virus Pandemic', *The American Journal of Bioethics*, 16(5), 1–4.

Hasan, S., Ahmad, S.A., Masood, R. and Saeed, S. (2019) 'Ebola Virus: A Global Public Health Menace: A Narrative Review', *Journal of Family Medicine & Primary Care*, 8(7), 2189–2201.

Herek, G., Capitanio, J. and Widaman, K. (2002) 'HIV-Related Stigma and Knowledge in the United States: Prevalence and Trends, 1991–1999', *American Journal of Public Health*, 92(3), 371–377.

Heymann, D., Chen, L., Takemi, K., Fidler, D., Tappero, J., Thomas, M. et al (2015) 'Global Health Security: The Wider Lessons from the West African Ebola Virus Disease Epidemic', *The Lancet*, 385(9980), 1884–1901.

Horton, R. (2019) 'The Mistakes We Made Over Ebola', *The Lancet*, 394(10208), 1494.

Huang, Q. (2021) 'The Pandemic and the Transformation of Liberal International Order', *Journal of Chinese Political Science*, 26, 1–26.

Huizar, M.I., Arena, R. and Laddu, D.R. (2021) 'The Global Food Syndemic: The Impact of Food Insecurity, Malnutrition and Obesity on the Healthspan amid the COVID-19 Pandemic', *Progress in Cardiovascular Diseases*, 64, 105–107.

Jamrozik, E. and Selgelid, M. (2018) 'Ethics, Health Policy, and Zika: From Emergency to Global Epidemic?', *Journal of Medical Ethics*, 44, 343–348.

Jedwab, R., Khan, A., Russ, J. and Zaveri, E. (2021) 'Epidemics, Pandemics, and Social Conflict: Lessons from the Past and Possible Scenarios for COVID-19', *World Development*, 147, 105629.

Kaldor, M. (2018) *Global Security Cultures*, Polity.

Kamradt-Scott, A., Harman, S., Wenham, C. and Smith, F. (2015) 'Saving Lives: The Civil-Military Response to the 2014 Ebola Outbreak in West Africa', University of Sydney, New South Wales, October.

Kathleen, S. and Field, M. (1988) 'AIDS and the Coercive Power of the State', *Harvard Civil Rights-Civil Liberties Law Review*, 139.

Kelly, A., Lezaun, J., Löwy, I., Corrêa Matta, G., de Oliveira Nogueira, C. and Teixeira Rabello, E. (2020) 'Uncertainty in Times of Medical Emergency: Knowledge Gaps and Structural Ignorance during the Brazilian Zika Crisis', *Social Science & Medicine*, 246, 112787.

Kirk, J. and McDonald, M. (2021) 'The Politics of Exceptionalism: Securitization and COVID-19', *Global Studies Quarterly*, 1(3), ksab024.

Lal, A., Erondu, N., Heymann, D., Gitahi, G. and Yates, R. (2021) 'Fragmented Health Systems in COVID-19: Rectifying the Misalignment between Global Health Security and Universal Health Coverage', *The Lancet*, 397, 61–67.

Lalot, F., Abrams, D. and Travaglino, G. (2021) 'Aversion Amplification in the Emerging COVID-19 Pandemic: The Impact of Political Trust and Subjective Uncertainty on Perceived Threat', *Journal of Community & Applied Social Psychology*, 31(2), 213–222.

Lin, C., Wu, C. and Wu, C. (2020) 'Reimagining the Administrative State in Times of Global Health Crisis: An Anatomy of Taiwan's Regulatory Actions in Response to the COVID-19 Pandemic', *European Journal of Risk Regulation*, 11(2), 256–272.

Luehrmann, A. and Rooney, B. (2021) 'Autocratization by Decree: States of Emergency and Democratic Decline', *Comparative Politics*, 53(4), 617–649.

Magri, P. (2020) 'Holding Back the Old Demons in the Euro-Mediterranean Region in Post-Pandemic Times: Populism and Authoritarianism', *IEMed Mediterranean Yearbook*, 119–124.

Mahajan, M. (2021) 'Casualties of Preparedness: The Global Health Security Index and COVID-19', *International Journal of Law in Context*, 17(2), 204–214.

Mao, F. and Illmer, A. (2021) 'Are Asia's Covid "Winners" Entering Shaky New Territory?', *BBC*, 18 June.

Marais, F., Minkler, M., Gibson, N., Mwau, B., Mehtar, S., Ogunsola, F. et al (2015) 'A Community-Engaged Infection Prevention and Control Approach to Ebola', *Health Promotion International*, 31(2), 440–449.

Mason, C., Barraket, J., Friel, S., O'Rourke, K. and Stenta, C.P. (2015) 'Social Innovation for the Promotion of Health Equity', *Health Promotion International*, 30(2), 116–125.

Matilla-Santander, N., Ahonen, E., Albin, M., Baron, S., Bolibar, M. and Bosmans, K. et al (2021) 'COVID-19 and Precarious Employment: Consequences of the Evolving Crisis', *International Journal of Health Services*, 51(2), 226–228.

Matthewman, S. and Huppatz, K. (2020) 'A Sociology of Covid-19', *Journal of Sociology*, 56(4), 675–683.

Maurice, J. (2016) 'The Zika Virus Public Health Emergency: 6 Months On', *The Lancet*, 388(10043), 449–450.

McCloskey, B. and Endericks, T. (2017) 'The Rise of Zika Infection and Microcephaly: What Can We Learn from a Public Health Emergency?', *Public Health*, 150, 87–92.

Mechler, R., Stevance, A.S., Deubelli, T., Linnerooth, B., Scolobig, A. and Irshaid, J. et al (2020) 'Bouncing Forward Sustainably: Pathways to a Post-COVID World: Governance for Sustainability', International Institute for Applied Systems Analysis and International Science Council. Available at: http://pure.iiasa.ac.at/id/eprint/16550/1/Background%20Paper%20 %20-%20Governance%20for%20Sustainability.pdf

Metinsoy, S. (2021) 'A Keynesian Revolution or Austerity? The IMF and the COVID-19 Crisis', *Global Perspectives*, 2(1), 24185.

Morgan, O., Aguilera, X., Ammon, A., Amuasi, J., Soce Fall, I., Frieden, T. et al (2021) 'Disease Surveillance for the COVID-19 Era: Time for Bold Changes', *The Lancet*, 397(10292).

Nelkin, D., Willis, D. and Parris, S. (1991) *A Disease of Society: Cultural and Institutional Responses to AIDS*, Cambridge University Press.

Newton, K. (2020) 'Government Communications, Political Trust and Compliant Social Behaviour: The Politics of Covid-19 in Britain', *The Political Quarterly*, 91(3), 502–513.

O'Manique, C. (2005) 'The "Securitisation" of HIV/AIDS in Sub-Saharan Africa: A Critical Feminist Lens', *Policy and Society*, 24(1), 24–47.

Oliveira, J., Pescarini, J., Rodrigues, M., Almeida, B., Henriques, C., Gouveia, F. et al (2020) 'The Global Scientific Research Response to the Public Health Emergency of Zika Virus Infection', *PLoS ONE*, 15(3), e0229790.

Pagliaro, S., Sacchi, S., Pacilli, M.G., Brambilla, M., Lionetti, F. and Bettache, K. et al (2021) 'Trust Predicts COVID-19 Prescribed and Discretionary Behavioral Intentions in 23 Countries', *PLoS ONE*, 16(3), e0248334.

Peisah, C., Byrnes, A., Doron, I., Dark, M. and Quinn, G. (2020) 'Advocacy for the Human Rights of Older People in the COVID Pandemic and Beyond: A Call to Mental Health Professionals', *International Psychogeriatrics*, 32(10), 1199–1204.

Philips, M. and Markham, A. (2014) 'Ebola: A Failure of International Collective Action', *The Lancet*, 384(1181).

Ramasubban, R. (1998) 'HIV/AIDS in India: Gulf Between Rhetoric and Reality', *Economic and Political Weekly*, 33(45), 2865–2873.

Rana, O., Llanos, J. and Carr, M. (2021) 'Lessons from the GDPR in the COVID-19 era', *Academia Letters*, Article 429.

Razavi, A., Erondu, N.A. and Okereke, E. (2020) 'The Global Health Security Index: What Value Does It Add?' *BMJ Global Health*, 5, e002477.

Reynolds, C., Pade, C., Gibbons, J., Otter, A., Lin, K.M., Muñoz Sandoval, D. et al (2022) 'Immune Boosting by B.1.1.529 (Omicron) Depends on Previous SARS-CoV-2 Exposure', *Science*, 10.1126/science.abq1841.

Ritchie, H., Mathieu, E., Rodés-Guirao, L., Appel, C., Giattino, C., Ortiz-Ospina, E. et al (2020) 'Coronavirus Pandemic (COVID-19)', OurWorldInData.org. Available at: https://ourworldindata.org/coronavirus

Rushton, S. and Youde, J. (eds) (2015) *Routledge Handbook of Global Health Security*, Routledge.

Sanders, D., Sengupta, A. and Scott, V. (2015) 'Ebola Epidemic Exposes the Pathology of the Global Economic and Political System', *International Journal of Health Services*, 45(4), 643–656.

Sauer, M., Truelove, S., Gerste, A. and Limaye, R. (2021) 'A Failure to Communicate? How Public Messaging Has Strained the COVID-19 Response in the United States', *Health Security*, 19(1), 65–74.

Schmelz, K. (2021) 'Enforcement May Crowd out Voluntary Support for COVID-19 Policies, Especially Where Trust in Government Is Weak and in a Liberal Society', *Proceedings of the National Academy of Sciences*, 118(1), e2016385118.

Seckinelgin, H. (2007) *International Politics of HIV/AIDS: Global Disease, Local Pain*, Routledge.

Šeško, Z. (2021) 'Eastern European Countries Adopting Authoritarian Measures in Face of Covid', *The Guardian*, 29 December. Available at: www.theguardian.com/world/2021/dec/29/eastern-european-countries-adopt-authoritarian-measures-covid

Singhal, A. and Rogers, E. (2003) *Combating AIDS: Communication Strategies in Action*, SAGE.

Siplon, P. (2002) *AIDS and the Policy Struggle in the United States*, Georgetown University Press.

Solomon, S. and Ganesh, A.K. (2002) 'HIV in India', *Topics in HIV Medicine*, 10(3), 19–24.

Southall, H., DeYoung, S. and Harris, C. (2017) 'Lack of Cultural Competency in International Aid Responses: The Ebola Outbreak in Liberia', *Frontiers in Public Health*, 5(5).

Stawicki, S., Firstenberg, M. and Papadimos, T. (2020) 'The Growing Role of Social Media in International Health Security: The Good, the Bad, and the Ugly', in A. Masys, R. Izurieta and M. Reina Ortiz (eds) *Advanced Sciences and Technologies for Security Applications*, Springer.

Stockton, M.A., Giger, K. and Nyblade, L. (2018) 'A Scoping Review of the Role of HIV-related Stigma and Discrimination in Noncommunicable Disease Care', *PLoS ONE*, 13(6), e0199602.

Sullivan, M., Rosen, A., Allen, A., Benbella, D., Camacho, G. and Cortopassi, A. et al (2020) 'Falling Short of the First 90: HIV Stigma and HIV Testing Research in the 90–90–90 Era', *AIDS Behaviour*, 24, 357–362.

Sun, S., Xie, Z., Yu, K., Jiang, B., Siwei, Z. and Xiaoting, P. (2021) 'COVID-19 and Healthcare System in China: Challenges and Progression for a Sustainable Future', *Global Health*, 17, 14.

Taggart, T., Ritchwood, T., Nyhan, K. and Ransome, Y. (2021) 'Messaging Matters: Achieving Equity in the HIV Response through Public Health Communication', *Lancet HIV*, 8(6), e376–e386.

Tham, E. (2022) 'China Bank Protest Stopped by Health Codes Turning Red, Depositors Say', *Reuters*, 14 June. Available at: www.reuters.com/world/china/china-bank-protest-stopped-by-health-codes-turning-red-depositors-say-2022-06-14/

UKCDR and GloPID-R (2020) *COVID-19 Research Project Tracker*. Available at: www.ukcdr.org.uk/funding-landscape/covid-19-research-project-tracker/

Van Dooren, W. and Noordegraaf, M. (2020) 'Staging Science: Authoritativeness and Fragility of Models and Measurement in the COVID-19 Crisis', *Public Administration Review*, 80(4), 610–615.

Vearey, J., de Gruchy, T. and Maple, N. (2021) 'Global Health (Security), Immigration Governance and Covid-19 in South(ern) Africa: An Evolving Research Agenda', *Journal of Migration and Health*, 3, 100040.

Wæver, O. (1995) 'Securitization and Desecuritization', in R. Lipschutz (ed) *On Security*, Columbia University Press.

Wenham, C. (2017) 'What We Have Learnt about the World Health Organization from the Ebola Outbreak', *Philosophical Transactions of the Royal Society London Series B Biological Science*, 372(1721), 20160307.

Wenham, C. (2021) *Feminist Global Health Security*, Oxford University Press.

Wenham, C., Arevalo, A., Coast, E., Correa, S., Cuellar, K. and Leone, T. et al (2019) 'Zika, Abortion and Health Emergencies: A Review of Contemporary Debates', *Global Health*, 15, 49.

Whitacre, R. (2021) 'How the Science of HIV Treatment-as-Prevention Restructured PEPFAR's Strategy: The Case for Scaling up ART in "Epidemic Control" Countries', in S. Bernays, A. Bourne, S. Kippax, P. Aggleton and R. Parker (eds) *Remaking HIV Prevention in the 21st Century: Social Aspects of HIV*, Springer, vol 5.

WHO (World Health Organization) (2016) *Pregnancy Management In The Context Of Zika Virus*. Interim Guidance, 3 2, Geneva, WHO.

Woodall, J. (2016) 'WHO Reform: Bring Back GOARN and Task Force "Scorpio"', *Infection Ecology & Epidemiology*, 6, 30237.

Xinhua News (2018) 'Xi Reaffirms China's Commitment to Peaceful Development Path', *Xinhua Net*. Available at: http://www.xinhuanet.com/english/2018-09/19/c_137479505.htm

Yan Zhong, H. (2005) 'The Politics of HIV/AIDS in China', prepared for the Freeman Asian Studies Symposium on China, 31 March.

Yong, E. (2022) 'The Pandemic's Legacy Is Already Clear', *The Atlantic*, 20 September 2022.

Zhao, Y. (2020) 'China, an Important Contributor in Fighting against COVID-19', *NOW Grenada*. Available at: https://nowgrenada.com/2020/04/china-an-important-contributor-in-fighting-against-covid-19/

Chapter 13: All for one

Adam, A. and Tsarsitalidou, S. (2022) 'Data Misreporting during the COVID19 Crisis: The Role of Political Institutions', *Economics Letters*, 213, 110348.

Afsahi, A., Beausoleil, E., Dean, R., Ercan, S.A. and Gagnon, J. (2022) 'Democracy in a Global Emergency', *Democratic Theory*, 7(2).

Agha, H., Khan, F.A. and Sherbaz, S. (2021) 'Globalization, Democracy and Child Health: Asia vs. Latin America', *Forman Journal of Economic Studies*, 17(1), 137–159.

Allen, L., Hatefi, A. and Feigl, A. (2019) 'Corporate Profits vs Spending on Non-Communicable Disease Prevention: An Unhealthy Balance', *Lancet Global Health*, 7(11), E1482–1483.

Altman, D. and Castiglioni, R. (2009) 'Democratic Quality and Human Development in Latin America: 1972–2001', *Canadian Journal of Political Science*, 42(2), 297–319.

Arne Westad, O. (2012) *Restless Empire: China and the World since 1750*, Bodley Head.

Baiocchi, G. (2005) *Militants and Citizens: The Politics of Participatory Democracy in Porto Allegre*, Stanford University Press.

Balbim, R. (ed) (2016) *The Geopolitics of Cities: Old Challenges, New Issues*, Institute for Applied Economic Research.

Bergh, A. and Nilsson, T. (2010) 'Good for Living? On the Relationship between Globalization and Life Expectancy', *World Development*, 38(9), 1191–1203.

Besley, T. and Kudamatsu, M. (2006) 'Health and Democracy', *American Economic Review*, 96(2), 313–318.

Besley, T. and Kudamatsu, M. (2008) 'Making Democracy Work', in E. Helpman (ed) *Institutions and Economic Performance*, Harvard University Press.

Bherer, L. (2010) 'Successful and Unsuccessful Participatory Arrangements: Why Is There a Participatory Movement at the Local Level?' *Journal of Urban Affairs*, 32(3), 287–303.

Bherer, L., Dufour, P. and Montambeault, F. (2016) 'The Participatory Democracy Turn: An Introduction', *Journal of Civil Society*, 12(3), 225–230.

Boese, V., Lindberg, S. and Lührmann, A. (2021) 'Waves of Autocratization and Democratization: A Rejoinder', *Democratization*, 28(6), 1202–1210.

Boese, V., Alizada, N., Lundstedt, M., Morrison, K, Natsika, N., Sato, Y. et al (2022) 'Autocratization Changing Nature?', *Democracy Report 2022*, Varieties of Democracy Institute.

Bollyky, T., Templin, T., Cohen, M., Schoder, D., Dieleman, J. and Wigley, S. (2019) 'The Relationships between Democratic Experience, Adult Health, and Cause-Specific Mortality in 170 Countries between 1980 and 2016: An Observational Analysis', *The Lancet*, 393(10181), 1628–1640.

Brocard, E., Mélihan-Cheinin, P. and Rusch, E. (2021) 'Health Democracy in Time of COVID-19: A Perspective from France', *Lancet Public Health*, 6(4), E201.

Burroway, R. (2016) 'Democracy and Child Health in Developing Countries', *International Journal of Comparative Sociology*, 57(5), 338–364.

Cassan, G. and Van Steenvort, M. (2021) 'Political Regime and COVID 19 Death Rate: Efficient, Biasing or Simply Different Autocracies?', *SSM – Population Health*, 16, 100912.

Cassani, A. (2017) 'Social Services to Claim Legitimacy: Comparing Autocracies' Performance', *Contemporary Politics*, 23(3), 348–368.

Cohen, J. (2009) 'Reflections on Deliberative Democracy', in L. Christiano and J. Christman (eds) *Contemporary Debates in Political Philosophy*, Wiley-Blackwell, pp 247–265.

Coppedge, M., Gerring, J., Knutsen, C.H., Lindberg, S., Skaaning, S.E., Teorell, J. et al (2018) 'The Methodology of Varieties of Democracy (V-Dem)'. Available at: https://ueaeprints.uea.ac.uk/id/eprint/72785/1/Accepted_Manuscript.pdf

Costa, A.M., Souto, L. and Rizzotto, M. (2017) 'Health is Democracy: Yesterday, Today and Always', *Saúde debate*, 41(115), 991–994.

Daniels, N. and Sabin, J. (2002) *Setting Limits Fairly: Can We Learn to Share Medical Resources?* Oxford University Press.

Deaton, A. (2006) 'Global Patterns of Income and Health: Facts, Interpretations and Policies', NBER Working Paper W12735.

Deaton, A. (2013) *The Great Escape: Health, Wealth, and the Origins of Inequality*, Princeton University Press.

Desai, M. (2003) 'India and China: An Essay in Comparative Political Economy', presented at the IMF Conference on India/China, New Delhi. Available at: http://www.imf.org/external/np/apd/seminars/2003/newdelhi/desai.pdf

Doucouliagos, H. and Ulubaşoğlu, M. (2008) 'Democracy and Economic Growth: A Meta-Analysis', *American Journal of Political Science*, 52, 61–83.

Dummer, T. and Cook, I. (2008) 'Health in China and India: A Cross-Country Comparison in a Context of Rapid Globalisation', *Social Science & Medicine*, 67(4), 590–605.

Eckersley, R. (2020) 'Ecological Democracy and the Rise and Decline of Liberal Democracy: Looking Back, Looking Forward', *Environmental Politics*, 29(2), 214–234.

Economist Intelligence Unit (2022) 'Democracy Index 2021: The China Challenge', *The Economist*. Available at: www.eiu.com/n/campaigns/democracy-index-2021/

Engler, S., Brunner, P., Loviat, R., Abou-Chadi, T., Leemann, L., Glaser, A. and Kübler, D. (2021) 'Democracy in Times of the Pandemic: Explaining the Variation of COVID-19 Policies across European Democracies', *West European Politics*, 44(5–6), 1077–1102.

Fins, J. (2021) 'Is Deliberative Democracy Possible during a Pandemic? Reflections of a Bioethicist', *Journal of Theoretical and Philosophical Psychology*, 41(4), 216–225.

Gerring, J., Bond, P., Barndt, W. and Moreno, C. (2005) 'Democracy and Economic Growth: A Historical Perspective', *World Politics*, 57(3), 323–364.

Goenaga, A. (2022) 'Who Cares about the Public Sphere?', *European Journal of Political Research*, 61, 230–254.

Grupe, C. and Rose, A. (2010) 'China, India, and the Socioeconomic Determinants of Their Competitiveness', *Hindawi Publishing Corporation Economics Research International*, article ID 860425.

Gugushvili, A. and Reeves, A. (2021) 'How Democracy Alters Our View of Inequality: And What It Means for Our Health', *Social Science & Medicine*, 283.

Heller, P., Harilal, K. and Chaudhuri, S. (2007) 'Building Local Democracy: Evaluating the Impact of Decentralization in Kerala, India', *World Development*, 35(4), 626–648.

Helliwell, J. (1994) 'Empirical Linkages Between Democracy and Economic Growth', *British Journal of Political Science*, 24(2), 225–248.

Honigsbaum, M. (2022) 'Bereaved Families Fear Covid Inquiry Cover-up after Ban on Testimony', *The Guardian*, 2 October. Available at: www.theguardian.com/uk-news/2022/oct/02/bereaved-families-fear-covid-inquiry-cover-up-after-ban-on-testimony

Hyland, J. (1995) *Democratic Theory: The Philosophical Foundations*, Manchester University Press.

IDEA (2019) *The Global State of Democracy 2019: Addressing the Ills, Reviving the Promise*, IDEA.

Jetter, M., Agudelo, A.M. and Hassan, A.R. (2015) 'The Effect of Democracy on Corruption: Income is Key', *World Development*, 74, 286–304.

Karabulut, G., Zimmermann, K., Huseyin Bilgin, M. and Cansin Doker, A. (2021) 'Democracy and COVID-19 Outcomes', *Economics Letters*, 203, 109840.

Kim, N.K. and Kroeger, A. (2018) 'Do Multiparty Elections Improve Human Development in Autocracies?', *Democratization*, 25(2), 251–272.

Kolstad, I. and Wiig, A. (2016) 'Does Democracy Reduce Corruption?', *Democratization*, 23(7), 1198–1215.

Koonings, K. (2004) 'Strengthening Citizenship in Brazil's Democracy: Local Participatory Governance in Porto Alegre', *Bulletin of Latin American Research*, 23, 79–99.

Kudamatsu, M. (2007) 'Political Economy of Development: Health as a Development Outcome, Micro Evidence, and Heterogeneity of Democracies and Autocracies', London School of Economics and Political Science; ProQuest Dissertations Publishing. Available at: http://etheses.lse.ac.uk/2020/1/U501707.pdf

Larry, D. (2022) 'Democracy's Arc: From Resurgent to Imperilled', *Journal of Democracy*, 33(1), 163–179.

Lima, V. (2019) 'The Limits of Participatory Democracy and the Inclusion of Social Movements in Local Government', *Social Movement Studies*, 18(6), 667–681.

Lin, C. (2015) 'Rethinking Land Reform: Comparative Lessons from China and India', in M. Mamdani (ed) *The Land Question: Socialism, Capitalism and The Market*, Makerere Institute of Social Research (MISR), Kampala, Uganda, pp 95–157.

Linz, J. and Valenzuela, A. (eds) (1994) *The Failure of Presidential Democracy*, vol 1, Johns Hopkins University Press.

López, M. and Dubrow, J. (2020) 'Politics and Inequality in Comparative Perspective: A Research Agenda', *American Behavioral Scientist*, 64(9), 1199–1210.

Lührmann, A., Tannenberg, M. and Lindberg, S. (2018) 'Regimes of the World (RoW): Opening New Avenues for the Comparative Study of Political Regimes', *Politics and Governance*, 6(1), 60–77.

Maclenbach, J.P. and McKee, M. (2013) 'Social-Democratic Government and Health Policy in Europe: A Quantitative Analysis', *International Journal of Health Services*, 43(3), 389–413.

Mackenbach, J.P., Hu, Y. and Looman, C. (2013) 'Democratization and Life Expectancy in Europe, 1960–2008', *Social Science & Medicine*, 93, 166–175.

Maerz, S., Lührmann, A., Hellmeier, S., Grahn, S. and Lindberg, S. (2020) 'State of the World 2019: Autocratization Surges – Resistance Grows', *Democratization*, 27(6), 909–927.

Marx, B., Pons, V. and Rollet, V. (2022) 'Electoral Turnovers', NBER Working Paper Series No 29766.

Mathonnat, C. and Minea, A. (2019) 'Forms of Democracy and Economic Growth Volatility', *Economic Modelling*, 81, 594–603.

McCann, K. and Tisch, D. (2021) 'Democratic Regimes and Epidemic Deaths', V-Dem Institute Working Paper 2021, 126, University of Gothenberg.

McGuire, J. (2020) *Democracy and Population Health*, Cambridge University Press.

Meisner, M. (1999) *The Significance of the Chinese Revolution in World History*, LSE Asia Research Centre.

Miller, M. (2015) 'Electoral Authoritarianism and Human Development', *Comparative Political Studies*, 48(12), 1526–1562.

Mitra, S. (2019) 'Fragmented Society, Stable Democracy: The Indian Paradox', in A. Croissant and P. Walkenhorst (eds) *Social Cohesion in Asia: Historical Origins, Contemporary Shapes and Future Dynamics*, Routledge, pp 101–121.

Mok, K.H. and Kang, Y.Y. (2019) 'Social Cohesion and Welfare Reforms: The Chinese Approach', in A. Croissant and P. Walkenhorst (eds) *Social Cohesion in Asia: Historical Origins, Contemporary Shapes and Future Dynamics*, Routledge, pp 26–49.

Montambeault, F. (2015) *The Politics of Local Participatory Democracy in Latin America: Institutions, Actors, and Interactions*, Stanford University Press.

Norheim, O., Abi-Rached, J., Bright, L., Bærøe, K., Ferraz, O. and Gloppen, S. et al (2021) 'Difficult Trade-offs in Response to COVID-19: The Case for Open and Inclusive Decision Making', *Nature Medicine*, 27, 10–13.

Nuffield Council on Bioethics (2020) 'Covid-19 and the Basics of Democratic Governance'. Available at: www.nuffieldbioethics.org/news/statement-covid-19-and-the-basics-of-democratic-governance

Ong, L. (2020) '"Land Grabbing" in an Autocracy and a Multi-Party Democracy: China and India Compared', *Journal of Contemporary Asia*, 50(3), 361–379.

Parvin, P. (2018) 'Democracy Without Participation: A New Politics for a Disengaged Era', *Res Publica*, 24, 31–52.

Patterson, A. and Veenstra, C. (2016) 'Politics and Population Health: Testing the Impact of Electoral Democracy', *Health & Place*, 40, 66–75.

Pearse, H. (2020) 'Deliberation, Citizen Science and Covid-19', *The Political Quarterly*, 91, 571–577.

Persad, G. (2019) 'Justice and Public Health', in A. Mastroianni, J. Kahn and N. Kass (eds) *The Oxford Handbook of Public Health Ethics*, Oxford University Press.

Pieters, H., Curzi, D., Olper, A. and Swinnen, J. (2016) 'Effect of Democratic Reforms on Child Mortality: A Synthetic Control Analysis', *Lancet Global Health*, 4(9), e627–e632.

Prah Ruger, J. (2020) 'Social Justice as a Foundation for Democracy and Health', *British Medical Journal*, 371, m4049.

Ross, M. (2006) 'Is Democracy Good for the Poor?', *American Journal of Political Science*, 50, 860–874.

Safaei, J. (2006) 'Is Democracy Good for Health?', *International Journal of Health Services*, 36(4), 767–786.

Sebhatu, A., Wennberg, K., Arora-Jonsson, S. and Lindberg, S. (2020) 'Explaining the Homogeneous Diffusion of COVID-19 Nonpharmaceutical Interventions across Heterogeneous Countries', *Proceedings of the National Academy of Sciences*, 117(35), 21201–21208.

Stasavage, D. (2020) 'Democracy, Autocracy, and Emergency Threats: Lessons for COVID-19 From the Last Thousand Years', *International Organization*, 74(S1), E1–E17.

Templin, T., Dieleman, J., Wigley, S., Mumford, J.E., Miller-Petrie, M., Kiernan, S. and Bollyky, T. (2021) 'Democracies Linked To Greater Universal Health Coverage Compared With Autocracies, Even In An Economic Recession', *Health Affairs*, 40(8), 1234–1242.

UNDP (2004) *Democracy in Latin America: Toward a Citizens' Democracy*, UNDP.

UNDP (2019) *Human Development Report: Gender Inequality Index*, UNDP.

UNICEF (2019) *The State of the World's Children*, UNICEF.

Wang, Y., Mechkova, V. and Andersson, F. (2019) 'Does Democracy Enhance Health? New Empirical Evidence 1900–2012', *Political Research Quarterly*, 72(3), 554–569.

Welander, A., Lyttkens, C. and Nilsson, T. (2015) 'Globalization, Democracy and Child Health in Developing Countries', *Social Science and Medicine*, 136, 52–63.

Whitehead, L. (ed) (2002) *Emerging Market Democracies: East Asia and Latin America*, Johns Hopkins University Press.

Wigley, S., Dieleman, J., Templin, T., Everett Mumford, J.E. and Bollyky, T. (2020) 'Autocratisation and Universal Health Coverage: Synthetic Control Study', *British Medical Journal*, 371, m4040.

Willis, R., Curato, N. and Smith, G. (2022) 'Deliberative Democracy and the Climate Crisis', *Wiley Interdisciplinary Reviews: Climate Change*, e759.

World Bank (2013) 'Why is China Ahead of India? A Fascinating Analysis by Amartya Sen'. Available at: https://blogs.worldbank.org/psd/why-china-ahead-india-fascinating-analysis-amartya-sen

Wu, C. and Wilkes, R. (2018) 'Local–National Political Trust Patterns: Why China is an Exception', *International Political Science Review*, 39(4), 436–454.

Zhengxu, W. (2005) 'Political Trust in China: Forms and Causes', in L. White (ed) *Legitimacy: Ambiguities of Success or Failure in East and Southeast Asia*, Word Scientific Press, pp 113–139.

Zhong, P. and Zhan, J.V. (2021) 'Authoritarian Critical Citizens and Declining Political Trust in China', *China Review*, 117–152.

Chapter 14: Who counts?

Adalberto, F. (2021) 'Communicating Corrected Risk Assessments and Uncertainty About COVID-19 in the Post-Truth Era', *Frontiers in Communication*, 6.

Adams, V. (2016) *Metrics: What Counts in Global Health*, Duke University Press.

Aldemer, R. (1985) 'Peirce's Thirteen Theories of Truth', *Transactions of the Charles S Peirce Society*, 21(1), 77–94.

Atkins, P. (1995) 'Science and Truth', *History of the Human Sciences*, 8, 97.

Atwood, K.C. (2003) '4th Naturopathy: A Critical Appraisal', *Medgenmed: Medscape General Medicine*, 5(4), 39.

Balmford, B., Bateman, I., Bolt, K., Day, B. and Ferrini, S. (2019) 'The Value of Statistical Life for Adults and Children: Comparisons of the Contingent Valuation and Chained Approaches', *Resource and Energy Economics*, 57, 68–84.

Balon, R., Beresin, E., Brenner, Coverdale, J., Guerrero, A. and Louie, A. et al (2016) 'Opportunities and Challenges of Global Mental Health', *Academic Psychiatry*, 40, 643–646.

Bill & Melinda Gates Foundation (2013) 'Annual Letter 2013'. Available at: https://www.gatesfoundation.org/ideas/annual-letters/annual-letter-2013

Bowker, G. (1996) 'The History of Information Infrastructures: The Case of the International Classification of Diseases', *Information Processing & Management*, 32(1), 49–61.

Broome, A. and Quirk, J. (2015) 'The Politics of Numbers: The Normative Agendas of Global Benchmarking', *Review of International Studies*, 41, 813–818.

Cameron, T. (2010) 'Euthanizing the Value of a Statistical Life', *Review of Environmental Economics and Policy*, 4(2).

Carney, T. and Bennett, B. (2014) 'Framing Pandemic Management: New Governance, Science or Culture?', *Health Sociology Review*, 23(2), 136–147.

Carpenter, M. (2021) 'Intersex Human Rights, Sexual Orientation, Gender Identity, Sex Characteristics and the Yogyakarta Principles Plus 10', *Culture, Health & Sexuality*, 23(4), 516–532.

Carr-Hill, R. (2013) 'Missing Millions and Measuring Development Progress', *World Development*, 46, 30–44.

Chan, M. (2012) 'From New Estimates to Better Data', *The Lancet*, 380(9859), 2054.

Chamberlain, K. and Lyons, A. (eds) (2022) *Routledge International Handbook of Critical Issues in Health and Illness*, Routledge.

Cislaghi, B., Weber, A.M., Gupta, G.R. and Darmstadt, G.L. (2020) 'Gender Equality and Global Health: Intersecting Political Challenges', *Journal of Global Health*, 10(1), 010701.

Clinton, C. and Sridhar, D. (2017) *Governing Global Health: Who Runs the World and Why?* Oxford University Press.

Cochrane, A.L. (1972) *Effectiveness and Efficiency: Random Reflections on Health Services*, Nuffield Trust.

Cook, H.J. (2010) 'Victories for Empiricism, Failures for Theory: Medicine and Science in the Seventeenth Century', in C.T. Wolfe and O. Gal (eds) *The Body as Object and Instrument of Knowledge*, Springer, pp 9–32.

Cookson, R., Griffin, S., Norheim, O. and Culyer, A. (eds) (2021) *Distributional Cost-Effectiveness Analysis: Quantifying Health Equity Impacts and Trade-offs*, Oxford University Press.

Cosentino, G. (2020) *Social Media and the Post-Truth World Order: The Global Dynamics of Disinformation*, Palgrave.

Coyle, D. (2019) 'Valuing Data is Tricky but Crucial for the Public Good', *Financial Times*, 20 November.

Deaton, A. and Cartwright, N. (2018) 'Understanding and Misunderstanding Randomized Controlled Trials', *Social Science & Medicine*, 210, 2–21.

Debanjan, B. and Meena, K. (2021) 'COVID-19 as an "Infodemic" in Public Health: Critical Role of the Social Media', *Frontiers in Public Health*, 9.

Dobson, G. (2020) 'Science and the War on Truth and Coronavirus', *Frontiers in Medicine*, 563.

Drummond, M., Brixner, D., Gold, M., Kind, P., McGuire, A. and Nord, E. (2009) 'Toward a Consensus on the QALY', *Value in Health*, 12(1), 98–103.

Farr, J. (2003) 'Political Science', in T. Porter and D. Ross (eds) *The Cambridge History of Science*, Cambridge University Press.

Feyerabend, P. (1975) *Against Method*, Verso.

Foucault, M. (1970) *The Order of Things*, Vintage Books.

Field, M. and Gold, M. (eds) (1998) 'Summarizing Population Health: Directions for the Development and Application of Population Metrics', Institute of Medicine, Committee on Summary Measures of Population Health, National Academy Press.

Formighieri Giordani, R.C., Giordani Donasolo, J.P., Both Ames, V.D. and Giordani, R.L. (2021) 'The Science between the Infodemic and Other Post-Truth Narratives: Challenges during the Pandemic', *Ciência de Saúde Coletiva*, 26(7), 2863–2872.

Fuller, S. (2020) *A Player's Guide to the Post-Truth Condition: The Name of the Game*, Anthem Press.

Gard, M. (2011) 'Truth, Belief and the Cultural Politics of Obesity Scholarship and Public Health Policy', *Critical Public Health*, 21(1), 37–48.

Gillett, G. (2006) 'Medical Science, Culture, and Truth', *Philosophical Ethics of Humanitarian Medicine*, 1, 13.

Glass, D.V. and Eversley, D. (eds) (1965) *Population in History: Essays in Historical Demography*, Edward Arnold.

Gold, M. and Muennig, P. (2002) 'Measure-Dependent Variation in Burden of Disease Estimates: Implications for Policy', *Medical Care*, 40(3), 260–266.

Gold, M., Stevenson, D. and Fryback, D. (2002) 'HALYs and QALYs and DALYs, Oh My: Similarities and Differences in Summary Measures of Population Health', *Annual Review of Public Health*, 23, 115–134.

Gutenschwager, G. (2021) 'Ambiguity, Misinformation and the Coronavirus', *Academia Letters*, article 1395.

Hill, A.B. (1937) 'Principles of Medical Statistics', *The Lancet*, 1937, 41–43.

Holmes, D., Murray, S., Perron, A. and Rail, G. (2006) 'Deconstructing the Evidence-Based Discourse in Health Sciences: Truth, Power and Fascism', *International Journal of Evidence Based Healthcare*, 4, 180–188.

Horton, R. (2013) 'Metrics for What?' *The Lancet*, 381, S1–S2.

Hunt, J. (2020) *The COVID-19 Pandemic vs Post-Truth*, Global Health Security Network.

Hussain, R., McGarvey, S. and Fruzzetti, L. (2015) 'Partition and Poliomyelitis: An Investigation of the Polio Disparity Affecting Muslims during India's Eradication Program', *PLoS One*, 10(3), e0115628.

Jackson, S. (1932) *Principles of Medicine*, Carey & Lea.

Jacobson, T. and Mackey, T. (2019) *Metaliterate Learning for the Post-Truth World*, Neal-Schuman Publishers.

Jewell, N.P., Lewnard, J.A. and Jewell, B.L. (2020) 'Caution Warranted: Using the Institute for Health Metrics and Evaluation Model for Predicting the Course of the COVID-19 Pandemic', *Annals of Internal Medicine*, 173, 226–227.

Keidl, P. and Melamed, L. (2020) *Pandemic Media: Preliminary Notes Toward an Inventory*, Meson Press.

Kertzer, D., Arel, D. and Hogan, D. (eds) (2001) *Census and Identity: The Politics of Race, Ethnicity, and Language in National Censuses*, Cambridge University Press.

Kwok, H., Singh, P. and Heimans, S. (2021) 'The Regime of "Post-Truth": COVID-19 and the Politics of Knowledge', *Discourse: Studies in the Cultural Politics of Education,* 44(1), 106–120.

The Lancet (2017) 'Editorial: Better Understanding of Youth Mental Health', 389, 1670.

Lee, K. (2015) 'Revealing Power in Truth: Comment on "Knowledge, Moral Claims and the Exercise of Power in Global Health"', *International Journal of Health Policy Management*, 4(4), 257–259.

Levi-Strauss, C. (1955) *Tristes Tropiques*, Librairie Plon.

Livi-Bacci, M. (1992) *A Concise History of World Population*, Blackwell.

Lundberg, O., Åberg Yngwe, M., Kölegård Stjärne, M., Björk, L. and Fritzell, J. (2008) 'The Nordic Experience: Welfare States and Public Health (NEWS)', Health Equity Studies No 12, Centre for Health Equity Studies (CHESS), Stockholm University/Karolinska Institutet.

MacKillop, E. and Sheard, S. (2018) 'Quantifying Life: Understanding the History of Quality-Adjusted Life-Years (QALYs)', *Social Science & Medicine*, 211, 359–366.

Mahajan, M. (2019) 'The IHME in the Shifting Landscape of Global Health Metrics', *Global Policy*, 10(S1), 110–120.

Mathers, C.D., Vos, T., Lopez, A.D., Salomon, J., Ezzati, M. (2001) (eds) *National Burden Of Disease Studies: A Practical Guide, Edition 2.0*, Geneva: World Health Organization. Available at: www.who.int/healthinfo/nationalburdenofdiseasemanual.pdf

Mathers, C.D. (2020) 'History of Global Burden of Disease Assessment at the World Health Organization', *Archives of Public Health*, 78, 77.

McDougall, J., Furnback, W., Wang, B. and Mahlich, J. (2020) 'Understanding the Global Measurement of Willingness to Pay in Health', *Journal of Market Access & Health Policy*, 8, 1.

McMichael, P. and Weber, H. (2021) *Development and Social Change: A Global Perspective*, 7th edn, SAGE.

Naghavi, M. on behalf of the Global Burden of Disease Self-Harm Collaborators (2016) 'Global, Regional, and National Burden of Suicide Mortality 1990 to 2016: Systematic Analysis for the Global Burden of Disease Study 2016', *British Medical Journal*, 364, l94.

Nally, D. (2022) 'Theorising Post-Truth in the COVID Era', *Journal of Education and Change*, 23, 277–289.

Nassir Ghaemi, S. (2009) *A Clinician's Guide to Statistics and Epidemiology in Mental Health*, Cambridge University Press.

Nay, O. and Barre-Sinoussi, F. (2022) 'Bridging the Gap between Science and Policy in Global Health Governance', *Lancet Global Health*, 10(3), E322–E323.

Nelson, F. (2022) 'The Lockdown Files: Rishi Sunak on What We Weren't Told', *Spectator*, 27 August.

Parmet, W. and Paul, J. (2020) 'COVID-19: The First Posttruth Pandemic', *American Journal of Public Health*, 110, 945–946.

Pastorino, R., De Vito, C., Migliara, G., Glocker, K., Binenbaum, I., Ricciardi, W. and Boccia, S. (2019) 'Benefits and Challenges of Big Data in Healthcare: An Overview of the European Initiatives', *European Journal of Public Health*, 29(3), 23–27.

Patel, V. (2014) 'Why Mental Health Matters to Global Health', *Transcultural Psychiatry*, 51(6), 777–789.

Pettitt, D.A., Raza, S., Naughton, B., Roscoe, A., Ramakrishnan, A. and Ali, A. et al (2016) 'The Limitations of QALY: A Literature Review', *Journal of Stem Cell Research Therapy*, 6, 334.

Pinker, S. and Mack, A. (2014) 'The World Is Not Falling Apart', *The Slate*, 22 December. Available at: https://slate.com/news-and-politics/2014/12/the-world-is-not-falling-apart-the-trend-lines-reveal-an-increasingly-peaceful-period-in-history.html

Polinder, S., Haagsma, J., Stein, C. and Havelaar, A. (2012) 'Systematic Review of General Burden of Disease Studies using Disability-Adjusted Life Years', *Population Health Metrics*, 10, 21.

Power, M. (2004) 'Counting, Control and Calculation: Reflections on Measuring and Management', *Human Relations*, 57, 765–783.

Prasad, A. (2022) 'Anti-Science Misinformation and Conspiracies: COVID–19, Post-Truth, and Science & Technology Studies (STS)', *Science, Technology and Society*, 27(1), 88–112.

Ramsey, F. (1927) 'Facts and Propositions', *Aristotelian Society*, supplementary volume 7, 153–170.

Ravallion, M. (2020) 'Should Randomistas (Continue to) Rule?', National Bureau of Economic Research, Working Paper 27554, July. Available at: http://www.nber.org/papers/w27554

Rosen, G. (1958) *A History of Public Health*, MD Publications.

Sarmiento, P.J., Yap, J.F., Espinosa, K.A., Ignacio, R. and Caro, C. (2021) 'The Truth must Prevail: Citizens' Rights to Know the Truth during the Era of COVID-19', *Journal of Public Health*, 43(2), e275–e276.

Schrödinger, E. (1935) 'Die gegenwärtige Situation in der Quantenmechanik', *Naturwissenschaften*, 23(48).

Scott, J. (2008) *Seeing Like a State: How Certain Schemes to Improve the Human Condition Have Failed*, Yale University Press.

Shelton, T. (2020) 'A Post-Truth Pandemic?' *Big Data & Society*, doi:10.1177/2053951720965612

Shiffman, J. (2014) 'Knowledge, Moral Claims and the Exercise of Power in Global Health', *International Journal of Health Policy Management*, 3, 297–299.

Shiffman, J. and Shawar, Y.R. (2020) 'Strengthening Accountability of the Global Health Metrics Enterprise', *The Lancet*, 395(10234), 1452–1456.

Shryock, R. (1969) 'Empiricism versus Rationalism in American Medicine 1660–1960', *The American Antiquarian Society*.

Sredl, D. (2011) 'QALY vs. DALY Quandary', *International Journal of Science in Society*, 2(4), 99–122.

Strmic-Pawl, H.V., Jackson, B.A. and Garner, S. (2018) 'Race Counts: Racial and Ethnic Data on the U.S. Census and the Implications for Tracking Inequality', *Sociology of Race and Ethnicity*, 4(1), 1–13.

Summerfield, D. (2012) 'Afterword: Against "Global Mental Health"', *Transcultural Psychiatry*, 49(3–4), 519–530.

Sundby, J. (1999) 'Are Women Disfavoured in the Estimation of Disability Adjusted Life Years and the Global Burden of Disease?', *Scandinavian Journal of Public Health*, 27(4), 279–285.

Supriya, M. and Chattu, V.K. (2021) 'A Review of Artificial Intelligence, Big Data, and Blockchain Technology Applications in Medicine and Global Health', *Big Data and Cognitive Computing*, 5, 41.

Sweis, N. (2022) 'Revisiting the Value of a Statistical Life: An International Approach during COVID-19', *Risk Management*, https://doi.org/10.1057/s41283-022-00094-x

Thomason, J. (2021) 'Big Tech, Big Data and the New World of Digital Health', *Global Health Journal*, 5(4), 165–168.

Tichenor, M. and Sridhar, D. (2019) 'Metric Partnerships: Global Burden of Disease Estimates within the World Bank, the World Health Organization and the Institute for Health Metrics and Evaluation', *Wellcome Open Research*, 4, 35, 10.12688/wellcomeopenres.15011.1

Todres, J. (2003) 'Birth Registration: An Essential First Step toward Ensuring the Rights of All Children', *Human Rights Brief*, 10(3), 32–35.

Torrance, G. (1986) 'Measurement of Health State Utilities for Economic Appraisal: A Review', *Journal of Health Economics*, 5(1), 1–30.

Trautmann, S., Xu, Y., König-Kersting, C., Patenaude, B., Harling, G. and Sie, A. et al (2021) 'Value of Statistical Life Year in Extreme Poverty: A Randomized Experiment of Measurement Methods in Rural Burkina Faso', *Population Health Metrics*, 19, 45.

UNICEF (2019) *Birth Registration for Every Child by 2030: Are We on Track?* UNICEF.

van den Tweel, J.G. and Taylor, C.R. (2010) 'A Brief History of Pathology', *Virchows Archiv*, 457, 3–10.

Venkataramakrishnan, S. (2020) 'The Real Fake News about COVID-19', *Financial Times*, 25 August.

Viscusi, W. and Masterman, C. (2017) 'Income Elasticities and Global Values of a Statistical Life', *Journal of Benefit-Cost Analysis*, 8(2), 226–250.

Visoka, G. and Gjevori, E. (2013) 'Census Politics and Ethnicity in the Western Balkans', *East European Politics*, 29(4), 479–498.

Voigt, K. and King, N. (2014) 'Disability Weights in the Global Burden of Disease 2010 Study: Two Steps Forward, One Step Back?', *Bulletin of the World Health Organization*, 92, 226–228.

Voigt, K. and King, N. (2017) 'Out of Alignment? Limitations of the Global Burden of Disease in Assessing the Allocation of Global Health Aid', *Public Health Ethics*, 10(3), 244–256.

von Mises, R. (1957) *Probability, Statistics, and Truth*, Dover Publications.

Weber, M. (1922) *Wirtschaft und Gesellschaft (Theory of Social and Economic Organisation)*, Tubingen.

Weber, A.M., Gupta, R., Abdalla, S., Cislaghi, B., Meausoone, V. and Darmstadt, G. (2021) 'Gender-Related Data Missingness, Imbalance and Bias in Global Health Surveys', *BMJ Global Health*, 6, e007405.

WHO (World Health Organization) (2001) *Mental Health: New Understanding, New Hope*, WHO.

Wieringa, S., Engebretsen, E., Heggen, K. and Greenhalgh, T. (2018) 'Rethinking Bias and Truth in Evidence-Based Health Care', *Journal of Evaluation in Clinical Practice*, 24(5), 930–938.

William Colglazier, E. (2020) 'Response to the COVID-19 Pandemic: Catastrophic Failures of the Science-Policy Interface', INGSA, 9 April.

Wittgenstein, L. (1953) *Philosophische Untersuchungen*, translated by G.E.M. Anscombe, Basil Blackwood.

Woods, B., Revill, P., Sculpher, M. and Claxton, K. (2016) 'Country-Level Cost-Effectiveness Thresholds: Initial Estimates and the Need for Further Research', *Value Health*, 19(8), 929–935.

Wyber, R., Vaillancourt, S., Perry, W., Mannava, P., Folaranmic, T. and Anthony Celid, L. (2015) 'Big Data in Global Health: Improving Health in Low- and Middle-Income Countries', *Bulletin of the World Health Organization*, 93, 203–208.

Zuboff, S. (2015) 'Big Other: Surveillance Capitalism and the Prospects of an Information Civilization', *Journal of Information Technology*, 30, 75–89.

Conclusion: crisis redux

Deaton, A. (2013) *The Great Escape: Health, Wealth, and the Origins of Inequality*, Princeton University Press.

Dember, W.N., Martin, S.H., Hummer, M.K., Howe, S. and Melton, R. (1989) 'The Measurement of Optimism and Pessimism', *Current Psychology*, 8, 102–119.

Easterly, W. (2006) *The White Man's Burden: Why the West's Efforts to Aid the Rest Have Done So Much Ill and So Little Good*, Oxford University Press.

Escobar, A. (1995) *Encountering Development: The Making and Unmaking of the Third World*, Princeton University Press.

Fanon, F. (1961) *Les Damnés de la Terre*, François Maspero.

Fukuyama, F. (2022) *Liberalism and its Discontents*, Profile Books.

Galor, O. (2020) 'The Journey of Humanity: Roots of Inequality in the Wealth of Nations', *Economics and Business Review*, 6(20), 2, 7–18.

Galor, O. (2022) *The Journey of Humanity: The Origins of Wealth and Inequality*, Bodley Head.

Gates, W. (2020) 'Is Inequality Inevitable?' *GatesNotes, the blog of Bill Gates*, 23 November. Available at: www.gatesnotes.com/Podcast/Is-inequality-inevitable

Hecht, D. (2013) 'The Neural Basis of Optimism and Pessimism', *Experimental Neurobiology*, 22(3), 173–199.

Helm, T. (2022) 'Britain faces chaos if it scraps EU laws, warns ex-Whitehall legal boss', 23 October, *The Guardian*. Available at: https://www.theguardian.com/world/2022/oct/23/britain-faces-chaos-if-it-scraps-eu-laws-warns-ex-whitehall-legal-boss

Kharas, H. (2019) 'Optimists and Pessimists on Global Development', *The Hill*. Available at: www.brookings.edu/opinions/optimists-and-pessimists-on-global-development/

Malthus, T. (1798) *Essay on the Principle of Populations as it Affects the Future Improvement of Society*, J. Johnson Printer.

Pinker, S. (2018) *Enlightenment Now: The Case for Reason, Science, Humanism & Progress*, Viking.

Pinker, S. (2021) 'Inequality and Progress', *Journal of Applied Corporate Finance*, 33(3), 28–41.

Romer, P. (1990) 'Endogenous Technological Change', *Journal of Political Economy*, 98(5), Part 2.

Roser, M. and Nagdy, M. (2014) 'Optimism and Pessimism', Our World in Data. Available at: https://ourworldindata.org/optimism-pessimism

Rosling, H. (2018) *Factfulness: Ten Reasons We're Wrong about the World – and Why Things are Better than We Think*, Flatiron Books.

Sachs, J. (2005) *The End of Poverty: How We Can Make It Happen in Our Lifetime*, Penguin Books.

Simon, J. (1981) *The Ultimate Resource*, Princeton University Press.

Singer, H. (1975) *Strategy of International Development: Essays in the Economics of Backwardness*, edited by A. Cairncross and M. Puri, Macmillan Press.

Postscript: crisis in the UK

Azzolini, L. and Evans, G. (2021) 'How Party Ideological Convergence Accentuates Class Differences in Voter Turnout: The Role of Age and Values', Nuffield Elections Unit, Working Paper, Nuffield College, January.

Ball, L., Furceri, D., Leigh, D. and Loungani, P. (2013) 'The Distributional Effects of Fiscal Consolidation', IMF Working Paper Research Department, WP/13/151, June. Available at: www.imf.org/external/pubs/ft/wp/2013/wp13151.pdf

Bell, E. (2010) 'From New Labour to New Conservative: The Emergence of a Liberal Authoritarian Consensus?', *Observatoire de la Société Britannique*, 9. Available at: http://journals.openedition.org/osb/1045

Bell, T. (2022) 'Liz Truss Thinks We Have to Choose between Inequality and Growth – but it Doesn't Have to be this Way', *New Statesman*, 7 September. Available at: www.newstatesman.com/quickfire/2022/09/liz-truss-redistribution-inequality-growth

BMA (2022) 'Valuing Health: Why Prioritising Population Health is Essential to Prosperity', BMA.

Booth, R. (2022) 'UN Poverty Envoy Tells Britain this is "Worst Time" for More Austerity', *The Guardian*, 2 November. Available at: www.theguardian.com/society/2022/nov/02/un-poverty-envoy-tells-britain-this-is-worst-time-for-more-austerity

Brandenburg, H. and Johns, R. (2014) 'The Declining Representativeness of the British Party System, and Why it Matters', *Poltical Studies*, 62(4), 704–725, https://doi.org/10.1111/1467-9248.12050

Campbell, D. (2022) 'Thérèse Coffey Scraps Promised Paper on Health Inequality', *The Guardian*, 29 September. Available at: www.theguardian.com/politics/2022/sep/29/therese-coffey-scraps-promised-paper-on-health-inequality

Crook, C. (2022) 'Is It Too Late for Truss to Repair the Damage?', *Bloomberg UK*, 29 September. Available at: www.bloomberg.com/opinion/articles/2022-09-29/uk-economic-crisis-is-it-too-late-for-truss-to-repair-the-damage

Dearden, N. (2022) 'Liz Truss's Neoliberal Blitz is Doomed to Fail', *Al Jazeera*, 30 September. Available at: www.aljazeera.com/opinions/2022/9/30/trusss-neoliberal-blitz-is-doomed-to-fail

The Economist (2022) 'Liz Truss Has Made Britain a Riskier Bet for Bond Investors', 11 October.

Elliott, L. (2022) 'The UK Economy is about to be Thrown into a Black Hole – by its Own Government', *The Guardian*, 2 November. Available at: www.theguardian.com/commentisfree/2022/nov/02/the-uk-economy-is-about-to-be-thrown-into-a-black-hole-by-its-own-government

English, P., Grasso, M.T., Buraczynska, B., Karampampas, S. and Temple, L. (2016) 'Convergence on Crisis? Comparing Labour and Conservative Party Framing of the Economic Crisis in Britain, 2008–14', *Politics and Policy*, 44, 577–603.

Evans, G. and Dirk de Graaf, N. (eds) (2013) *Political Choice Matters: Explaining the Strength of Class and Religious Cleavages in Cross-National Perspective*, Oxford University Press.

Financial Times (2022) 'Editorial: Truss and Kwarteng's Embarrassing U-Turn', 3 October. Available at: www.ft.com/content/c8715aa6-03d7-4ddb-85ea-28df149dfbe8

Foy, S., Gifford, C., Rees, T., Bo, H. and Oliver, M. (2022) 'Jacob Rees-Mogg Leads Backlash against Plan to Increase Capital Gains Tax', *The Telegraph*, 4 November. Available at: www.telegraph.co.uk/business/2022/11/04/jacob-rees-mogg-leads-backlash-against-plan-increase-capital/

Furceri, D., Loungani, P. and Ostry, J. (2020) 'How Pandemics Leave the Poor Even Farther Behind', *IMF Blog*, 11 May. Available at: www.imf.org/en/Blogs/Articles/2020/05/11/blog051120-how-pandemics-leave-the-poor-even-farther-behind

Ghitis, F. (2022). 'Opinion: Why the World has to Worry about Liz Truss', *CNN*, 30 September. Available at: https://edition.cnn.com/2022/09/30/opinions/liz-truss-economic-policy-disaster-ghitis/index.html

Giles, C. (2020) 'Global Economy: The Week that Austerity was Officially Buried', *Financial Times*, 16 October. Available at: www.ft.com/content/0940e381-647a-4531-8787-e8c7dafbd885

Hutton, W. (2022) 'The Future Offers Only Variants on Austerity? Bunk. There are Ways to Invest and Grow', *The Observer*, 23 October. Available at: www.theguardian.com/commentisfree/2022/oct/23/the-future-off ers-only-variants-on-austerity-bunk-there-are-ways-to-invest-and-grow

Isaac, A. (2022) 'Brexit a Major Cause of UK's Return to Austerity, Says Senior Economist', *The Guardian*, 14 November. Available at: www.the guardian.com/politics/2022/nov/14/brexit-a-major-cause-of-uks-return-to-austerity-says-senior-economist

Lancet Public Health (2022) 'Editorial: Liz Truss, Friend or Foe? The Jury is Out', *Lancet Public Health*, 7(10), E801, 1 October.

Lansley, S. (2021) *The Richer, The Poorer: How Britain Enriched the Few and Failed the Poor. A 200-Year History*, Policy Press.

Lin, K-H. and Neely, M. (2020) 'Why the Great Recession Made Inequality Worse', *OUPblog*, 10 February. Available at: https://blog.oup.com/2020/02/why-the-great-recession-made-inequality-worse/

McKee, M., Karanikolos, M., Belcher, P. and Stuckler, D. (2012) 'Austerity: A Failed Experiment on the People of Europe', *Clin Med*, 12(4), 346–350.

Nelson, E. (2022) 'Britain's Economic Experiment Stumbles at the Start', *New York Times*, 4 October. Available at: www.nytimes.com/2022/10/04/business/truss-tax-cuts-britain.html

Ortiz, I., Cummins, M., Capaldo, J. and Karunanethy, K. (2015) 'The Decade of Adjustment: A Review of Austerity Trends, 2010–2020, in 187 Countries' (Extension of Social Security Series No. 53), International Labour Office.

Stiglitz, J. and Welsbrot, M. (2022) 'Argentina and the IMF Turn Away From Austerity', *Foreign Policy*, 1 February. Available at: https://foreign policy.com/2022/02/01/argentina-imf-austerity-debt-economics-inflation/

The Telegraph (2022) 'Comment: Hunt Must Rethink Attack on Taxpayers', 5 November. Available at: www.telegraph.co.uk/opinion/2022/11/05/hunt-must-rethink-attack-taxpayers/

Temple, L., Grasso, M.T., Buraczynska, B., Karampampas, S. and English, P. (2016) 'Neoliberal Narrative in Times of Economic Crisis: A Political Claims Analysis of the UK Press, 2007–14', *Politics and Policy*, 44, 553–576, https://doi.org/10.1111/polp.12161

Van Reenan, J. (2015) 'Austerity in the UK: Past, Present and Future', *LSE Blogs*, 11 March. Available at: https://blogs.lse.ac.uk/politicsandpolicy/austerity-past-present-and-future/

Wise, J. (2022) 'Public Health: What is its Future under Truss's Government?', *BMJ*, 379, o2482, doi: 10.1136/bmj.o2482

Index

References to figures show both the page number and 'f' (193f).
References to endnotes show both the page number and the note number (184n17).

'developed' countries *see* advanced countries

developing countries 13, 15, 23n4, 215, 223n19, 226
  democracy 190, 193
  economic growth 32, 34, 41, 42, 52n10, 56, 62f, 64n3, 65n12
  freedom 71, 73, 77, 95, 96, 102n2
  justice, 114, 115, 123, 125, 130, 140, 143, 145

development *see* economic development; human development, technological development

development assistance 43f

devolution *xii*, 63, 142

diabetes 47, 85n7, 87, 135, 145n1, 204n8

diagnostic testing 7, 174

diarrhoeal diseases 123

DICE *see* dynamic integrated climate economy

Dichlorodiphenyltrichloroethane (DDT) 183n16

Dickens, Charles 4

Dieleman, J. et al 159f, 160f

'difference principle' 119n16

diphtheria 77, 85n3, 129f

disability 77, 110, 118n8, 138f, 217

'disability-adjusted life years' (DALY) 214, 222n12–13

'disability-free life expectancy' (DFLE) 222n12

disease distribution 3, 211f, 212–213, 222n7–8

domestic energy security 232

domestic hygiene 37

domestic spending 42

Don Quixote (Cervantes) 3

double-entry bookkeeping 30, 38n4

DPT1 (diphtheria, pertussis and tetanus toxoid) vaccination 129f

drug misuse 163n5, 173

dynamic integrated climate economy (DICE) 39n9

dysentery 6

E

'Earthrise' 213f, 222n10

East Africa 2

Ebola 6–7, 52n6, 53n22, 79, 123, 162, 165n15
  risk and 174–176, 184n18, 184n21, 184n24

Ebola Interim Assessment Panel (2015) 166n26

ecomodernism 56

economic development 29, 41, 57, 153, 154, 175, 196–197, 200
  freedom and 70–71, 72f, 73–74, 75n1–9, 76n10–15, 90

economic growth *xii*, 20, 29f, 30–32, 33f, 34, 51n1, 69, 232
  COVID-19 and 61, 62f, 63–64, 65n13, 101
  crisis and 226, 228, 231
  democracy and, 191, 193, 196
  development goals 41, 42, 44, 45, 51n2, 52–53n13–15, 73
  health and 34–35, 36f, 37–40
  limitations to 55–57, 58f, 59f, 65n5, 65n8
  trade and 48–50

Economic Opportunity, Office of (United States) 164n7

economics and economists 30–31, 38n6, 39n9

Economist Finance and Economics, The 147n18

education and educational services 37, 113, 120n23, 136, 147n17
  security and 181, 182, 183n16

Egypt 1, 12, 15

electoral participation 15, 17, 18f, 24n9–10, 190–191, 197f, 203

'elephant curve': income levels 16f

'El idioma analitico de John Wilkins' (Borges) 221n1

Eliot, George 3

'elites' 18–19, 30

Emancipation Proclamation (1863) (United States) 75n7

embryology 1

Emergency Committee (World Health Organization) 176

emerging diseases 61, 63

emerging economies 11, 15, 16f, 61, 62f, 91, 115, 153, 167n27

empiricism 212, 213, 219

Energy Information Agency 12f

enforcement: vaccination 81–82, 84

Enlightenment, The 30, 70, 226, 227

environmental issues 6, 111, 126, 162, 182n1, 200, 204n16
  economic growth 33, 37, 41, 45, 53n14, 56, 57, 61, 64, 65n16

'Environmental Land Management Scheme' 235n1

'equal world' worldview 147n15

Ethiopia 52n10, 128

ethnic minorities 19, 143

Europe 15, 23n5, 30, 65n8, 80, 148n28

'evidence-based medicine' 212

evolutionary science 107

Exchange Rate Mechanism (ERM) 236n4

Expanded Programme on Immunisation (EPI) 77, 128

extraterritorial executions 19, 25n13

extremism 20

F

face masks 220

'fake news' *see* truth